THE GROWTH OF
HUMANITY

Foundations of Human Biology

Series Editors

Matt Cartmill
Kaye Brown

Department of Biological Anthropology and Anatomy
Duke University Medical Center
Durham, North Carolina

THE GROWTH OF HUMANITY

Barry Bogin
Department of Behavioral Sciences
University of Michigan, Dearborn
Dearborn, Michigan 48128
bbogin@umich.edu

 **WILEY-LISS**

A John Wiley & Sons, Inc., Publication

New York · Chichester · Weinheim · Brisbane · Singapore · Toronto

This book is printed on acid-free paper. ∞

Published simultaneously in Canada.

For ordering and customer service, call 1-800-CALL-WILEY.

Library of Congress Cataloging-in-Publication Data:

Bogin, Barry.
    The growth of humanity/by Barry A. Bogin.
        p.   cm.
    Includes index.
    ISBN 0-471-35448-1 (pbk.)
    1. Human growth.   2. Population.   3. Physical anthropology.   4. Demographic anthropology.
    5. Infants—Growth.   6. Youth—Growth.   7. Life cycles (Biology)   I. Title.

    GN62.9 .B62 2001
    599.9—dc21
                                                                                    00-043852

Printed in the United States of America.

10 9 8 7 6 5 4 3 2 1

To my parents, Marvin and Florence Bogin—
loving, responsible people who make this world
a better place for all of us.

Contents

THREE
How People Grow   63

FOUR
Evolution of the Human Life History   98

FIVE
Food, Demography, and Growth   143

SIX
Migration and Human Health   189

SEVEN
Growth of Humanity   229

EIGHT
The Aging of Humanity · 263

Glossary · 281
References · 289
Index · 313

Acknowledgments

My deepest appreciation goes to my colleague and partner, Inês Varela Silva. Inês read all chapters, offered many ideas, supplied statistical information on Portugal, and wrote the boxed text features on Cape Verde in Chapter 6. Most importantly, Inês provided constant support for the writing of this book. Joseph Gaughan, my colleague at the University of Michigan-Dearborn, provided ethnographic and historical sources on the Irish famine and Irish society. Bibiana Orden of Argentina assisted with several illustrations while she worked with me as a postdoctoral student. Richard Steckel, Ohio State University, and John Komlos, University of Munich, provided many sources on anthropometric history. Several colleagues provided very helpful criticism of the early proposal for this book. For their suggestions I thank Fatimah L. Jackson, Lynette E. Leidy, Timothy B. Gage, Robert C. Bailey, Peter T. Ellison, Leslie Sue Lieberman, Darna L. Dufour, Andrew Hill, Michael A. Little, Dennis H. O'Rourke, and Andrea S. Wiley. Benjamin Campbell read a draft of the manuscript when it was nearing completion. His comments helped to improve the final text. Matt Cartmill and Kaye Brown invited me to write this book. I much appreciate their confidence in me and their encouragement. Finally, I thank Luna Han, my editor at John Wiley & Sons, for patience and support during the two years it took to write this book.

Series Introduction

Human beings are more than what we are as animals. But what we are as animals guides and limits what else we can be; and so the proper starting place for the study of humanity is the study of our biology.

The series Foundations of Human Biology was conceived as a suite of five interrelated books that would cover the fundamental facts of biological anthropology, the science that deals with the biology of human beings in a cultural context. Our aim in creating this series was to present the core knowledge of biological anthropology to students through the work of its leading practitioners and best authors. Subsequent volumes in the series will focus on the human body, the human genome, the fossil record of human evolution, and the evolution of human behavior.

We are delighted to inaugurate our series with Barry Bogin's daring and innovative work, which integrates the studies of human growth, nutrition, and demography with each other and with our current scientific understanding of the human fossil and archaeological record. Barry Bogin is known for seeing clearly in all matters relating to the growth and development of humans. His views on the evolution of childhood and adolescence have become an important part of the study of human biology. His meticulous work on the causes of height variability among Guatemalan children has become the standard by which we judge investigations of comparative stature. Bogin is a careful investigator who has always asked questions of importance both for humanity and for evolutionary biologists. We hope that this book will serve to bring his work to an even greater audience.

The reader will find *The Growth of Humanity* to be much more than an authoritative text, skillfully written. It is a powerful vision of how ontogeny and phylogeny have interacted in the history of human populations. In *The Growth of Humanity*, Bogin presents a pathbreaking synthesis that ranges through all the subdisciplines of biological anthropology to yield a new, interdisciplinary understanding of the evolution of human life history and population growth. His book will teach you to look at the world around you with new wisdom, and sensitize you to the ways in which the sociocultural world molds and shapes human bodies and lives. Through this book, you will come to see how wars, disease, and economics translate into changes in stature, body composition, and growth rates in a population, and how these changes affect differential reproduction and evolution. You will begin to understand why ancient hunters and gatherers, living in small, mobile groups, led remarkably healthy lives, and why technological progress and disease have until very recently been opposite sides of one coin. You will gain a new perception of childhood and adolescence—not as mere labels for arbitrary age classes, but as evolutionary novelties as important to the human adaptation as the acquisition of fire and language. Perhaps most importantly, this book will impress on its readers that the real population crisis the world faces in the century ahead is not a matter of uncontrolled growth, but of the unequal distribution of human reproduction and human resources.

Barry Bogin has given all of us a wonderfully readable book dealing with some of the critical issues of the day in a language that is accessible to everyone. We are fortunate to have this important contribution as the first work in our series. We feel sure that your perceptions of the human world will be transformed by reading *The Growth of Humanity*.

Kaye Brown
Matt Cartmill
Series Editors
Foundations of Human Biology

THE GROWTH OF HUMANITY

ONE

OF POPULATIONS
AND PEOPLE

Somewhere on this globe, every ten seconds, there is a woman giving birth to a child. She must be found and stopped.

SAM STEVENSON, AMERICAN COMEDIAN

My purpose in this book is twofold: first, to provide an introduction to the key concepts, methods of research, and essential discoveries of the fields of human demography and human growth and development, and second, to show that demography and human growth are two closely related fields, indeed, that only by considering both simultaneously can we come to understand much of the biological and social history of the human population. The target audiences are junior- and senior-level undergraduate students, graduate students, their professors, and the literate public. This book is part of the *Foundations of Human Biology* textbook series. This series is designed to present the core knowledge of the fields of physical anthropology and human biology.

There is no single book that treats the material included in *The Growth of Humanity*. Demographers write mainly for other demographers. Human growth and development researchers, sometimes also called auxologists,[1] write mainly for each other as well. This is not unusual in an academic world segregated into disciplines and departments and where research is funded by agencies that often also specialize by disciplinary interest. But, both demographers and auxologists also write for public health workers, medical researchers, social policy makers, economists, educators, and, sometimes, the interested public. Unfortunately, demographers rarely write for auxologists, or vice versa. There was a time, during the first third of the twentieth century, when an attempt was made to link demography and auxology. This was during the infancy of a field that is now called human biology. The idea that demography and human growth are affiliated disciplines originated

---

[1] From the word: **aux.in**, *n* [fr. Gk *auxein*] **1:** any of various acidic organic substances that promote cell elongation in plant shoots and regulate other growth processes (as root initiation) **2:** plant hormone—**aux.in.ic**, *adj* (from *Merriam-Webster' Collegiate Dictionary*, online 1999).

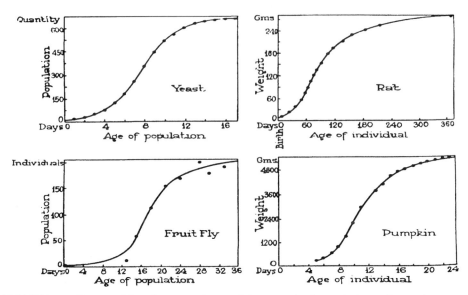

FIGURE 1.1 Raymond Pearl's comparisons of the growth of populations of organisms and of individual organisms (Pearl, 1925).

in the 1920s with the work of Raymond Pearl (1925), one of the founders of the field of human biology. Some of Pearl's original data are reproduced here as Figure 1.1. It may be seen that the curves of growth both for populations—yeast and fruit flies—and for individuals—weight growth for rats and pumpkins—follow almost identical curves.

Pearl believed that the growth of the human population would also follow this curve, and Pearl predicted that the population of the United States would reach a stable maximum of about 190 million people. That number was exceeded in 1965, and the U.S. population continues to grow, as is seen in Figure 1.2. Pearl neglected the major contribution that migration makes to the growth of the U.S. population. More globally, the growth of the total human population also differs from that of yeast and fruit flies. Figure 1.3 illustrates the growth of the total human population over the past 2,000 years. Graph A is a linear scaling of population against time, and graph B is a logarithmic scaling. Note that the human population curve does not resemble the S-shaped curve seen in Figure 1.1. Until A.D. 1000, the human population remained stable, or even declined; then it increased to A.D. 1350. The bubonic plague pandemic reduced world population for the next 50 years or so. Following the plague, the human population began an exponential increase in numbers that continues unabated to the present day.

Chapter 2 examines the history of world population growth in more detail. The analysis shows that since the 1960s, the rate of world population growth has been declining. Pearl's prediction of a stable population for the United States may yet be realized, but at a number well above 190 million. The prospects for a stable world population are also discussed in Chapter 2.

Pearl and his followers, such as Samuel Brody (1945), also made predictions about human growth and development. These predictions were based on the S-

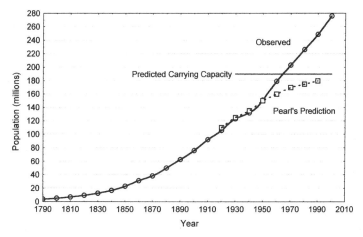

FIGURE 1.2 Pearl's predicted population growth for the United States and the real population growth (from Ellison and O'Rourke, 2000).

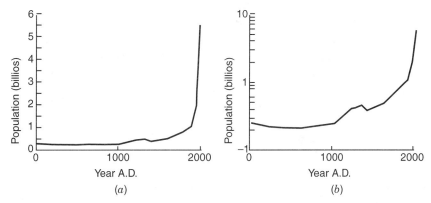

FIGURE 1.3 Growth of the human population of the world (from Ellison and O'Rourke, 2000).

shaped curves of growth for rats, pumpkins, and other nonhuman species. As for the population growth predictions, these predictions for individual growth in height, weight, and other body dimensions were also wrong. Pearl and Brody did not know, or did not understand, that the human curve of growth, from birth to maturity, does not follow an S-shaped curve. The classic curves of normal human growth are shown in Figure 1.4. The human "distance" curve, showing the amount of growth in height from birth to age 22 years, is labeled on the right side of the graph. This curve has three phases: an initial phase of rapid growth during infancy, a second prolonged phase of moderate and near-constant growth during the childhood and juvenile stages, and a third phase with the adolescent growth spurt.

These phases are more clearly seen in the velocity curves. The increments of the velocity curve, which represents the rate of growth in height during any year, is labeled on the left side. Changes in the velocity of growth may be divided into five phases, or stages, of human development. Below the velocity curve are symbols

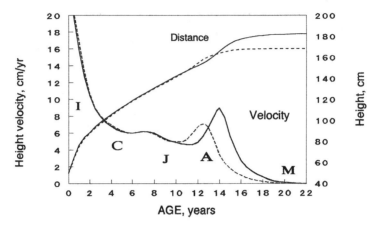

FIGURE 1.4 Distance and velocity curves of growth for human beings. The stages of post-natal growth are abbreviated as follows: I = infancy, C = childhood, J = juvenile, A = adolescence, M = mature adult (Bogin, 1999a).

indicating the average duration of each stage of development. These are (1) infancy, (2) childhood, (3) juvenile, (4) adolescent, and (5) adult stages. In addition to changes in growth rate, each stage may also be defined by characteristics of the dentition, by changes related to methods of feeding, by physical and mental competencies, and by maturation of the reproductive system and sexual behavior. I explain these aspects of human growth and development in detail in Chapter 3. At this point my focus is only on changes in the rate of growth.

The most rapid velocity of growth of any of the postnatal stages characterizes **infancy**,[2] a stage that begins at birth and lasts until about age three years. The infant's rate of growth is also characterized by a steep decline in velocity, a deceleration. The infant's curve of growth, rapid velocity and deceleration, is a continuation of the fetal pattern, in which the rate of growth in length actually reaches a peak in the second trimester of gestation and then begins a deceleration that lasts until childhood (Fig. 3.6 shows the fetal pattern of growth rate). The **childhood** stage follows infancy, encompassing the ages of about three to seven years. The growth deceleration of infancy ends at the beginning of childhood, and the rate of growth levels off at about 5 cm per year. This leveling off in growth rate is unusual for mammals, as virtually all other species continue a pattern of deceleration after infancy. This slower and steady rate of human growth maintains a relatively small-sized body during the childhood years.

Another feature of the childhood phase of growth is the modest acceleration in growth velocity at about six to eight years, called the **midgrowth spurt** (shown in Fig. 1.4). Some studies note the presence of the midgrowth spurt in the velocity curve of boys but not girls. Others find that up to two-thirds of boys and girls have midgrowth spurts. The midgrowth spurt is linked with an endocrine event called **adrenarche**, which results in a progressive increase in the secretion of adrenal androgen hormones. We will explore the ramifications of adrenarche in Chapter 3.

---

[2] Formal definitions for all words and phrases set in **boldface** may be found in the Glossary.

The human **juvenile** stage begins at about age 7 years. The juvenile stage is characterized by the slowest rate of growth since birth. In girls, the juvenile period ends, on average, at about the age of 10, two years before it usually ends in boys, the difference reflecting the earlier onset of adolescence in girls. Human **adolescence** is the stage of life when social and sexual maturation takes place. In terms of growth, both boys and girls experience a rapid acceleration in the growth velocity of virtually all of the bones of the body. This is called the **adolescent growth spurt**. Adolescence ends and early **adulthood** begins with the completion of the growth spurt, the attainment of adult stature, and the achievement of full reproductive maturity, meaning both physical and psychosocial maturity. Height growth stops when the long bones of the skeleton (e.g., the femur, tibia, humerus) lose their ability to increase in length.

LIFE HISTORY: THE LINK BETWEEN DEMOGRAPHY AND GROWTH

Clearly, human population growth and the growth of individual people follow patterns that are strikingly different from the S-shaped curves of other animals and plants. The reason for this differences lies in the nature of the human course of life, that is, the fact that humans add new stages to life that are not found in any other primate or mammal. The study of the evolution and function of life stages is called **life history theory**. A central theme of this book is that life history theory makes the connection between demography and growth especially clear. Life history may be defined as the strategy an organism uses to allocate its energy toward growth, maintenance, reproduction, raising offspring to independence, and avoiding death. For a mammal, it is the strategy of when to be born, when to be weaned, how many and what type of prereproductive stages of development to pass through, when to reproduce, and when to die.

Different species of living things have greatly different life history strategies, and understanding what shapes these histories is one of the most active areas of research in whole-organism biology. One focus of this research links the way in which people grow up with human reproductive success, which is greater than that of any other mammal. The social mammals, such as wolves, lions, and elephants, rear about 12 to 18 percent of their live-born offspring to adulthood. Our closest living relative, the chimpanzee, rears about 36 percent of its live-born offspring to maturity. But human hunter-gatherers and horticulturists, living in traditional societies without the benefits of modern medical care, rear about 60 percent of their infants to adulthood. Industrial societies of North America and Western Europe successfully rear at least 95 percent of live-born infants to maturity.

My own research on the evolution of human life history helps to explain this extraordinary human reproductive success (Bogin, 1999a). It seems that during human evolution, perhaps about two million years ago (MYA), our ancestors added a childhood stage to the life cycle. Within the last 100,000 years our ancestors added a distinct adolescent stage to the life cycle. Even though these additional stages prolonged the total time from birth to adulthood and thus delayed the age at reproduction, they provided people with a reproductive advantage. Chimpanzees must care for an infant for five years until the mother may again reproduce. With the addition of a childhood stage of life, people reduce this infant-care period to no more than three years, because children have biological and behavioral capacities to survive under the care of people other than the mother. This frees the mother to have another baby. People can have three or four offspring in the time it takes chimps to have two.

Equally importantly, more human babies survive because people have adolescence, a biologically defined stage of life that allows teenage boys and girls to learn and practice social and reproductive skills before they start having babies. Chimpanzees have to "learn on the job," so to speak, how to be successful mates and mothers, which results in a higher rate of death, especially for first-born offspring. Later in this book (Chapter 4), I will explain the evolution and significance of human childhood and adolescence in detail and show how these new stages of life history lead inextricably to growth of the entire human population.

WHY DO ANTHROPOLOGISTS STUDY HUMAN GROWTH AND DEMOGRAPHY?

Anthropology and Growth

The study of human growth has been a part of anthropology since the founding of the discipline. European anthropology of the early to mid-nineteenth century was basically anatomy and anthropometry, the science of human body measurements (Malinowski and Wolanski, 1985). Early practitioners of American anthropology, especially Franz Boas (1858–1942), are known as much for their studies of human growth as for work in cultural studies, archaeology, or linguistics. One of Boas's interests was the effect of migration from Europe to the United States on changes in body size and shape. At the time of those studies, around 1910, most anthropologists and anatomists believed that stature and other measurable dimensions of the body, such as head shape, could be used as "racial" markers. The word "race" refers to the scientifically discredited notion that human beings can be organized into biologically distinct groups based on **phenotypes** (the physical appearance and behavior of a person). According to this fallacious idea, northern European "races" were tall and had relatively long and narrow heads, while southern European "races" were shorter and had relatively round skulls. Boas found that, generally, the children of Italian and Jewish European migrants to the United States grew up to be significantly taller and heavier than their parents. The children of the migrants even changed the shape of their heads; they grew up to have long narrow heads.

Boas (1911, 1912) was able to show that in the new environment of the United States, the children of these recent immigrants from southern Europe grew up to look less like their own parents and more like the descendants of immigrants from northern Europe. Most of the northern Europeans had come to America two or three generations ago. Boas used the changes in body size and shape to argue that environment and culture are more important than heredity or "race" in determining the physical appearance of people. In terms of the environment, Boas pointed out that life in the United States afforded better nutrition than was available in southern Europe, in terms of both the quantity and the variety of food. There were also greater opportunities for education and wage-paying labor. Today, it is well known that these nutritional and socioeconomic gains are associated with larger body size.

In terms of culture, migration to America brought many changes, especially some changes in child-rearing practices. In much of Europe, infants were usually wrapped up tightly and placed on their backs to sleep, but the American practice, at the turn of the century, was to place infants in the prone position. In order to be "modern," the European immigrant parents often adopted the American practice. One effect on the infant was a change in skull shape, since pressure applied to the back of the infant's skull produces a rounder head, while pressure applied to the side of the skull produces a longer and narrower head. Studies in Europe by Walcher (1905) demonstrated the sleeping position effect on skull shape. Boas extended those studies to immigrants to the United States. His research showed that human biology interacted with the environmental, socioeconomic, and cultural changes that followed migration.

Boas effectively demonstrated that human beings had to be studied as both biological and cultural entities. Anthropologists, with training in anatomy and other areas of human biology, as well as training in social, cultural, and linguistic disciplines are well suited to study human growth and development.

Anthropological Demography

Demography, in its traditional sense, has been defined as the "study of mortality, fertility, and migration, and their relationship to population growth, family formation, and human ecology" (Gage, 2000, p. 507). Demographers study some of the most essential aspects of human life—birth, death, mating and marriage, household formation, and movement from place to place. Anthropology and anthropologists play a key role in demographic research because (from Brown University brochure, "Graduate Study in Anthropological Demography, 1999):

> Birth, death, marriage, household organization and migration are central to the lives of all people, and they have been at the core of anthropology since it became a discipline. Practices and beliefs surrounding birth, the study of marriage and domestic groups, as well as illness and death are of long-standing interest to anthropologists. Both internal migration—especially movement from rural to urban areas—and international migration have attracted anthropological attention for decades.

These topics, which form the core of demographic research, are of interest to many other disciplines. Accordingly, demography is an interdisciplinary field and includes sociology, economics, history, political science, and public health, as well as social anthropology, archaeology, and biological anthropology. In broad perspective, **anthropological demography** is the study of the biosocial characteristics of a human population and their development through time.

Anthropological demography adds to traditional demography the comparative, evolutionary, and holistic approaches of anthropology to the study of the human population. Using these approaches, anthropological demographers make connections between cross-cultural variations in social behavior, biology, and population dynamics. From social anthropology comes the use of **participant-observation** as a methodology for the collection of demographic and other social data. Participant-observation requires the researcher to live with the people being studied and to learn their language and rules for behavior. This methodology allows the researcher to produce **qualitative data** about the demographic processes at work in a group of people. Traditional demography produces **quantitative data**, usually in the form of statistics on births, deaths, marriages, and migrations. Qualitative data help to explain these quantitative statistics in human terms. For example, sets of narratives that detail the life history of individuals within a human group provide a qualitative picture of how demographic processes actually work. Qualitative data also provide information about the cultural construction of gender, age, and ethnic groups and about the impact of religion, kinship, and marriage on the demographic decisions that people make during their lives. These qualitative social data may come from hundreds of different cultures, and this allows for comparisons between cultures for shared and unusual population patterns.

Additional benefits of anthropological demography come from the historical and biological perspectives of the field. **Archaeology** is one of the major subfields of anthropology. From archaeology comes the historical time-depth required to ascertain if current population problems are of recent or ancient origin and if current trends are merely local distortions or the true long-term patterns of population behavior. Biological anthropology provides the fundamental knowledge of human biology relating to fertility, growth and development, adaptation, physiological variability, health, disease, and mortality. The integration of these biological variables with the social data leads to the formation of biosocial models of human population dynamics.

ANTHROPOLOGICAL PERSPECTIVE ON HIV/AIDS

An example of the place of anthropology within demographic research is useful here. The following example is about acquired immunodeficiency syndrome, or AIDS, which is an infectious disease, meaning that it is transmissible from person to person. The disease is caused by the human immunodeficiency virus (HIV). Once the body is infected, HIV slowly attacks and usually destroys the immune system, the body's defense against disease, leaving the individual vulnerable to other infections. Indeed, one indication that a person has HIV is when he or she has a combination of bacterial and viral infections, such as tuberculosis and the rare cancer Kaposi's sarcoma. It is these secondary infections that eventually cause death.

AIDS was first diagnosed in 1981 in a small population of homosexual men. Today, AIDS has spread to the general population and affects heterosexual males and females with multiple sex partners, hemophiliacs, and people addicted to intravenous drugs. Even infants and small children are susceptible and have become one of the fastest growing groups at risk. In adults, children, and infants HIV is spread by exchange of infected blood or blood products. It may also be passed between partners during sexual intercourse. Infected pregnant women may spread the virus to a fetus through the placental wall. Nursing mothers can infect an infant through breast milk. Neither the exchange of saliva nor the transmission of blood via insect bites is known to spread HIV.

From this list of the modes of infection it is clear that with the exception of maternal–fetal transfer, human behaviors are the cause of the spread of HIV. Modifying the behaviors that place people at risk for HIV infection could, in principle, completely eradicate the disease. This principle is, in practice, a far too simplistic notion. Anthropologists understand that human behaviors, especially those related to sexual and reproductive behavior, additive behaviors, and infant and child-rearing practices, are deeply ingrained in the basic nature of each culture. It may be unrealistic to expect these behaviors, which are often imbued with deep symbolic meaning, to change quickly—even in the face of a terrifying and debilitating disease such as HIV.

A look at the demographics of HIV/AIDS around the world shows that the distribution of the disease is not uniform. Figure 1.5 depicts the number of adults and children estimated to be living with HIV/AIDS as of the end of 2000. The World Health Organization (WHO) estimates that 33.4 million people of all ages were living with HIV/AIDS. Sub-Saharan Africa represents 70 percent of all cases, and 80 percent of all deaths due to AIDS in 2000 occurred in this region. But, sub-Saharan Africa has only 10.3 percent of the world's population. What are the biocultural factors that may explain this uneven distribution of HIV/AIDS prevalence and deaths? The United Nations Programme on HIV/AIDS (UNAIDS) report, "AIDS Epidemic Update: December 1998," highlights four factors that drive the HIV/AIDS epidemic: (1) migrant labor, (2) conflict, (3) danger, and (4) stigma (the full report is located at the Internet site *http://www.who.int/emc-hiv/ december1998/wadr98e.pdf*).

Adults and children estimated to be living with HIV/AIDS as of end 2000

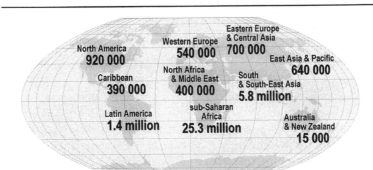

Total: 36.1 million

FIGURE 1.5 Number of people, of all ages, estimated to be living with HIV/AIDS as of the end of 2000 (World Health Organization; Internet site: *http://www.who.int/emc-hiv*).

Migrant Labor

The migration of people from place to place in search of work is not a new phenomenon, but the pace of migration has increased during the past 50 years (Bogin, 1988). Rural-to-urban migration is very common in much of the world, including Africa. These urban migrants are usually adolescents or unmarried young adults who find themselves alone in the city. Their loneliness and the boredom of low-paying, menial jobs (e.g., domestic servants) lead many to seek comfort in sexual liaisons. The men often seek sex with prostitutes and become infected with HIV from them. These infected men may pass on the infection to young migrant women or take it back to their rural village when they return home to visit. Compounding this mode of disease transmission are social values. The UNAIDS report notes that in some areas of South Africa it is almost expected that men and women separated from their families will have sex outside of the primary relationship.

Another type of migrant mentioned in the UNAIDS report are gold miners in South Africa (p. 11):

> Carltonville, at the heart of South Africa's gold mining industry, is home to 88,000 mine workers, 60% of them migrants from other parts of South Africa or from nearby countries: Lesotho, Malawi and Mozambique. With the miners come wages. Some US$ 18 million is paid out to workers every month in Carltonville. With wages come all manner of goods and services, including, of course, drugs and sex. Some 400–500 sex workers service the Carltonville mines. And with the drugs and sex comes HIV.

The miners live in single-sex dormitories and have a dangerous job. The use of drugs and sex to ameliorate their loneliness and fear is understandable, and warnings about the dangers of a slow, prolonged death due to HIV infection have little impact on men who might die suddenly in the mines. With a ratio of approximately one sex worker for every 175 men, the rapid spread of any sexually transmitted disease (STD) is inevitable. Visits by the miners to their hometowns further increase the spread of the epidemic to wives and other women back at home. The UNAIDS report states that in one South African rural community, where 60 percent of the households have one or more male migrants, the rate of HIV infection among pregnant women reached 26 percent in 1997 and continues to rise.

Conflict and Danger

Conflict and danger are the second and third factors driving the HIV/AIDS epidemic mentioned in the UNAIDS report: "Wars and armed conflicts generate fertile conditions for the spread of HIV" (p. 12). Warfare between Hutu and Tutsi ethnic groups in Rwanda is a case in point. Prior to start of the hostilities in the mid-1990s, the rate of HIV infection was about 10 percent in urban areas and 1.3 percent in rural areas. By 1997, both urban and rural populations had rates of 11 percent—a sixfold increase for the rural population. The war displaced much of the population, mixing people from urban and rural areas into refugee camps or other states of homelessness: "Overcrowding, violence, rape, despair and the need to sell or give away sex to survive are all likely to have contributed to this huge leap in infection" (p. 12). The rate of increase in HIV infection was greatest at the earliest ages, especially 12-, 13-, and 14-year-olds—an age group at risk for dangerous behavior because of lack of education and experience.

Rwanda is just one African nation, and a relatively small nation, with a recent history of conflict. The situation in the larger neighboring nations at war (such as the Republic of Congo) is likely to be worse. And conflicts are not confined to Africa. Regional warfare in Eastern Europe, Southeast Asia, and the Americas places even more people at risk for infection.

Stigma

The fear of HIV/AIDS and the shame that infection brings to the individual and his or her family are powerful stigmas that create a social environment promoting the further spread of the disease. Some HIV-positive individuals refuse to alter the high-risk behaviors that caused their infection because it might be interpreted as an admission of having the disease. Men with HIV may refuse to use a condom with their wives because they are afraid of admitting that they have had extramarital relationships and afraid of acknowledging their disease status. Women with HIV may fear being beaten or left homeless if they confess to family members. Concealing her HIV status may mean that the disease is transferred to her fetus or nursing infant. According to the UNAIDS report, in the city of Mutare, Zimbabwe, there are an estimated 30,000 people with HIV. The city has one HIV support group with just 70 members. Those who know they are infected fear the social stigma of revealing their status. Many people surveyed say they fear that they may be infected but are even more afraid to find out.

A South African effort to help overcome the stigma of HIV/AIDS infection is given in Box 1.1.

BIOCULTURAL MODEL OF HIV/AIDS

The list of social factors that help to fuel the epidemic of HIV/AIDS may be expanded beyond these four described in the UNAIDS report. The spread of industrialization, urbanization, and capitalistic market economies to the Third World (I use this phrase to characterize the less economically developed countries of the world) leads to fundamental change in the way people live. In many parts of the world, for example in much of sub-Saharan Africa, this type of "modernization," as defined by the most industrialized and market-oriented nations of the world, leads to the break-up of traditional social systems. Under these traditional systems, food, clothing, shelter, education, and other goods and services were provided by family-based economies of labor and exchange. Industrialized and urbanized economies transform the family-based systems of exchange into market commodities. To find cash-paying employment to pay for such commodities, family members are often separated from each other. As documented in the UNAIDS report, separation may lead to high-risk behaviors for the spread of STDs.

Many social and cultural factors may lead to the spread of STDs, but these diseases are not social variables. They are biological entities. HIV/AIDS, which is a type of virus, is only one of many STDs. Others are genital herpes, another virus, and syphilis, gonorrhea, and chlamydia, which are bacterial infections. These STDs may have existed in the population prior to modernization, or visitors from the industrialized nations may have introduced them. When left untreated, these STDs

---

BOX 1.1
"HIV/AIDS Is Among Us"

South Africa, which in 1998 accounted for nearly 1 in 10 of the new HIV infections estimated to have occurred worldwide, is the latest country in the ranks of those seeking to break through the shroud of stigma and shine a light on the human disaster of AIDS: "For too long we have closed our eyes as a nation, hoping the truth was not so real," South African Deputy President Thabo Mbeki (now President) told South Africans in October 1998. "For many years, we have allowed the human immunodeficiency virus to spread.... At times we did not know that we were burying people who had died from AIDS. At other times we knew, but chose to remain silent.

[Now] we face the danger that half of our youth will not reach adulthood. Their education will be wasted," Mbeki said. "The economy will shrink. There will be a large number of sick people whom the healthy will not be able to maintain. Our dreams as a people will be shattered."

Appealing to South Africans to change "the way we live and how we love," Mbeki called for abstinence, fidelity, and condom use and urged a caring, nondiscriminatory attitude to those already infected with or affected by HIV. The speech was nationally televised, and the whole nation was urged to stop work to listen to it. Many private companies gave workers a day off. Flags flew at half mast on government buildings and religious leaders, youth, trade unionists, women's organizations, and business leaders committed themselves to the President's Partnership Against AIDS.

SOURCE: Quoted from "Aids epidemic update: December 1998," UNAIDS Joint United Nations Programme on HIV/AIDS, Geneva.

often cause infertility and therefore have demographic impacts. People living in traditional cultures usually value high fertility, and the worth of a woman or a man is measured, in part, by the number of children they produce. Faced with infertility, due to the widespread nature of STDs, many people in traditional cultures seek multiple partners to ensure their parenthood. This behavior, which seems completely reasonable and desirable to the practitioners, increases the rate of the spread of the STDs, which leads to further infertility. In societies where men value high fertility and many adult women are infected with STDs, such as in much of sub-Saharan Africa, there is an attempt to find ever-younger sexual partners in the hope that these young women are uninfected and will produce offspring. Young female sexual partners are also desired in many parts of Asia because older men believe they are less likely to be infected with STDs, and hence the men may have lower risk for infection. In fact, however, the men are often infected, and their beliefs and behaviors only serve to increase the spread of STDs, including HIV/AIDS, to the younger generation of women and girls.

These interactions between social beliefs, cultural values, behavior, and biology illustrate the **biocultural** nature of human health and disease. Human demography and human growth and development are also biocultural in nature. Since the late-nineteenth century, anthropologists have used biocultural models. An example of such use is given in Box 1.2.

BOX 1.2
Human Growth in Biocultural Perspective

The biocultural nature of human growth may be appreciated by the following example, based on my own research in Guatemala and the United States on the impact of the economic and political environment on the growth and development of Maya children (Bogin and Loucky, 1997). Two samples of Maya are compared: one a group living in their homeland of Guatemala and the other a group of migrants living in the United States. Both groups include individuals between the ages of 5 and 14 years old. The Guatemalan sample live in a village with an irregular supply of water, no safe drinking water, and unsanitary means for waste disposal. The parents of these Maya children are employed, predominately, as tailors or seamstresses by local clothing manufacturers and are paid minimal wages. There is one public health clinic in the village, which administers treatment to infants and preschool children with clinical undernutrition—an omnipresent problem. The incidence of infant and childhood morbidity and mortality from infectious disease is relatively high. Deaths due to political repression, especially the civil war of the late 1970s to the early 1980s, are common for the Maya of Guatemala. The residents of this particular Maya village were caught up in the military hostilities of that time but escaped the worst of the civil war. They also suffered from reduced food availability due to the collapse of the Guatemalan economy during the 1980s (Bogin and Keep, 1999).

The U.S. sample reside in two places, Indiantown, a rural agricultural community in central Florida, and Los Angeles, California. The political status of the Maya in the United States is heterogeneous. Some have applied for, and a few have won, political asylum. Others have temporary legal rights to reside and to work, but many remain undocumented. Adults in the Florida community work as day laborers in agriculture, landscaping, construction, child care, and other informal sector jobs. Many of the Los Angeles Maya work in the "sweatshops" of the garment industry, although a few have jobs in the service sector or technical professions.

The growth in height, weight, and body composition of Maya children and youths living in Guatemala is significantly retarded compared with U.S. National Center for Health Statistics (NCHS) reference data.[3] Figure B1.1 illustrates the mean height and weight of the Guatemalan Maya from the village of San Pedro during two time periods. Some researchers argue that the small size and delayed maturation of malnourished populations such as the Maya are genetic adaptations to their poor environmental conditions. If this argument were true, then a change in the economic, social, or political environment would not influence growth. The notion that the small size of the Maya is primarily genetic is clearly wrong, for as also shown in Figure B1.1, the U.S. Maya are significantly taller and heavier than Maya children living in Guatemala. The Maya in the United States attain virtually the same weight as the NCHS sample. The average increase in height is 5.5 cm between Maya in the United States and Maya in Guatemala. This increase occurred within a single generation, that is, as children moved from Guatemala to the United States. Moreover, the change in average stature is, perhaps, the largest such increase ever recorded. By contrast, the immigrant children measured by Boas averaged about 2.0 cm taller than their European-born parents.

The reason for the increase in body size of the Maya children is the same as for the European immigrant children measured by Boas. In the United States

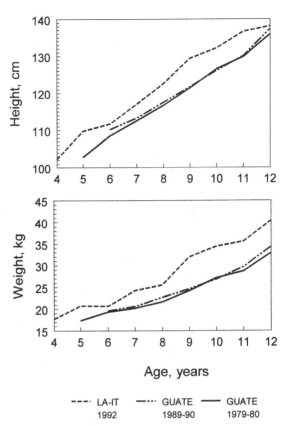

FIGURE B1.1 Mean height or weight by age of the Los Angeles and Indiantown Maya sample (LA-IT) and the Maya samples from Guatemala measured in 1979 to 1980 and 1989 to 1990 (GUATE). Data for boys and girls within all samples are combined. Note that there is virtually no change in the mean size of the Guatemala-living Maya. This indicates that the generally poor environmental conditions for growth remained unchanged for that decade. The Maya population in the United States is significantly taller and heavier than the Maya in Guatemala.

there is both more food and a greater variety of food than in rural Guatemala. In the United States there are also social services that are unavailable in rural Guatemala, including health care, food supplementation programs, schools, and job training programs. All of these differences improve the biological and social environment for human growth. The most important differences, however, are safe drinking water and the conditions that go with less political repression. The public supply of safe drinking water in the United States eliminates the constant exposure to bacteria, parasites, agricultural pesticides, and fertilizers that contaminate drinking water in rural Guatemala. The relative political freedom for Maya in the United States allows parents to pursue their goals for the healthy growth and development of their children. LeVine (1977), an anthropologist of the family and of children, proposed a universal evolutionary hierarchy of human parental goals. The primary goal is to encourage the survival and the health of a child. Secondary goals relate to developing the child into a self-supporting adult and instilling cultural beliefs and behavioral norms. Economic and political conditions in Guatemala make it difficult for parents to achieve these goals for their children. The political economy of the United States offers real possibilities for success, and Maya parents seize upon these, just as other immigrants have done before them.

As Boas argued for nearly 50 years, the study of human growth provides a mirror of the human condition. Reflected in the patterns of growth of human populations are the "material and moral conditions of that society" (Tanner, 1986, p. 3). The forces holding back growth in Guatemala are severe indeed, and the growth differences between the Maya of Guatemala and the United States may be used as a measure to assess the magnitude of change in political and socioeconomic conditions.

---

[3] NCHS reference data represent the growth status of a healthy, well-nourished population from the United States in the year 1977. These reference data are recommended by the World Health Organization for the evaluation of human growth for all populations so as to provide a common baseline for international comparison. The NCHS reference data are used throughout this book for all such comparisons.

With the discovery of the nature of deoxyribonucleic acid (DNA) and other fundamentals of developmental biology, the use of biocultural models became increasingly common in anthropology. The models of the 1960s and 1970s considered the biocultural nature of human beings to be essentially linear. By "linear," I mean, first, that human variation in growth and development, or in fertility and mortality, started with a biological substrate and, second, that substrate was influenced to a greater or lesser extent by the social and cultural environment. In the last 10 years or so, a newer, expanded biocultural view of human nature has replaced the older linear model. The newer biocultural model posits that there is a recurring interaction between human biology and the sociocultural environment. Not only does the latter influence the former, but human biological variation modifies social and cultural processes as well. It is now understood, for example, that environmental forces, including the social, economic, and political environment, regulate the expression of DNA as much, or more so, than DNA regulates human biology (Goodman and Leatherman, 1998; Bogin, 1999a).

In addition to the biocultural interactions between people and STDs mentioned so far, there are some other biological and cultural factors that help to explain the rapid and devastating effect of HIV/AIDS in tropical Africa and Asia. These regions are plagued by malaria, which is another devastating infectious disease. Malaria is caused by a parasitic infection that destroys blood cells and has many other harmful effects on the human body. One way to treat these effects is with blood transfusions, which prior to the HIV/AIDS epidemic was an efficacious treatment. During the 1980s, the dangers of blood tainted with HIV/AIDS were unknown in many of the malarial regions of Africa and Asia, even though the information was available in the industrialized countries. Even when the dangers were known, the precautions taken when administering blood transfusions were often not sufficient to prevent the spread of HIV/AIDS. The lack of appropriate medical technology and health education in most of Africa, due, largely, to persistent economic, social, and political instability, allowed the epidemic to spread. Together, these biosocial factors resulted in the current HIV/AIDS burden that is crippling much of Africa.

DEMOGRAPHIC IMPACT OF HIV/AIDS

HIV/AIDS is a fatal disease. The UNAIDS program estimates that from the beginning of the epidemic in 1981 to the end of 2000, 21.8 million people had died of HIV/AIDS. Of this total, 17.5 million were adults (8.5 million men and 9 million women) and 4.3 million were children and youth under 15 years old. In 2000 alone, 3 million people of all ages died of HIV/AIDS. Worldwide, AIDS is already the fourth leading cause of death. With 36.1 million people still living with HIV/AIDS, UNAIDS predicts that rate of mortality from HIV/AIDS will increase in the next decade.

By the late 1980s there was both scientific and popular concern that the HIV/AIDS epidemic might cause negative population growth. Some people thought this would be restricted to certain regions of the world, such as Africa. Others wondered if the world population might be affected. By 1992, papers were presented at the International Conference on AIDS that attempted to model and predict population growth in relation to the HIV/AIDS epidemic. Way and Stanecki (1992), working at the U.S. Bureau of the Census, predicted that negative population growth due to the epidemic "is not particularly likely, especially in Sub-Saharan Africa" (p. C326). Their prediction was based on a complex mathematical model of the epidemic, which included "demographic, behavioral, and epidemiological inputs" (p. C326). Way and Stanecki argued that negative population growth would require an epidemic two to three times more severe than existed in urban Africa in 1992. They added that "such an epidemic is possible with only implausible behavioral and/or transmission parameters" (p. C326).

By 1996, the implausible became reality. Low-Beer et al. (1996) presented the first report of severe, negative population change due to the HIV/AIDS epidemic. Their results were limited to relatively small districts within the African nation of Uganda, but their findings were startling. Uganda is a nation with very high population growth, but some districts had lost 27 percent of their population. The most severely impacted regions had 50 percent deficits for adult men in the 40- to 44-year-old age group and adult women in the 35- to 39-year-old group. The most likely reason for the deficits in expected population size is mortality due to HIV/AIDS. Even more "implausible" is that the epidemic had infected and estimated 40 percent of the population in these districts. The impact on future fertility was unknown at that time. The researchers urged careful monitoring to ascertain if these types of severe population declines were spreading to larger areas.

Papers presented at the 1998 International Conference on AIDS showed that the "implausible reality" of Uganda was an international phenomenon. Way and Stover (1998) reported that "AIDS is substantially reducing levels of life expectancy in many countries. National levels of HIV infection of 10 percent or less can result in a doubling in the number of deaths and the crude death rate and a reduction of 20 years in life expectancy" (p. 943). The first author of this paper is the same Dr. Way who said in 1992 that the HIV/AIDS epidemic was unlikely to have such severe demographic impact. I point this out to show that the science is a self-correcting process. Disciplines that use the scientific method will change their interpretations and expectations of how things work in response to the accumulation and further analysis of empirical data. Furthermore, the results of these analyses will lead to the formulation of new theoretical positions. In science, this type of change is expected and is good.

In another paper, Stover and Way (1998) state that, by the year 2005, AIDS deaths in the most severely affected African countries will result in population declines of 13 to 59 million people. By the year 2025 the population loss may reach 120 million. Other studies found HIV-infected adults have up to a threefold increase in total mortality, and death rates may be even higher for young adults. One severe impact of this is seen in the decline of life expectancy. The UNAIDS projections for changes in life expectancy in some sub-Saharan countries are given in Figure 1.6. Life expectancy at birth is a key indicator of social and economic development. Many political and social agencies use the human development index to assess the quality of life in a country. This index takes into account a nation's wealth, literacy, and life expectancy. Due to the HIV/AIDS epidemic, life expectancy in Botswana has declined so much (Fig. 1.6) that Botswana dropped 26 places on the human development index.

Boerma et al. (1998) reported that women infected with HIV die at earlier ages than men. Moreover, women infected with HIV have lower fertility than non-infected women (Zaba, 1998). Together, higher female mortality and lower fertility will reduce population growth and, maybe, even population size. The demographic impact of the HIV/AIDS epidemic is further compounded by the raising number of cases of infection among people 15 to 24 years old. Almost one-half of new HIV infections occur in this age group around the world. In several industrialized nations, including the United States, Spain, Canada, and Denmark, HIV/AIDS is a leading cause of death for people under 40 years old, rivaling automobile accidents, firearms, and other traumatic causes. Researchers in both the industrialized nations and in

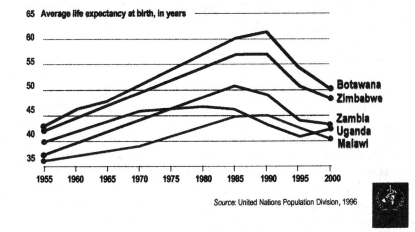

FIGURE 1.6 Projected life expectancy at birth in several sub-Saharan countries. The declines in life expectancy are mostly due to the effects of the HIV/AIDS epidemic (data from United Nations Population Division, 1996; Internet site: *http://www.who.int/emchiv/december1998/wadr98e.pdf*).

the Third World are concerned about the potential years of life lost (PYLL) due to the HIV epidemic. This concern is not only about lowering life expectancy but also about the loss of reproduction and economic productivity. The biocultural effects of lowered fertility in women of prime childbearing ages (20 to 29 years) often drive men to seek younger sexual partners. As described above, this only enhances the spread of the epidemic to younger women, further lowering total fertility and increasing the PYLL.

ECONOMIC EFFECTS OF THE HIV/AIDS EPIDEMIC

The economic effects of the PYLL are difficult to measure, but it is clear that the HIV/AIDS epidemic takes a significant economic toll. The **morbidity** (i.e., ill health) and mortality of the epidemic often decimate the pool of skilled workers, waste investments in education, divert money away from social and business investment, and reduce the size of the economically active and consumer-oriented segment of the nation. Traditional biocultural models of disease need to be revised in the face of the HIV/AIDS epidemic. In the United States, for example, mortality from heart disease and cancer are each greater than mortality from HIV/AIDS. More money is allocated to research and treatment of heart disease and cancer than to HIV/AIDS. An analysis by Lai et al. (1997) shows that lowering the death rate from heart disease and cancer would lengthen life after age 65 years, but lowering mortality from HIV/AIDS would lengthen life during the working years (15 to 65). The economic impact of HIV/AIDS mortality is, then, much greater than for the other two diseases combined. The authors advocate an approach to policy for research funding that emphasizes the PYLL and economic impacts more than a simple approach based on number of deaths.

IMPACT OF HIV/AIDS ON FAMILY STRUCTURE AND HUMAN DEVELOPMENT

Perhaps the most insidious and pernicious effect of the HIV/AIDS epidemic is on family structure. HIV/AIDS kills young adults, the people most likely to be parents of dependent infants, children, and juveniles. The number of people less than 15 years old orphaned by AIDS since 1981 is estimated to be 13.2 million. This number will increase greatly in the next decade because the prevalence of orphaning due to HIV/AIDS deaths lags at least 10 years behind the spread of the epidemic (Gregson et al., 1998). The geographic distribution of these orphans is shown in Figure 1.7. Africa is home to 92 percent of these orphans. In some African cities more than 15 percent of all people under age 15 years are orphans. The impact of these staggering levels of orphanhood on human development and national development is barely known. Research in both the industrialized nation and the Third World indicates that so-called street children, who may be orphaned, abandoned, or run-aways, suffer from poor physical growth and development (Panter-Brick et al., 1996). In the United States, children in need of foster care often suffer from inadequate nutrition, which causes growth failure (Wyatt et al., 1997).

Cumulative number of children estimated to have been orphaned by AIDS at age 14 or younger at the end of 1999

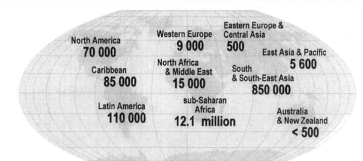

North America
70 000

Western Europe
9 000

Eastern Europe &
Central Asia
500

East Asia & Pacific
5 600

Caribbean
85 000

North Africa
& Middle East
15 000

South
& South-East Asia
850 000

Latin America
110 000

sub-Saharan
Africa
12.1 million

Australia
& New Zealand
< 500

Total: 13.2 million

FIGURE 1.7 Estimated number of people under age 15 years who have been orphaned by the HIV/AIDS epidemic since 1981 (UNAIDS/WHO, 1998; Internet site: *http://www.who.int/emc-hiv*).

In Africa and Asia, the number of orphaned infants and children is so great that traditional family systems cannot take care of all those in need. While most orphans have adult relatives, these adults have their own families and many live in poverty. Gregson et al. (1998) note that lower fertility among HIV-infected women will reduce the number of orphans. However, they predict that the total burden of orphans "will remain substantial" (p. 482). One solution may be to build orphanages, but institutionalized care has many problems. The most immediate problem is the cost of building and administrating such places. The longer term costs are to human development. The available research is mostly from the industrialized nations. Halfon et al. (1995) investigated the medical history of orphans and foster children in California. They found that over 80 percent of orphans living in institutions had developmental, emotional, or behavioral problems. The most common were physical growth abnormalities (low weight and height), neurological problems, and asthma. Almost one-third of the orphans had three or more problems. Frank et al. (1996) reviewed the health of orphans living in institutions. The authors covered research published during the prior century. They were especially interested in "five areas of potential biologic and social risk to infants and young children in orphanage care: (1) infectious morbidity, (2) nutrition and growth, (3) cognitive development, (4) socioaffective development, and (5) physical and sexual abuse" (p. 569). The authors found "that infants and young children are uniquely vulnerable to the medical and psychosocial hazards of institutional care, negative effects that cannot be reduced to a tolerable level even with massive expenditure. Scientific experience consistently shows that, in the short term, orphanage placement puts young children at increased risk of serious infectious illness and delayed language development. In the long term, institutionalization in early childhood increases the likelihood that impoverished children will grow into psychiatrically impaired and economically unproductive adults" (p. 569). If this loss of human development and economic productivity occurs in the United States, imagine the losses that will occur in the Third World.

INTEGRATED STUDY OF HUMAN DEMOGRAPHY AND GROWTH

Throughout this book, I will take an approach to the study of human demography and human growth and development that combines perspectives from life history theory and biocultural anthropology. Earlier in this chapter I described briefly topics to be covered in Chapters 2, 3, and 4. Before moving on to those chapters, I will outline the topics covered in all the remaining chapters in greater detail.

Chapter 2 begins with an overview of some ideas that lead to the development of the methods and principles of demography. Readers will be introduced to the methods that demographers use to construct, interpret, and analyze **life tables**. These tables are a mathematical expression of births, deaths, rates of aging, and population structure. Ways to extend the use of life tables to study human risk for disease and to analyze growth and development are also presented. Principles of fertility and mortality are reviewed (migration is treated in Chapter 5).

Chapter 3 provides readers with the principles of individual human growth and development. Essential concepts are reviewed, such as amount versus rate of growth and chronological age versus biological age. An emphasis is placed on the biocultural interactions between the environmental, genetic, and hormonal determinants of growth.

Chapter 4 begins with a detailed discussion of life history theory and its application to human demography and physical growth. The chapter next details what is known about the evolution of the human curve of growth, especially how the special human stages of childhood and adolescence evolved. Throughout this chapter, the discussion connects evolutionary change in patterns of growth with their demographic consequences.

Chapter 5 discusses how the evolution of human nutrition, systems of food production, human growth, and population regulation are all connected. Readers will learn how the social, economic, and political environment, in which people live, influences the supply and distribution of critical resources. The nature of this distribution, in turn, strongly influences the dynamics of population regulation and the growth of individual human beings. The nutritional and economic transitions—from foraging and horticulture, to intensive agriculture, to industrial, and now postindustrial societies—are described. Demographic transitions associated with these nutritional and economic changes are also detailed. The real connections, spurious connections, and lack of connections between these two kinds of transitions will be explained. Two of the overarching questions that shape this chapter are (1) What is overpopulation? and (2) Will overpopulation cause the ultimate famine, or will the human population continue to overcome the dire predictions of Malthus?

Chapter 6 discusses migration, a major demographic force that takes people, and their genetic, physiological, social, and cultural make-up, from place to place. As such, migration can seriously alter the ecology of both the sending and receiving populations. One cause and consequence of migration is disease. Fear of disease is one of the forces that drive human movement, and this influences human and population growth. Some of the history of disease and people will be detailed. Other factors, such as money, marriage, and mayhem (warfare), also push and pull people from place to place, and these will also be treated. Special attention will be paid to the effects of urbanization and the diseases of urban lifestyle on the growth of individuals and the human population. The case of migration from the Cape Verde Islands, presented in several text boxes within this chapter, provides an example of an anthropological approach to migration and demography.

Chapter 7 describes how anthropologists, economists, and historians are using past records of human growth and population dynamics to reconstruct the physical, social, and political well-being of people over the past 50,000 years or so. Research is showing that our ancient ancestors, living in small foraging groups, were taller and more massive, on average, than human beings alive today. Why did human body size shrink even as our population size increased? This chapter will discuss that question and also explore more recent cases of height, health, and population change. The reader will be introduced to the new and highly productive field of "anthropometric history." The methodology of anthropometric history is applied to an analysis of the economic and political history of Latin America during the past 8,000 years, to a reanalysis of the causes and consequences of the Irish Famine, and finally to a discussion of the desertification of rural Portugal and its link to the physical growth of the Portuguese.

Finally, Chapter 8 deals with two sets of questions. The first set is: Why are some human populations, especially in the richest nations, now in a period of zero or negative growth? How are physical and social resources to be allocated in populations with unprecedented numbers of old people? A life history approach is taken to the value of a postreproductive stage in the human life cycle for the health of the human population. The case of Japan is presented in terms of the prospects for the biocultural stability and well-being of new generations of Japanese. The second set is: How big can the human population grow? How big, and how fast, can people grow? Do people need to voluntarily regulate the growth of individuals and populations? Will Mother Nature do it for us? These questions guide a final discussion of the interactions of the growth of individuals and population. Some lessons from the past are probably our best sources of information and inspiration about the future of the human population.

TWO

HOW POPULATIONS GROW: HISTORY, METHODS, AND PRINCIPLES OF DEMOGRAPHY

There is no bound to prolific nature in plants and animals but what is made by their crowding and interfering with each other's means of subsistence.

T. R. MALTHUS (1798)

POPULATION PROBLEM

Thomas Robert Malthus (1766–1834) was an English clergyman, an economist, and a demographer. Malthus studied philosophy, mathematics, and theology at Cambridge University from 1784 to 1788. In 1790 he took holy orders in the Anglican Church, and by 1798 he became the curate of the parish of Albury, in Surrey, England. During that period he wrote his most well known work, *Essay on the Principle of Population* (1798). The impact of this essay on political and economic thinking in England, the rest of Europe, and elsewhere no doubt helped Malthus to secure his final position. In 1805 he became professor of history and political economy at the East India College near London.

The quote that opens this chapter comes from the *Essay*. If we think for a moment about plants and animals "crowding and interfering with each other's means of subsistence," then it may soon become apparent that Malthus's essay must have a somber character. Indeed it does, and Malthus, writing in the third person, states in the Preface to the *Essay*: "The view which he has given of human life has a melancholy hue, but he feels conscious that he has drawn these dark tints from a conviction that they are really in the picture, and not from a jaundiced eye or an inherent spleen of disposition." To use current vernacular, Malthus believes that he is correct to have a "bad attitude" about the human condition. Malthus was one of the first people to think clearly about the effect of population growth on the welfare of humanity. The full title of his book is *An Essay of the Principle of Population, as it Affects the Future Improvement of Society with Remarks on the Speculations of Mr. Godwin, M. Condorcet, and Other Writers*. His "remarks" were, in fact, an attack on the ideas of William Godwin and the Marquis de Condorcet's notions of eternal human progress. These hopeful ideas stem from the Enlightenment movement and its belief that people are rational and society is perfectible. The Enlightenment also predicted that high fertility would lead to population growth and economic prosperity—more workers, producing more goods, leading to a better life for all. If this were true, then eventually poverty, misery, disease, and war would cease to exist.

Malthus had a different view. He wrote in the Preface to the *Essay*, "It is an obvious truth... that population must always be kept down to the level of the means of subsistence" For Malthus, poverty, misery, disease, and war are the mechanisms by which population size is maintained below the means of subsistence. The reason for all this human suffering, the "obvious truth" referred to by Malthus, is that the food supply required by any group of organisms can only increase by arithmetic units, that is, a progression of 1, 2, 3, 4, 5, and so on. In contrast, said Malthus, the population will increase in geometric units: 1, 2, 4, 8, 16, and so on. These mathematical relationships are shown in Figure 2.1. Once the population exceeds the food supply, the rate of suffering and, eventually, death must increase. Malthus was not in favor of human suffering. Indeed, one of his reasons for writing the *Essay* was to offer a way to avoid such suffering. In 1803 Malthus published a revised edition of the *Essay* in which he offered a specific remedy, which he called "moral restraint." By this Malthus urged that people, especially from the poorer and working classes, delay marriage to a relatively

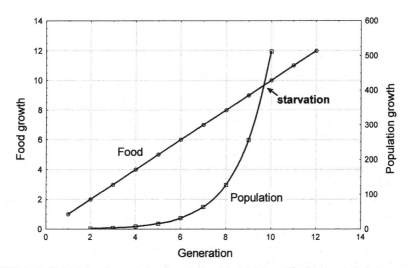

FIGURE 2.1 "Principle of population" as defined by Malthus. The food supply increases arithmetically, while the size of the population increases geometrically. Unless population growth is checked, it will surpass the food supply. Malthus predicted that starvation, civil unrest, increased mortality, and the like will ensue as people compete for scarce resources.

late age and practice conjugal abstinence. These behaviors, he hoped, would slow the rate of birth, help to reduce population size, and lead to greater prosperity for all.

Because he pointed to population growth as the cause of human suffering, Malthus was bitterly attacked by supporters of the Enlightenment. He was also attacked by the social reform movement, which saw the avarice and greed of capitalists of the Industrial Revolution as the reason for the spread of poverty and suffering. To be sure, Malthus also had many supporters, including David Ricardo, who helped develop modern economy theory. The fields of political science, sociology, and some branches of history also owe a debt to Malthus. Even biology was forever changed, as Malthus influenced Charles Darwin. Darwin reserved judgment about the applicability of Malthus's "principle of population" to human beings. But, Darwin enthusiastically embraced the principle when applied to the rest of the biological world. In the Introduction to his book *Origin of Species* (1859; 1979) Darwin writes, "the Struggle for Existence amongst all organic beings throughout the world . . . inevitably follows from their high geometrical powers of increase . . . This is the doctrine of Malthus, applied to the whole animal and vegetable kingdoms" (p. 68 of 1979 reprint). The doctrine formed the basis for Darwin's hypothesis of natural selection.[1]

Some supporters of Malthus elaborated on his ideas, taking them far beyond what Malthus ever intended. By the middle of the nineteenth century a neo-Malthusian movement started in Europe. The proponents of this movement advocated birth control, including abortion, for the poor and also for "undesirable" segments of the population. The Malthusian League, founded in 1877, was a popular and strong advocate of these methods of population control. "Undesirables" could be any ethnic, religious, or national group despised by the majority population or by the group in power. In the minds of many, the poor were undesirable because they were poor, that is, their poverty was prima facie evidence of their biological, mental, and moral deficiencies. It is important to emphasize that all of this occurred well after Malthus died. During his life, Malthus never accused the poor, or any social group, of being undesirable and never considered human reproduction to be, in and of itself, a problem. He advocated only fertility regulation for the entire human population.

Many social reformers eventually embraced the Malthusian position, but they turned the argument on its head and said that only through birth control could the plight of the poor be improved. Margaret Sanger, in the United States, and Marie Stopes, in Britain, were two such social reformers. Sanger was a nurse with first-hand experience of the misery of the poor in the New York City region. In 1914 she started publishing a magazine, *The Woman Rebel*, that disseminated information about birth control. In 1916 she opened a family planning clinic in Brooklyn, New York. The police soon closed it. After considerable legal work such clinics were

---

[1] Darwin (1859) defines natural selection as follows: "As many more individuals of each species are born than can possibly survive; and as, consequently, there is a frequently recurring struggle for existence, it follows that any being, if it vary however slightly in any manner profitable to itself, under the complex and sometimes varying conditions of life, will have a better chance of surviving, and thus be naturally selected. From the strong principle of inheritance, any selected variety will tend to propagate its new and modified form." (p. 68 of 1979 reprint).

allowed to open, but only if a licensed physician was on staff. Stopes was born to a middle-class family in Edinburgh, Scotland. She was the first woman to earn a doctorate in Botany, from the University of Munich in 1904. While Sanger looked outward, to the plight of the poor, for her inspiration, Stopes seems to have looked inward. The biases against women, including those she must have faced in order to earn a doctorate, led her to write a book titled *Married Love*. In this book she appealed for sexual equality and personal fulfillment for married women. Sanger and Stopes knew each other, and it was Sanger who suggested that Stopes add a chapter on birth control to her book. Stopes did so, with the hope that married women of all social classes could better manage the physical strain of pregnancy and motherhood and the health risks of excessive childbearing.

WAS THERE A POPULATION PROBLEM?

Did the size of the human population in 1798 exceed the level of subsistence? The answer to this question is, no. There are many more people alive today than in the time of Malthus. To be sure, there is still an unacceptable level of hunger, disease, warfare, and other miseries. But, we know today that these are not due to an excess of population above the capacity of the planet to produce food. Rather, all this suffering is due to social, economic, and political inequalities that deny some people access to food, to education, and to the ability to live in peace. To some readers, my assertion that social inequalities are the cause of much human suffering may appear to be political rhetoric. I detail these assertions with empirical evidence in Chapters 5, 6, and 7. Suffice it to state here that Malthus predicted the total destruction of civilization, and the death of most people, at a population size less than one-third that which exists today (about 6 billion). Malthus could not predict that technological devices and strategies for the production of food and other essentials have allowed the human population to increase about sixfold since 1798 (there were about 1 billion people back then).

HOW MANY PEOPLE?

How can we know the size of the human population today? How might we know the size of the human population in 1798? No one knows, for sure. Malthus was hampered by the fact that there were no empirical counts of the number of people alive in 1798. There were not even counts of the number of people living in London. One legacy of the work of Malthus, and the controversy that followed publication of his *Essay*, is that methods to accurately enumerate the size of the human population were developed. These methods are discussed in some detail in the next section of this chapter. Even though the number of people alive 200 years ago is not known with accuracy, there are estimates. The U.S. Bureau of the Census published several of these estimates at their web site (*http://www.census.gov/*). For the year 1800 the lowest estimate is 813 million and the highest estimate is 1.125 billion people. Most of the estimates, and there are six, cluster around 950 million people.

How is it possible to calculate the size of the human population for the year 1800 when there are no accurate data for the number of people alive then? The most recent of the six estimates mentioned above was performed by Haub (1995). Haub's methodology is a mix of mathematics and mysticism. He first assumes that population growth has been constant, rather than periodic. Famines, disease, and major warfare might be causes of periodic decreases in the rate of population growth. But, it is extremely difficult to account for these variables, so Haub assumes a constant rate. Next he asks two questions: (1) how long have people lived on the planet and (2) what was the average population size at the starting point? He comes up with almost Biblical answers. People first appear on the planet at 50,000 B.C. and there were just two at that time. Human paleontologists and geneticists are not in agreement about when the first members of the species *Homo sapiens* appeared on the planet. Genetic evidence pushes that date as far back as 250,000 B.P. (years before present) and fossil evidence places that date at about 125,000 B.P. So, a starting date of 50,000 B.C. (48,000 B.P.) for our species may be too young. More difficult to accept is the starting number of two—Haub does not say, but we must suppose this was one woman and one man! Even Haub is suspicious of this "Adam and Eve" approach, but he defends it by saying that a population size of two people for the starting point is a common assumption of demographers. It is referred to as a "minimalist approach."

Haub then applies some additional assumptions about human population size in the past. One is that at 8000 B.C. there were 5 million people, and at A.D. 1 there were 300 million people. It seems that these are also "magic numbers," in the sense that demographers use them as standard population benchmarks. Haub then begins to apply some of his own "guesstimates" (his own choice of words) about population growth. He sets the rate of birth at 80 per 1,000 people for the time period from 50,000 B.C. to A.D. 1 and at 60 per 1,000 from A.D. 2 through 1750. Haub justifies these rates on the basis that they are needed to maintain population size in the face of very high mortality. The balance between births and deaths means that there is only very slow increase in total population size. Slow population growth prior to the year A.D. 1000 is a generally accepted fact by most demographers (see Fig. 1.3). Haub assumes that after A.D. 1750 death rates decline due to "the arrival of modern medicine, better diet, and improved sanitation" (p. 4). This is another arguable assumption. Nevertheless, Haub uses it to propose that birth rates decline to 24 per 1,000 people. That rate continues to 1998. Given all of the assumptions, Haub generates estimates of the total size of the human population. His results are given in Table 2.1. With these data Haub shows that about 110 billion people have ever lived on the planet, and of this total about 5.5 percent are alive today. He says that this is a fairly large percentage, but nowhere near the popular notion that 75 percent of the people that ever lived are alive today. Haub says, "Because of the many assumptions, the study should be taken in the spirit of an interesting intellectual exercise rather than a scientific fact. The results will surely be revised when and if new information becomes available" (p. 4).

HUMAN POPULATION SIZE TODAY

The United Nations declared July 11, 1999, as "World Population Day." One purpose of this act was to begin a countdown that ended on October 12, 1999—the day that the world population reached 6 billion people. No one really knew, of course, if the

TABLE 2.1
Estimates of Total Human Population and Rate of Birth from 50,000 B.C. to A.D. 1998

Year	Population	Births/1,000	Births between Benchmarcks
50,000 B.C.	2	80	
8,000 B.C.	5,000,000	80	1,137,789,769
A.D. 1	300,000,000	80	46,025,332,354
1200	450,000,000	60	26,591,342,000
1650	500,000,000	60	12,782,002,453
1750	795,000,000	50	3,171,931,513
1850	1,265,000,000	40	4,046,240,009
1900	1,656,000,000	40	2,900,237,856
1998	5,902,706,742	24	5,427,305,000

Note: Total ever born: 109,947,781,641; percent of total ever born living in 1998: 5.46%.
Source: From Haub (1995).

human population achieved this exact figure on that particular day. Demographers working for the UN estimated these figures based on past knowledge of population size and population growth. The most basic method that demographers use to ascertain the size and rate of growth of a population is a **census**. A census is a count. One can count the number of houses in a neighborhood, the number of fast-food restaurants in a city, the number of firms that manufacture widgets, the number of swallows that return to Capistrano, or any other number of things or organisms that may be found in a given region at a particular time. When the word census is used without additional qualifiers, the term usually refers to an enumeration of people.

POPULATION CENSUS

The **population census** is the most common type of count of people used today. The history of the modern population census began in the seventeenth century. Now, it is certainly true that enumeration of people, livestock, and other property was carried out before then, but the reasons for these more ancient censuses and the methods used were different from modern ones. The most important difference was that these counts were made to control wealth and labor. For example, the ancient Romans enumerated citizens and their property every five years to determine taxes due to the state. Another example is the Doomsday Book, which is a type of census of landlords and their holdings in England in the year 1086. William the Conqueror ordered this inventory after acquiring these new lands. Because of the nature of these ancient censuses, it is not surprising to learn that many people provided inaccurate information, and, hence, these inventories are generally considered to be unreliable.

Another difference between the ancient and modern censuses is that the former is not representative of the general population. In an ancient census only property owners or young men of military age would be counted. A modern population census usually attempts to enumerate every person within a well-defined geographic region, such as a city, county, or nation. This type of census requires a detailed map, with both the boundaries of the region and the distribution of people within it clearly specified. The lack of such maps prior to the seventeenth century is another reason why the modern census begins after that time. It is not possible to identify "the first modern census." The idea of a census, its methods, and the uses to which the data are put changed over time. Something like a modern census may have been first used in the European colonies of the New World. Enumerations of the entire population in French Canada were undertaken in the mid-1600s. But, "the United States made history when it took its first census in 1790, not only because of the size of the area enumerated and the effort to obtain data on characteristics of the population but also because of the political purpose for which it was undertaken—namely, representation in Congress on the basis of population" ("census," *Encyclopedia Britannica Online*, 1999, *http://www.eb.com:180/bol/topic?eu=22402&sctn=1&pm=1*). The following section, which provides a very brief history of the U.S. census, serves as an example to explain some of the basic principles of census methodology.

The Constitution of the United States, adopted in 1787, specifies that a census of the population be taken every 10 years. The purpose of this enumeration is to obtain the population counts needed to apportion seats in the House of Representatives. The Congress of the U.S. federal government is comprised of two groups of elected officials. The U.S. Senate has two elected officials from each state, regardless of the geographic size or population of the state. The House of Representatives has a variable number of elected officials from each state. The population of the state is divided into congressional districts, and one representative is elected from each district. More densely populated states, as determined by the census, have more districts and, hence, more representational voting power. We see here that in the early years of the United States demographic methods were used to determine the apportionment of political power. This is clearly a cultural use of demography. Biological concerns, such as fertility and mortality, did not become part of the reason for the U.S. census until later.

The first decennial census of the U.S. population was taken in 1790. This first official census found that the non-Native portion of the United States numbered 3,929,214 people. The population of Native Americans[2] was not included in the federal census until 1890. The European, sometimes called White, population of the 1790 census numbered 3,143,571 people. Approximately half of this White population of the original 13 states was of English origin; the rest were Scots-Irish, German, Dutch, French, Swedish, Welsh, and Finnish. A fifth of the population, or 785,643 people, was enslaved Africans (Gibson and Lennon, 1999).

There are two ways to count the number of people living in a given region. The first is called a **de jure census**, which is a tally of people according to their regular or legal residence, even if they are living elsewhere at the time of the census. The second type is called a **de facto census**, which is a count of people living at a

---

[2] The term *Native*, with a capital "N," is used here to denote the inhabitants of the Americas prior to the European voyages of discovery and conquest. The U.S. census uses the term *native*, with a lower case "n," to denote any person born in the United States, regardless of the place of origin of his or her ancestors.

given location at the time of the census. From the start, the U.S. census has been taken on a de jure basis rather than on a de facto basis. A de jure census introduces some bias and probable error into the population count. People may not be at their usual place of residence at the time of the census and therefore are missed in the count. Births and deaths to people away from home may not be accurately recorded. Since the apportionment of political power lies at the core of the U.S. census, it is hardly surprising that these errors have been of considerable concern to many political groups (see the U.S. Bureau of the Census web site, at *www.census.gov*, for examples of these political concerns for the year 2000 census). In this regard, the U.S. census is not unusual, because most demographic data are biased and/or inaccurate. In fact, all census data collected prior to 1850 are considered poor by current standards. In the U.S. decennial census prior to 1850, and in the census of European nations, the data were collected not for individuals, but rather as tallies at the household level. These tallies were based on predefined categories on the census questionnaire. For example, the census taker might ask about the number of household members who were white females under five years old or the number of adults who were employed in commerce. The 1850 census of the United States introduced a major change by collecting data for each individual. This census was also the first to allow write-in responses, which could be coded later into a large number of categories (Gibson and Lennon, 1999). These innovations allowed for more detailed analysis of census data and led to the development of more refined census methodologies. In Box 2.1 are listed some common topics used in many types of modern census procedures.

Even today, census data from many parts of the world are of limited quality or nonexistent. As of 1998, two countries, Chad and Oman, have never even conducted a census (Gage, 2000). The poorer, Third World, nations often census only part of their population. A majority, perhaps, of the traditional cultures of the world have never been counted, especially hunting and gathering and tribal and chiefdom societies. When such social groups are counted, additional problems, such as inaccurate age reporting, are common. Many traditional peoples do not calculate age as is done in the developed world. Each of these problems needs to be considered when using census data for demographic analysis.

USING CENSUS DATA: DEFINING THE POPULATION

No matter the motivation for a census or the use to which census data are put, the most basic outcome of any census is a count of the **population**. There are many types of populations and many definitions of this word. Biologists use one fairly narrow definition: a group of individuals of a species that occupies a well-defined geographic area and, in sexually reproducing species, interbreeds. This definition fits the needs of human demography and human growth very well and will be the definition used throughout this book. Despite the clarity of this definition, there are many difficulties identifying biological populations. Some of these difficulties are geographic. The boundaries that separate one population from another may not be clearly demarcated. Topic 19 of the sample census questionnaire concerns the distribution of the urban and rural population. Where, for example, might we draw the line between the urban and rural population of France or any other First World nation? Is it

BOX 2.1
Questions Found on a Modern Census

There is no such thing as an "ideal" or "standard" census. Every group that conducts a census has its own motivations. These may be economic, political, social, humanitarian, or punitive. The following is one list of desirable topics, suggested by the United Nations, for inclusion in a general nationwide census. The list is divided into direct topics and derived topics. The former are obtained by asking people to answer questions. The later are calculated from the answers given to the direct topic questions. Each topic area is followed by one or more variables, consecutively numbered.

Part A: Direct Topics

Geographic—(1) place enumerated and/or place of usual residence
Familial—(2) relation to head of household or family
Demographic—(3) sex, (4) age, (5) marital status, (6) children ever born, (7) birthplace
Economic—(8) type of activity, (9) occupation, (10) industry, (11) employer-employee status
Social and political—(12) citizenship, (13) language, (14) ethnic or religious affiliation
Educational—(15) literacy or level of education, (16) school attendance

Part B: Derived Topics

(17) Total population
(18) Population of towns and local areas
(19) Urban–rural distribution
(20) Household or family composition

Possible additional topics include (21) prior place of residence (for understanding internal migration), (22) farm-tenure status, (23) income, (24) labor force participation, (25) duration of marriage, and (26) number of prior marriages.

In fact, this list of direct and derived topics can be greatly expanded. However, the expense and logistic difficulties of doing a census, managing the data, and producing analyses, even on a relatively small population, can be enormous. Accordingly, the list is usually kept as small as possible to answer the questions and satisfy the motivations for the census.

simply a matter of where people live? Probably not, for many people with country homes may spend a great deal of time in the city at work and play. We might settle this geographic problem by ascertaining the facts about interbreeding. If the urban workers only reproduce with other urban workers, and the rural workers only reproduce with other rural workers, regardless of where each person lives, then we may divide people into two reproductive populations. In practice, such simple groupings are unlikely. Just consider the case of a married couple with one person employed in the city and one in the countryside. This problem becomes even more acute in Third World countries, where people regularly migrate to and from rural villages to the urban areas.

The identity of human populations is further obscured by many cultural behaviors. People may live within the same well-defined geographic region but have little chance of interbreeding. Religious prohibitions or social class differences may effectively block the opportunity for social and sexual intercourse. Conversely, people who live hundreds, even thousands, of miles apart may be very likely to reproduce if they are members of social or religious groups that practice arranged marriages. Clearly, human populations must be defined using both biological and cultural criteria. Malthus knew this and in a way took a biocultural approach to human demography. He believed that biologically there was little that could be done to control the rate of population increase. He therefore advocated cultural methods (late marriage and abstinence) to curb population growth. A biocultural approach to demography does not change our definition of the population. It does mean that we must consider social, economic, political, religious, and other cultural factors when we attempt to delineate and study populations.

Census data may be critical in the biocultural definition of a population. The list of direct and derived topics included in the sample census of Box 2.1 includes all sorts of biocultural information. The sample census is recommended for the study of national populations. The aggregation of people into a political entity, such as a nation, is one way that political scientists and economists carry out demographic analysis. However, the citizens and residents of any nation may be comprised of many distinct biological populations. By associating the cultural data with biological outcomes, such as fertility and mortality, demographers can identify biocultural populations within larger aggregations of people. In later chapters we will see how the biocultural definition of human populations leads to important discoveries about the growth of humanity.

USING CENSUS DATA: THE LIFE TABLE

For now it is essential that we examine another standard use of census data. This is the construction of a **life table**. Life tables are mathematical devices designed to measure the duration of some phenomenon. In demography, life tables usually measure the duration of life. But, the same mathematical formulas may be used to measure the duration of marriages, the time it really takes to get through a "four-year" college program, and the duration of a measles epidemic. Life table analysis is often also called **event history analysis**, because it is so widely applicable to the duration of almost any process.

A life table may also be considered as an "enhanced" frequency distribution table. Frequency tables represent the simplest method for analyzing categorical data. For example, if we asked 200 people if they preferred apples or oranges, we might find the following results:

Preference	Count	Cumulative Count	Percentage	Cumulative Percentage
Apples	72	72	36	36
Oranges	84	156	42	78
Both	40	196	20	98
Neither	4	200	2	100

The table above shows the number, percentage, and cumulative percentage of respondents who characterized their preferences for the two fruits.

Life tables are "enhanced" frequency distributions in the sense that they provide more information and more detailed information. In demography, life tables show how rates of birth, growth, and development of individuals, age at reproduction, and death influence the overall growth rate of a population. Mortality life tables for the United States and for Haiti are given in Tables 2.2 to 2.5. The census data used to construct these tables are for the year 1970. This is the most recent year for which data are available for Haiti. The data in these tables are presented in columns, which represent various statistics used by demographers to describe population dynamics. There are many ways to organize these statistics. The tables given here use the style of organization of the U.S. Bureau of the Census International Database. These tables use the standard statistical terminology employed by professional demographers. This terminology, and the abbreviations used by demographers for each statistic, is a bit daunting at first, so I will explain these in some detail. I present the tables as they are found in the International Database at the Census Bureau web site (*www.census.gov*). Interested readers may wish to visit the site to examine life tables for other years and for other countries.

TABLE 2.2
Life Table for U.S. Males of All Ages (1970)

Age, years	$1,000(q_x)$	d_x	$1,000(m_x)$	l_x	L_x	e_x
0–1	22.5	2,246	22.9	100,000	97,976	67.1
1–5	3.7	358	0.9	97,754	390,193	67.6
5–10	2.5	243	0.5	97,396	486,333	63.9
10–15	2.6	250	0.5	97,153	485,260	59
15–20	7.9	769	1.6	96,903	482,793	54.2
20–25	11.2	1,080	2.3	96,134	478,003	49.6
25–30	10.1	958	2	95,054	472,836	45.1
30–35	11.5	1,080	2.3	94,096	467,873	40.6
35–40	15.6	1,448	3.1	93,016	961,682	36
40–45	23.9	2,190	4.8	91,568	452,728	31.5
45–50	37.2	3,325	7.6	89,378	439,115	27.2
50–55	57.5	4,949	11.8	86,053	418,694	23.2
55–60	89.1	7,228	18.6	81,104	388,424	19.4
60–65	130.9	9,673	27.9	73,876	346,191	16.1
65–70	187.6	12,045	41.3	64,203	291,736	13.1
70–75	257.7	13,439	59	52,158	227,635	10.6
75–80	356.2	13,793	86.9	38,719	158,754	8.3
80–85	469.1	11,693	124.2	24,926	94,152	6.6
85+	1,000	13,233	188	13,233	70,379	5.3

Note: Birth to age one year is presented in the first row. Thereafter, the data are presented by five-year age groups. Abbreviations as follows: $1,000(q_x)$, deaths between ages x and $x + n$ per 1,000 persons ages x to $x + n$ (age-specific central death rate); d_x, number of deaths occurring between ages x and $x + n$; $1,000(m_x)$, deaths between ages x and $x + n$ per 1,000 persons surviving to age x (age-specific mortality rate); l_x, number of survivors at age x; L_x, number of person-years lived between ages x and $x + n$; e_x, life expectancy at age x.
Source: U.S. Bureau of the Census, International Database, *www.census.gov*.

TABLE 2.3
Life Table for U.S. Females of All Ages (1970)

Age, years	$1,000(q_x)$	d_x	$1,000(m_x)$	l_x	L_x	e_x
0–1	17.6	1,759	17.9	100,000	98,426	74.7
1–5	3	293	0.7	98,241	392,275	75.1
5–10	1.7	168	0.3	97,948	489,285	71.3
10–15	1.5	145	0.3	97,780	488,574	66.4
15–20	3.1	301	0.6	97,635	487,474	61.5
20–25	3.8	369	0.8	97,334	485,763	56.7
25–30	4.4	426	0.9	96,965	483,795	51.9
30–35	5.9	570	1.2	96,539	481,359	47.1
35–40	9.1	875	1.8	95,969	477,807	42.4
40–45	13.6	1,297	2.7	95,094	472,436	37.8
45–50	21	1,965	4.2	93,797	464,362	33.2
50–55	30.6	2,813	6.2	91,832	452,526	28.9
55–60	44.5	3,961	9.1	89,019	435,712	24.7
60–65	64	5,446	13.2	85,058	412,418	20.7
65–70	97.8	7,782	20.5	79,612	379,705	17.0
70–75	151.2	10,862	32.6	71,830	333,451	13.5
75–80	239.2	14,585	54.1	60,968	269,750	10.5
80–85	361.8	16,783	88.3	46,383	190,173	8.0
85+	1,000	29,600	165.1	29,600	179,327	6.1

Note: See Table 2.2 for definition of symbols.
Source: U.S. Bureau of the Census, International Database, *www.census.gov*.

TABLE 2.4
Life Table for Haitian Males of All Ages (1970)

Age, years	$1,000(q_x)$	d_x	$1,000(m_x)$	l_x	L_x	e_x
0–1	137	NA	150.85	NA	NA	47.64
1–5	88.63	NA	23.6	NA	NA	54.15
5–10	35.97	NA	7.33	NA	NA	55.30
10–15	14.32	NA	2.88	NA	NA	52.27
15–20	24.07	NA	4.87	NA	NA	47.99
20–25	32.19	NA	6.54	NA	NA	44.12
25–30	27.29	NA	5.53	NA	NA	40.50
30–35	34.22	NA	6.96	NA	NA	36.57
35–40	38.39	NA	7.83	NA	NA	32.77
40–45	44.98	NA	9.2	NA	NA	28.98
45–50	56.42	NA	11.61	NA	NA	25.23
50–55	74.22	NA	15.42	NA	NA	21.59
55–60	98.66	NA	20.76	NA	NA	18.12
60–65	140.65	NA	30.26	NA	NA	14.83
65–70	194.91	NA	43.19	NA	NA	11.85
70–75	283.9	NA	66.17	NA	NA	9.11
75–80	405.17	NA	101.62	NA	NA	6.73
80+	1,000	NA	217.01	NA	NA	4.61

Note: See Table 2.2 for definition of symbols; NA = not available.
Source: U.S. Bureau of the Census, International Database, *www.census.gov*.

TABLE 2.5
Life Table for Haitian Females of All Ages (1970)

Age, years	$1,000(q_x)$	d_x	$1,000(m_x)$	l_x	L_x	e_x
0–1	124	NA	134.87	NA	NA	48.31
1–5	94.16	NA	25.18	NA	NA	54.10
5–10	37.19	NA	7.58	NA	NA	55.59
10–15	13.73	NA	2.76	NA	NA	52.64
15–20	24.48	NA	4.96	NA	NA	48.34
20–25	32.43	NA	6.59	NA	NA	44.49
25–30	32.89	NA	6.69	NA	NA	40.90
30–35	33.65	NA	6.85	NA	NA	37.21
35–40	37.67	NA	7.68	NA	NA	33.41
40–45	43.76	NA	8.95	NA	NA	29.62
45–50	54.41	NA	11.19	NA	NA	25.87
50–55	70.89	NA	14.7	NA	NA	22.21
55–60	93.33	NA	19.58	NA	NA	18.71
60–65	131.74	NA	28.21	NA	NA	15.38
65–70	181.05	NA	39.81	NA	NA	12.34
70–75	262.66	NA	60.47	NA	NA	9.51
75–80	375.59	NA	92.49	NA	NA	7.01
80+	1,000	NA	211.78	NA	NA	4.72

Note: See Table 2.2 for definition of symbols; NA = not available.
Source: U.S. Bureau of the Census, International Database, *www.census.gov*.

These tables are arranged in seven columns. The first column indicates the sex and age of the sample. Life tables are constructed separately for males and females because each sex has different life history characteristics (such as different probabilities for death at any age). Birth to age one year is presented in the first row. Thereafter, the data are presented by five-year age groups. This is done because there is a high rate of death in the first year of life in many populations. The second column, labeled $1,000(q_x)$, provides one indication of the rate of death. The symbol q_x is used by demographers to indicate the **age-specific central death rate**. This is the probability that an individual who survives to age x will die within the next age interval, for example from birth to age one year, age one year to five years, and so on. This probability is multiplied by 1,000 to give a more readable number. From Table 2.2, we can see that for boys in the United States the probability of death during the first year of life is 22.5. For girls the corresponding value is 17.6. In Haiti the value for boys is 137 and for girls it is 124. Beyond the obvious fact that the probability for death in the first year of life is higher in Haiti than in the United States, these probability values make little sense until we see how they relate to the actual number of deaths.

The next three columns of the tables provide that information. The symbol d_x denotes the number of deaths occurring in the age interval. For the interval birth to one year, Tables 2.2 and 2.3 show, respectively, that in the United States in the year 1970, 2,246 boys and 1,759 girls died out of a starting population of 100,000 live births. The 100,000 is an arbitrary figure. Life tables are traditionally constructed to represent an imaginary population of individuals. The demographers that constructed these life tables chose a starting population size of 100,000. That information is given in the fifth column of Tables 2.2 and 2.3, labeled l_x. At birth, both life tables begin with a population of 1000,000 live-born infants. As the population ages, the number of individuals surviving to the beginning of the next age interval decreases. So, the statistic l_x shows the size of the population at the beginning of an age interval and also provides one indication of the number of deaths in the previous age interval. If you subtract the value of d_x from the value of l_x in any age interval, you will get the value of l_x for the next age interval.

The fourth column provides yet another type of mortality statistic. This column, labeled $1,000(m_x)$, indicates the number of deaths in an age interval per 1,000 persons surviving to age x. This statistic is called the **age-specific mortality rate**. This mortality rate differs from the age-specific central death rate in that m_x is a standardized value representing the actual number of deaths per 1,000 population, while q_x is an unstandardized probability, meaning that it does not take into consideration the population size. The last two columns are labeled L_x and e_x, where L_x is the number of person-years lived during a given age interval and e_x is the life expectancy at age x. Using Table 2.2 as an example (boys in the United States), we see that from birth to age one year the death rate results in 97,976 person years lived and that these boys have a life expectancy at birth of 67.1 years.

Note that the life tables for Haiti (Tables 2.4 and 2.5) do not provide all of these demographic statistics. Information for d_x, l_x, and L_x is not available. Census data for Third World nations, such as Haiti, are often incomplete. Some reasons for this are that there was not enough money or trained personnel to collect all of the data or the data were collected but not analyzed sufficiently to produce all of the statistics. Despite the lack of some information, it is still possible to compare the life tables for the United States and Haiti for the year 1970. Mortality rates, measured by m_x, during the first year of life in Haiti were about 6.5 times greater for boys and 6.8 times greater for girls than in the United States. The data for both countries are graphed in Figure 2.2. It may be seen from this figure that mortality rates remain higher in Haiti at virtually all ages. As a consequence, the expectation of life at birth is 19.46 years greater for men and 26.39 years longer for women residing in the United States.

Insurance companies were the first to develop and use life tables. The companies needed a way to predict how long people, within a given age range, could be expected to live. Knowing this, the companies could structure their premiums to assure sufficient income to both pay claims and make a profit. Demographers adopted life tables to make predictions about life expectancies of human and nonhuman populations, including plant, animal, and even microbial populations.

When life tables for different populations of the same species are compared, the numbers provide far more information than just expected longevity. The numbers for the United States and Haiti, for example, provide a very general indication about the quality of life in these two nations. Life in Haiti is far more precarious than it is in the United States. The expectation for life is much less in Haiti, and the life tables show that deaths during the first year of life account for most of the difference in longevity (Fig. 2.2). The poverty of the vast majority of Haitians in 1970 is the major reason for the very high infant mortality rate. Poverty is much more than just a lack of money. Poverty is always associated with low levels of

Mortality by age group - Haiti and USA

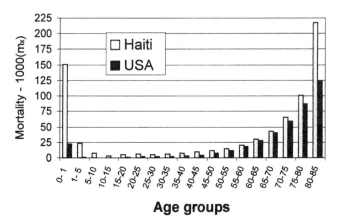

Age groups

FIGURE 2.2 Mortality for males as measured by $1,000(m_x)$ for Haiti and the United States. Data are from Tables 2.2 and 2.4.

education, poor sanitation, inadequate nutrition for people of all ages, and insufficient medical care. Separately and together, these deficiencies in the standard of living reduce a newborn's chances of surviving to age one year. Those who do survive are often so debilitated in infancy by poverty that they retain a high risk for death at later ages. Because life table numbers reflect the quality of life of a human population, they are employed by many disciplines in addition to life insurance and demography. These disciplines include public health, medicine, economics, sociology, anthropology, and others that study the human condition.

MEDICAL EXAMPLE OF THE USE OF LIFE TABLES

In public health and medicine, life tables may be used to predict "the likelihood of developing or dying of a disease . . . at a given age" (Bunker et al., 1998). Many women in the United States and the United Kingdom are alarmed when they read that the risk for developing breast cancer is 1 in 8 and 1 in 12, respectively. These risk figures are correct for women who survive to the age of 75 to 80 years. In other words, the 1-in-12 figure for women living in England and Wales only holds for a rather old age cohort—one that has survived all of the other risks for death at all younger ages. Using a life table analysis, a team of physicians working in London show that the risk of developing breast cancer for women in England and Wales changes markedly with age. Women under 35 years old have a risk of 1 in 625. By age 50 years the risk increases to 1 in 56, then 1 in 18 at age 65, and finally 1 in 13 at age 75 (Bunker et al., 1998). Even these figures need to be tempered with information about other predisposing factors that may increase a woman's risk for the disease, such as a family history of breast cancer, age at menarche, age at first pregnancy, age at menopause, alcohol consumption, and use of oral contraceptives.

More to the point, many women want to know not only the risk of developing breast cancer but also the risk of dying if they do develop the disease. Bunker

TABLE 2.6
Life Table for Cumulative Probability of Death from Breast cancer in England and Wales in 1995 per 100,000 women

Age Interval	Number of Deaths in Each Interval/ 100,000 women	Cumulative Number of Deaths	Probability of Death by End of Interval
25–34	34.6	34.6	1/2873
35–44	176.3	210.9	1/474
45–54	522.5	733.4	1/136
55–64	794.7	1,528.1	1/65
65–74	1,060.4	2,588.0	1/39
75–84	1,189.5	3,778.0	1/26

Source: Data from Bunker et al. (1998).

et al. (1998) use life tables to put the risk of breast cancer mortality in perspective. Their findings for women living in England and Wales are shown in Table 2.6. Note that this life table uses descriptive phrases as headings for each column, rather than the jargonistic abbreviations of the previous tables.

This life table shows that the risk of death is relatively low for younger women; indeed it is matched or exceeded by the risk for death from heart disease and lung cancer in women who smoke. The authors point out that fewer women fear lung cancer, even though the cure rate is less than 5 percent. The cure rate for breast cancer, as measured by survival after treatment for at least 10 years, is 70 percent. In this example, life tables show that fear of breast cancer may outweigh the actual risks of the disease.

LIFE TABLE ANALYSIS OF GROWTH AND DEVELOPMENT

Life tables are not often used in studies of human growth and development, but they may be so used. After all, life tables measure the duration of any phenomenon. Applied to human development, a life table may be constructed to measure the duration of a stage, or stages, of life history. Here I construct a life table for the duration of the preadolescent stages of postnatal life, that is, infancy, childhood, and juvenile stages. The length of the preadolescent stages may be measured by calculating the age at which the velocity curve of growth changes from deceleration during the juvenile stage to the acceleration of adolescence (see Fig. 1.4). This point is often called "**take-off**," referring to the take-off in velocity increase of the adolescent growth spurt. The point of take-off may be estimated by fitting a mathematical formula to real growth data. The example used here is based on my own study of two Guatemalan samples. Technical details of the mathematical procedures may be found in the original publication of this study (Bogin et al., 1992). The two groups studied are a sample of high-socioeconomic-status (SES) Ladino boys and girls and a group of low-SES Maya boys and girls. Ladinos are one of the major ethnic groups of Guatemala. Ladinos trace their descent from Spanish conquistadors. Ladinos speak Spanish and, generally, follow "western" (European) cultural values in terms of family organization, religion, and world outlook. The living Maya people trace descent from the ancient Maya culture. They speak one of several Maya languages and follow traditional (nonwestern) values and practices in family organization, religion, and other aspects of life. The distinctions between Ladinos and Maya are mostly of social and cultural origin. There are no known genetic differences of any importance, especially of importance to physical growth. The Ladino boys and girls of this sample come from very wealthy Guatemalan families, and they enjoy good health. The Maya boys and girls come from very poor families. My research shows that these Maya are poorly nourished and suffer from poor health (Bogin and MacVean, 1984).

I calculated life tables for the duration of the preadolescent stages by using a commercially available statistics program called *Statistica*. The program has a module for event history analysis, including the estimation of standard life tables. The results are presented in Table 2.7 for the Maya and Table 2.8 for the Ladinos. I combined boys and girls together for these life tables in order to focus on the SES differences between the two samples. It should be remembered, however, that, on average, girls enter adolescence about two years earlier than do boys. As for Table 2.6, I use descriptive headings for the columns rather than jargonistic abbreviations.

The life tables show that the preadolescent stages of life last for more years for the Maya sample than for the Ladino sample. The first column represents one year age groups, starting with birth at "0" years. The second column presents the total number of boys and girls entering each age group: 58 Maya and 182 Ladinos were included in the study. The next column presents the number of boys or girls "dying" in each age group (this corresponds to the statistic d_x in Tables 2.2 to 2.5.

TABLE 2.7

Life Table Analysis of Duration of Preadolescent Stages of Postnatal Life for Low-SES Maya (Guatemalan) Boys and Girls

Age, years	Number Entering	Number "Dying"	Cumulative Percentage Surviving	Hazard Rate
0	58	0	100	0.009
1	58	0	99.1	0.009
2	58	0	98.3	0.009
3	58	0	97.4	0.009
4	58	0	96.6	0.009
5	58	0	95.8	0.009
6	58	1	94.9	0.009
7	57	0	93.3	0.009
8	57	1	92.5	0.018
9	56	7	90.8	0.135
10	49	16	79.5	0.396
11	33	15	53.5	0.597
12	18	12	29.2	1.014
13	6	5	9.7	1.449
14	1	0	1.6	0.676
15	1	1	0.8	

TABLE 2.8
Life Table Analysis of Duration of Preadolescent Stages of Postnatal Life for High-SES Ladino (Guatemalan) Boys and Girls

Age, years	Number Entering	Number "Dying"	Cumulative Percentage Surviving	Hazard Rate
0	182	0	100	0.003
1	182	0	99.7	0.003
2	182	0	99.5	0.003
3	182	0	99.2	0.003
4	182	0	98.9	0.003
5	182	0	98.6	0.003
6	182	2	98.4	0.011
7	180	24	97.3	0.139
8	156	52	84.3	0.389
9	104	61	56.2	0.806
10	43	32	23.2	1.151
11	11	9	5.9	1.345
12	2	1	1.1	0.648
13	1	0	0.5	0.648
14	1	0	0.3	0.648
15	1	1	0.1	

The children are not dying; rather the term *dying* refers to the end of the preadolescent stages, that is, the age at which boys or girls reach the point of take-off of the adolescent growth spurt. No Maya or Ladino boys and girls die during the first six years of life. One Maya and two Ladinos die during the age-seven interval, meaning that they enter adolescence. The number of Ladinos entering adolescence increases with each succeeding age for the Ladinos, and all but two individuals, or 98.9 percent of the sample, have died by age 13 years. The onset of Maya adolescence is delayed compared with the Ladinos. The majority of Maya do not end the preadolescent stages until age 11, with 16 "deaths," or later ages. At age 13, only 70.8 percent of Maya have entered the adolescent stage of life.

The next column shows the cumulative percentage of the sample "surviving" to the next age group. Again, surviving in this case means that the boys and girls are still in the preadolescent stages of life. More Maya survive to later ages than Ladinos. The survival rate for preadolescence is presented graphically in Figure 2.3, which shows more clearly the later age of entry into adolescence for the Maya. The last column is called the **hazard rate**. In event history analysis, the hazard rate is defined as the probability per time unit that a case that has survived to the beginning of the respective interval will fail in that interval. In our analysis of the duration of the preadolescent stages of life, a "case" is an individual boy or girl, and "fail" refers to the age interval in which the juvenile stage of life ends and the adolescent stage begins. In essence, the hazard rate may be used to show changes in the age distribution for the onset of adolescence.

For the Maya the age interval for the maximum "hazard" for adolescence is 13 years, and for the Ladinos it is an age interval of 11 years. The 2-year difference is most likely due to the better nutritional status and health of the high-SES Ladino

Survival of preadolescent stages -Maya

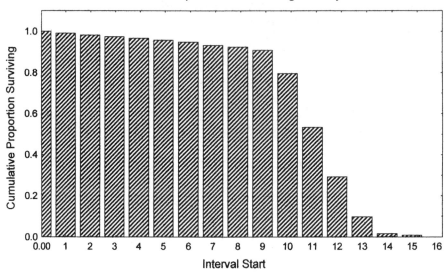

Survival of preadolescent stages - Ladino

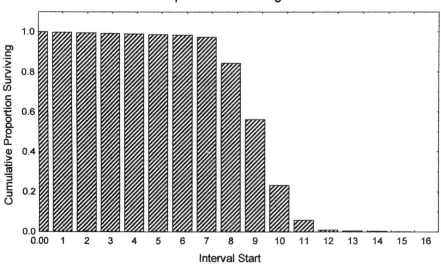

FIGURE 2.3 Survival of preadolescent stages of life for Mayan and Ladino Guatemalan boys and girls.

sample. The life table not only reveals this 2-year gap between the Ladinos and the Maya but also shows the progression of the "hazard for adolescence" as the samples of boys and girls age. This provides more information than a standard frequency analysis, which would not include the hazard estimates.

The examples of life table analysis given in this section show the traditional use of life tables for the analysis of census data, the value of life tables in the evaluation of risks for disease, and a less traditional use to document the duration of the life stages during human growth and development. With this background, we will be able to use and interpret life tables as needed in the following sections of this book.

FROM MALTHUS TO GOMPERTZ

Malthus was overwhelmed with a fear of a world in which human beings would be "crowding and interfering" with each other's hopes for a decent life. Malthus wanted to slow the fertility of people, so that the human population might find a way to avoid his principle of population. In essence, concern with fertility and overpopulation leads to the creation of the discipline of demography, to the development of the census and the life table. I explained earlier in this chapter that in the nineteenth century many demographers used these techniques for apportionment of political power. I also noted that actuaries working for insurance companies employed these techniques to calculate risks for death and the price of insurance policy premiums. These uses of demographic data diverted interest away from the biology of human populations. In the year 1825, one British actuary, Benjamin Gompertz, tried to return some biology to the use of life tables. Gompertz (1825) believed he had discovered that a "law of geometrical progression pervades, in an approximate degree, large portions of different tables of mortality" (p. 514). Gompertz compared life tables based on death records from populations in England, Sweden, and France. He limited his analysis of mortality to people between the ages of 20 and 60 years. His work resulted in a simple formula that describes the exponential increase in mortality for this age range. The formula is commonly referred to today as the **Gompertz equation**. In its modern formulation the equation takes the form $m(t) = \exp(mt)$, where m is the mortality rate and t is time as measured by age in years. What this formula means is that as people age, there is a regular and progressive increase in the rate of death. Because Gompertz noted the same progression in the rate of death in several European populations, he believed that his formula represented a universal **law of mortality**. Gompertz's law of mortality is, in many ways, the compliment to Malthus's principle of population. Malthus attempts to describe a universal pattern of fertility, and Gompertz tries to describe a universal pattern of mortality. Moreover, whereas Malthus made a link between arithmetic increases in the food supply and geometric increases in population growth, Gompertz believed he discovered a link between arithmetic increases in age and geometric increases in the likelihood for death.

I recommend that readers interested in a brief detailed history of the impact of Gompertz's work read the article "Ever since Gompertz" (Olshansky and Carnes, 1997). Here I will present a few of the highlights of this article. Just as Malthus's "principle" captured the attention of biologists, sociologists, politicians, and the public, the "law" of Gompertz was heralded widely by scientists, insurance companies, and the public. Another similarity between the two demographers is that, with time, their work was attacked, discredited, but eventually revived in modified form.

Gompertz looked beyond the evidence provided by life tables, and he tried to find the biological reasons for the consistency in mortality he observed between the ages of 20 and 60 years. He proposed that death is due to two causes acting simultaneously. The first he called deterioration, which he defined as the progressive inability of the person to withstand bodily destruction. Deterioration was due to the natural *intrinsic* decline of some vital force that maintained life. Gompertz proposed that the rate of decay of this vital force was constant in all human beings. This would explain the similarity in rates of mortality in different populations. It seems that Gompertz never identified or defined exactly what the vital force may be. The second cause is chance—people die from accidents, from exposure to lethal disease, predation, murder, and other *extrinsic* causes. Chance mortality explains the departures from the intrinsic law of mortality.

In the late-nineteenth and early-twentieth centuries, several scientists tried to extend and clarify Gompertz's proposals. Experimental evidence, based on nonhuman populations (varying from bacteria to domesticated farm animals) allowed investigators to propose testable hypotheses about aging and death. Two notable figures in this work are Samuel Brody and Raymond Pearl, whose work on demography and human growth was reviewed in the previous chapter. Brody (1924) was able to show that the Gompertz formula of exponential rates of mortality could also be applied to an exponential decline with age for milk production in cows and the rate of egg production in chickens. This exponential pattern of change was also found in laboratory experiments that measured the rate of change of monomolecular chemical reactions. At the time of this research it was generally accepted that all life processes depended on a series of these monomolecular chemical reactions. Brody (1924) concluded that both growth and senescence "follow the same exponential law—the law of monomolecular change in chemistry; and that the two processes are simultaneous and consecutive" (p. 248).

Without the benefit of our current knowledge of genetics and biochemistry, Brody was still able to propose a hypothesis for the underlying causes of both growth and aging that is remarkably similar to some current hypotheses (such as the free radical hypothesis; see Chapter 8). But was Brody's hypothesis correct, that is, does it account for a universal pattern of mortality? According to the work of Pearl, the answer is no. Pearl compared the rates of mortality of several species. He found that when the total life span of each species was scaled so that species could be compared, human beings had a higher expectancy for life at every age. Pearl believed that human culture, our ability to modify and control some aspects of our environment, explained the human advantage. But, even the other species differed in the shape of their mortality curves. After 20 years of research, Pearl concluded that a universal law of mortality, as proposed by Gompertz and defended by Brody and others, did not exist (Pearl and Miner, 1935).

FALL AND RISE OF BIODEMOGRAPHY

Following this declaration, the quest for the proof of the law of mortality languished. Today, however, the search for the underlying causes of mortality has been revived in the form of a field of research called **biodemography**. Olshansky and Carnes (1997, p. 6) define biodemography as "an attempt to discover a biological pattern to the dying-out of individuals within a population." Biodemographers are not looking for the universal curve of mortality imagined by Gompertz and proved wrong by Pearl. Rather, they are trying to answer questions such as "why do deaths concentrate at about 1,000 days for laboratory mice, at 5,000 days for most dogs, and at about 28,000 days for modern humans? Why do some individuals die shortly after birth whereas others live to ripe old ages? Why does the risk of death decline to its lowest point at sexual maturity for many species, and thereafter increase along a predictable path?" (p. 6).

Modern biodemography combines a biological perspective of the life table (the pattern of the hazard rate for death of a population) with the **epidemiology** of populations. Epidemiology is the study of disease in populations, including the origins, the spread, and the consequences of disease for human groups. Epidemiologists study both the *extrinsic* causes of disease and death, such as the introduction of bacterial pathogens or new lifestyles (e.g., automobiles), the *intrinsic* causes of disease and death, such as genetically based variation in risk for cancer, and the interaction between these factors. Since about the year 1990, biodemographers have gone even further in the quest for an understanding of mortality. They now link the demographic principles of the life table with both epidemiology and evolutionary biology. [Weiss (1990) wrote a classic article describing this three-part combination of disciplines.] Biodemographers Olshansky and Carnes (1997) state that this combination of disciplines helps to reveal the intrinsic patterns of reproduction (fertility), growth and development, senescence, and death in any species. Furthermore, these two researchers suggest that once all of the extrinsic causes of reproduction, growth, aging, and death are removed from consideration, modern biodemographic methods may reveal the elusive law of mortality proposed by Gompertz. I would take this further, and suggest that modern biodemographic methods may reveal laws pertaining to life history in general, including fertilty, growth, aging, and death.

FERTILITY AND MORTALITY[1]

With this understanding of the history of demography, from Malthus to Gompertz to biodemography, we can review current knowledge of the two most fundamental factors that control population growth—fertility and mortality. The size of a **closed population**, one which experiences neither immigration nor emigration of people, is governed by the rate of birth and the rate of death. At the simplest level, demographers use the crude birth rate and crude death rate. These are calculated as the number of births or deaths in a given population during a given time period (such as January 1–December 31) divided by the total population and multiplied by one thousand. Crude birth and death rates provide limited information about the population as a whole. They provide no understanding of the age structure of the population, that is, the age of women giving birth or the age of the people dying. Life tables are better suited to study population growth. We can construct a life table that shows the average number of offspring left by a woman at each age interval. If we also include the proportion of individuals suiviving to each age, that is we account for mortality, then we may calculate the rate at which the population increases or decreases in number over time.

---

[1] This section is adapted from Thompson (1999) and from Gage (2000).

Estimating Mortality

The life table is the standard method used for analyzing mortality in human populations (Gage, 2000). Demographers sometimes use a model life table to estimate mortality. The model life table is a mathematical construction based on the pattern of age-specific mortality from the wealthier developed nations of the world. This tends to impose the pattern of mortality of the industrial nations on the poorer, less industrialized nations and the small traditional societies of the world. Infant mortality rates (the probability of and the small traditional societies of the world. Infant mortality rates (the probability of death in the first year of life) are one example of problems that may result from this imposition. Many poor nations have infant mortality rates above 100 per 1000—that is, more than 10% of the infants die in their first year. In richer nations, with effective health and educational systems, infant mortality rates are about 15 per 1000, or even lower. The infant mortality rate has a powerful effect on the biological structure of a population and on the mathematical structure of a life table. Use of an incorrect infant mortality rate may lead to meaningless data. Unfortunately, the use of the model life table is often necessary because very little reliable data on mortality is available from the poorer nations, and no data may be available for the small traditional societies. This is an area where demographic and anthropological field study is urgently needed.

Gage (2000) reviewed the research available on worldwide variation in patterns of mortality. In general, the risk of death at any given age is less for girls and women than for boys and men. The mortality advantage of women is characteristic of contemporary population, but there is evidence that in the past women had higher mortality than men at many ages. Even today, during the childbearing years women in poorer nations have a higher mortality rate than do men of the same age. In the wealthy nations of North America, Western Europe, Japan, and Australia women have lower mortality even during the childbearing years. There are economic, social, political, and cultural reasons for the sex differences in mortality. In the contemporary world we know that money can provide better health care for pregnant women, but only if that money is applied to the needs of women's health. The concept of "women's health needs" is defined socially and politically in terms of each culture's ideology. In the United States, for example, the inclusion of women and children in federally funded medical research studies was not necessary until the late twentieth century. Prior to this, research on men was used to develop health policy for women and children, despite the fact that significant differences in biology according to sex and age were known to exist. In almost all societies, the risk of death for both sexes is high immediately after birth, diminishes during childhood, and reaches a minimum at 10 to 12 years of age. The risk then begins to rise again, and by the age of 50 to 60 years it surpasses that of the first year of life. Graphically, this pattern of mortality gives rise to a J-shaped curve (see Figure 2.2).

Biocultural Regulation of Mortality

The expectation of life at birth is the most efficient index of the general level of mortality of a population. Gage's (2000) review finds that life expectancy at birth has varied from a low of 15 years in some prehistoric populations to a high of more than 80 years in some nations today. The prehistoric populations cluster in a narrow range of 18 to 25 years for life expectancy at birth. That range is similar for populations who made their living by hunting and gathering, horticulture, and agriculture. Paleodemographers (those who study ancient populations) often conclude from this that mortality was uniformly high in the past, and mortality did not vary much over time or place to place. In later chapters I describe in more detail the connections between subsistence systems (the way people make their living) and demographic patterns in prehistoric and historic times. Here I wish to mention that a few attempts have been made to find a simple set of reasons for the variation in mortality. Gage divides the reasons for mortality into two categories, proximate and ultimate causes. Proximate causes have to do with the types of diseases and other risks for death that people are likely to encounter. Ultimate causes have to do with the quality of the biosocial environment in which people live. Measles is a proximate cause of death in many populations. In parts of rural Guatemala during the 1960s measles epidemics accounted for up to 50% of all deaths to children under 5 years of age. Measles alone, however, cannot explain this massively high death rate, as measles did not kill children at anywhere near this rate in the United States or other wealthy nations. In Guatemala the rural population suffered from undernutrition, poor sanitation, a low level of formal education, lack of reasonable medical care and, in general, poverty. These were the first-level ultimate causes of death. Measles epidemics were only the final blow to a population already suffering from poor health. The second-level ultimate cause of death was a political system that maintained the rural population in poverty and plunged the nation into a bloody civil war in the 1970s. The political system of Guatemala has been changing since the end of civil war in the country in 1986. Mortality from infectious diseases has declined noticeably since then.

Some proximate causes of death for the United States in the year 1900 and 1998 are shown in Table 2.9. The 10 leading causes of death are given for each year. Diseases of the heart are in first place and liver diseases in tenth place on both lists. But the eight categories between first and last place changed a great deal over the century. Infectious diseases (influenza, pneumonia, tuberculosis, diphtheria, typhoid, paratyphoid, and measles) accounted for five of the leading causes in 1900. In 1998, only one infectious disease category, "pneumonia and influenza," is on the list. Cancers (malignant neoplasms) accounted for 64 deaths per 100,000 population in 1900, but increased to 200 per 100,000 in 1998. Several chronic diseases are on the 1998 list, including cerebrovascular disease, pulmonary diseases, diabetes, and kidney diseases (nephritis). Accidents are on both lists, but the type of accidents that killed people changed over time. In 1900 few people died in motor vehicle accidents, while in 1998 almost one-half of accident deaths were due to motor vehicles. Finally, suicides make the 1998 list, and account for almost as many deaths as did measles in 1900.

The changing pattern of mortality in the United States in the twentieth century had major impact on demographic structure of the population. The prominent infectious diseases of 1900 killed mostly infants and children. The control of these diseases by improvements in public health, especially sanitation and vaccination campaigns, sharply reduced infant and child mortality and increased life expectancy at birth. In 1998, life expectancy reached an all time high of 76.7 years for the United States population as a whole. But, all people die sooner or later, and an older

TABLE 2.9
Leading Causes of Death in the United States for the Years 1900 and 1998

1900		1998	
Cause of Death	Death Rate	Cause of Death	Death Rate
Diseases of heart and blood vessels	345	Diseases of the heart	268
Influenza and pneumonia	202	Malignant neoplasms	200
Tuberculosis	194	Cerebrovascular diseases	59
Accidents	72	Chronic obstructive pulmonary diseases	42
Diseases of stomach and intestines	143	Accidents and adverse effects (motor vehicle accidents)	36 (16)
Cancer	64	Pneumonia and influenza	34
Diphtheria	40	Diabetes mellitus	24
Typhoid and paratyphoid fever	31	Suicide	11
Measles	13	Nephritis, nephrotic syndrome, and nephrosis	10
Cirrhosis of the liver	13	Chronic liver disease and cirrhosis	9

Death rates are presented as the number of deaths per 100,000 population.

population will tend to die from chronic diseases that act over many years to debilitate the body.

The ultimate causes of death in 1998 are not only due to an aging population. Lifestyle variables such as diet and physical activity play a role. The generally sedentary lifestyle and high caloric intake of Americans leads to specific diseases, such as diabetes mellitus and heart disease, and may also lead to obesity. A lifestyle that results in excess body weight, especially if it is in the form of body fat, contributes to all of the diseases on the top 10 list for 1998. Industrial activity associated with the production and use of the automobile results in the high rate of death from motor vehicle accidents and also to some of the mortality from malignant neoplasms and from chronic pulmonary disease. Carcinogenic substances that are by-products of industrial activity induce many cancers. The air pollution caused by industry and by the exhaust of motor vehicles contributes to both the cancer rate and the rise of lung diseases. The relatively high rate of suicide in 1998 may reflect other ultimate causes of death. The proximate reasons why people choose suicide are many and varied. The ultimate causes, however, may reflect the social, economic, and political structures of the population which promote self-destruction, and the cultural values that sanction suicide as an acceptable means of death.

Measuring Fertility

The average number of offspring that a woman leaves during her lifetime may be measured in several ways. One method calculates what is called the **total repro-**

ductive rate (**TRR**) per woman. If all women of a given birth cohort survived to the oldest possible reproductive age for that population (generally 50 years), then the total reproductive rate is simply the average number of all offspring left by all women. Because men do not become pregnant or give birth, demographers also calculate the **gross reproductive rate (GRR)**. The GRR is the average number of female children that a woman would produce if she lived to the end of her potential reproductive years. In real populations, however, some girls and women die during each age interval, thus reducing the number of possible births if all females survived passed age 50 years. To account for this, demographers may also calculate the **net reproductive rate (NRR)**. This is done by multiplying the proportion of women surviving to each age (l_x using the terminology of Tables 2.2 and 2.3) by the average number of offspring produced at each age (b_x) and then adding the products from all the age groups. The NRR takes into account both birth and deaths.

An easily accessible source for fertility data is the International Data Base at the U.S. Census Bureau web site (*www.census.gov*). At this site the demographic data for TRR and GRR for women are reported for most years, but the data for NRR are reported only sporadically. Nevertheless, the difference between GRR and NRR is almost always a matter of a few hundredths of a decimal. We may then use the GRR as if it were the NRR. A gross or net reproductive rate of 1.0 indicates that a population is neither increasing nor decreasing but replacing its numbers of women exactly. Any number below 1.0 indicates a decrease in population; any number above indicates an increase.

The total reproductive rate and gross reproductive rate for a few countries in the year 1999, representing a range of values, are given below. The values for TRR and GRR are the average number of offspring born per 1,000 women. In this way, populations of very different total sizes may be compared:

Country	Total Reproductive Rate	Gross Reproductive Rate
Zambia	6.3471	3.1267
Guatemala	4.7360	2.3102
Haiti	4.5858	2.2370
Kenya	3.8800	1.9113
Columbia	2.8740	1.4130
United States	2.0705	1.0109
Japan	1.4785	0.7212
Russia	1.3356	0.6515
Portugal	1.3352	0.6475

The total range of values is relatively large. The population of Zambia is tripling each generation, and the populations of Guatemala and Kenya are more than doubling each generation. Columbia is growing, but at a more moderate rate. The United States is at about replacement each generation, while the populations of Japan is shrinking by about 25 percent each generation. The populations of Russia and Portugal are decreasing by about one-third each generation. None of these values includes the effects of migration. Migration into a country from another nation would increase the population. Migration out of the country would have the opposite effect.

Generation length in each of these countries is not identical. Demographers usually calculate a statistic called the **mean generation time** (*T*). Generation time is the average interval between the birth of an individual and the birth of its offspring. To determine the mean generation time of a population, the age of the individuals (*x*) is multiplied by the proportion of females surviving to that age (l_x from Tables 2.2 to 2.5) and the average number of offspring left by females at that age (b_x). This calculation is performed for each age group, and the values are added together and divided by the NRR. The mean generation time for human beings varies from population to population, but in no case is it much earlier than 19 years. The age at first marriage and childbirth clusters around 19 years for women from such diverse cultures as the Kikuyu of Kenya, Mayans of Guatemala, Copper Eskimo of Canada, and both the Colonial period and contemporary United States (Bogin, 1994). The reason for this clustering is that both the biological maturation of a woman's reproductive system and the sociocultural maturation of a woman's place in society take about 19 years to complete. The reason for this is explained later in this chapter in the section titled "Biocultural Regulation of Human Fertility."

With knowledge of the NRR and the mean generation time (*T*), it is possible for population biologists to calculate the value of the **Malthusian parameter** (*r*), also called the intrinsic rate of natural increase. Very simply, *r* is equivalent to the number of births minus number of deaths per generation time, in other words, the reproduction rate less the death rate. Values above zero indicate that the population is increasing; the higher the value, the faster the growth rate. The Malthusian parameter can be used to compare growth rates of populations of a species that have different generation times. Some human populations have lower intrinsic rates of natural increase partially because individuals in those groups begin reproducing later than those in other groups, the gross reproductive rate is lower, or the death rate is higher.

In the United States the intrinsic rate of natural increase, or *r*, is –0.7 for the entire population (National Center for Health Statistics, 1999). For the segment of the population that is classified as "white" (a "racial" category used on official census forms) the value of *r* is –1.8, while for all other "races" the value of *r* is +3.7 (the other so-called "races" are officially labeled as Hispanic, black, American Indian, and Asian or Pacific Islander). As an anthropologist and human biologist I deplore the use of "race" to categorize people into biologically distinct groups. Definable biological distinctions between so-called "races" do not exist at the genotypic or phenotypic level (Bogin, 1993). "*Race*" does have some value as a short-hand term to categorize people into groups that differ in economic opportunities, social organization and resources, and political power. In the United States those people who are classified as white enjoy, on average, greater economic opportunities and political power. This has an impact on social resources and on demographics.

The difference in the *r* values between the so-called "white race" and the "other races" is revealed in the demographic data for births and deaths. The intrinsic rates of birth and death, respectively, for whites are 12.2 and 14.0 (subtracting the two gives the value of *r* of –1.8). The intrinsic rates of birth and death, respectively, for "other races" are 16.1 and 12.4. The "other races" have both higher intrinsic birth rates and lower intrinsic death rates than the whites. The reasons for these disparities are not completely known. The average age of the white population is older than that of the "other races," and this may explain both higher death rates and lower birth rates. But, shorter generation times and a desire for larger families among the "other races" probably also explain part of the differences.

Finally, the Malthusian parameter may also be used to compare different species. Mice have higher intrinsic rates of natural increase than elephants because they reproduce at a much earlier age and have a much shorter mean generation time.

POPULATION PYRAMIDS

If the intrinsic rate of natural increase of a population is equal to zero, then it is neither growing nor declining in numbers. Such a population has a stable age distribution. A growing population has more individuals in the lower age classes than does a stable population. In contrast, a declining population has more individuals in the older age classes than does a stable population. These types of populations may be depicted in the form of **population pyramids**. Figure 2.4 illustrates the changing shape of such pyramids for the population of Portugal at three times: 1991, 2010, and 2050. The width of each blue histogram bar indicates the number of people within each age group. The data for females are on the right-hand side, and the data for males are on the left-hand side of each graph. Of course, only the data for 1991 are known with some certainty, that is, based on a census. The pyramids for 2010 and 2050 are based on estimates of demographic change using the known census data. The pyramids show that the population structure of Portugal is changing. For at least three decades prior to 1991, Portugal experienced a trend of immigration of its citizens to other countries, especially other countries of Europe and the United States. Birth rates within Portugal also declined in the same period. Consequently, by 1991 the population was still relatively young, with modal ages under 30 years as indicated by the "bulge" of the histogram. But, the number of people in the youngest age groups, from birth to 14 years, was already shrinking. If recent population trends continue to the year 2010, then the population should show signs of aging, as the bulge move up the graph and the modal age is 40 to 50 years. This trend is predicted to continue so that by 2050 Portugal may have a very old population, with a modal age over 65 years for men and over 70 years for women.

Portugal is typical of many highly industrialized nations, such as most of the countries in the European Community and Japan, which are experiencing negative trend in the intrinsic rate of population growth. The total population size of some of these nations remains stable, or even grows slightly, due to immigration from other countries. Population growth in the United States, for example, is due primarily to immigration. Migration is an extrinsic determinant of population growth that is discussed in Chapter 4. In contrast to the industrialized nations, many human populations in the less developed nations are currently undergoing population increase, far exceeding a stable age distribution. The biocultural reasons for the change in population dynamics from increasing, to stable, to declining are explored in Chapter 6, under the topic of demographic transitions. The remainder of this chapter reviews some fundamentals of human demography that are needed to understand population regulation.

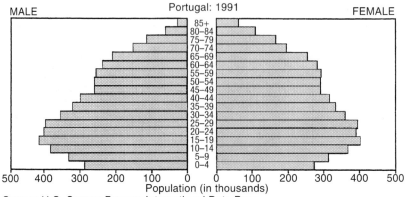

Source: U.S. Census Bureau, International Data Base.

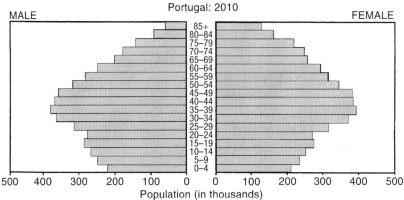

Source: U.S. Census Bureau, International Data Base.

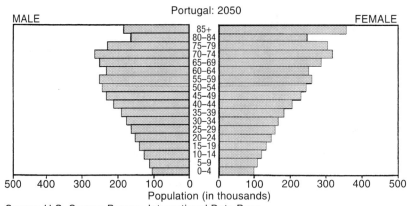

Source: U.S. Census Bureau, International Data Base.

FIGURE 2.4 Population pyramids for Portugal at three time periods.

POPULATION REGULATION: LIMITS TO POPULATION GROWTH

Malthus noted that in an ideal environment one that has no limiting factors, populations grow at a geometric, or exponential, rate. The growth curve of these populations is smooth and becomes increasingly steeper over time (Fig. 1.3). The steepness of the curve depends on the intrinsic rate of natural increase for the population. Human population growth in the twentieth century shows all the signs of exponential growth. The growth of all populations is eventually limited by some factor. This might be competition for food or some other resources, disease, or some other ecological factor. If growth is limited by resources such as food, the exponential growth of the population begins to slow as competition for those resources increases. The growth of the population eventually slows nearly to zero as the population reaches the carrying capacity (K) for the environment. The result is an S-shaped curve of population growth known as the logistic curve. We saw such curves in Figure 1.1.

As noted above, the human population, while not immune to death from starvation and disease, has found the means to overcome the limits to population growth that are imposed on most nonhuman species. Consequently, the logistic curve of population growth does not apply to the human species. People have **culture**, which may be defined as technological, sociological, and ideological strategies to exploit and enhance resources required for survival. Cultural behavior allows people to increase the carrying capacity of many natural environments. Examples of these would be the agricultural revolution (technology) and urbanization (sociological) that allow for dense concentrations of human populations. Both of these involved ideological change as well, such as the rise of monotheistic religions in societies with intensive irrigation agriculture. Monotheistic religion provided a supernatural justification for the centralized bureaucratic political organization needed to administer irrigation agriculture. Another example of ideological change is the invention of the concepts of individuality and privacy rights in congested urban settings. These new concepts replaced ideals of egalitarianism and communality found in less densely populated and rural societies.

There is evidence that the total human population is now entering a period of slower growth, which is due to continuing changes in technology, social organization, and ideology. These changes slow the rate of population-growth in three fundamental ways: (1) they lower the rate of unwanted births, (2) they lower the desired family size, and (3) they raise the average age at which women begin to bear children or reduce the number of births below the level that would replace current human populations (e.g., two children per woman). Some of these population-limiting changes include improvements in the technology of contraception coupled with new ideologies regarding the acceptability of contraception, social and ideological changes in attitudes about women's place in society that lead to greater amounts of formal education for women, and new attitudes about the value versus the costs of children. As with all other species, the human population is regulated in size and rate of growth, but with humans the regulation is as much cultural in nature as it is biological.

BIOCULTURAL REGULATION OF HUMAN FERTILITY

Human fertility is constrained primarily by the **fecundity** of women. Fecundity refers to the biological potential for childbearing, and this is determined by a complex set of physical and cultural variables. Age is one such variable.

Age

Numerous studies show that age patterns of fecundity are similar across a wide variety of populations, but with marked differences in levels of absolute fertility. Fecundity rates increase in the teen years and early twenties and then decrease after the midthirties. These patterns are illustrated in Figure 2.5 for married women in so-called **natural fertility populations**. These are defined as societies without conscious family size limitations due to contraception or induced abortion. Only married women are represented in this figure, as in natural fertility populations it is more likely that married women will reproduce than unmarried women. The Hutterites are a religious order in North America who prize high fertility of women. Adherents marry after age 15 years and do not practice any form of birth control. The curve labeled "Henry's 13" represents 13 natural fertility small societies studied by the French demographer Louis Henry (1961), who first noted the relatively constant shape of the age-specific fertility rate in different populations. The Chinese farmers represent a group of rural villagers and the !Kung are a society of hunters and gathers living in the Kalahari desert of Botswana in southern Africa. While the rural Chinese farmers and the !Kung are considered to be "natural fertility," note that their levels of fertility are lower at all ages than the other two groups. In fact, !Kung women are known to use herbal medicines and other means to prevent or terminate pregnancies. Lower fertility among the rural Chinese and the !Kung may

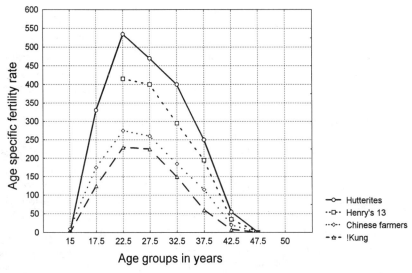

FIGURE 2.5 Age-specific fertility rates for married women in natural fertility populations (redrawn from Ellison and O'Rourke, 2000).

also be due to nutritional stress (Howell, 1979; also see the sections on energetics and lactation below).

Demographers like to contrast natural fertility societies with **controlled fertility populations**, that is, groups where family planning measures are routinely used. In practice, few societies fall neatly into one or the other group. Most people practice some type of fertility regulation in order to maintain desired family size. For example, many traditional societies, including foragers, horticulturists, and preindustrial agriculturists, make use of herbal medicines to limit or enhance fertility (Moerman, 1986; see also the electronic database Medicinal Plants of Native America, *http://probe.nal.usda.gov:8000/related/aboutmpnadb.html*). It may be better to consider societies as falling along a continuum from natural to controlled fertility, with the small traditional societies, such as the Hutterites, at one end and the large highly industrialized societies at the other end.

The groups depicted in Figure 2.6 represent the middle- and the low-fertility end of this continuum. The data in this figure are for national populations, rather than small societies, and all women, married and unmarried, are represented. Despite these differences, the fertility curves for Guatemala and Haiti overlap broadly with those for the Chinese farmers and the !Kung depicted in Figure 2.5. Some fertility control, varying from high-technology medical procedures to traditional medicine, is practiced in Haiti and Guatemala. The majority of the population of both these nations live in rural areas and in poverty. In contrast, the United States and Japan are wealthy industrialized nations. After age 25 years, fertility in both the United States and Japan follow essentially similar patterns. Prior to age 25 years, fertility is much lower in Japan. In fact, the shape of the age-specific fertility curve in Japan prior to age 25 is unlike that of any of the other societies or national populations: Note that the shape of the curve is convex rather than concave as in all of the other curves. Japanese women obviously delay age at first birth; however,

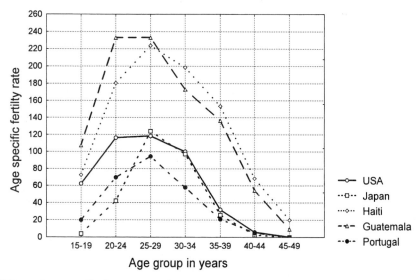

FIGURE 2.6 Age-specific fertility rate for all women in semicontrolled and controlled fertility populations.

the reasons why they do so are not clear. The demands of education and employ-ment may be in competition with the desire for childbirth, but other more subtle social, economic, and ideological constraints on fertility are also likely to be at work. Finally, Portugal is an extreme case of controlled fertility (but not the most extreme, as Spain, Bulgaria, and Latvia have total fertility rates of 1.2 births per woman). Already mentioned above is the effect of out migration of young women on low-ering fertility. The curve of age-specific fertility shows that even those women who remain in Portugal have very low fertility rates at all ages. Portugal is one of the poorest nations in the European Community and in many ways was similar to a developing nation up to about the year 1990. Until the peaceful revolution of 1974, Portugal was essentially a rural, agricultural nation ruled for centuries by a royal family and later by a series of dictators. Since the late 1980s, the country has been in a period of transformation toward a modern industrialized state. The net effect of these political, social, and economic changes has had a profound effect on the Portuguese people. One of the consequences is extremely low fertility.

Developmental Biology of Fertility

Despite the variation in the absolute levels of fertility depicted in Figures 2.5 and 2.6, the constancy in the shape of the age-specific fertility curves is remarkable (with the exception of Japan prior to age 25 years). The pattern of rising fertility after age 15 is due to the increase in the number of young women who reach full reproductive maturation. The term *full reproductive maturation* means the biologi-cal, social, and psychological maturation of the woman have reached the point where risks of pregnancy are near the minimum for both the mother and her off-spring. **Menarche**, the first menstruation, occurs at a median age that varies from 12.1 to 13.5 years in healthy populations (the normal range in age at menarche is 8 to 17 years). But, the average age at full sexual maturation occurs at age 17 or 18 years. Fertility may occur earlier, even as early as six months after menarche. Fer-tility, however, does not equal reproductive maturity. Becoming pregnant is only a part of the business of reproduction. Maintaining the pregnancy to term and raising offspring to adulthood are equally important. Girls under 17 years old have diffi-culty with both of these, since the risks for spontaneous abortions, complications of pregnancy such as high blood pressure in the mother, and low-birth-weight babies are more than twice as high as those for women 20 to 24 years old. The likelihood of these risks declines, and the chance of successful pregnancy and birth increases, markedly after age 18.

One reason for this is that female fertility tracks the growth of the pelvis. Ellison (1982) and Worthman (1993) find that age at menarche is best predicted by **biiliac width**, the distance between the iliac crests of the pelvis. A median width of 24 cm is needed for menarche in American girls living in Berkeley, California, Kikuyu girls of East Africa, and Bundi girls of highland New Guinea. The pelvic width constant occurs at different ages in these three cultures, about 13 years in California versus 16 to 17 years in Kenya and New Guinea due to chronic malnutri-tion and disease among the Kikuyu and the Bundi. Marquisa LaVelle (Moerman, 1982) also reports a special human relationship between growth in pelvic size and reproductive maturation. She finds that the crucial variable for successful first birth is size of the **pelvic inlet**, the bony opening of the birth canal. LaVelle measured pelvic x-rays from a sample of healthy, well-nourished American girls who achieved menarche between 12 and 13 years. These girls did not attain adult pelvic inlet size until 17 to 18 years. Quite unexpectedly, the adolescent growth spurt, which occurs before menarche, does not influence the size of the pelvis in the same way as the rest of the skeleton. Rather, the female pelvis has its own slow pattern of growth, which continues for several years even after adult stature is achieved. LaVelle's research indicates that the one cause of the high risks of adolescent pregnancy is a small pelvic inlet.

While there are several other risks, a study by Tague (1994) provides support to the effect of pelvic inlet size. Tague examined the relationship between pelvic size and age at death in three prehistoric Native American populations. The populations, called Indian Knoll, Pecos Pueblo, and Libben, are represented by sizable collections of skeletal material from people who died from infancy to old age. Only adults were studied by Tague. He found that the female pelvis continues to grow and remodel in adulthood for a longer time than the male pelvis. The age at death for women was assessed by pelvic morphology (changes in the appearance of the pubic symphysis and the auricular surface of the ilium) and by dental wear. Age at death correlates with pelvic inlet size—women with smaller inlets died at younger ages. Tague states that complications of pregnancy and birth were a leading cause of mortality in prehistoric populations. The correlation between pelvic inlet size and age at death in his sample of adult women, all of childbearing age, seems to show that inlet size is a major predictor of reproductive success.

Another variable influencing fertility is the frequency of ovulation. It is often assumed that following menarche an ovulation occurs with each menstrual cycle. But, this is not the case. Most girls experience one to three years of anovulatory menstrual cycles following menarche, meaning that they cannot become pregnant. Two studies of girls and young women living in Switzerland and Finland examined the frequency of ovulation for 4.5 years following menarche (reviewed in Worthman, 1993). Ovulation frequency varied from zero to 10 percent of menstrual cycles at six months postmenarche. The frequency increased to about 30 percent after 1.5 years, varied between 40 and 55 percent after 2.5 years, and leveled off at 60 to 65 percent after 4.5 years. Since the mature level of ovulatory frequency is about 65 percent of menstrual cycles, it appears that following menarche it takes about 5 years for healthy, well-nourished girls to achieve adult maturity for fertility.

Cross-cultural studies of reproductive behavior shows that human societies acknowledge (consciously or not) this special pattern of pelvic growth and ovulatory maturation. As mentioned earlier in this chapter, the age at first marriage and childbirth clusters around 19 years for women from a diversity of cultures. Why it takes the postmenarcheal adolescent girl up to five years to reach full reproductive maturity is not completely understood. One likely reason is that it provides time for teenage girls to practice and learn the economic, social, sexual, and political skills they will need to be successful mothers. Adolescent girls, and the adults around them, may or may not be aware of the period of "adolescent sterility." Everyone in the social group is aware of the dramatic changes in growth and development taking place in the adolescent girl. By the middle of the adolescent stage of life, girls achieve nearly all of their adult size in stature and develop most of their secondary sexual characteristics (e.g., breasts and body hair grow). These changes certainly stimulate both the girls and adults around them to participate in adult social, sexual, and economic behavior. Sexual activity, in particular, is "low risk" in terms of pregnancy during this time. The investment that the teenage girl makes in this practice and learning pays off in successful reproduction. Indeed, human women have the highest rate of reproductive success of any mammalian species (I develop these ideas in greater detail in Bogin, 1999a).

The decline in fertility after the midtwenties is sometimes explained as a function of less frequent intercourse. This notion is being challenged by new research indicating that the fertility decline is likely due to aging of the female reproductive system. Women over 30 years produce lower levels of ovarian hormones and their ova are of lower quality than is the case for younger women. These changes make it more difficult for older women to conceive.

Energetics

A woman's energy balance is a critical influence on her **fecundity**, that is, her biological potential to become pregnant and maintain that pregnancy until birth. Women who are poorly nourished may be unable to conceive. Poor nutrition may be due to inadequate intake of both food in general and one or more **essential nutrients** (defined as those vitamins, minerals, amino acids, fats, carbohydrates, and water that must be supplied by the diet). Women faced with an energy imbalance, that is, a food intake that is either much greater or much less than their energy expenditure, may also be subfecund. Other fecundity problems result from energy flux, which results from relatively sudden changes in either food intake or energy expenditure. In the real world these problems are often combined. For example, the fecundity of women in agricultural societies varies with the work load. During the season of heaviest physical labor fecundity declines due, in part, to a sudden upward flux in energy expenditure. When this is combined with existing levels of moderate undernutrition, the effects on subfecundity are exaggerated. Much research shows that the effect of energetics on fecundity is the result of changes in the production of reproductive hormones and ovarian function (Ellison and O'Rourke, 2000).

Birth seasonality among the Lese is a clear example of these relationships. The Lese are subsistence farmers, meaning that the food they produce is for their own consumption and not for sale. They live in the Ituri forest of northeast Congo (the former Zaire). A study by Bailey et al. (1992) investigated a significant pattern of Lese birth seasonality. The monthly distribution of conceptions for the Lese is shown in Figure 2.7. This pattern follows changes in rainfall and food production. Seasons of low rainfall cause a reduction in garden size and the production of food. This leads to declines in energy balance that may be measured by weight loss in women. Bailey and colleagues also measured seasonal changes in ovarian function in the Lese women by analyzing levels of the hormone progesterone in saliva. A significant rise in salivary progesterone indicates that an ovulation took place in the two weeks prior to menstruation. Progesterone levels and ovulations declined in direct relation to losses of weight. In June the average weight of the 40 women studied was at its lowest point, and only 65 percent of these women were ovulating. This pathway from rainfall to fertility is shown in Figure 2.8. Further details of the relation between energetics and demography are given in Chapter 5.

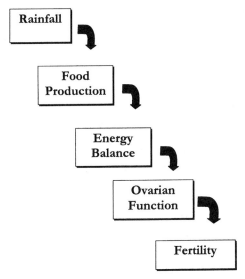

FIGURE 2.7 Cascade of events that influence energetics and fertility in Lese farming women (from Bailey et al., 1992).

Lactation

The production of milk to feed her infant represents a considerable energetic demand to a woman. Well-nourished women, in energy balance, may be able to meet this demand by increasing food intake or decreasing work. Undernourished women or women in negative energy balance may have to sacrifice some of her own body reserves. These women may have to convert fat tissue into carbohydrates for energy, skeletal tissue into minerals, and muscle tissue into amino acids in order to supply high-quality milk to the infant. A new pregnancy during the period of lactation would add a substantial energetic burden to the mother, one that would compromise the health of the current infant, the new pregnancy, and the mother. It is not surprising, then, that much research shows a negative relationship between lactation and fecundity.

The relationship is not simple. The frequency of nursing, the mother's nutritional status, and the introduction of supplemental foods to the infant are just three of the factors that interact in complex ways to influence fecundity during lactation. !Kung women living a traditional foraging lifestyle in Botswana, for example, nurse their infants every 15 minutes, on average, throughout the day. They experience a period of **postpartum amenorrhea** (the absence of menstrual cycles following birth) that lasts more than three years. These !Kung women are under considerable nutritional stress, as evidenced by short stature, low weight, and very thin subcutaneous skinfolds (a measure of the fat layer that lies just under the skin). !Kung women living on farms and cattle ranches in southern Africa and Australian aborigine women on reservations or farms nurse their infants as frequently as the foraging !Kung women. These women, however, resume menstrual cycles in about half the time as the women living as foragers. The women living a more settled life are much heavier than the foraging !Kung women. Presumably, their better nutritional status allows for an earlier resumption of cycling.

   The mechanism by which nutritional status regulates fecundity is not known. What is known is that levels of undernutrition and nursing frequency correlate with the levels of the hormone **prolactin**. As its name indicates, prolactin stimulates milk production in nursing women. Women in the African nation of Gambia were studied for prolactin levels and postpartum amenorrhea in relation to nutrition. In an experiment, one group of women were given a food supplement during pregnancy and lactation. A second group was given the supplement during lactation only, while a control group was given no supplement at any time. All three groups were followed for more than 80 weeks of lactation. The unsupplemented group maintained the highest levels of prolactin and the longest period of amenorrhea during the experiment. The group receiving the supplement during both pregnancy and lactation had the lowest levels of prolactin and the shortest period of amenorrea. The group receiving the supplement during lactation only was intermediate in both prolactin levels and length of postpartum amenorrhea. As all women nursed for the entire 80 plus weeks, nursing did not directly cause the variation in prolactin or amenorrhea. Some interaction between pregnancy, nursing, nutritional status, and other untested variables determined these relationships. Still, as Ellison and O'Rourke (2000) comment in their review of this experiment, prolactin levels "may be a good indicator of how hard a woman's metabolism must be pushed to produce the milk the baby needs" (p. 572). As women are pushed harder, fecundity may be suppressed so as to concentrate all available resources on the survival of the current infant.

Disease and Fertility

Several diseases have a direct effect on fertility and fecundity. As mentioned in Chapter 1, many sexually transmitted diseases (STDs), including gonorrhea and chlamydia, can cause infertility or subfecundity. Malaria, which is one of the most widespread infectious diseases in the world, leads to problems of placental function and fetal loss. Specific nutrient deficiencies cause not only malnutrition in the mother but also developmental problems for any pregnancy she may carry. Iodine deficiency can disrupt ovarian function and folate deficiency can cause life-threatening developmental abnormalities in the fetus. In fact, the impact of disease on fertility may be modulated by the nutritional status of the woman. A malnourished woman is likely to be less able to fight off infectious diseases to which she is exposed. Once infected, even with diseases that in and of themselves have no direct effect on fecundity, her nutritional state may deteriorate further as her body uses resources to fight the disease. This may plunge her below the nutritional reserve threshold required to become pregnant or maintain the pregnancy to term.

Male Fertility

The number of fecund and reproductively active women in a population is the major determinant of human fertility. The fecundity and fertility of men are of little consequence to the growth of human populations. Perhaps this is why much less is known about the factors that may influence male fecundity. It is known that age, energetics, and disease seem to have much less impact on men than on women. In general, male fecundity is much less sensitive to the environment. Nevertheless, there is considerable variation in the fertility of individual men in many human populations. In many traditional societies, men of high social status father significantly more offspring than men of lower social status. A well-known case in anthropology is that of the Yạnomaö man named "Shinbone" (Chagnon, 1983). The Yạnomaö are a tribal people living in the rain forests of southern Venezuela and northern Brazil. The Yạnomaö allow men to have several wives, a practice called polygyny. Shinbone had 11 wives and fathered many children, of whom 43 lived long enough to be remembered by other people. Shinbone's father was also very successful reproductively. So much so that when Chagnon collected detailed genealogies from the Yạnomaö villages with descendents of these two men, he found that 75 percent of the 541 people then alive were descendents of Shinbone and his father.

This level of differential fertility between men is rare in the industrialized nations. First of all, polygyny is uncommon or even prohibited. This results in a more even distribution of marriages among men, meaning more men are in fact married. Then there are numerous economic and social constraints on family size, such as the high costs associated with rearing children. The next section explores some of these issues.

TABLE 2.10
Social Factors Regulating Human Fertility

Part A: Factors Regulating Intercourse

1. *Age at marriage.* Late age at marriages tends to reduce fertility.
2. *Monogamy versus polygyny.* There is some evidence that wives of polygynous marriages have lower fertility. This may be due to lower coital frequency or older age of the husband and his loss of libido (see factor 8 below).
3. *Separation and divorce.* These often result in periods of low exposure to intercourse, especially in societies that sanction births only within legal unions.
4 *Widowhood.* Some societies have strong prohibitions against remarriage, especially of women. Where the life expectancy of men is relatively short, high rates of widowhood for still fertile women may slow population growth.
5. *Postpartum abstinence.* Some societies prohibit coitus between husband and wife for a period of time following birth. The period may last from a few weeks to more than one year. Adherence to these prohibitions varies widely however.
6. *Ceremonial abstinence.* Intercourse may be prohibited during some holy days, during the hunting season, during periods of mourning, and during other ceremonial times. These prohibitions will have an effect on fertility only if they are of long duration.
7. *Celibacy.* Young men in several societies (e.g., Zulu in Africa, several Plains Indians groups in North America) are required to be celibate while serving as warriors but marry by their mid-twenties. Ritual and religious specialists in a few societies, usually men, remain celibate all their lives (e.g., Roman Catholic and Buddhist priests). This type of celibacy has virtually no effect on fertility of the population. In some complex agroindustrial societies a class of permanent spinsters may arise, for example in Ireland and Victorian England during the nineteenth century. In some postindustrial nations today, such as Japan, Portugal (see Fig. 2.6), Lativia, and

Spain, many women are choosing not to reproduce and even not to marry. Spinsterhood, delayed marriage for women, and voluntary sterility for women do have consequences for fertility and may even lower the birth rate for the entire population below the replacement level.

8. *Frequency of coitus*. Ritual and work patterns may influence the frequency of intercourse. Factors 5 and 6 are examples of ritual abstinence. When wives of husbands are required to travel to distant locations for work, such as migrant agricultural workers or business consultants, coital frequency between the spouses will decrease. But, there is only sporadic evidence that coital frequency has any real impact on fertility (Bailey et al., 1992).

Part B: Factors Influencing Likelihood of Conception and Birth Following Intercourse

1. *Contraception*. Many societies employ methods of contraception, but the effectiveness of these methods varies tremendously. Already discussed in the text is the use of herbal medicines to limit fertility. Some of these are quite effective, and the original "pill" developed by western pharmaceutical scientists is derived from an herbal contraceptive. Mechanical means, such as condoms and diaphragms, have only partial success in preventing pregnancy (80 percent or so). *Coitus interruptus* is widely practiced but has even lower success than mechanical means. Benedict (1972) considers social rules that prohibit sexual contact, even any form of social contact, between men and women in specific kinship relations as a form of contraception. These incest taboos, which are usually considered to structure social, economic, and political relations, may also reduce reproductive opportunities brought on by propinquity. Taboos between cousins, both parallel and cross cousins, residing in the same village or neighborhood may be examples of this type of social contraception.

2. *Abortion*. Some type of abortion is practiced in virtually every society. Abortion is usually initiated at the discretion of women and often without knowledge of the father or other men. The covert nature of abortion is necessary because in general it is overtly prohibited or disapproved of by most societies. Abortion practices vary from limiting childbirth after a woman decides she has "enough" children, as is done in Southeast Asia, to "space" births in the traditionally desired manner, as is done in many parts of Africa (Ellison and O'Rourke, 2000). At the level required to have a significant impact on population growth, abortion carries risks to women's health, and this usually outweighs its benefits.

3. *Infanticide*. Demographers are divided on the place of infanticide in population regulation. Benedict (1972) considers infanticide to be a social regulation of fertility, but Ellison and O'Rourke (2000) state that since it occurs postnatally, infanticide is not properly a fertility control measure. This distinction not withstanding, infanticide has been and still is an effective means of population regulation. This is especially the case when female infants are targeted for death. Yąnomaö groups practicing warfare prefer male infants, as they would grow to be warriors. In areas of rural China and India where patrilocal residence is practiced, male infants are preferred because girls are perceived as an economic burden. At marriage, the parents of girls must supply large amounts of bride wealth to the groom's family, and the daughter will move to the husband's village. In these societies female infanticide may skew the sex ratio. On a worldwide basis there are approximately 105 boys born for every 100 girls. By age 20 years the ratio is usually equal. But, in parts of China and India and among the Yąnomaö, the sex ratio for the birth to five-year-old age group may reach 135 boys for every 100 girls. Only infanticide and female neglect (less food and care going to daughters, which results in infant mortality) can account for such a skewed sex ratio.

Source: After Benedict (1972).

Social Regulation of Fertility

Many social, cultural, and personality factors influence male fertility. Social prestige influences a man's access to critical resources, which in turn influences his desirability as a mate to women. Similarly, the fertility of women is also subject to social regulation, albeit there are often marked differences between the sexes in the particular factors. Still, many demographers describe two major ways in which fertility may be regulated socially. The first is the regulation of intercourse, and the second is the likelihood that conception or birth will take place even after intercourse.

A partial list of ways in which human social groups regulate the conditions under which reproductive unions may take place is given in Table 2.10. An example

---

Box 2.2
Social Regulation of Fertility in the Mormon Church

The following is taken from Nag (1980). It is a comment on the article by Nag. The comment was written by L. R. Stucki and was published along with Nag's article. The comment is quoted in its entirety, except that the references cited in the comment have been removed.

As I have stated in the past leaders of [certain ethnic and religious] groups often deliberately seek to keep birth rates high in order to maximize their share of the total economic, social, and political "pie." Granted that many of these attempts fail, some do succeed. For example, the Mormon Church as late as 1977 still had a crude birth rate of 31.66 per thousand . . . despite the presence of such generally accepted fertility reducing factors as very high average educational levels, severe economic penalties associated with child rearing, and delayed marriage patterns . . . In fact, the almost 100% Mormon Provo-Orem Standard Metropolitan Statistical area in Utah in the 1970 census led the nation in high-school graduates while 11.7% of its population had income below the poverty level as compared to the national average of 8.7% . . . Further, despite sizable non-Mormon minorities in the Salt Lake and Ogden areas and the absence of a significant nonwhite or rural population, Utah led the nation in the 1970 census in number of families with three or more children under the age of 18 . . . , an anomaly that had even been more pronounced in the 1950 census when there been been many fewer non-Mormons in the state . . .

Outsiders frequently find it difficult to understand why so many Mormon families, often today under severe economic stress, continue to want large numbers of children and frequently sacrifice almost every economic asset they have to meet the direct and indirect financial burdens (often 15 to 20% of a family's gross income) required by the church to remain in good standing, even before paying debts to outside creditors for the basic necessities of life . . . Also surprising to many is the continued rapid growth rate of this very demanding religion in the United States and elsewhere (the highest of any major denomination in the United States . . . Certainly it would be wise for us to examine carefully the highly successful combination of doctrine, dedication, and organization that so fully controls the lives of the 3,200,000 American and the 1,500,000 foreign members of this remarkable church, which has fully embraced modern technology and the free-enterprise system yet mounts very effective national campaigns against such fertility-reducing practices as artificial contraception, abortion, and homosexuality . . .

of social regulation of fertility in a religious denomination, the Mormon Church of the United States, is presented in Box 2.2. In later chapters we will explore the ways in which these social factors influence population growth during specific times in human history (Chapter 6), within specific human groups, such as the Irish (Chapter 7), and for the human population as a whole (Chapters 8 and 9). Suffice it to state here that while most societies have some means to limit fertility, the biological and social mechanisms at their disposal are either ineffective or not often applied. Because of this, and despite the recent history of population decline in some nations, the human population has increased almost continuously throughout history. Its growth has skyrocketed since the Industrial Revolution (see Fig. 1.3). No other animal population has shown such steady growth.

THREE

HOW PEOPLE GROW

If there is a "secret" to life, it is hidden in the process that converts a single cell, with its complement of **deoxyribonucleic acid (DNA)**, into a multicellular organism composed of hundreds of different tissues, organs, behavioral capabilities, and emotions. That process is no less wondrous when it occurs in an earthworm, a whale, or a human being. The fact that this process happens repeatedly, creating populations of similar organisms, generation after generation, serves to increase our sense of amazement. Because this book is about human biology, this chapter focuses on the process of human growth and development; however, the reader must be aware that much of what we know about human growth, both of individual people and of populations, is derived from research on nonhuman animals. The two reasons for this are ethical limits on the kind of experimental research that may be performed on human beings and the evolutionary history that connects all living organisms.

Many growth processes that occur in humans are identical to those in other species and attest to a common evolutionary origin. Powerful evidence for the common evolutionary origin of the eye, for example, came in 1995 with the discovery of PAX-6 a "master-control gene" for eye growth and development (Halder et al., 1995). This gene is common to species as diverse as marine worms, squid, fruit flies, mice, and humans. Other organs, and the mechanisms that control their growth and development, also are shared among many diverse species. Some events in the human life cycle may be unique, such as the childhood stage of development and menopause, and they attest to the ongoing evolution of our species.

Biological evolution is the continuous process of genetic adaptation of organisms to their environments. **Natural selection** determines the direction of evolutionary change and operates by **differential mortality** between individual organisms prior to reproductive maturation and by **differential fertility** of mature organisms. Thus, genetic adaptations that enhance the survival of individuals to reproductive age and that increase the production of similarly successful offspring will increase in frequency in the population. The unique stages and events of human growth and development evolved because they conferred reproductive advantages to our species. In the next chapter we explore the evolution of the human life cycle and its impact on population dynamics. The remainder of the present chapter reviews some of the basic principles of human growth and development.

BASIC PRINCIPLES OF HUMAN GROWTH AND DEVELOPMENT

Human beings, like all animals, begin life as a single cell, the fertilized ovum. Guided by the interaction of the genetic information provided by each parent and the environment, this cell divides and grows. It differentiates and develops into the embryo, fetus, child, and adult.

Although growth and development may occur simultaneously, they are distinct biological processes. **Growth** may be defined as a quantitative increase in size or mass. Measurements of height or weight indicate how much growth has taken place in a child. Additionally, the growth of a body organ, such as the liver or the brain, also may be described by measuring the number, weight, or size of cells present. **Development** is defined as a progression of changes, either quantitative or qualitative, that lead from an undifferentiated or immature state to a highly organized, specialized, and mature state. **Maturity** is measured by functional capacity, such as the development of motor patterns in an infant, because these capacities are related to development of the skeletal and muscle systems. Even though these definitions are broad, they allow us to consider the growth, development, and maturation of organs (e.g., kidneys), systems (e.g., the reproductive system), and the person.

The process of growth and development from fertilized ovum to human newborn is counterintuitive to our expectations, which are formed on the basis of our experience with child growth after birth. In fact, throughout much of human history, scholars and physicians did not know or believe that it occurred. Preformation (Fig. 3.1) was a popular belief about the nature of human growth. In 1651, William Harvey, a physician, presented some evidence that the embryo is not a preformed adult. Incontrovertible evidence against preformation was presented in 1799, when S. T. Sommerring published drawings of the human embryo and fetus from the fourth week after fertilization to the fifth month. These drawings clearly showed that the embryo is not a miniature human being; rather, during development, each new life passes through a series of embryological stages that are distinct in appearance from the form visible just before and after birth [Bogin (1999a) provides greater historical detail and references].

STAGES IN THE LIFE CYCLE

Many of the basic principles of human growth, development, and maturation are best presented in terms of the events that take place during the life cycle. Chapter 1 presented an overview of the five stages of human life from birth to adulthood. This chapter describes in greater detail the stages of the complete life cycle. One of the many possible ordering of events is given in Table 3.1, in which growth periods are divided into developmentally functional stages. For convenience, the life cycle may be said to begin with fertilization and then proceed through prenatal growth and development, birth, postnatal growth and development, maturity, senescence, and death. In truth, however, the course of life is cyclical; birth, the onset of sexual maturation in the adolescent boy or girl, and even death are each fundamental

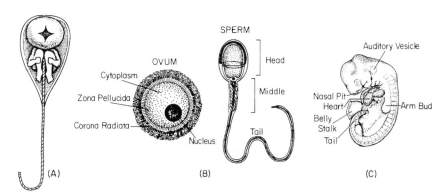

FIGURE 3.1 (*a*) Preformationist rendering of a human spermatozoan, from a drawing published by Hartsoeker in 1694 (Singer, 1959). (*b*) Diagram of human actual appearance of human ovum and spermatozoan (not to scale). (*c*) Diagram of human embryo 32 days after fertilization. The union of sperm with ovum initiates the process of growth by hyperplasia and hypertrophy. Development also begins soon after fertilization as groups of cells differentiate, or specialize, and become functional cell types and tissues.

attributes of the cycle of life. In the fetus, child, and adult, old cells die and degrade so that their molecular constituents may be recycled into new cells formed by mitosis. At the population level, people grow, mature, age, and die even as new individuals are conceived and born. Declaring one moment, such as fertilization, to be a beginning to life is arbitrary in a continuous cycle that passes through many stages, both in the individual person and in generation after generation.

In the following sections the stages of prenatal and postnatal life are described. The timing of growth events is presented, usually in the form of mean, median, or modal ages. The reader should bear in mind that these ages indicate the central tendency and not the normal range of variation that occurs naturally in the timing of many growth events. Research may find, for example, that the median age at menarche (first menstruation) is 12.6 years in a sample of girls. The actual age at menarche for individual girls in the sample may range from 8.0 to 15.0 years, and both the earliest and latest ages represent perfectly normal variation. When the range of variation in the timing of growth events is important in terms of the basic principles of human growth, it will be given in this chapter.

Prenatal Stages

The course of pregnancy may be divided into three periods of roughly three months duration called **trimesters**. During the first trimester, one of the major events is the multiplication of a single cell, the fertilized ovum, into tens of thousands of new cells. At first, cell division may produce exact copies of the original parent cell, but within hours of the first division, distinct groups of cells begin to form. Variations in the rate of cell division may be seen in the separate groups. Eventually these groups of cells form different kinds of tissue (the "germ layers" of endoderm, mesoderm, and ectoderm) that will constitute the growing embryo. Thus growth (an increase in cell number or cell size) and development (cellular differentiation) begin soon after conception. After the initial embryonic tissues are formed, the first

TABLE 3.1
Stages in Human Life Cycle

Stage	Growth Events/Duration (approximate or average)
Prenatal Life	
Fertilization	
First trimester	Fertilization to 12th week: embryogenesis
Second trimester	Fourth through 6th lunar month: rapid growth in length
Third trimester	Seventh lunar month to birth: rapid growth in weight and organ maturation
Birth	Transition to extrauterine life
Postnatal Life	
Neonatal period	Birth to 28 days: extrauterine adaptation, most rapid rate of postnatal growth and maturation
Infancy	Second month to end of lactation, usually by age 36: rapid growth velocity, steep deceleration in velocity with time, feeding by lactation, deciduous tooth eruption, many developmental milestones in physiology, behavior, and cognition
Childhood	Third to 7th year: moderate growth rate, dependency for and feeding, midgrowth spurt, eruption of first permanent molar and incisor, cessation of brain growth by end of stage
Juvenile	Ages 7–10 for girls and 7–12 for boys: slower growth rate, capable of self-feeding, cognitive transition leading to learning of economic and social skills
Puberty	Occurs at end of juvenile stage and is an event of short duration (days or a few weeks): reactivation of central nervous system mechanism for sexual development, dramatic increase in secretion of sex hormones
Adolescence	Five to 8 years after the onset of puberty: adolescent growth spurt in height and weight, permanent tooth eruption virtually complete, development of secondary sexual characteristics, sociosexual maturation, intensification of interest and practice adult social, economic, and sexual activities
Adulthood	
Prime and transition	From 20 years of age to end of childbearing years: homeostasis in physiology, behavior, and cognition, menopause for women by age 50 years
Old age and senescence	From end of childbearing years to death: decline in the function of many body tissues or systems

trimester is taken up with **organogenesis**, the formation of organs and physiological systems of the body. During the first few weeks after conception the embryo has an external appearance that is "mammalian," that is, many mammalian embryos share these same external features. By the eighth week the embryo has many phenotypic characteristics that may be recognized as human.

Though the human body is composed of dozens of different kinds of tissues and organs, their generation and growth during prenatal life, and postnatal life as well, take place through a few ubiquitous processes. Goss (1964) described two types of cellular growth: **hyperplasia** and **hypertrophy**. Hyperplasia involves cell division by mitosis. For example, epidermal cells of the skin form by the mitotic division of **germinative cells** (undifferentiated cells) in the deep layers of the skin. Hypertrophic growth involves the enlargement of already existing cells, as in the case of adipose cells growing by incorporating more lipid (fat) within their cell membranes. Goss (1964) also described three strategies of growth employed by different tissues: renewal, expansion, and stasis. **Renewing tissues** include blood cells, gametes (sperm and egg cells), and the epidermis. Mature cells of renewable tissue are incapable of mitosis and have relatively short lives; for example, red blood cells (erythrocytes) survive in circulation for about six months. The supply of red blood cells is constantly renewed by a two-step process: first, the mitotic division of pre-erythrocyte cells of the bone marrow and, second, the differentiation of some of these into mature red blood cells. Goss (1986) points out that the undifferentiated cells are sequestered in a growth zone that is "spatially distinct from the differentiated compartment" (p. 5). This two-step process and the growth zone for undifferentiated cells are common physiological features of many types of renewing tissues.

Expanding tissues include the liver, kidney, and endocrine glands, the cells of which retain their mitotic potential even in the differentiated state. In the liver, for example, there is no special germinative layer or compartment, and most liver cells are capable of hyperplasia to replace other cells lost by damage. Relatively large portions of a diseased liver may be excised surgically, as a proliferation of new cells will eventually occur to meet physiological demands. Perhaps it is no coincidence that in Greek mythology the gods punished Prometheus, who gave the secret of fire to the mortals, by binding him to a rock and sending an eagle to peck out his liver each day for all eternity.

Mitotically **static tissues**, such as nerve cells and striated muscle, are incapable of growth by hyperplasia once they have differentiated from precursor germinative cells. Because the reserve of the germ cells is limited and usually depleted early in life, the pool of static tissues cannot be renewed if damaged or destroyed. However, unlike renewable tissues, which have short lives, static tissues usually live as long as the person survives. Static tissues can grow by hypertrophy; for example, individual nerve cells may grow to relatively great lengths during normal development and, if not fatally damaged by accidents or surgery, regrow new interconnections. The physique of body-building enthusiasts results from hypertrophy of existing muscle cells and not from the formation of new muscle cells. These tissues are static in the sense that they cannot undergo mitosis, but they are reconstituted by a turnover of material at the subcellular and molecular levels. Studies of dietary intake and excretion of nitrogen provide an estimate of protein metabolism in the body. This is because most of the body's store of nitrogen is in protein molecules. As muscle tissue forms the largest mass of protein in the body, measures of nitrogen balance may be used as indicators of muscle turnover and renewal. Data published by Cheek (1968) and Young et al. (1975) indicate that in young adult men, about 2 to 3 percent of the muscle mass is renewed each day. In infancy, when new muscle tissue is forming by hyperplasia, the rate of protein renewal is about 6 to 9 percent per day. The magnitude of this metabolic renewal may be appreciated by the fact that much of the basal metabolic rate of the body (which may be measured by the heat that the body produces when at complete rest) is due to protein turnover. A similar turnover of cellular material occurs in other "static" tissues, such as nerve cells in the body, the brain, and expanding tissues. The renewing tissues may also undergo a turnover of protein molecules during their relatively short lives, but the major metabolic dynamic of these tissues is their mitotic proliferation and eventual death.

Thus, the biological substrate of the individual is not permanent, and from embryonic life through adulthood the human body is in a constant state of decomposition and reorganization. Tanner (1978, p. 26) observed that "this dynamic state enables us to adapt to a continuously changing environment, which presents now an excess of one type of food, now an excess of another; which demands different levels of activity at different times; and which is apt to damage the organism. But we pay in terms of the energy we must take in to keep the turnover running . . . Enough food must be taken in to provide this energy, or the organism begins to beak up." To be sure, different tissues turn over at different rates, so that in muscle cells nitrogen is replaced in a few days to a few weeks, while the calcium in bone cells is replaced over a period of months. During the years and decades of life, sufficient turnover and renewal of the molecular constituents of the body's cells must take place to rejuvenate the entire human being.

The metabolic dynamic of the human organism is most active during the first trimester of prenatal life. The multiplication of millions of cells from the fertilized ovum, and the differentiation of these cells into hundreds of different body parts, makes this earliest period of life highly susceptible to growth pathology caused by either the inheritance of genetic mutations or exposure to harmful environmental agents that disrupt the normal course of development (e.g., certain drugs, malnutrition, and disease that the mother may experience). Because of this, it is estimated that about 10 percent of human fertilizations fail to implant in the wall of the uterus, and of those that do so about 50 percent are spontaneously aborted (Bierman et al., 1965; Werner et al., 1971). Most of these spontaneous abortions occur so early in pregnancy that the mother, and father, is usually unaware that they have happened.

By the start of the second trimester of pregnancy the differentiation of cells into tissues and organs is complete and the embryo is now a fetus. During the first trimester, the embryo grows slowly in length, often measured as **crown–rump length** (CRL, the distance from the top of the head to the buttocks). At 18 days post-conception the embryo has a CRL of about 1.0 to 1.5 mm and by 12 weeks post-conception the CRL is about 53 mm. The rate of growth in length increases during the second trimester. By the fourth month the CRL is about 205 mm, by the fifth month 254 mm, and by the sixth month between 356 and 381 mm, which is about 70 percent of average birth length. Increases in weight during this same period are also rapid. At eight weeks the embryo weighs 2.0 to 2.7 g and at six months the fetus weighs 700 g. This is about 20 percent of birth weight, so relative to size at birth the growth in length during the second trimester exceeds the growth in weight. During the third trimester of pregnancy growth in weight takes place at a relatively faster rate. During the last trimester, the development and maturation of several physiological systems, such as the circulatory, respiratory, and digestive systems, also occur, preparing the fetus for the transition to extrauterine life following birth.

Birth

Birth is a critical transition between life in utero and life independent of the support systems provided by the uterine environment. The **neonate** moves from a fluid to a gaseous environment, from a nearly constant external temperature to one with potentially great volatility. The newborn is also removed from the supply of oxygen and nutrients that have been provided by the mother's blood passed through the placenta and that also handle the elimination of fetal waste products and must now rely on his or her own systems for digestion, respiration, and elimination. The difficulty of the birth transition may be seen in relation to the percentage of deaths by age during the **neonatal period** (the first 28 days postpartum), as shown in Figure 3.2. Of course, most of these deaths were not due to the birth process itself; rather the leading factor associated with neonatal death is inadequate growth and development during the prenatal period. Excessive prenatal growth also carries higher risk for neonatal death, but the discussion here is confined to inadequate growth as this is correlated with the leading cause of death in all human populations. The most common indicator of inadequate prenatal growth is **low birth weight** (defined as a weight less than 2,500 g at birth). During the 1980s, about four out of five neonatal deaths in the United States were due to low-birth-weight babies (Emanuel et al., 1989). An index of relative mortality during the neonatal period by birth weight is given in Figure 3.3. Relative mortality is defined as the percentage of deaths in excess of the number that occur for infants within the normal birth weight range of 3.0 to 4.5 kg. These data are for infants at all gestational ages. **Prematurity**, defined as birth prior to 37 weeks gestation, may cause additional complications that increase the chances of neonatal death. Some infants are small for gestational age (SGA), which is often defined as a birth weight less than the 10th percentile for completed week of gestation. Newborns who are both SGA and premature are usually at a greater risk of death than a premature child of the expected weight for gestational age.

The causes of low birth weight, prematurity, and SGA are many and not all are well understood. It is known that one set of causes may be **congenital** (heredi-

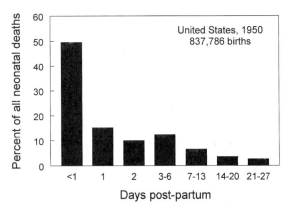

FIGURE 3.2 Percent of deaths occurring during the neonatal period (birth to day 28). Data from the United States, all registered births for 1950 (Shapiro and Unger, 1965). These data are presented in lieu of more recent data as the technology for extraordinary neonatal medical care in existence today reduces neonatal deaths.

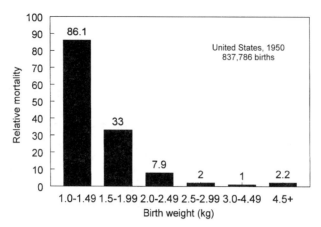

FIGURE 3.3 Index of relative mortality by birth weight (kg) during the neonatal period. Data from the United States, all registered births for 1950 (Shapiro and Unger, 1965). Relative mortality is calculated as the risk of death for an infant born at a given weight. Infants of normal birth weight, 3.0 to 4.5 kg, have a relative mortality of 1.0. Infants born at 2.5 to 3.0 kg have twice the risk of death as normal birth weight infants, and so on.

tary or inborn) problems with the fetus. Another set of causes may be placental insufficiency, or maternal conditions including undernutrion, disease, smoking, or alcohol consumption. Whatever the cause, low birth weight, with or without prematurity, is associated with **socioeconomic status** (SES) of the mother. Socioeconomic status is a concept devised by the social sciences to measure some aspects of education, occupation, and social prestige of a person or a social group. A higher or lower SES does not, by itself, influence birth weight; rather the attitudes and behaviors of people are associated with SES, and it is these attitudes and behaviors that influence diet, health, smoking, alcohol consumption, and other determinants of birth weight. Any measure of SES will only partially account for all of the social and cultural factors that affect growth. Nevertheless, SES serves as a proxy for these more specific determinants, and at a gross level the effect of SES is obvious; for example, the incidence of low birth weight in the wealthier, higher SES nations averages 5.9 percent of all live births; in the poorer, lower SES nations the incidence averages 23.6 percent (Villar and Belizan, 1982). The Netherlands has one of the lowest rates at 4.0 percent; Bangladesh has the highest rate at 50 percent (World Resources Institute, 1994).

At a finer level, within the developed nations, the socioeconomic relationship with birth weight is still strong. When educational attainment is used to estimate general SES, researchers in the United States found that 10.1 percent of births to women with less than 12 years of schooling are low birth weight compared with 6.8 percent of births to women with 12 years and 5.5 percent to those with 13 or more years of formal education (Taffel, 1980). Blacks and other nonwhite minority groups show consistently lower average birth weights compared with whites, and part of this difference is accounted for by the lower SES of the nonwhite groups. However, when white (European-American) and black (African-American) women are matched for socioeconomic status, black women still give birth to a higher percentage of low-birth-weight infants. To some researchers, the white–black differences suggest that genetic factors are major determinants of birth weight, but others point to nongenetic factors.

There is so much concern about birth weight because it is a strong predictor of later events in life. Low birth weight (LBW) often leads to smaller physical size, especially in height, later in life. It is also associated with reduced cognitive development and poor school performance. Work productivity and economic advancement is impaired by LBW. Research by Barker (1994) shows that LBW increases the risk of death by heart disease and diabetes when the individual is an adult. Birth weight is also an important demographic variable, as populations with an excess of LBWs also tend to have high fecundity, a young demographic profile, and other characteristics typical of the fast-growing, lower income nations.

The debate about the genetic versus environmental determinants of birth weight is important because it reflects the more general question of heredity and environment in human affairs. To place this debate in perspective, it is first necessary to state more clearly what is known about the factors that produce variation in birth weight. Based on a variety of evidence and many research studies, Robson (1978) estimates the variance in birth weight due to fetal genotype to be 10 percent and the variance due to parental genotype to be 24 percent. Most of the remaining 66 percent of the total variance is due to nongenetic maternal and environmental factors. There are many environmental factors that act directly on the developing embryo and fetus. Some obvious factors, briefly mentioned above, are smoking (Garn, 1985; Schell and Hodges, 1985), alcohol consumption (Able, 1982), and famine (Stein et al., 1975). There is also evidence that exposure to urban pollution in the form of noise, lead, and polychlorinated biphenyls can reduce gestation length leading to premature births and cause LBW in full-term infants (Schell, 1991).

Emanuel and colleagues (1989) found that these relationships may hold across so-called "racial" lines, influencing births to both white and black women, but the relative amount of influence on birth weight is not equal (the term "race" and similar terms are set in quote marks to indicate that for human beings "racial" categories denote socially defined groups and not biologically or genetically justifiable classifications). It is well established that in any given year more black infants are LBW than white infants, even when black and white mothers are matched for SES variables (e.g., income, education, housing, and occupation). Even more curious are the findings for so-called "biracial" infants. One study by Migone et al. (1991) examined all "biracial" single births reported in the United States in the year 1983. Such births were to either white mothers and black fathers or black mothers and white fathers. The percentage of LBWs for these "biracial" couples was compared to samples of single births to same-"race" parents. The results, shown in Table 3.2, indicate a statistically significant trend. The "race" of either parent contributes to this trend; however, the mother's "race" is a stronger predictor of birth weight than the "race" of the father. The data in Table 3.2 are unadjusted for known confounding variables, but the significant trend remained even when the authors of the study adjusted for mother's age, education, marital status, prenatal care, live birth order, previous fetal deaths, babies' sex, and gestational age. Another study reports that in a sample of low-SES women (defined as likely to be unmarried and live on incomes of less than

TABLE 3.2
Total Number of Births, Number of Low-Weight Births (<2,500 g), and Proportion of Low-Weight Births for each Parental "Racial" Group

Parental Groups (mother–father)	Total Births	Low-Weight Births	
		Number	%
White–white	24,059	1,027	4.3
White–black	18,004	1,108	6.2
Black–white	5,617	459	8.2
Black–black	15,220	1,629	10.7

$10,000 per year), 14 percent of infants born to black mothers with white fathers were LBW, compared with 9 percent of infants born to white mothers with black fathers (Collins and David, 1993).

What does the "race" effect seen in these studies mean? The social conditions of life for same-"race" or different-"race" parents are likely not to be equivalent. This is especially true for the two groups of women studied by Collins and David. Moreover, the differences or similarities in living conditions between the various combinations of parents are likely to be quite complex and not easily summarized by a statistic such as current SES. Recognizing these complexities, Emanuel and colleagues (1992) tried to explain the reason for the persistence of LBWs for infants born to black mothers by the "intergenerational effect hypothesis." By this, the researchers mean that the SES matching is valid only for the current generation of adult women. The mothers and grandmothers of these black and white women were less likely to be equally matched for SES. Given the social history of the United States and Britain, previous generations of black women were likely to be of lower SES than their white counterparts. The intergenerational effect hypothesis predicts that the poor growth and development of women from older generations will have a lasting effect on the current generation.

There is considerable support for the intergenerational effect hypothesis. In several studies, Emanuel and his colleagues working with both British (Emanuel et al., 1992) and U.S. data (Sanderson et al., 1995) found that the mother's own birth weight, her health history during infancy and childhood, and her adult stature (which reflects the total history of her growth and development) are strong predictors of the birth weight of her offspring. These results were confirmed in a similar study of all births in Norway since 1967 (Skjaervern et al., 1997). The authors of the study linked the birth weight records of women with the birth weight of their own infants and produced a sample of 101,264 mother–infant birth weight pairs. Mother's birth weight was strongly associated with the weight of their infant.

Other Measures of Growth at Birth

Weight at birth is just one measurement commonly taken to indicate the amount of growth that took place during prenatal life. Recumbent length, the circumference of the head, arm, and chest, and skinfolds are others. Recumbent length is similar to stature; however the person measured is lying down and is stretched out fully by having the examiner apply pressure to the abdomen and knees. The maximum distance between the vertex of the head and the soles of the feet constitutes the measurement. This can be measured at a very young age or under other circumstances when stature (standing height) is impossible to determine. Circumferences measure the contribution made by a variety of tissues to the size of different body parts. For example, head circumference measures the maximum girth of the skull and hence, indirectly, the size of the brain. This is because of the intimate conformity between the brain and the tissues that surround and protect it and the dominant role of the brain in determining head size. Similarly, arm circumference includes the measurement of bone, muscle, subcutaneous fat, and skin. For infants of the same weight and length, variations in arm circumference are chiefly due to variations in the amounts of muscle and, especially, subcutaneous fat.

Some representative data for several measures of size at birth and at 18 years of age are given in Table 3.3. These average figures show that, at birth, boys are a bit longer, heavier, and larger headed than girls, but the girls have slightly more subcutaneous fat at birth than the boys. In reality there is such a wide range of variation in actual birth dimensions that the small average sexual dimorphism in size is biologically insignificant. At 18 years of age, on average, men and women display well-marked sexual dimorphism in all of these growth variables, except head circumference. Another difference between the infant and the adult is in body proportions. For children born in the United States, head circumference at birth averages about 70 percent of length at birth. By age seven years, head circumference averages 42 percent of length, and at maturity the average value falls to about 30 percent. The reason for this change in percentage over time is that during the fetal, infant, and childhood stages of life the growth of the brain proceeds at a faster rate than the growth of the body (Scammon, 1930). For the average child in the United States, head circumference reaches 80 percent of mature size by about seven years of age, though length of the body is only 68 percent complete at the same age

TABLE 3.3
Mean Size at Birth and Age 18 years for Children Born in the United States

	At Birth		At 18 years	
	Boys	Girls	Boys	Girls
Recumbent length/stature,[a] cm	49.9	49.3	176.6	163.1
Weight,[a] kg	3.4	3.3	71.4	58.3
Head circumference,[b] cm	34.8	34.1	55.9	54.9
Triceps skinfold, mm	3.8[c]	4.1[c]	8.5[d]	17.5[d]
Subscapular skinfold, mm	3.5[c]	3.8[c]	10.0[d]	12.0[d]
Arm muscle area at age 1 year,[e] mm^2	20.4	19.6	75.0	57.2

[a] Hamill et al. (1977).
[b] Nellhaus (1968).
[c] Johnston and Beller (1976).
[d] Johnson et al. (1981).
[e] Frisancho (1990).

(Hamill et al., 1977; Nellhaus, 1968). There are also proportional changes in the length of the limbs, which become longer relative to total body length during growth. The proportional changes are illustrated in Figure 3.4.

The composition of the newborn's body in terms of adipose tissue and muscle tissue has been determined. The newborn's total body weight is about 12 percent body fat and 20 percent muscle mass. By adulthood, men average 15 to 17 percent body fat and 40 percent muscle mass; women average 24 to 26 percent fat and 35 to 37 percent muscle mass (Bogin, 1999a). The composition of the newborn, the adolescent, and the adult in terms of other soft tissues and a variety of chemicals is also available (Fomon et al., 1966; Forbes, 1986) and shows marked differences between birth and adulthood. The study of the formation and maturation of hard tissues, such as the skeleton, during prenatal and postnatal life is another means of describing different stages of development. Most bone forms from cartilage that becomes calcified (calcium and phosphorous minerals are added) and, then, ossified (hardened) into mature skeletal tissue. Bone formation takes place throughout the growing years. A record of the process can be captured on radiographs, since at certain x-ray exposure levels cartilage is "invisible" but calcified and ossified bone is radio-opaque (Fig. 3.5). Radiographs of skeletal development of normally growing children from the United States and England have been compiled into atlases, which may be used to assess the stage of bone maturation of other children (Greulich and Pyle, 1959; Roche et al., 1975; Tanner et al., 1983).

The importance of these contrasts between early and later life is twofold. First, they allow clinicians and researchers to assess a child's stage of biological maturation for different organs, tissues, or chemicals independent of chronological age. Biological maturation is used to help determine if a child is developing too slowly or quickly, either of which may indicate the presence of some disorder. Second, the contrasts between early and later life are also conceptually important. They show that the infant may take any one of several paths for growth, maturation, and functional development. Adult human morphology, physiology, and behavior are **plastic** (Lasker, 1969) and in no way rigidly predetermined. **Plasticity** refers to the ability of an organism to modify its biology or behavior to respond to changes in the environment, particularly when these changes are stressful. People, of course, cannot sprout wings or breathe water, but the sizes, shapes, colors, emotions, and intellectual abilities of people can be significantly altered by environmental stress, training, and experience.

When the biology and behavior of people are considered together (a biocultural perspective), it seems that human beings are, perhaps, the most plastic of all species. In part, this is because the human life span is long, relative to most other animals, and the adult human phenotype is achieved after many years during which a variety of factors may influence their final outcome. This makes people highly variable and adaptable.

Postnatal Life

In contrast to the widely used trimester system for prenatal growth and development, many ways have been proposed to divide life after birth into distinct periods. Following from my previous work (Bogin, 1999a), I prefer a five-stage system from birth to adulthood. These five stages are infant, child, juvenile, adolescent, and adult.

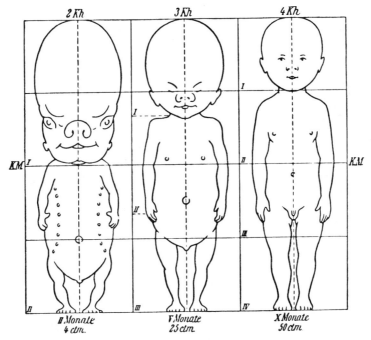

Fig. 3.   Proportionen des Fötus.

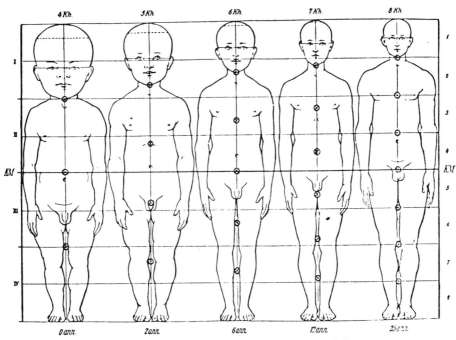

Fig. 6.   Wachstumsproportionen nach der Geburt bis zur Reife.

FIGURE 3.4 Changes in body proportions of human beings that occur during prenatal and postnatal growth. Depicted in the top graphic is, from left, a fetus aged two, five, and ten months; in the bottom graphic, from left, is a newborn aged zero, two, six, twelve, and twenty-five years. Human body segments (head, trunk, arms, legs) grow at different rates and mature, generally, from a head-to-foot direction (Stratz, 1909).

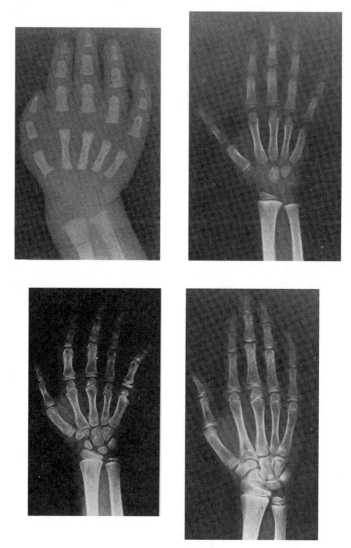

FIGURE 3.5 Radiographs of the hand and wrist at different skeletal ages illustrating the sequence of bone maturation events. (*a*) Newborn; at this age most wrist bones and the growing ends of the finger bones (called epiphyses) are formed of cartilage. At certain x-ray exposures this cartilage is "invisible." The newborn has no ossification centers (places where bone is present) in the wrist and no visible epiphyses. (*b*) Three years old; some wrist ossification centers present, epiphysis of radius present, most epiphyses of hand calcified (i.e., forming bone). (*c*) Eight years old; all ossification centers calcified, epiphyses of the radius and ulna are not as wide as their diaphyses. (*d*) Thirteen years old; all bones have assumed final shape, epiphyses of the radius and ulna are almost as wide as their diaphyses, the growth in size and closure of all epiphyses remains to be completed (Lowery, 1986).

Although any stage model is somewhat arbitrary (life is a continuous process), the use of stages aids description and analysis of the life cycle. The rationale for the five-stage model begins with an analysis of the amount and rate of growth from birth to adulthood that was presented in Chapter 1 (Fig. 1.4). These stages of growth are also outlined in Table 3.1. Each stage may also be defined by characteristics of the dentition, by changes related to methods of feeding, by physical and mental competencies, and by maturation of the reproductive system and sexual behavior.

Infancy Stage

The infancy stage occupies the first three years of human postnatal life. Infancy is characterized by the most rapid velocity of growth of any of the postnatal stages. During the first year of postnatal life infants may add 28 cm in length and 7 kg in weight, which represents more than 50 percent of birth length (about 50 cm) and 200 percent of birth weight (about 3.4 kg). The rate of decrease in velocity, or deceleration, is also very steep, which makes infancy the life stage of most rapidly changing rate of growth. The infant's curve of growth, rapid velocity and deceleration, is a continuation of the fetal pattern, in which the rate of growth in length actually reaches a peak in the second trimester and then begins a deceleration that lasts until childhood (Fig. 3.6).

As for all mammals, human infancy is the period when the mother provides all or some nourishment to her offspring via lactation or by some culturally derived

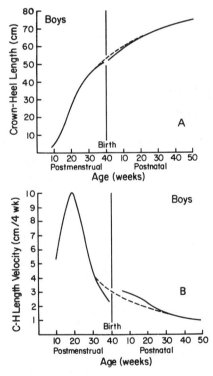

FIGURE 3.6 (*a*) Distance and (*b*) velocity curves for growth in body length during human prenatal and postnatal life. The figure is diagrammatic, as it is based on several sources of data. The interrupted lines depict the predicted curve of growth if no uterine restriction takes place. In fact, such restrictions do take place toward the end of pregnancy, and this may impede the flow of oxygen or nutrients to the fetus. Consequently, growth rate slows, but rebounds after birth and returns the infant to the size she or he would be without any restriction (Tanner, 1990).

TABLE 3.4
Median and Range in Age of Eruption of Deciduous Teeth for French-Canadian Infants

Teeth	Males		Females	
	Median Age (months)	Range (months)	Median Age (months)	Range (months)
Maxillary				
I^1	8.49	5.70–11.84	9.42	6.19–13.33
I^2	9.81	5.87–14.74	10.53	6.13–16.12
C	17.56	12.44–23.56	18.31	13.28–24.15
M^1	15.20	11.26–19.74	15.06	11.51–19.09
M^2	27.04	19.95–35.20	27.86	20.67–36.11
Mandibular				
I_1	6.86	3.90–10.63	7.31	3.96–11.68
I_2	11.48	6.95–17.13	12.54	7.70–18.57
C	17.77	12.98–23.30	18.58	13.14–24.96
M_1	15.25	11.49–19.54	15.32	11.67–19.48
M_2	26.13	19.19–34.14	26.90	20.22–34.54

Note: Abbreviations for the teeth are I_1 = central incisor, I_2 = lateral incisor, C = canine, M_1 = first molar, M_2 = second molar.
Source: After Demirjian (1986).

imitation of lactation. One reason for this is that infants do not have teeth and thus cannot eat solid food. During infancy the deciduous dentition (the so-called milk teeth) emerges through the gums. Infants will erupt five deciduous teeth in each quadrant of their mouth, the central incisor, lateral incisor, canine, first molar, and second molar (I_1, I_2, C, M_1, M_2). Table 3.4 provides the median age of emergence and range in age of these teeth for French-Canadian infants. The deciduous teeth of boys emerge about one month earlier than girls. This is noteworthy only because in most other aspects of physical growth and maturation girls are, on average, ahead of boys.

One surprising feature of human growth during infancy is the similarity that most infants show in both amount and rate of growth in length and weight during the first six months of life. One might expect that variation in hereditary and environmental factors between individual infants and populations would lead to marked differences in amounts and rates of growth. But, Habicht et al. (1974) and Van Loon et al. (1986) show that the growth of infants of normal birth weight from a wide variety of ethnic and socioeconomic classes in both the developed and developing nations is remarkably similar during the first six months of life. Perhaps breast feeding, which supplies the nutrient, immunity, and psychological needs of the infant, overrides the effect of variations in other aspects of the environment. After six months of age, when breast milk alone no longer meets the nutritional demands of the growing infant and other specially prepared infant foods must be supplemented, infants from the developed nations or higher socioeconomic classes may become significantly larger than their less privileged age mates from poorer environments. If alleviated by improved nutrition and health status early on, the disadvantaged children may catch up in size (first shown by Pagliani in 1876, cited in Bogin, 1999a). Otherwise, the differences in size between the well-off and the deprived become greater and greater, and by childhood the differences may have become irreversible.

Motor patterns and abilities (what a baby can do physically) develop rapidly during infancy. At birth, states of wakefulness and sleep are not sharply differentiated and motor coordination is variable and transient. By 1 month the infant can lift its chin when prone and by 2 months lift its chest by doing a "push-up." By 4 months the infant can sit with support, by 7 months sit without support, by 8 months crawl, and by 12 months walk with support. By 2 years of age the infant can walk well and turn the pages of a book, one at a time. By 3 years of age, the end of the infancy stage, the youngster can run smoothly, pour water from a pitcher, and manipulate small objects, such as blocks, well enough to control them. There is a similar progression of changes in the problem-solving, or cognitive, abilities of the infant.

The development of the skeleton, musculature, and the nervous system accounts for all of these motor and cognitive advancements. The rapid growth of the brain, in particular, is important. The human brain grows more rapidly during infancy than almost any other tissue or organ of the body (Fig. 3.7). All areas of the brain seem to take part in this fast pace of growth and maturation, including those structures that control the reproductive system. The **hypothalamus**, a center of neurological and endocrine control, is one of these brain structures. During fetal life and early infancy the hypothalamus produces relatively high levels of gonadotropin-releasing hormone (GnRH). This hormone causes the release of luteinizing hormone (LH) and follicle-stimulating hormone (FSH) from the **pituitary**. Luteinizing hormone and FSH travel in the blood stream to the gonads (ovaries or testes), where they stimulate the production and release of estrogen or androgen hormones (Fig. 3.8). These gonadal hormones are, in part, responsible for the rapid rate of growth during early infancy. By late infancy, however, the hypothalamus is inhibited for reasons as yet not completely known. Then GnRH secretion virtually stops and the levels of the sex hormones fall, which suspends reproductive maturation (see

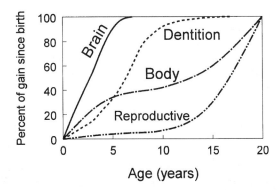

FIGURE 3.7 Growth curves for different body tissues. The "brain" curve is for total weight of the brain (Cabana et al., 1993). The "dentition" curve is the median maturity score for girls based on the seven left mandibular teeth (I1, I2, C, PM1, PM2, M1, M2) using the reference data of Demirjian (1986). The "body" curve represents growth in stature or total body weight, and the "reproductive" curve represents the weight of the gonads and primary reproductive organs (Scammon, 1930).

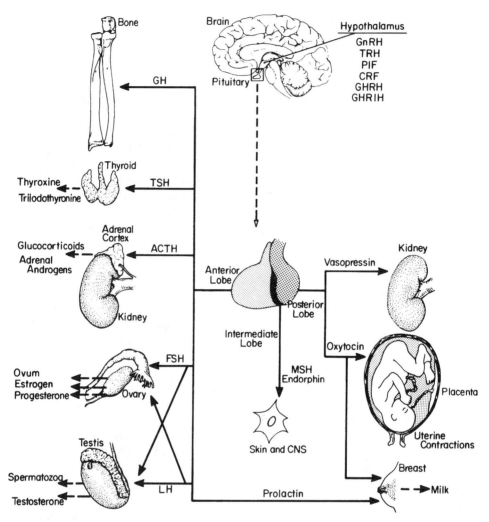

FIGURE 3.8 Location of the hypothalamus and pituitary within the brain and a schematic of the target organs and tissues of the pituitary hormones. Abbreviations: GnRH, gonadotropin-releasing hormone; TRH, thyrotropin-releasing hormone; PIF, prolactin-release inhibiting factor; CRF, adrenocorticotropin-releasing factor; GHRH, growth hormone–releasing hormone; GHRIH, growth hormone release–inhibiting hormone; GH, growth hormone; TSH, thyroid-stimulating hormone; ACTH, adrenocorticotropic hormone; FSH, follicle-stimulating hormone; LH, luteinizing hormone; MSH, melanocyte-stimulating hormone. (Schally et al., 1977).

Fig. 3.7 "reproductive" curve). The hypothalamus is reactivated just before **puberty**, the event of development that marks the onset of sexual maturation.

The age of emergence of the last deciduous tooth, usually M_2, is important for this is one of the events that signals the end of infancy. Emergence of all of the deciduous teeth allows the infant to switch from dependence on breast feeding (or formula/infant food feeding) to eating appropriate weaning foods. The strict definition of **weaning** used in this book is the termination of breast feeding. In preindustrialized societies, such as hunters and gatherers, horticulturists, and pastoralists, weaning occurs between 24 and 36 months of age. By this age all the deciduous teeth have erupted, even for very late maturing infants. Thus, by 36 months of age there occur both biological developments (tooth emergence) and behavioral changes in the mother–infant relationship (weaning) that signal the end of infancy.

Childhood Stage

The childhood stage follows infancy, encompassing the ages of about three to seven years. Childhood may be defined by its own pattern of growth, feeding behavior, motor development, and cognitive maturation. The rapid deceleration in rate of growth that characterizes infancy ends at the beginning of childhood, and the rate of growth levels off at about 5 cm per year. In terms of feeding, children are weaned from the breast, or bottle, but are still dependent on older people for food and protection. Most mammalian species move rapidly from infancy and its association with dependence on nursing from the mother to a stage of independent feeding. Postweaning dependency is found in several species of social mammals, especially carnivores (such as lions, wild dogs, hyenas) and in some species of primates. Lion cubs, for example, are weaned at about 6 to 8 months old but remain dependent on their mothers until about 24 months old. During that time the cubs must learn how to hunt for themselves. Many species of primates must also learn to hunt for high-quality foods, such as insects, and learn how to open fruits and seeds with tough skins. This learning also requires a period of postweaning dependence on the mother and sometimes the father (as for marmosets and tamarins).

Postweaning dependency is, by itself, not a sufficient criteria to define human childhood. Human children do, of course, learn how to find and prepare food, but there are a suite of features that define the childhood stage. Not all of these features are found for the social carnivores and nonhuman primates. Human children require specially prepared foods due to the immaturity of their dentition, the small size of their stomachs and intestines, and the rapid growth of their brain (Fig. 3.7). The metabolic activity of the human brain is especially important. The newborn uses 87 percent of its resting metabolic rate (RMR) for brain growth and function. By age five years the percent RMR usage is still high, at 44 percent, while in the adult human the figure is between 20 and 25 percent of RMR. At the comparable stages of development the RMR values for the chimpanzee are about 45, 20, and 9 percent, respectively (Leonard and Robertson, 1992).

The human constraints of immature dentition and small digestive system necessitate a childhood diet that is easy to chew and swallow and low in total volume. The child's relatively large and active brain, almost twice the size of an adult chimpanzee's brain, requires that the low-volume diet be dense in energy, lipids, and proteins. Children do not yet have the motor and cognitive skills to prepare such a diet for themselves. Children are also especially vulnerable to disease and accidents and thus require protection. In past times, and in some areas of the world today, children were also targets for predatory birds and mammals. There is no society in which children survive if deprived of this care provided by older individuals. So-called wolf children (referring to children reared by wolves or children living "wild" on their own) and even "street children," who are sometimes alleged to be living on their own, are either myths or, in fact, not children at all. A search of the literature finds no case of a human child that is a youngster under the age of six living alone either in the wild or on urban streets.

One of the more striking features of human growth in height, weight, and body composition during the childhood years is predictability, both within individuals and between populations. The distance and velocity curves for height depicted in Figure 1.4 are examples of the predictability of childhood growth, as they describe a pattern that is common to all healthy individuals. Another example is that of the first lon- gitudinal study of human growth. The study "sample" consists of one French boy, the son of the Count Montbeillard. The boy was born in 1759 and was measured until his 18th birthday in 1777. The boy was raised in the French countryside, under near-optimal conditions for that time. Though this study represents but a single child, the pattern of his growth is essentially that shown in Figure 1.4 for both amount and rate of growth. For example, the boy gained 59.9 cm in height between his 2nd and 12th birthdays (Scammon, 1927). Children of generally middle socio- economic class born in the United States during the 1960s and early 1970s average a 61.6-cm gain in height between their 2nd and 12th birthdays (Hamill et al., 1977). The difference between the gains in height of the French boy and the U.S. sample is not statistically significant. The similarity in growth between a child and a sample of children across time periods and across geographic boundaries emphasizes the common pattern of growth shared by all normal children and the predictability of this pattern. These features of human growth have important practical implications. For instance, they form the basis of epidemiological and clinical examinations that detect pediatric health disorders by searching for deviations in the expected trajec- tory of growth.

Though the pattern of childhood growth is predictable, there are several factors that may influence the amount and rate of growth of the individual child or groups of children. These factors include heredity, nutrition, illness, socioeconomic status, and psychological well-being. Chapters 5, 6, and 7 are devoted to a detailed discussion of the action of some of these factors and their combined interactions on growth and development as well as on population dynamics. Here it may be briefly stated that, all other factors being equal, short or tall parents are likely to have chil- dren who achieve similar stature. However, malnutrition, chronic illness, poor living conditions, and chronic psychological stress are each capable of retarding the growth of a child.

Two of the important physical developmental milestones of childhood are (1) the replacement of the deciduous teeth by the emergence of the first permanent teeth and (2) completion of growth of the brain in weight. First molar eruption (eruption is usually defined as first appearance of the tooth through the gingival, or gum, surface) takes place, on average, between the ages of 5.5 and 6.5 years in most human populations. Eruption of the central incisor quickly follows, or sometimes precedes, the eruption of the first molar. There is some variation between human populations in the age of eruption, but by the end of childhood, usually at age seven years, most children have erupted the four first molars and, in addition, permanent incisors have begun to replace "milk" incisors. Within another year the four lateral incisors will also erupt, replacing the milk teeth that had been in that position. Along with growth in size and strength of the jaws and the muscles for chewing, these new teeth provide sufficient capabilities to eat a diet similar to adults. The mean age of eruption of the permanent dentition of boys and girls is given in Table 3.5.

TABLE 3.5
Mean Age and Standard Deviation for Eruption of Permanent Teeth for North American Boys and Girls

Teeth	Males		Females	
	Mean (years)	Standard Deviation (years)	Mean (years)	Standard Deviation (years)
Maxillary				
I^1	7.34	0.77	6.98	0.75
I^2	8.39	1.01	7.97	0.91
C	11.29	1.39	10.62	1.40
P^3	10.64	1.41	10.17	1.38
P^4	11.21	1.48	10.88	1.56
M^1	6.40	0.79	6.35	0.74
M^2	10.52	1.34	11.95	1.22
M^3	20.50	—	20.50	—
Mandibular				
I_1	6.30	0.81	6.18	0.79
I_2	7.47	0.78	7.13	0.82
C	10.52	1.14	9.78	1.26
P_3	10.70	1.37	10.17	1.28
P_4	11.43	1.61	10.97	1.50
M_1	6.33	0.79	6.15	0.76
M_2	12.00	1.38	11.49	1.23
M_3	19.80	—	20.40	—

Note: Abbreviations for the teeth are I_1 = central incisor, I_2 = lateral incisor, C = canine, P_3 = first premolar, P_4 = second premolar, M_1 = first molar, M_2 = second molar.

A close association between human dental development and other aspects of growth and maturation was noted many years ago by anatomists and anthropologists. More recently, Holly Smith (1991a, 1992) analyzed data from humans and 20 other primates species and found that age of eruption of the first molar is highly associated with brain weight and a host of other growth and maturation variables. The correlation coefficient between age of eruption of the first molar and adult brain weight is $r = 0.98$ ($r = 1.00$ is a perfect relationship). The big brain of humans predicts a late age of first molar eruption. Other research, based on direct measurements of victims of accidents and disease, shows that human brain growth in weight is complete at a mean age of seven years (Cabana et al., 1993), confirming Smith's statistical analysis. At about age seven years, then, the child becomes capable dentally of processing an adult-type diet. The end of brain growth in weight means that nutrient requirements for brain growth diminish.

During late infancy and childhood human locomotion develops and matures. Nakano and Kimura (1992) review previous research on human and nonhuman primate locomotive development and present some of their own new research. At age three years, the beginning of childhood, the human is still a "toddler," that is, able to walk bipedally but without the efficiency and characteristic gait of the adult. Nakano and Kimura find that by age seven years, on average, humans are able to walk with the adult-type efficiency and gait. A study by Kramer (1998) examined the energy costs of locomotion in children and juveniles. Children use more energy per kilogram of body weight when walking than do adults. Five- to six-year-old children are about 85 percent efficient as adults. Seven- to eight-year-old juveniles have more than 90 percent the efficiency of adults. The onset of adult-style locomotion, the eruption of the first permanent teeth, and the end of brain growth are all indicators that the physically dependent child is moving on to independence.

The end of childhood is also marked by a small increase in velocity, depicted in Figure 1.4, called the midgrowth spurt (Tanner, 1947). This small increase in growth velocity was first noted by Backman (1934). Since then, some studies have found the midgrowth spurt and others have not. Varying methods of statistical analysis may explain the differences in findings between these studies. Especially important are the effect of data-"smoothing" techniques often used in longitudinal analysis that would tend to obliterate the midgrowth spurt. Curve fitting is also used commonly in longitudinal analysis, and many curve-fitting routines assume that the midgrowth spurt does not exist. The Edinburgh Longitudinal Growth Study, carefully analyzed to detect all growth spurts, found that all of 80 boys and all but one of 55 girls showed a midgrowth spurt. The median age of the spurt was 7.0 years for the boys and 6.7 years for the girls (Butler et al., 1990).

Juvenile Stage

Juveniles may be defined as "prepubertal individuals that are no longer dependent on their mothers (parents) for survival" (Pereira and Altmann, 1985, p. 236). This definition is derived from ethological research with social mammals, especially non-human primates, but applies to the human species as well. In contrast to infants and human children, juvenile primates can survive the death of their adult caretaker. The human primate is no exception to this, as ethnographic research shows that juvenile humans have the physical and cognitive abilities to provide much of their own food and to protect themselves from accidents and disease (Blurton-Jones, 1993; Weisner, 1987). Remember those so-called street children mentioned above— they are in fact "street juveniles!" During the juvenile stage the rate of growth declines once more. This decline follows the midgrowth spurt in those children who experience it. But even in children without a detectable midgrowth spurt, the rate of growth declines. Thus, juveniles grow at the slowest rates since birth. This slow rate of growth applies to global measures of size, such as stature and weight, and also to individual tissues, organs, and body systems.

Juvenile growth is also predictable, stable, and harmonious. The growth in height and weight of two groups of Guatemalan juveniles between the ages of 7 and 13 years, shown in Figures 3.9 and 3.10, is an example of a predictable and stabilized difference in size. Both groups live in Guatemala City and attend school. The larger juveniles are from high-SES families, the smaller juveniles are from low-SES families. Juveniles in the high-SES group are about the same size as healthy, well-nourished juveniles from the United States (Johnston et al., 1973). The families of the low-SES group are known to suffer from inadequate nutrition, primarily a shortage of total food intake, poor living conditions in terms of health care, the supply of potable water, and education (Bogin and MacVean, 1978, 1981a, 1983). Though unequal in size, these children all display a similar regularity in their growth as may

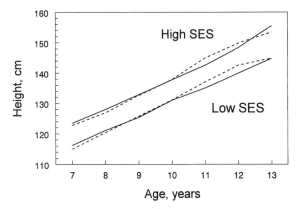

FIGURE 3.9 Mean heights of Guatemalan boys (solid lines) and girls (dashed lines) of high and low socioeconomic status (SES) (Bogin and MacVean, 1978).

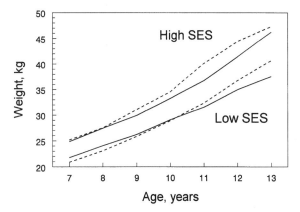

FIGURE 3.10 Mean weights of Guatemalan boys (solid lines) and girls (dashed lines) of high and low socioeconomic status (SES) (Bogin and MacVean, 1978).

be seen from the mean values plotted in the figures. The differences in size between girls and boys are not of biological importance at these ages. Even so, the pattern of growth by sex is virtually identical in both high- and low-SES samples, which is further evidence of the predictability of juvenile growth. Generally changes in size from age to age are similar for both of the SES groups. Indeed, a formal statistical comparison using the technique of tracking analysis (i.e., does the pattern of growth in one sample parallel, or track, the pattern in another sample) finds a high degree of tracking between the groups. The parallel tracking means that the differences in height and weight between these two groups were established prior to age seven years. Most likely this difference is the result of growth retardation in infancy and childhood due to the undernutrition of the low-SES group. Growth during the juvenile stage maintains the stable and predictable differences between these two SES groups.

The harmony of juvenile growth is shown in Figure 3.11. Juveniles from both SES groups have the same height-for-weight proportionality regardless of absolute

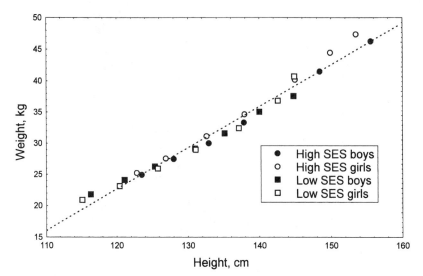

FIGURE 3.11 Relationship of height to weight for Guatemalan boys and girls aged 7.00 to 13.99 years old of high and low socioeconomic status (SES). The broken line is the linear regression, the "best fitting" straight line running through the data points (Bogin and MacVean, 1978).

size. The "regression line" drawn in Figure 3.11 represents the best-fitting straight line (estimated by the statistical method of least squares) drawn through the data points for the high-SES juvenile boys and girls. The data points of the low-SES juvenile boys and girls show no statistically significant deviations from the regression line. The maintenance of proportionality under the stress of low-SES reflects the stability, predictability, and harmony of juvenile growth. Since both height and weight are equally affected in the low-SES Guatemalan juveniles, it is likely that some common mechanism is regulating the growth of several different tissues (e.g, bone, muscle, adipose). The exact nature of this mechanism is not known.

Widdowson (1970) observed that to some extent a harmony of growth is displayed in the normal development of many body parts, not only during the juvenile stage of life, but also during all stages of human growth and development. For example, from childhood to adulthood there is a coordinated growth of the teeth and the craniofacial complex of bones (mandible, maxilla, etc.) that maintains the functional integrity of the masticatory system. Without a harmony of growth of these bones and the teeth the growing individual would not be able to eat. Another example is the phenomenon of **catch-up growth** (Prader et al., 1963). This is a rapid increase in growth velocity following a short-term period of starvation or illness that slowed or stopped growth. The increase in growth velocity usually restores a youngster to the size he or she would have achieved had there been no growth delay, and then the rate of growth slows and returns to its former level. Many segments of the body, such as the head, neck, truck and extremities, participate in this catch-up growth, and each segment maintains its normal pattern of growth, that is, the affected individual does not end up with one leg shorter than the other or with arms stunted but legs of normal length. The nearly global nature of this harmony of growth has stimulated several researchers to propose a theoretical concept of growth as biologically self-regulating (Bogin, 1999a; Goss, 1978; Tanner, 1963).

In girls, the juvenile period ends, on average, at about the age of 10, two years before it usually ends in boys, the difference reflecting the earlier onset of adolescence in girls. The juvenile period is often accompanied by a pronounced but short-lived decrease in rate of growth. The data for the health boys and girls used in Figure 1.4 show such a dip in velocity. The cause of this decrease in growth rate is not known. The nadir of this dip marks the end of the juvenile stage, for once the rate of growth begins to again increase, the growing individual has entered the adolescent stage of growth.

Adolescent Stage

The transition from the juvenile to the adolescent stage of growth and development is signaled by a reversal in the rate of growth, from deceleration to acceleration (Fig. 1.4). Human adolescence is also the stage of life when social and sexual maturation takes place. In fact, adolescence begins with puberty, or more technically with **gonadarche**, which is the reinitiation of activity of the hypothalamic–pituitary–gonadal system of hormone production. The current understanding of the control of gonadarche is that one or perhaps a few centers of the brain change their pattern of neurological activity and their influence on the hypothalamus. The hypothalamus, which has been basically inactive in terms of sexual development since about age two years, is again stimulated to produce GnRH. It is not known exactly how this change takes place. As stated above, the production of GnRH by the hypothalamus is inhibited by about age two years. The "inhibitor" has not been identified but likely is located in the brain, certainly not in the gonads. Human children born without gonads, or rhesus monkeys and other primates whose gonads have been surgically removed, still undergo both the inhibition of the hypothalamus in infancy and the reactivation of the hypothalamus at puberty (Fig. 3.12*a*). The transition from juvenile to adolescent stages requires not only the renewed production of GnRH but also its secretion from the hypothalamus in pulses (Fig. 3.12*b*). Gonadarche is triggered when the pulsatile secretion reaches both the necessary frequency (number of pulses in a given time period) and amplitude (peak amount of secretion during each pulse).

None of these hormonal changes can be seen without sophisticated technology, but the effects of gonadarche can be noted easily since visible signs of sexual maturation appear. One such sign is a sudden increase in the density of pubic hair (indeed the term "puberty" is derived from the Latin *pubescere*, "to grow hair"). Another sign, for girls, is the development of the breast bud, the first stage of breast development. The pubescent boy or girl, his or her parents, and other relatives, friends, and sometimes everyone else in the social group can observe these signs of early adolescence.

Sexual Development

The adolescent stage includes development of other **secondary sexual characteristics**, such as development of the external genitalia, sexual dimorphism in body size and composition (Fig. 3.13), deepening of the voice in boys, and the onset of greater interest and practice of adult patterns of sociosexual behavior and food production.

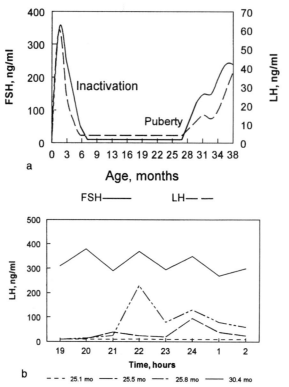

FIGURE 3.12 (*a*) Pattern of secretion of follicle-stimulating hormone (FSH) and luteinizing hormone (LH) in a male rhesus monkey (genus *Macaca*). The testes of the monkey were removed surgically at birth. The curves for FSH and LH indicate the production and release of gonadotropin-releasing hormone (GnRH) from the hypothalamus. After age 3 months (i.e., during infancy) the hypothalamus is inactivated. Puberty takes place at about 27 months and the hypothalamus is reactivated. (*b*) Development of hypothalamic release of GnRH during puberty in a male rhesus monkey with testes surgically removed. At 25.1 months of age the hypothalamus remains inactivated. At 25.5 and 25.8 months there is modest hypothalamic activity, indicating the onset of puberty. By 30.4 months adult pattern of LH release is nearly achieved. The pattern of LH release shows both an increase in the number of pulses of release and an increase in the amplitude of release. In human beings a very similar pattern of infant inactivation and late juvenile reactivation of the hypothalamus takes place (redrawn, with some simplification, from Plant, 1994).

Some of these physical and behavioral changes occur with puberty in many species of social mammals. What makes human adolescence unique are two important differences. The first is the length of time between puberty and adulthood, that is, full reproductive maturity. Humans take five to eight years for this transition. Monkeys and apes take less than three years. The second human difference is that during this life stage, both boys and girls experience a rapid acceleration in the growth velocity of virtually all skeletal tissue—the adolescent growth spurt (see Fig. 1.4). The magnitude of this acceleration in growth was calculated for a sample of healthy Swiss boys and girls (112 boys and 110 girls) measured once a year, near their birthdays, between the ages of 4 and 18 years (Largo et al., 1978). At the peak of their adolescent growth spurt the average velocity of growth in height was +9.0 cm/year

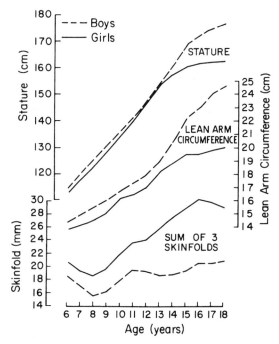

FIGURE 3.13 Mean stature, mean lean arm circumference, and median of the sum of three skinfolds for Montreal boys and girls (Baughan et al., 1980). Note that sexual dimorphism increases markedly after puberty, about age 12 to 13 years.

for boys and +7.1 cm/year for girls. Similar average values are found for healthy adolescents in most human populations. In contrast to humans, other primate species either have no acceleration in skeletal growth or an increase in growth rate that is very small (Bogin, 1999b).

The change in the velocity and acceleration of growth at adolescence affects almost all parts of the body, including the long bones, vertebrae, skull and facial bones, heart, lung, and other visceral organs. Not all parts of the body experience the adolescent spurt at the same time. Different regions of the skeleton, for example, reach the peak rate of growth during adolescence at different ages (reviewed by Satake et al., 1994). In a nationally representative sample of 18,004 girls from the former East Germany, measured by Greil (1997), the average age at peak velocity of the spurt occurred at about 9.0 years for foot length, 10 years for the hand length, 10.5 years for leg length, and 12 years for arm length, standing height, and trunk length. The sample of boys measured by Greil, totaling 18,123 individuals, followed the same general sequence of peak velocities, but the boys reached those peak values 2 to 3 years later than the girls.

Muscle mass of boys also undergoes a spurt at adolescence, and it is relatively greater than the spurt for growth in height. After the peak of the skeletal spurt, the rate of bone growth declines more steeply than the rate for muscle growth, meaning that adolescent boys continue to increase their muscle mass at a faster rate than they grow in stature. Expressed another way, the average healthy boy reaches 91 percent of his adult height by his age at peak-height velocity (PHV) during adolescence, typically about 14 years of age. However, the same average boy achieves only 72 percent of his total muscle mass at the age of PHV and takes about 4 more years to reach 91 percent of his adult value (Buckler, 1990).

Some body parts and tissues do not evidence an adolescent growth spurt, for example, adipose tissue, both subcutaneous fat and the deep body fat, decreases in mass during adolescence in almost all boys and perhaps in many girls as well. Lymphatic tissues and the thymus show no adolescent increase in growth rates (Scammon, 1930). Another body part unaffected by the adolescent growth spurt is the female pelvis (as described in Chapter 2).

Changes in stature, muscle mass, and fatness that typically occur from childhood through adolescence are illustrated in Figure 3.13 for a longitudinally measured sample of French-Canadian children (Baughan et al., 1980). Muscle mass is an estimate of the amount of muscle at the midpoint of the arm. This estimate is derived from measurements of upper arm circumference and triceps skinfold. These measurements are usually taken at the midpoint of the upper arm, halfway between the olecronon process (the "elbow") of the ulna and the acromion process (the "shoulder") of the scapula. The circumference measures the amount of skin, subcutaneous fat, muscle, and bone in a cross section of the arm. The triceps skinfold estimates the contribution of skin and subcutaneous fat to arm circumference. If it is assumed that the arm is cylindrical in shape, simple geometry may be used to calculate the lean arm circumference, which is the circumference of the muscle and bone at the midpoint of the upper arm. Gurney and Jelliffe (1973) give the following three formulas to make this calculation (readers with access to a skinfold caliper and tape measure may take the measurements and apply the formulas for themselves):

1. Arm muscle diameter (mm) = (arm circumference in mm/π) − triceps skinfold in mm
2. Arm muscle area (mm^2) = ($\pi/4$) × (arm muscle diameter)^2
3. Arm fat area (mm^2) = (arm circumference)$^2/4\pi$ − arm muscle area

If it is also assumed that the circumference of the humerus is equal for all individuals, variation in lean arm circumference represents differences in the amount of muscle at this site. Though the arm is not cylindrical in shape and the circumference of the humerus is not equal in all individuals, the differences between reality and the assumptions of the technique are small enough so that when applied to groups of individuals the estimate of average muscle mass at the midarm is reliable and accurate.

In Figure 3.13 fatness is represented by the sum of three subcutaneous skinfolds: triceps, subscapular, and suprailiac. While skinfold measurements do provide a good estimate of subcutaneous fat, their relationship to the deep body fat is questionable. Recent studies using computed tomography to measure deep fat show a lack of correlation in the amount of fat held in the two reserves (Borkan et al., 1982; Davies et al., 1986). Nevertheless, since during the childhood, juvenile, and adolescent stages most fat is subcutaneous, a measurement of the amount of subcutaneous fat is a fair estimate of total fat.

It may be seen in Figure 3.13 that there is little difference in average stature between boys and girls until adolescence, after which boys are typically taller than girls. Girls usually begin their adolescent growth spurt about two years earlier than boys, which means that on average girls are taller than their male age-mates for a couple of years. Boys have greater average muscle mass at all ages, though the differences become absolutely greater, and biologically important, at adolescence. Conversely, girls tend to have more subcutaneous fat at all ages, and again, the difference in fatness increases during adolescence. On average, girls add fat mass continuously from age 8 to 18, with a slowing or possible loss of fat at the time of the adolescent growth spurt (about age 11 to 12 years, as shown in Fig. 3.13). Most boys experience an absolute loss of total fat mass during adolescence and may have no more fat at age 18 than they had at age 6. The adolescent spurt in muscle mass in boys is usually accompanied by an increase in bone density, an increase in cardiopulmonary function, larger blood volume, and greater density of red blood cells. Increases in each of these also occur in girls, but at levels relatively and absolutely lower than for boys.

As may be seen in Figure 1.4, the shape of the adolescent growth spurt is not symmetrical. The rise to PHV is relatively slower than the fall after the peak. The size of the spurt is usually greater in boys than in girls, although there is much individual and population variation in this. The size of the spurt and the age when peak velocity is reached are not related to final adult height. In fact, some normal but slow-maturing individuals and people with certain endocrine disorders do not have a growth spurt but may reach normal adult height (Prader, 1984). This fact makes the otherwise universal nature of the adolescent growth spurt an even more striking human characteristic. The evolutionary, demographic, and biocultural significance of the human adolescent growth spurt are discussed in Chapter 4.

On average, adult men are taller and heavier than adult women. Alexander et al. (1979) surveyed 93 societies, including Western and non-Western cultures, and found that the stature of women averages between 88 and 95 percent the stature of men. In England, women average 93 percent of the height of men, and this average difference is identical for men and women in the tallest (97th percentile), median (50th percentile), and shortest (3rd percentile) height groupings (Marshall and Tanner, 1970). One study in Switzerland (Largo et al., 1978) found that the difference between men and women in adult height is 12.6 cm. Since this study had followed the growth of the subjects longitudinally from the age of 4 years, it was possible to calculate how much of the adult difference in height occurred in the various stages of postnatal growth. It was found that four factors accounted for the difference: the boys' greater amount of growth prior to adolescence added 1.6 cm, the boys' delay in the onset of adolescence added 6.4 cm, the boys' greater intensity of the spurt added 6.0 cm, and the girls' longer duration of growth following the spurt subtracted 1.4 cm from the final difference.

Due to the interplay of these factors, the regulation of size may be more precisely controlled and the "harmony of growth" evidenced during infancy and childhood is continued during adolescence. For instance, Boas (1930) discovered that the age at which adolescent growth begins is inversely correlated with the size of the spurt, meaning that early-maturing children have higher PHVs than late-maturing children (Fig. 3.14). This observation has been confirmed for American children, British children, and Swedish children (Bogin, 1999a). Another compensating mechanism, described for Swiss children by Largo et al. (1978), is that a child with slow growth prior to puberty will tend to have a longer lasting growth spurt during ado-

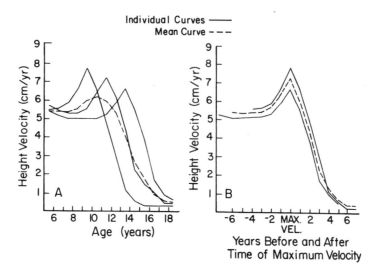

FIGURE 3.14 (*a*) Individual velocity curves of growth (solid lines) and mean velocity curve during the adolescent growth spurt. The mean velocity curve does not represent the true velocity of growth of any individual. (*b*) The same curves plotted against time before and after peak-height velocity (maximum velocity) of each individual. The mean curve accurately represents the average velocity of the group.

lescence than a child who achieves a greater prepubertal percentage of adult height. Where chronic undernutrition, disease, and child labor are endemic, height at every age is reduced compared with less stressed populations. However, the total span of the growth period is prolonged, up to age 25 or 26 years, so that a greater adult height may be achieved than if growth stopped at 18 to 21 years, as it does for healthy individuals in the United States. Presumably, these growth-adjusting mechanisms are present in all children.

Patterns of Secondary Sexual Development

In both sexes, the onset of puberty is followed within a few months by the appearance of the secondary sexual characteristics. In boys these include changes in size of the penis and scrotum, the growth of pubic, axillary, and facial hair, the "breaking of the voice," and seminal emission. In girls the secondary sexual characteristics include the growth of the breasts, appearance of pubic and axillary hair, **menarche** (first menstruation), and development of the uterus, vagina, and vulva to their mature size and appearance. One of the common methods used to assess the secondary sexual development of boys and girls is the Tanner Puberty Stage classification system (Tanner, 1962). This system divides the development into five stages. For both boys and girls there are five stages of pubic hair development: PH1 indicates no visible pubic hair, PH2 the first appearance of pubic hair, and PH3 to PH5 the progressive growth of pubic hair to the adult stage. For boys there are five stages for the development of the penis, testes, and scrotum that rate their changes in size and coloration. This genital rating proceeds from G1, the prepubertal stage, to G5, the adult stage. For girls there is a breast development scale that begins at B1, no breast development, and proceeds to B2, initiation of the breast bud, to B5, the adult form of the breast (including areola and nipple). Differences exist between these populations in the timing of onset of the stages of adolescent maturation. But, the amount of variation in the age at which healthy individual adolescents achieve any maturational stage is greater within a given sample than between samples. The between-population differences are of little biological importance (Bogin, 1999a).

All of these studies report findings for, generally, healthy adolescents of middle to upper socioeconomic class. There are also studies of the sexual development of South African adolescents who had been severely malnourished (requiring hospitalization) when they were between 5 months and 4 years, 4 months old (Cameron et al., 1988, 1990). These former patients were followed up at 10 years and 15 years after their hospitalization and compared with a control sample of adolescents from similar low socioeconomic and poor nutritional circumstances who had not developed clinical signs of severe malnutrition. Amazingly, both the former patients and the controls show an identical sequence in the order of appearance and timing of the secondary sexual characteristics. From this, one can conclude that severe malnutrition at an early age does not seem to disrupt the basic human pattern of secondary sexual development.

Common Control of Adolescent Development

As the sequence of appearance of secondary sexual characteristics is so highly predictable in people, much research has attempted to find a common control mechanism for adolescent development. To date, this research supports the idea that adolescent maturation is controlled by some central organ or system within the body. The data also demonstrate that there is a human pattern of adolescent growth and development that is shared by all people. The reasons for the universal pattern of adolescent maturation is the subject of Chapter 4, which discusses the evolution and ecology of human growth and demography.

Adult Stage

The attainment of adult stature is one of the hallmarks used to mark the transition from adolescence to adulthood. In the United States, young women and men of middle to upper socioeconomic status reach adult height at about 18 and 21 years of age, respectively (Roche and Davila, 1972). These ages may be close to the lower limit for onset of adulthood. In other populations growth continues to later ages. Hulanicka and Kotlarz (1983) studied a sample of 221 young men from Wroclaw, Poland, an industrial city of 600,000 people, and found that only 54 percent of the subjects reached final adult height by age 19 years. The other 46 percent added an average of 2.13 cm in height between the ages of 19 and 27 years. It is well known that individuals suffering from undernutrition, chronic diseases, and certain drug therapies may continue to grow in height until reaching about 26 years of age. Though these individuals may grow for a longer period of time, they usually achieve less total growth and end up shorter than their more privileged or healthier age mates.

Height growth stops when the long bones of the skeleton (e.g., the femur and tibia) lose their ability to increase in length. Usually this occurs when the **epiphysis**, the growing end of the bone, fuses with the **diaphysis**, the shaft of the bone. As shown in Figure 3.5, the process of epiphyseal union can be observed from radiographs of the skeleton. In their study of Polish men, Hulanicka and Kotlarz (1983) found that the amount of growth that occurred after age 19 was a function of **skeletal maturation**; that is, late maturers grew more than average or early maturers. This fact has been known for many years, and an estimate of skeletal maturation, often called **skeletal age**, is incorporated into equations used to predict the adult height of children. The fusion of epiphysis and diaphysis is stimulated by the gonadal hormones, the androgens and estrogens. However, it is not the fusion of epiphysis and diaphysis that stops growth, for children without gonads or whose gonads are not functional never have epiphysial fusion but they do stop growing (Tanner, 1978). Rather, it is a change in the sensitivity to growth stimuli of cartilage and bone tissue in the **growth plate region** (Fig. 3.15) that causes these cells to lose their hyperplastic growth potential.

Reproductive maturity is another hallmark of adulthood. The production of viable spermatozoa in boys and viable oocytes in girls is achieved during adolescence, but these events mark only the early stages, not the completion, of reproductive maturation. For girls, menarche is usually followed by a period of one to three years of adolescent sterility. That is, there are menstrual cycles, which are often

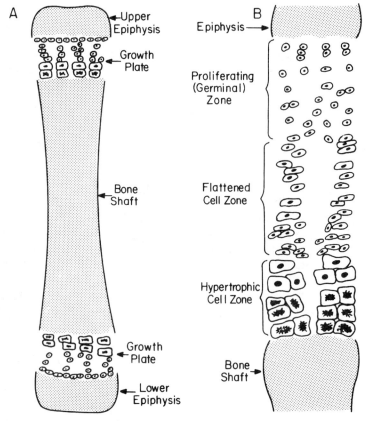

FIGURE 3.15 (*a*) A limb bone with its upper and lower epiphyses. (*b*) Enlargement of the growth plate region: new cells are formed in the proliferation zone and pass to the hypertrophic zone to add to the bone cells accumulating on top of the bone shaft (Tanner, 1990).

irregular in length, but there is no ovulation. So, the average girl is not fertile until 14 years of age or older. Fertility, of course, does not indicate reproductive maturation. Becoming pregnant is only a part of reproduction: Maintaining the pregnancy to term and raising offspring to adulthood are equally important aspects of the total reproductive process. Adolescent girls who become pregnant have a high percentage of spontaneous abortions and complications of pregnancy. This is true for girls in developed nations such as the United States as well as developing nations. Teenage mothers also have higher rates of low-birth-weight infants than older mothers, and consequently, these infants suffer high rates of mortality. There are many reasons for the reproductive difficulties faced by teenage girls, ranging from physiological immaturity of the reproductive system to socioeconomic and psychological trauma induced by the pregnancy. The fact that the mother is still growing means that the nutritional needs and hormonal activity of her body may compete and interfere with the growth and development of the fetus. This problem was suggested by Pagliani over 100 years ago and confirmed by Frisancho et al. (1985). For all these reasons, most researchers agree that female reproductive maturity is reached at the end of the adolescent stage of life, which occurs, on average, at 19 years.

Analysis of urine samples from boys 11 to 16 years old show that they begin producing sperm at median ages that cluster between 13.4 and 14.5 years (Muller et al., 1989). Whether this event marks the onset of fertility is not known. The quality of viable sperm from teenage boys is also unknown, though one may speculate that pubertal endocrine activity in the boy may have some effect on his sperm cells. Even if fertile, the average boy of 14 years is less than halfway through his adolescent growth spurt, and therefore, his developmental status is incomplete. In terms of physical appearance, physiological status, and psychosocial development, he is still more of a child than an adult. The cross-cultural evidence shows that few boys successfully father children until they are into their third decade of life (Bogin, 1993, 1994). In the United States, for example, only 3.09 percent of live-born infants in 1990 were fathered by men under 20 years of age (National Center for Health Statistics, 1994). A notorious exception occurred in 1997 when a 13-year-old school boy in the state of Washington fathered a child with his teacher, a married woman who had already given birth to four children.

The transition to adulthood is marked by dramatic events, such as the cessation of height growth and full reproductive maturity. In contrast, the course of growth and development during the prime reproductive years of adulthood are relatively uneventful. Most tissues of the body lose the ability to grow by hyperplasia (cell division), but many may grow by hypertrophy (enlargement of existing cells). Exercise training can increase the size of skeletal muscles, and caloric oversufficiency will certainly increase the size of adipose tissue. However, the most striking feature of the prime adult stage of life is its stability, or **homeostasis**, and its resistance to pathological influences, such as infectious disease and psychological stress.

Senescence and Old Age

Following the prime reproductive years of adulthood, the process of aging becomes more noticeable. Aging, or **senescence**, is a process of decline in the ability to adapt to environmental stress. The pattern of decline varies greatly between individuals.

Though specific molecular, cellular, and organismic changes can be measured and described, not all of these occur in all people and rarely do they follow a well-established sequence. **Menopause** may be the only event of the later adult years that is experienced universally by women who live past 50 years of age; men have no similar event. Further discussion of menopause and the postreproductive life stage of people are presented in Chapter 4. The evolution and possible demographic value of menopause and postreproductive life for men and women are described in Chapter 8.

There are many hypotheses about the aging process and about why we must age at all. One explanation for why we must age is called the "pleiotropy hypothesis." In now classic works on the biology of senescence, Medwar (1952) and Williams (1957) argued that aging is "due to an accumulation of harmful age-specific genes . . . [or] pleiotropic genes which have good effects early in life, but have bad effects later" (Kirkwood and Holiday, 1986, p. 371). Kirkwood (1977), Charlesworth (1980), and others refined this hypothesis further in terms of a general theory of aging. Some of the empirical experimental support for the pleiotropic hypothesis links aging with the limited mitotic (cell duplication) ability of hyperplastic cells. Hayflick (1980) found that when raised in tissue cultures, human embryo hyperplastic cell lines double in number by mitotic division only 50 (±10) times and then die. Tissue cultures of cells from adult humans have an even more limited mitotic potential, doubling only 14 to 29 times before dying. This doubling limit of hyperplastic cells provides a theoretical limit to life. In practice, few cells and few people ever reach this limit (Austad, 1997). Many cells die as part of normal physiology, not senescence. These cell deaths appear to be programmed by gene–environment inter-

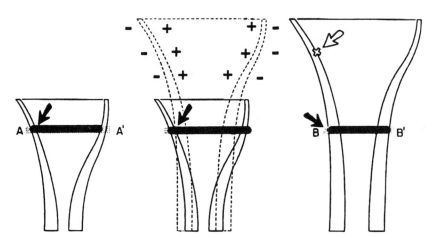

FIGURE 3.16 Representation of remodeling in a limb bone. As the bone grows in length, the level indicated by the line AA' becomes repositioned into level indicated by the line BB'. The relative level of AA' in the larger bone is indicated by an X. The structural remodeling of the bone occurs by the process of resorption (minus signs) and deposition (plus signs). One result of the subtraction and addition of bone is that the point indicated by the black arrow at level AA' has been relocated from the inner side of the cortex of the bone to the outer side of the cortex in BB'. As the bone continues to grow in length and new bone tissue replaces the older bone tissue, the point will eventually be lost by continued resorbtion. (From Enlow [1963], with permission of the author and publisher.)

actions, a process called **apoptosis**. In many cases cell death is required to bring about the mature form of a tissue or organ. An excess of brain cells are produced during prenatal growth and after birth, and apparently in response to many environmental stimuli, groups of brain cells die in order to create the functional architecture of the brain. Another example of apoptosis occurs during the growth of the mammalian skeleton. To maintain the form and efficient function of long bones as they grow, existing bone cells must die so that as the bone lengthens it does not also become wider, a process called bone remodeling (Fig. 3.16). People, as a whole organism, do not reach an age that would place them at or near Hayflick's theoretical limit. Rather, death occurs due to the inability of one or more cell types, including nerve, muscle, and other nonreplicating cells, to use nutrients and repair damage.

Other candidates for "agents of aging" are (1) free radicals, chemical by-products of metabolic activity, that accumulate with time and can damage DNA, proteins, and cell membrane; and (2) the amassed burden of DNA mutations caused by ionizing radiation or chemical pollutants. Undoubtedly, aging is a multicausal process, but unlike the biological self-regulation of growth prior to adulthood, there may not be a biological plan for the aging process. There may be no biological reason to age in any particular way. It is only recently, in the evolutionary history of our species, that an appreciable number of individuals have come to live past the prime adult years. Throughout prehistory, death by predation, disease, and trauma caused by violence and accidents was probably more common than death due to old age. Death is inevitable, but nature did not have the time or the selection pressures to mold our manner of death into a predictable pattern.

In contrast to the process of aging and death, growth and development from conception to adulthood follow a predictable pattern. It was during the evolutionary history of our species, and those species ancestral to ours, that selective pressures operated to shape our pattern of growth. To understand why we grow the way we do, we must examine some of the events that occurred during human evolution. The next chapter describes the evolution of the human pattern of growth.

FOUR

EVOLUTION OF THE HUMAN LIFE HISTORY

The basic pattern of human growth is shared by all people and is the outcome of the 4-million-year evolutionary history of the **hominids**, living human beings and our fossil ancestors. In this chapter we explore how the human pattern of growth and the human **life cycle** evolved. The life cycle of any organism includes all the stages of growth, development, and maturation from conception to death. In the following discussion the focus is on the stages of postnatal life because the most profound changes in the evolution of the human life cycle have occurred to the stages of life after birth.

The pattern of human growth evolved in the context of the biological and social **ecology** of our ancestors. The term "ecology" is used here to refer to the relationship that an individual organism, or group of individuals of a species, has with its physical, biological, and social environment. At the core of any ecological system are two sets of behaviors; the first is directed toward how an organism acquires food and the second is directed toward how the organism reproduces. All organisms are alike in that they share behaviors related to what may be called simply "food and sex." Social mammals, including most primates, satisfy their needs for food and reproduction through a complex ecology of biological and social relationships with their conspecifics (i.e., members of the same species) and their environment. The environment includes both other biological species as well as the physical surroundings. Human beings also share in this biosocial ecology and add to it a significant cultural component. Human beings are **cultural animals**, meaning that we possess all the potentials and limitations of any living creature, to which we add a cultural trilogy of (1) dependence on technology, (2) codified social institutions such as kinship and marriage, and (3) ideology. In its anthropological sense, ideology refers to a set of symbolic meanings and representations particular to any society, through which its members view and interpret nature. Elements of the human capacity for culture may be found in many other species of animals, such as tool use and some aspects of language, but only in the human species do all three aspects of the cultural trio become so intensified, elaborated, and universal. Because of this, human growth and demography may be best understood by using a **biocultural** and anthropological perspective.

HUMAN LIFE CYCLE

Anthropologists have become increasingly interested in explaining the significance of life-cycle characteristics of the human species. This is because the human life cycle stands in sharp contrast to other species of social mammals, even other primates. Several of these contrasts, such as the midgrowth spurt and the adolescent growth spurt, both of which are experienced almost universally by boys and girls, were described in previous chapters. Any theory of human growth needs to explain how and why humans successfully combined these growth spurts along with relatively helpless newborns, a short duration of breast feeding coupled with a vastly extended period of offspring dependency, delayed onset of reproduction, relatively short birth intervals, unusual secondary sexual characteristics (such as the peculiar distribution of both hair and fat in women and men), and menopause. A central question is, did these characteristics evolve as a package or as a mosaic? The present evidence suggests that the stages and events of the human life cycle evolved as a mosaic and may have taken form over more than a million years.

Life History and Stages of the Life Cycle

Life history refers to major events that occur between the conception and death of an organism. The events of life history "govern natality and mortality" (Cole, 1954, p. 103). More specifically, life history may be defined as the strategy an organism uses to allocate its energy toward growth, maintenance, reproduction, raising offspring to independence, and avoiding death. Living things on earth have greatly different life history strategies, and differences in life history characteristics can have profound effects on the growth dynamics, ecology, and evolution of populations. The field of life history theory, which is the scientific study of life-cycle strategies and their evolution, provides a way to unify systematic research of both growth and demography. One of the best introductions to life history theory is provided by Stearns (1992), who explains the goals of both organisms and the biologists who study them in the following way (p. vii):

> Consider a zygote that is about to begin its life and imagine that all opportunities are open to it. At what age and size should it start to reproduce? How many times in its life should it attempt reproduction—once, more than once, continuously, seasonally? When it does reproduce, how much energy and time should it allocate to reproduction as opposed to growth and maintenance? Given a certain allocation, how should it divide those resources up among offspring? Should they be few in number but high in quality and large in size, or should they be small and numerous and less likely to survive? Should it concentrate its reproduction early in life and have a short life as a consequence, or should it make less reproductive effort in any given attempt and live longer?

From this quotation we may see that questions of demography and growth are the core of life history theory. The key elements of life history theory are shown in Table 4.1. These key points are divided into two columns in the table. The left column lists the basic principles that guide the evolution of life history for any species. The right column lists the **trade-offs** that shape the particular life history strategy of a

TABLE 4.1
Life History Principal Traits and Trade-offs

Principles	Trade-offs

1. Size at birth
2. Growth patterns
  • Number of life-cycle stages
  • Duration of each stage
3. Age at maturity
  • Age at first reproduction
4. Sexuality: asexual, sexual,
  pathenogenesis?
5. Size at maturity
6. Number, size, and sex ratio of
  offspring
7. Age-, sex-, and size-specifrc
  reproductive investments
8. Age-, sex-, and size-specific mortality
  schedules
9. Length of life
  • Reproductive life span
  • Rate of aging/senescence
	1. Current reproduction vs. future
	  reproduction
	2. Current reproduction vs. survival
	3. Number, size, and sex of offspring
	4. Parental reproduction vs. growth
	5. Number vs. size of offspring
	6. Parental condition vs. offspring growth
	7. Offspring growth, condition, and
	  survival
	8. Parental vs. offspring reproduction

Note: This is a partial list of the most important traits. The list is based on the discussion in Cole (1954) and Stearns (1992), who provide additional traits.

species or members of a species. A trade-off may be thought of as the competition between two biological or behavioral traits. Stearns (1992) says that "trade-offs occur when two traits compete for materials and energy within a single organism" or "when selection for one trait decreases the value of a second trait" (p. 223). An example of the first type of trade-off is competition between organs or tissues of the body during growth. For example, should energy and materials be devoted to growing a large set of muscles or a larger brain? An example of the second type of trade-off is the choice of producing one large offspring or many, smaller offspring. All living things face these trade-off decisions. Some occur on a day-to-day basis; others occur over longer periods of time. Those that have reproductive consequences and occur over generations are subject to natural selection, and the effected traits may evolve over time.

Human beings are no exception to the questions of life history. People share many life history traits and trade-offs with other mammals. As for all mammals, people have evolved strategies of when to be born, when to be weaned, how many and what type of prereproductive stages of development to pass through, when to reproduce, and when to die. Human reproduction serves as a good example of life history traits and trade-offs. In contrast to most other mammals, people begin to reproduce relatively late in life, about two decades after fertilization. The lag between birth and age at first birth is, in part, a trade-off between the growth of the parent and the growth of offspring. Human beings usually begin to reproduce after their own growth and development are, essentially, complete. This is a wise trade-off, as earlier reproduction, especially pregnancy for teenagers 15 years old or younger, often leads to serious health problems or death for both the mother and her fetus and infant.

Once started women may reproduce more than a dozen times, and may do so continuously, as there are no seasonal constraints (e.g., due to changes in temperature or day length) on reproductive biology. However, there may be cultural constraints that lead to seasonal reproduction, such as religious practices or periodic separation of the sexes due to labor migration. But, the possible maximum number of pregnancies is rarely realized. Pregnancy and then the care of the infant and child take a toll on the mother. When pregnancies are spaced too closely, women may suffer from **maternal depletion**. This condition results when the mother becomes pregnant again before she has been able to recover from the physiological drain caused by a previous pregnancy, birth, and lactation.

Women usually give birth to a single infant and invest heavily in the resources needed to develop that infant into a high-quality and relatively large adult. Women can and do produce multiple births, which would seem to be a way to maximize reproductive potential. But, twin, triplet, and higher pregnancies compromise the health of both the mother and the offspring. One of the reasons for this is **sibling competition**, meaning that the brothers and sisters of multiple pregnancies are each vying for the same limited set of resources available from the mother. Sibling competition also occurs between brothers and sisters from different pregnancies. Among the poor populations of the developing countries, short birth intervals (less than 23 months) compromise the health of both the infant and the mother (Huttly et al., 1992; St. George et al., 2000). A major negative effect on the infant is low birth weight, which is known to impair both physical growth and cognitive development during childhood and later life stages (Grooks, 1995; Garn et al., 1984; Kliegman, 1995).

Older women and men have less success at reproduction. While women often remain fertile until age 45 to 50 years, there is much evidence for increased neonatal mortality when mothers are older than 35 years (St. George et al., 2000). Accordingly, in most cultures, women and men concentrate their efforts at reproduction between the ages of 20 and 35 years. All women who live long enough eventually reach the age of menopause and cease reproduction. Menopause is a clear trade-off between a woman's own reproduction and that of the next generation. Postmenopausal women may continue to invest in their own offspring, their grandchildren, or the offspring of nonkin. Menopause may also involve a more subtle trade-off. Compared with other species of mammals, human beings have much greater survival during the prereproductive stages of life. Wood et al. (1999) propose that the energy and other resources required to enhance prereproductive survival come at the expense of reproductive termination, that is, menopause, later in life.

Human life history theory is a very active area of research. It is still too early to write the definitive story of the evolution of human life history traits and trade-offs. Good reviews of the current knowledge of demographic aspects of human life history research were written by Gage (1998) and Hill and Kaplan (1999). My previous work (Bogin, 1999a) concentrated on the growth and development aspects of primate, especially human, life history. The goal in the remainder of this book is to integrate both the demography and growth of human life history. Early theorists and experimentalists, such as Pearl and Brody, were on the verge of a unified theory of growth and demography. They were searching for a type of "grand unification theory" that would unite the developmental biology of all animal species within one grand pattern of individual and population growth [see Bogin (1999b) for a detailed historical review]. Pearl, Brody, and their followers failed to appreciate the diversity of strategies and patterns that living things employ to grow and develop.

The importance of this diversity, and its consequences for growth and demography, became clear with the publication of seminal papers by Cole (1954) and Williams (1957, 1966). Cole's paper was a landmark not only for its focus on diversity but also because he attempted to bridge the gap between theoretical demography and empirical biology. Biologists working in the field often eschewed the mathematical musings of the theoreticians, as the mathematical formulas did not seem to apply to the seemingly infinite variety of behavior in real organisms. Cole showed how theory could be used to organize and categorize the tremendous variation of nature into a more manageable series of life history strategies. For example, Cole showed how mathematics could be used to understand why many individuals in species of sexually reproducing animals are sterile, as in the social insects, or choose not to reproduce, as in wolves and humans. Cole's application of mathematical theory to human beings also showed that a woman's lifetime reproduction and the healthy development of her offspring are optimized when she gives birth to one infant at a time, rather than having multiple births. With this approach, life history theory was born. I turn now to a discussion of what is known about the evolution of human life history. The discussion focuses on the evolution of the human pattern of growth and reproduction after birth. For a discussion of the evolution of prenatal patterns of growth and reproductive biology, see Bogin (1999a).

EVOLUTION OF HUMAN LIFE HISTORY: GROWTH AND DEMOGRAPHY

Human life history, with nearly two decades of infant dependency and extended childhood, juvenile, and adolescent stages prior to social and sexual maturation, has long been considered to be advantageous for our species because it provides

1. an extended period for brain development,
2. time for the acquisition of technical skills (e.g., tool making and food processing), and
3. time for socialization, play, and the development of complex social roles and cultural behavior.

These statements are standard "textbook" rationalizations for the value of the pattern of human growth. They emphasizes the value of learning, an idea that Spencer (1886) popularized but that actually goes back to the dawn of written history (Boyd, 1980). Learning as the reason for the evolution of several prolonged life stages prior to maturation was nicely summarized by Dobzhansky (1962): "Although a prolonged period of juvenile helplessness and dependency would, by itself, be disadvantageous to a species because it endangers the young and handicaps their parents, it is a help to man because the slow development provides time for learning and training, which are far more extensive in man than in any other animal" (p. 58). The learning hypothesis for human ontogeny was also invoked by Allison Jolly (1985), author of *The Evolution of Primate Behavior*. She writes that "human evolution is a paradox. We have become larger, with long life and immaturity, and few, much loved offspring, and yet we are more, not less adaptable" (p. 44). In an attempt to resolve the paradox of human evolution and our peculiar life history Jolly concludes in the next sentence that "mental agility buffers environmental change and has replaced reproductive agility" (p. 44).

The reference to reproductive agility means that we are a reproductively frugal species compared with those that lavish dozens, hundreds, or thousands of offspring on each brood or litter. It is fairly easy to argue that humans, with relatively low wastage of offspring, are somehow more "efficient" than other species. But a paradox still remains, for the learning hypothesis does not explain how the pattern of human growth evolved. It does not provide a causal mechanism for the evolution of human growth. Rather, it is a tautological argument for the benefits of the simultaneous possession of brains that are large relative to body size, complex technology, and cultural behavior. Specifically, the learning hypothesis does not explain the following questions: (1) Why not produce more offspring, instead of few mentally agile offspring? (2) Why do our offspring take so long to reach reproductive age? (3) Why is our path of growth and development from birth to maturity so sinuous, meandering through alternating periods of rapid and relatively slow growth and development? (4) Why do human women often live for many years past the age of reproduction? A theory of human growth and demography must answer these and other questions about the presence of human life history events and their timing during the life cycle.

EVOLUTION OF ONTOGENY

How did the human pattern of growth evolve? To ask this question is nearly the same as asking how the human species evolved. The ontogeny of an individual organism is, metaphorically, a scrapbook of the biological history of that species. Ontogeny refers to the process of growth, development, and maturation of the individual organism from conception to death. The metaphor of a scrapbook is used here to indicate that embodied in ontogeny are fragments of our biological past, fragments that have been pasted into our book of life history. These scraps of biological history, which are technically called structural and regulatory genes, are somewhat like scrap metal. Such metal is collected to be reworked in new forms and newer, more useful objects. During hominid evolution the form and function of our ancestors' structural and regulatory DNA was reworked to produce the genetic basis for the ontogeny of the human species.

The literature is replete with proposals for how the reworking occurred. One tradition looks for a single major cause or process. It has been argued that humans evolved when we became big-brained apes, terrestrial apes, killer apes, hunting apes, aquatic apes, tool-making apes, symbolic apes, monogamous apes, food-sharing apes, and, even, apes with ventral–ventral copulatory behavior. None of these, or any other single-factor hypothesis, proves to be helpful to understand human evolution, for a nonhuman primate exception can always be found.

Another tradition looks instead at the pattern of ontogeny. In the book *Size and Cycle*, J. T. Bonner (1965) develops the idea that the stages of the life cycle of an individual organism, a colony, or a society are "the basic unit of natural selection." Bonner's focus on life-cycle stages follows from the research of several nineteenth- and twentieth-century embryologists who proposed that speciation is often achieved by altering rates of growth of existing life stages and by adding or deleting stages. Bonner (1993) states that we should not think in terms of organisms *with* a life cycle, but rather think of organisms *as* life cycles: "The great lesson that comes from thinking of organisms as life cycles is that it is the life cycle, not just the adult, that evolves. In particular, it is the building period of the life cycle—the period of development—that is altered over time by natural selection. It is obvious that the only way to change the characters of an adult is to change its development" (p. 93).

A history of research on life-cycle evolution was published by S. J. Gould (1977) in the book *Ontogeny and Phylogeny*. Gould handily summarizes the mechanisms for biological change over time by stating, "Evolution occurs when ontogeny is altered in one of two ways: when new characters are introduced at any stage of development with varying effects upon subsequent stages, or when characters already present undergo changes in developmental timing. Together, these two processes exhaust the formal content of phyletic change" (p. 4). Gould contends that it is the second process that accounts for human evolution. This process is called **heterochrony**. Quoting Gould again, "this book is primarily a long argument for the evolutionary importance of *heterochrony*—changes in the relative time of appearance and rate of development for characters already present in ancestors" (p. 2, author's italics). In the discussion that follows, the focus will be on whether the human life cycle evolved by altering "characters already present" in our ancestors or whether it evolved by introducing new characters. The evidence argues strongly in favor of childhood and adolescence as new characters in the human life cycle.

Gould explains that there are several types of heterochronic processes, but only one accounts for human evolution. This is **neoteny**, defined in the glossary of Gould's book as "paedomorphosis (retention of formally juvenile characters by adult descendants) produced by retardation of somatic development." In a subsequent publication, Gould provides a somewhat more readable definition: "In neoteny rates of development slow down and juvenile stages of ancestors become adult features of descendants. Many central features of our anatomy link us with the fetal and juvenile stages of [nonhuman] primates" (Gould, 1981, p. 333). Following Gould, we must add neoteny to the list of other single-cause hypotheses as the reason, or at least the mechanism, for human evolution.

Another heterochronic process, called **hypermorphosis**, is favored by other researches as the mechanism for human evolution. Hypermorphosis may be defined, at this point, as an extension of the growth and development period of the descendant beyond that of the ancestor. The differences between neoteny and hypermorphosis may be summarized as follows. Neoteny is a slowing down of the *rate* of development. Neoteny produces an adult descendant that retains the immature body shape, and even the immature behavioral characteristics, of its ancestor. Hypermorphosis is a prolongation of the *time* for development, and this extra time for ontogeny produces a descendant with features that are hypermature compared with the ancestor.

I have reviewed the evidence for and against neoteny and hypermorphosis in other publications (Bogin, 1999a, 1999b). My conclusion, and that of several other researchers, is that neither of these mechanisms can account for the pattern of human growth or the traits and trade-offs of human life history. I find that the work of Shea (1989) presents the single most compelling case against a simple heterochronic mechanism for human evolution. Figure 4.1 is a summary of Shea's findings. The figure shows estimates for body size and shape as a consequence of neoteny and two types of hypermorphosis. None of these acting as a single process can produce the human adult size and shape from the human infant size and shape.

To accomplish this required, in Shea's view, several genetic changes or adjustments during human evolution. These would be the changes and adjustments to the structural and regulatory DNA that are preserved in the "scrapbook" of human ontogeny. Since the hormones that regulate growth and development are, virtually, direct products of DNA activity, Shea proposes that the best place to look for evidence of the evolution of ontogeny is in the action of the endocrine system. According to Shea and others (e.g., Bogin, 1999a), the endocrine differences between humans and other primates negate neoteny or hypermorphosis as unitary causal processes and instead argue for a multiprocess model for human evolution. For example, I review evidence (Bogin, 1999a) showing that human and chimpanzee males have relatively small differences in testosterone levels during puberty but relatively large differences in the rate of growth of arms and legs at that time, with humans growing about five times faster than chimpanzees. The heterochronic models of neoteny and hypermorphosis predict that a greater or lesser amount of time for growth produces the differences in size and shape between humans and chimpanzees. But, the empirical data gathered from growth and endocrine research show that it is the sensitivity of specific skeletal parts to testosterone, determined by DNA and cellular activity, that results in the differences in limb size and shape between adult humans and chimpanzees. The time available for growth is largely irrelevant.

One point to stress at this juncture is that Gould (1977) defined another way for life stages to evolve. This is "when new characters are introduced at any stage of development." Some stages of the human life cycle, namely childhood and adolescence, may well be such new life-cycle stages. If this is true, then these new stages were inserted de novo into human life history sometime in the past. The next sections of this chapter show that some types of heterochrony can account for the evolution of the juvenile life stage. It is also shown that neither the Peter Pan scenario of neoteny nor the Methuselah-like development of hypermorphosis is adequate to account for the evolution of the entire human life cycle. Moreover, neither neoteny nor hypermorphosis can unravel the paradox of human evolution. To resolve the puzzle of why we have so few offspring, why they take so long to develop and reproduce, and why our rate of growth takes a serpentine path to adulthood requires a multicausal, and more "mature," view of human ontogeny and human evolution.

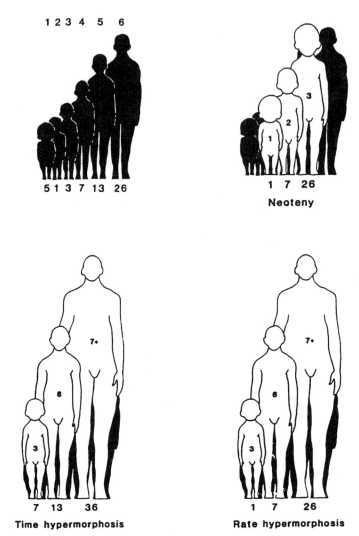

FIGURE 4.1 Silhouettes of size and shape change during human growth. Numbers under silhouettes indicate age in years. Numbers above or on silhouettes indicate relative shape. Top left: actual size and shape change during normal human development. Top right: neoteny; note that at adult size shape 3 is still maintained. Bottom left: time hypermorphosis; the growth period is extended to 36 years, yielding a peramorphic giant (size and shape of the descendant beyond that of the ancestor). Bottom right: rate hypermorphosis; growth ends at age 26 but proceeds at a faster rate, producing another peramorphic giant. Note that in both cases the adult shape at 7+ is outside the range of normal development. (From Shea [1989] with permission.)

CASE FOR *DE NOVO* CHILDHOOD

Forgotten by all parties in the litigation surrounding heterochrony is that there is another process by which evolution works. To requote Gould, "Evolution occurs when ontogeny is altered in one of two ways": the first is "when new characters are introduced at any stage of development with varying effects upon subsequent stages" (the second is by heterochrony). Much of human evolution, especially the evolution of childhood and adolescence, the human capacity for symbolic language, and culture, is the result of the introduction of new life stages into the general pattern of primate growth and development.

As discussed in previous chapters, human growth and development from birth to reproductive maturity may be characterized by five stages: (1) infancy, (2) childhood, (3) juvenile, (4) adolescence, and (5) adulthood. It was explained in Chapter 1 how each stage may be defined by rate of growth. This chapter shows that additional life history traits, such as characteristics of the dentition, methods of feeding, the development of physical and mental competencies, maturation of the reproductive system, and sexual behavior, also define the stages of human postnatal growth. The following discussion focuses on why and when the stages of childhood and adolescence were added to the human pattern of growth.

HUMAN CHILDHOOD

Human beings are not "permanent children" (as neoteny would have us), but we do pass through a childhood stage of growth and development. The onset of the childhood stage is marked by a change in growth rate, from the rapid decline during infancy to a more steady period of gentle decline, the eruption of all of the deciduous teeth, weaning (the end of breast feeding), and maturation of both new motor and cognitive skills. Though weaned, children are still dependent on older individuals for feeding and protection. The end of childhood is proclaimed by several biological events: eruption of the first permanent molar, the end to brain growth in weight, attainment of adult-style locomotion, and a small increase in growth velocity (the midgrowth spurt). Childhood's end is also associated with new levels of cognitive maturity, the so-called five- to seven-year old shift.

Weaning

Childhood begins after the infant is weaned. Weaning is defined here as the termination of lactation by the mother (other researchers may define weaning as the process of shifting from lactation to eating solid foods). In human societies the age at weaning varies greatly. Industrialized societies provide a poor indication of weaning age because bottle feeding and the manufacture of "baby foods" allow either early termination of breast feeding or no breast feeding at all. Preindustrialized human societies, herafter called traditional societies, provide a better indication of the age at weaning, and hence the transition from infancy to childhood. In a review of traditional societies Dettwyler (1995) found that the termination of breast feeding occurs at a median age of 36 months. Another review of the age at human weaning (Lee et al., 1991) found that in so-called food-enhanced societies, that is, those where nutritional intake is good, weaning takes place as early as 9 months of age. In "food-limited" societies, where chronic undernutrition occurs, weaning takes place at 36 month median age.

The age at weaning has important demographic implications. For virtually all mammals, including women living in traditional societies, the biological demands of lactation inhibit a new pregnancy. In traditional societies nursing is usually done on-demand, 24 hours per day. Many mothers nurse their infants to soothe them as much as to feed them. The hormonal consequences of such regular nursing result in a pause in ovulation. This makes sense, as a new pregnancy would deplete the mother's nutritional reserves and compromise the health of the current infant(s), the new pregnancy, and the mother. Yet, women are unlike other mammals, even other species of primates, in that they wean their infants at a relatively early stage of development, that is, before the first permanent tooth erupts. This occurs even in traditional societies, including food-limited groups such as the !Kung and the Ache hunter-gatherers. Early weaning allows the mother to become pregnant that much sooner. We will return to a discussion of these demographic implications later in this chapter. But first, a few more words about the consequences of early weaning on the evolution of human childhood.

Teeth, Guts, and Brains

For all of the other primates, and virtually all other mammals, weaning is coincident with first molar eruption. Human mothers can wean their infants at an earlier stage of growth because the mother, or other people, will provide her child with specially prepared postweaning foods. Children require specially prepared foods due to the immaturity of their dentition. The deciduous dentition, often called "milk teeth," have thin enamel and shallow roots compared with the permanent dentition. Smith (1991a) and Smith et al. (1994) report that given this dental morphology, young mammals with only the deciduous dentition cannot process the adult-type diet. Smith also found that mammals with some permanent teeth are able to process the adult diet and are independent in terms of feeding. When human infancy ends, the deciduous dentition is still in place; thus the human child still requires a special diet and remains dependent on older individuals for food.

Children also require a special diet due to the small size of their digestive tracts relative to that of the adult. Children cannot process the adult-type diet, which is usually based on high-fiber foods that require a large digestive tract to digest and absorb the nutrients. Research in Guatemala, in Thailand, and many other similar studies show that without the use of appropriate weaning foods children will suffer calorie insufficiency leading to undernutrition, developmental delays, and growth retardation (Bogin, 1999a).

Another reason that children need a special high-energy diet is due to the rapid growth of their brain (Fig. 3.7). Leonard and Robertson (1992) estimate that due to this rapid brain growth, "a human child under the age of 5 years uses 40–85% of resting metabolism to maintain his/her brain [adults use 16–25%]. Therefore, the consequences of even a small caloric debt in a child are enormous given the ratio of energy distribution between brain and body" (p. 191). In a related study, Leonard and Robertson (1994) also show that the size of the human brain relative to total body size necessitates an energy-dense diet. At all stages of life after birth, human beings have brains that are significantly larger than expected given the human body size (Fig. 4.2). These large, metabolically active brains demand a larger percentage of energy than any other primate.

Aiello and Wheeler (1995) refine the relationship between human brain size, body size, and metabolic costs by noting that, relative to total body size, adult human

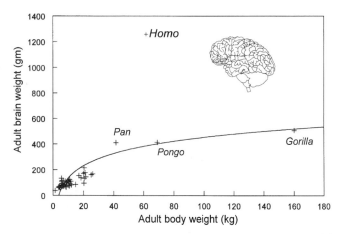

FIGURE 4.2 Adult body weight and brain weight plotted for 61 species of Cercopithecidae (Old World monkeys), apes, and people. The curve is a logarithmic regression fitted to the data for all species. Each part of the human brain enlarged during evolution, especially the size of cerebral cortex (data from Harvey et al., 1986).

beings have an unexpectedly small gastrointestinal tract (gut) as well as an unexpectedly large brain (Fig. 4.3). In contrast, the size of other organs, such as the liver, kidney, and heart, are about as big as expected. Aiello and Wheeler show that both brain tissue and gut tissue are "expensive," meaning that both types of tissue have relatively high metabolic rates. Aiello and Wheeler present estimates of the percentage of total body basal metabolic rate for several tissues utilized by the typical 65-kg adult human male. For the brain the value is 16.1 percent and for the gut the value is 14.8 percent. Given these values, Aiello and Wheeler propose that during human evolution the gut decreased in size as a trade-off allowing, in part, for expansion of brain size. Had the gut remained as large as expected for a primate of human size, the metabolic costs would have been too great to also support a large brain. The trade-off in size between brain and gut means that humans have a total metabolic rate that is about average for a placental mammal of our size.

Even with this trade-off, the large and metabolically expensive human brain still requires a constant supply of energy. A smaller than expected gut size for humans means that less total food can be processed in a given amount of time. This presents humans with the problem of eating just the right kind of food to meet the nutritional demands of the brain and the rest of the body. Both Leonard and Robertson (1994) and Aiello and Wheeler (1995) conclude that the way human beings satisfy nutritional demands is to consume a diet that is nutrient dense, especially in energy, and easy to digest. Human beings meet these dietary requirements in two ways. The first is by selection of appropriate foods. The human ability to include foods such as seeds, roots, and meat, which are rare in the diet of other primates, increases quality, as these are nutrient-dense foods. The second way humans meet nutritional requirements is by processing food to extract, concentrate, and enhance its nutritional content.

The human dietary pattern is ancient. Since at least the time of *Homo habilis* (about 2 million years ago), hominids have depended on technology to do this

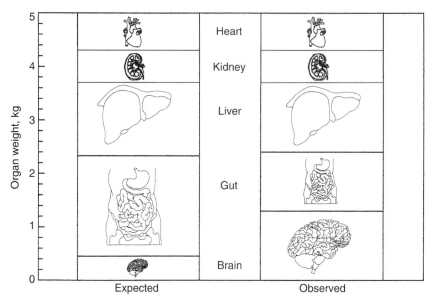

FIGURE 4.3 Expected and observed weight of several human organs. The histograms provide a comparison of the weight of the heart, kidney, liver, digestive system (gut), and brain. The observed sizes of the human heart, kidney, and liver are about equal to the expected sizes. The human gut is much smaller than expected, while the human brain is much larger than expected. The last three organs are shown pictorially in relative size. The expected size of the organs are based on the actual sizes of these organs in more than 20 species of monkeys and apes. The data are from Aiello and Wheeler (1995), where the details of data selection, sample sizes, and methods of analysis are described.

preparation (e.g., the hand-axes and fire used by *Homo erectus* or the food processors and microwave ovens of *Homo sapiens*). By about 20,000 years ago Paleolithic foragers living in western Europe consumed about 30 percent of total energy from animal protein (Bogin, 1997). I have hypothesized that the evolution of childhood provided the impetus for these special features of the human diet (Bogin, 1999a, and below). Added together, all the constraints of childhood—an immature dentition, a small digestive system, a calorie-demanding brain that is both relatively large and growing rapidly, and feeding dependency—necessitate a special diet, one that must be procured, prepared, and provided by older members of the social group. If my correlation between diet and childhood is correct, then the evolution of childhood is ancient as well—childhood evolved at the time of *H. habilis* (further evidence for this conclusion is presented later in this chapter).

Passage from Childhood and the Midgrowth Spurt

Important developments that allow children to progress to the juvenile stage of growth and development are the eruption of the first permanent molars and completion of growth of the brain (in weight). First molar eruption takes place, on average, between the ages of 5.5 and 6.5 years in most human populations (Jaswal, 1983; Smith, 1992). Functional occlusion occurs some weeks to months thereafter. Recent morphological and mathematical investigation shows that brain growth in weight is complete at a mean age of seven years (Cabana et al., 1993). Thus, significant milestones of dental and brain maturation take place at about seven years of age. At this stage of development the child becomes much more capable of processing dentally an adult-type diet (Smith, 1991a). Furthermore, nutrient requirements for the maintenance and growth of both brain and body diminish to less than 50 percent of total energy needs.

The midgrowth spurt is another important milestone that signals the end of human childhood. This spurt is associated with an endocrine event called adrenarche, the progressive increase in the secretion of adrenal androgen hormones. Adrenal androgens produce the midgrowth spurt in height, a transient acceleration of bone maturation, and the appearance of axillary and pubic hair and seem to regulate the development of body fatness and fat distribution (Katz et al., 1985; Parker, 1991). There is a little story that links the midgrowth spurt with neoteny. Louis Bolk (1926), the "father" of the scientific hypothesis for human evolution via neoteny, speculated that for our early human ancestors sexual maturation took place at about six to eight years of age. The midgrowth spurt was first reported by Backman (1934), and following its discovery, several of Bolk's followers, without any additional supporting evidence, opined that the midgrowth spurt and adrenarche are vestiges of sexual maturation from our evolutionary past. We now understand that the midgrowth spurt is associated with adrenarche, a maturation event of the adrenal gland, and not with gonadarche, the maturation of the gonads. Much research, from clinical medicine to anthropological fieldwork, shows that there is virtually no connection between adrenarche and gonadarche, as each are independently controlled events (Parker, 1991; Smail et al., 1982; Weirman and Crowley, 1986, Worthman, 1986).

Bolk's idea about sexual maturation in the past may be wrong, but a connection between the midgrowth spurt and the evolution of the human pattern of growth is still a possibility. The mechanism controlling adrenarche is not understood, as no known hormone appears to cause it. There are connections, however, between the production of adrenal hormones, growth, and maturation. Cutler et al. (1978) and Smail et al. (1982) measured the plasma concentration of the adrenal androgens dehydroepiandrosterone (DHA), dehydroepiandrosterone sulfate (DHAS), and delta^4-androstenodine (D^4) before and after sexual maturation in 14 species. These species include samples of rodents (rat, guinea pig, hamster), domestic animals (rabbit, dog, sheep, pig, goat, horse, cow), primates [macaques (including 76 *Macaca mulatta* and 80 *M. nemestrina*), a few baboons, and 52 chimpanzees), and the chicken. Cutler and colleagues (1978) found that the plasma concentrations of DHA, DHAS, and D^4 were significantly higher in sexually mature primates species than in any of the other animals. However, the serum level of these adrenal androgens was not related to sexual maturation. Rhesus monkeys aged one to three years old and not sexually mature had the same high concentrations of all three adrenal androgens as older, sexually mature monkeys. The same was true for baboons. In contrast, chimpanzees seven years old or older had adrenal androgen concentrations that were, on average, 4.7 times greater than those for chimpanzees less than four years old. Cutler and colleagues concluded that among the animals examined so far, the chimpanzee and the human being are the only species that show adrenarche. Smail and colleagues (1982) generally confirmed the findings of Cutler et al. (1978) but also measured adrenal function in sexually mature *M. nemestrina* monkeys. In the oldest group of these monkeys, ages six to nine years, there was a significant increase in the serum concentration of both DHA and DHAS. The authors state that this shows clearly that, like chimpanzees and humans, this species of macaque has adrenarche. But, in the monkey adrenarche occurs *after* gonadarche, meaning that the adrenal changes and sexual maturation are completely independent.

Only human beings are known to have both adrenarche and a midgrowth spurt. The primate data reported by Cutler et al. (1978) and Smail et al. (1982) suggest a possible function for adrenarche. In those primate species with adrenarche, serum levels of adrenal androgens are relatively low after infancy and prior to adrenarche. Moreover, chimpanzees and humans have relatively slow growth and a long delay prior to the onset of sexual maturation. Given that one biological action of adrenal hormones is to speed up skeletal growth and maturation, perhaps the evolution of reduced adrenal androgen production prior to adrenarche may be explained as a mechanism that maintains slow epiphyseal maturation and skeletal growth in the face of the prolongation of the prepubertal stages of growth. In the human being, the delay is so protracted that it becomes possible to insert the childhood stage of development between the infancy and juvenile stages.

Synthesizing all of these data, it is possible to view the combination of adrenarche and the human midgrowth spurt as life history events marking the transition from the childhood to the juvenile stage of growth. In terms of physical growth, the effects of the adrenal androgens, to increase rate of skeletal growth, stimulate body hair growth, and regulate body fat distribution, are short-lived and quite small. Even so, these physical changes may be noticed by the child and his or her intimates, such as parents, and recognized as markers of developmental maturation. More to the point is the fact that while adrenarche may have only transient effects on physical development, there is a more permanent and important effect on cognitive function. Psychologists have long been interested in what is called the five- to seven-year-old shift in cognition (Rogoff et al., 1975; Weisner, 1996; White, 1965). Weisner (1996, p. 295) states that "the 5–7 shift involves changes in internal states and competencies of the maturing child—shifts in cognitive capacities, self concept, visual/perceptual abilities, or social abilities. The transition marks the emergence of increasing capabilities for strategic and controlled self-regulation, skills at inhibition, the ability to maintain attention and to focus on a complex problem, and planfullness and reflection."

Using the terminology of Piaget, the five- to seven-year-old shift moves the child from the preoperational to concrete operational stage of cognition. This five- to seven-year-old shift is found in all cultures so far investigated (Rogoff et al., 1975). The shift has never been reported in any other primate species (Parker, 1996) and thus seems to be a human species phenomenon. Ethnographic and psychological research shows that juvenile humans have the physical and cognitive abilities to provide much of their own food and to protect themselves from environmental hazards such as predation (children in foraging societies and rural agricultural societies are especially vulnerable to predation due to small body size) and disease (Blurton-Jones, 1993; Weisner, 1987). In addition to self-care and feeding, the post-shift juvenile becomes increasingly involved with domestic work and "caretaking interactions with other children" (Weisner, 1996, p. 296). The association of adrenarche, the midgrowth spurt, and the five- to seven-year-old shift seems to mark the progression of the child to the juvenile stage of development.

HOW AND WHEN DID HUMAN CHILDHOOD EVOLVE?

The stages of the life cycle may be studied directly only for living species. However, there are lines of evidence that may be used to reconstruct the life cycle of extinct species. The fossil evidence of skeletons and teeth provides direct and tangible clues to the life cycle of extinct species. Indirect evidence comes from the fields of comparative anatomy, comparative physiology, comparative ethology, and archaeology. We know from fossil evidence that one human characteristic, bipedalism, appears relatively early in hominid evolution—about 4 MYA. There are many hypotheses for the evolution of hominid bipedalism, but in the context of this discussion one of these is most important. Bipedalism "allows individuals to walk long distances and carry objects" (Zihlman, 1997, p. 185). Zihlman explains that "objects" include infants. There are significant connections between human infancy and bipedalism. During infancy, when the child is dependent on the mother for care and feeding, the rate of leg growth and the maturation of corresponding nerve cells in the motor-sensory cortex of the brain are slow relative to the growth of the head, the arms, and the nerve cells that control movement in the upper half of the body. By about two years of age, there is an acceleration in both the rate of leg growth and the maturation of the motor-sensory cortex region devoted to the legs (Tanner, 1978). At the time the child is weaned (about three years of age in traditional societies), independent locomotion takes on greater importance for the child and the rate of leg growth becomes faster than the rate of arm growth (Hansman, 1970; Scammon and Calkins, 1929).

Another method used to reconstruct life histories for extinct hominids is by analyzing teeth. Teeth are covered by enamel, the hardest substance in a mammal's body, which protects teeth from destruction. The jaw (mandible and maxilla) that supports the teeth is composed of fairly dense and durable bone, and therefore both teeth and jaws (either in whole or part) are more likely to be preserved in the fossil record than any other body parts. This is fortuitous for the study of life history because the morphology and development of the dentition is highly conservative in evolution and the pattern of tooth development reveals a great deal about life history. The use of teeth to reconstruct the evolution of hominid life history is a very active area of research with a burgeoning literature that cannot be adequately reviewed in this book. Interested readers should consult Mann et al. (1990) and Winkler and Anemone (1996) for reviews, details of methodology, and alternative interpretations of the evidence. One example of this research is the work of Holly Smith. Smith (1991b) found a significant correlation between age of eruption of the first molar (M1) and adult brain size across a large number of mammalian species. She also found high correlations between age at M1 eruption and age at weaning ($r = 0.93$) and age at sexual maturity for both males ($r = 0.93$) and females ($r = 0.93$). Such high correlations mean that these life history events are linked to some more fundamental developmental process and that a change in the timing of one of these events will probably result in a change in the timing of them all. We may conclude, then, that even though age at weaning and sexual maturity cannot be seen directly in the fossil record, they can be reconstructed based on the dentition.

Another example of the methods used to reconstruct the evolution of life history may be found in the work of Martin (1983, 1990) and Harvey et al. (1986) on patterns of brain and body growth in apes, humans, and their ancestors. Martin showed that Old World monkeys and apes have a pattern of brain growth that is rapid before birth and relatively slower after birth. In contrast, humans have rapid brain growth both before and after birth (Fig. 4.4). This difference may be appreciated by comparing ratios of brain weight divided by total body weight (in grams). At birth this ratio averages 0.09 for the great apes and 0.12 for human neonates. At adulthood the ratio averages 0.008 for the great apes and 0.028 for people. In other words, relative to body size human neonatal brain size is 1.33 times larger than the great apes, but by adulthood the difference is 3.5 times. The human–ape difference is not due to any single heterochronic process, that is, not the result of delay, prolongation, or acceleration of a basic apelike pattern of growth. Rather it is due to new patterns of growth for the human species. The rate of human brain growth exceeds that of most other tissues of the body during the first few years after birth (Fig. 3.7). Martin (1983, 1990) and Harvey et al. (1986) also show that human neonates have remarkably large brains (corrected for body size) compared with other primate species. Together, relatively large neonatal brain size and the high postnatal growth rate give adult humans the largest encephalization quotient (an allometric scaling of brain to body size) of all higher primates (Fig. 4.2).

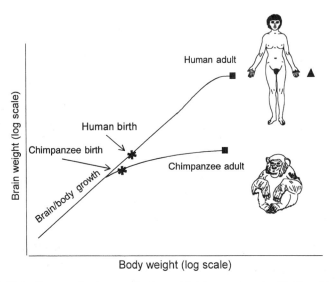

FIGURE 4.4 Growth curve for human brain and body compared with the chimpanzee. The length of the human fetal phase, in which brain and body grow at the same rate for both species, is extended for humans. Chimpanzee brain growth slows after birth, but humans maintain the high rate of brain growth during the postnatal phase. In contrast, the rate of human body growth slows after birth. If human brain/body growth rates were equal to the chimpanzee rate, then adult humans would weigh 454 kg and stand nearly 3.1 m tall (indicated by the "▲" symbol). After Martin (1983).

Martin (1983) hypothesizes that a "humanlike" pattern of brain and body growth becomes necessary once adult hominid brain size reaches about 850 cm³. This biological marker is based on an analysis of head size of fetuses and birth canal dimensions of their mothers across a wide range of social mammals, including cetaceans, extant primates, and fossil hominids (Martin, 1983, pp. 40–41). Given the mean rate of postnatal brain growth for living apes, an 850-cm³ adult brain size may be achieved by all hominoids (living and extinct apes and humans) by lengthening the fetal stage of growth. At brain sizes above 850 cm³ the size of the pelvic inlet of the fossil hominids, and living people, does not allow for sufficient fetal growth. Thus, a period of rapid postnatal brain growth and slow body growth—the human pattern—is needed to reach adult brain size.

Martin's analysis is elegant and tenable. Nevertheless, the difference between ape and human brain growth is not only a matter of velocity but also a matter of life history stages. Brain growth for both apes and human beings ends at the start of the juvenile stage, which means that apes complete brain growth during infancy. Human beings, however, insert the childhood stage between the infant and juvenile stages. Childhood may provide the time and the continuation of parental investment necessary to grow the larger human brain. Following this line of reasoning, any fossil human, or any of our fossil hominid ancestors, with an adult brain size above Martin's "cerebral Rubicon" of 850 cm³ may have included a childhood stage of growth as part of its life history.

Given this background, Figure 4.5 is a summary of the evolution of the human pattern of growth and development from birth to age 20 years (the evolution of adolescence is discussed later in this chapter). Figure 4.5 must be considered as "a work in progress" for two reasons. The first is that only the data for the first and last species (the chimpanzee *Pan* and *H. sapiens*) are known with some certainty. The second is that this version of the figure supercedes earlier versions that were

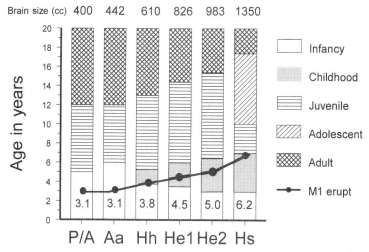

FIGURE 4.5 Evolution of hominid life history during the first 20 years of life. Abbreviated nomenclature as follows: P/A, Pan and *Australopithecus afarensis*; Aa, *Australopithecus africanus*; Hh, *Homo habilis*; He1, early *Homo erectus*; He2, late *Homo erectus*; Hs, *Homo sapiens*. Mean brain sizes are given at the top of each histogram. Mean age at eruption of the first permanent molar (M1) is graphed across the histograms and given below the graph.

prepared without the advantage of more recent information about patterns of growth for fossil hominids (e.g., Bogin, 1994, 1995, 1997; Bogin and Smith, 1996). Even with the latest information available, the patterns of growth of the fossil hominid species are tentative reconstructions, based on published analyses of skeletal and dental development of fossil specimens that died before reaching adulthood.

Known ages for eruption of the M1 are given for *Pan* and *H. sapiens*. Estimated ages for M1 eruption in other species were calculated by Smith and Tompkins (1995). Age of eruption of M1 is an important life history event that correlates very highly with other life history events. Known or estimated adult brain sizes are given at the top of each bar; the estimates are averages based on reports in several textbooks of human evolution. Following Martin's (1983, 1990) analysis, brain size is another crucial influence on life history evolution. One major message to take from the figure is that the prolongation of the total time for growth that plays such a prominent role in the hypotheses of neoteny and hypermorphosis is definitely a part of human evolution. However, I find that time prolongation is not sufficient to account for the insertion of the new stages of childhood and adolescence that are part of human growth.

Australopithecus afarensis appears in the fossil record about 3.9 MYA and is one of the oldest hominid fossil species. *Australopithecus afarensis* shares many anatomical features with nonhominid pongid (ape) species including an adult brain size of about 400 cm^3 (Simons, 1989) and a pattern of dental development indistinguishable from extant apes (Bromage and Dean, 1985; Conroy and Vannier, 1991; Smith, 1991b). Therefore, the chimpanzee and *A. afarensis* are depicted in Figure 4.5 as sharing the typical tripartite stages of postnatal growth of social mammals—infant, juvenile, adult (Pereira and Fairbanks, 1993). Following the definitions used throughout this book, infancy represents the period of feeding by lactation, the juvenile stage represents a period of feeding independence prior to sexual maturation, and the adult stage begins following puberty and sexual maturation. The duration of each stage and the age at which each stage ends are based on empirical data for the chimpanzee. A probable descendent of *A. afarensis* is the fossil species *A. africanus*, dating from about 3.0 MYA. To achieve the larger adult brain size of *A. africanus* (average of 442 cm^3) may have required an addition to the length of the fetal and/or infancy periods. Figure 4.5 indicates an extension to infancy of one year.

The first permanent molar (M1) of the chimpanzee erupts at 3.1 years, but chimpanzees remain in infancy until about age five years. Until that age the young chimpanzee is dependent on its mother and will not survive if the mother dies or is otherwise not able to provide care and feeding (Goodall, 1983; Nishida et al., 1990). After erupting M1 the young chimpanzee may be able to eat adult-type foods but still must learn how to find and process foods. Learning to successfully open fruits that are protected by hard shells and to extract insects from nests (such as ants and termites) require more than one year of observation and imitation by the infant of the mother. For these reasons, chimpanzees extend infancy for more than one year past the eruption of M1. Based on brain size details of dental anatomy, the mean age of M1 eruption and eruption of M2 and M3 for *A. afarensis* and *A. africanus* is estimated to be identical to the chimpanzee. It is likely that these early hominids followed a pattern of growth and development very similar to chimpanzees. Behavioral capacities of these fossil hominids also seem to be similar to living chimpanzees. For these reasons, the early hominids also may have extended infancy for at least one year beyond the age of M1 eruption.

About 2.2 MYA fossils with several more humanlike traits, including larger cranial capacities and greater manual dexterity, appear. Also dated about this time are stone tools of the Oldowan tradition. Given the biological and cultural developments associated with these fossils they are considered by most paleontologists to be members of the genus *Homo* (designated as *H. habilis, H. rudolfensis,* or early *H. erectus*—refered to collectively here as *H. habilis*). The rapid expansion of adult brain size during the time of *H. habilis* (650 to 800 cm³) might have been achieved with further expansion of both the fetal and infancy periods, as Martin's "cerebral Rubicon" was not surpassed. However, the insertion of a brief childhood stage into hominid life history may have occurred. Christine Tardieu (1998) shows that *H. habilis* has a pattern of growth of the femur that is distinct from that of the australopithecines but consistent with that of later hominids. The distinctive femur shape of the more recent hominids is due to the addition of a prolonged childhood stage of growth. Then, *H. habilis* may have had a short childhood stage of growth.

Childhood and Fertility

A childhood stage of growth for the earliest members of the genus *Homo* is also supported by a comparison of human and ape reproductive strategies. There are limits to the amount of delay possible between birth and sexual maturity and between successful births that any species can tolerate. The great apes are examples of this limit. Chimpanzee females in the wild reach menarche at 11 to 12 years of age and have their first births at an average age of 14 years (Goodall, 1983). The average period between successful births in the wild is 5.6 years, as infant chimpanzees are dependent on their mothers for about five years (Goodall, 1983; Nishida et al., 1990; Teleki et al., 1976). Actuarial data collected on wild-living animals indicate that between 35 percent (Goodall, 1983) and 38 percent (Nishida et al., 1990) of all live-born chimpanzees survive to their midtwenties. Although this is a significantly greater percentage of survival than for most other species of animals, the chimpanzee is at a reproductive threshold. Goodall (1983) reports that for the period 1965 to 1980 there were 51 births and 49 deaths in one community of wild chimpanzees at the Gombe Stream National Park, Tanzania. During a 10-year period at the Mahale Mountains National Park, Tanzania, Nishida et al. (1990) observed "74 births, 74 deaths, 14 immigrations and 13 emigrations" in one community. Chimpanzee population size in these two communities is, by these data, effectively in equilibrium. Any additional delay in age of females at first birth or the time between successful births would likely result in a decline in population size. Galdikas and Wood (1990) present data for the orangutan that show that these apes are in a more precarious situation. Compared with the 5.6 years between successful births of chimpanzees, the orangutan female waits up to 7.7 years, and orangutan populations are in decline. Lovejoy (1981) calls the state of great ape reproduction a "demographic dilemma" (p. 211).

The great apes, and fossil hominids such as *Australopithecus*, may have reached this demographic dilemma by extending the length of the infancy stage and forcing a demand on nursing to its limit (Fig. 4.5). Early *Homo* may have overcome this reproductive limit by reducing the length of infancy and inserting childhood between the end of infancy and the juvenile period. Free from the demands of nursing and the physiological brake that frequent nursing places on ovulation (Ellison, 1990), mothers could reproduce soon after their infants became children. This certainly occurs among modern humans. An often-cited example, the !Kung, are a traditional hunting and gathering society of southern Africa. A !Kung woman's age at her first birth averages 19 years and subsequent births follow about every 3.6 years, resulting in an average fertility rate of 4.7 children per woman (Howell, 1979; Short, 1976). Women in another hunter-gatherer society, the Hadza (Blurton-Jones et al., 1992), have even shorter intervals between successful births, stop nursing about one year earlier, and average 6.15 births per woman.

For these reasons, a brief childhood stage for *H. habilis* is indicated in Figure 4.5. This stage begins after the eruption of M1 and lasts for about one year. That year of childhood would still provide the time needed to learn about finding and processing adult-type foods. During this learning phase, *H. habilis* children would need to be supplied with special weaning foods. There is archaeological evidence for just such a scenario. *Homo habilis* seems to have intensified its dependence on stone tools. There are more stone tools, more carefully manufactured tools, and a greater diversity of stone tool types associated with *H. habilis* (Klein, 1989). There is considerable evidence that some of these tools were used to scavenge animal carcasses, especially to break open long bones and extract bone marrow (Potts, 1988). This behavior may be interpreted as a strategy to feed children. Such scavenging may have been needed to provide the essential amino acids, some of the minerals, and especially the fat (dense source of energy) that children require for growth of the brain and body (Leonard and Robertson, 1992).

Continuing Evolution of Childhood

Further brain size increase occurred during *H. erectus* times, which begin about 1.6 MYA. The earliest adult specimens have mean brain sizes of $826\,cm^3$, but many individual adults had brain sizes between 850 and $900\,cm^3$. This places *H. erectus* at or above Martin's "cerebral Rubicon" and seems to justify insertion and/or expansion of the childhood period to provide the biological time needed for the rapid, human-like, pattern of brain growth. It should be noted from Figure 4.5 that the model of human evolution proposed here predicts that from the *Australopithecus* to the *H. erectus* stage the infancy period shrinks as the childhood stage expands. Perhaps by early *H. erectus* times the transition from infancy to childhood took place before M1 eruption. Of course, it is not possible to know if this was the case or to state the cause of such a life history change with any certainty. Maybe the evolution of ever larger brains led to a delay in M1 eruption, which in turn led to both the need for a childhood stage and the expansion of the childhood stage as brains continued to enlarge. Alternatively, a delay in dental maturation may have precipitated the need for childhood and in turn the biocultural ecology of childhood and its effects on hominid social learning and behavior selected for ever larger brains. No matter what the cause of childhood may be, if an expansion of childhood led to a shrinking of the infancy stage, then *H. erectus* would have enjoyed a greater reproductive advantage than any previous hominid. This seems to be the case, as *H. erectus* populations certainly did increase in size and begin to spread throughout Africa and into other regions of the world.

Later *H. erectus*, with average adult brain sizes of 983 cm^3, are depicted with further expansion of the childhood stage. In addition to bigger brains (some individuals had brains as large as 1,100 cm^3), the archaeological record for later *H. erectus* shows increased complexity of technology (tools, fire, and shelter) and social organization (Klein, 1989). These technosocial advances, and the increased reliance on learning that occurs with these advances, may well be correlates of changes in biology and behavior associated with further development of the childhood stage of life (Bogin and Smith, 1996). The evolutionary transition to archaic and, finally, modern *H. sapiens* expands the childhood stage to its current dimension. Note that M1 eruption becomes one of the events that coincides with the end of childhood. Perhaps no further extension of childhood beyond M1 eruption is possible, given the significant biological, cognitive, behavioral, and social changes that are also linked with dental maturation and the end of childhood. With the appearance of *H. sapiens* comes evidence for the full gamut of human cultural capacities and behaviors. The technological, social, and ideological requisites of culture necessitate a more intensive investment in learning than at any other grade of hominid evolution. The learning hypothesis for childhood, while not sufficient to account for its origins, certainly plays a significant role in the later stages of its evolution. The *H. sapiens* grade of evolution also sees the addition of an adolescent stage to postnatal development. The evolution of human adolescence is discussed later in this chapter.

WHO BENEFITS FROM CHILDHOOD?

Brain sizes of extant and fossil apes and hominids provide some idea of when human life stages may have evolved but do not explain why they evolved. Bonner (1965) shows that the presence of a stage and its duration in the life cycle relate to such basic adaptations as locomotion, reproductive rates, and food acquisition. To make sense out of the pattern of human growth, one must look for the "basic adaptations" that Bonner describes. The most basic of these adaptations are those that relate to evolutionary success. This is traditionally measured in terms of the number of offspring that survive and reproduce. Biological and behavioral traits do not evolve unless they confer upon their owners some degree of reproductive advantage in terms of survivors a generation or more later. Three "textbook" reasons for the evolution of human childhood were listed at the start of this chapter. These reasons emphasized the role of learning in human adaptation, and they are valid reasons inasmuch as learning does confer an adaptive advantage to preadult individuals. However, the "textbook" explanations cannot account for the initial impetus for the insertion of childhood into human life history. A childhood stage of development is not necessary for the type of learning listed here. The prolonged infancy and juvenile period of the social carnivores (Bekoff and Byers, 1985) and apes (Bogin, 1994) can serve that function. Rather childhood may be better viewed as a feeding and reproductive adaptation for the parents, a strategy to elicit parental care after infancy, a strategy to minimize the risks of starvation for the child, a means of shifting the care of offspring from the parents, especially the mother, to juveniles and older, postreproductive, adults (i.e., grandmothers), and a mechanism that allows for more precise "tracking" of ecological conditions via developmental plasticity during the growing years.

Thus in addition to the three "textbook" explanations given at the beginning of this chapter, I propose that there are at least five additional reasons for the evolution of childhood:

1. Childhood Is a Feeding and Reproductive Adaptation

A childhood growth stage may have originally evolved as a means by which the mother, the father, and other kin could provision dependent offspring with food. This frees the mother from the demands of nursing and the inhibition of ovulation related to continuous nursing. This decreases the interbirth interval and increases reproductive fitness.

A little life history theory will help to understand the importance of a reduced interbirth interval (Thompson, 1999):

> Of the many differences in life history that occur among populations, age at the time of first reproduction is one of the most important for understanding the dynamics and evolution of a population. All else being equal, natural selection will favor individuals that reproduce earlier than other individuals within a population, because by reproducing earlier an individual's genes enter the gene pool sooner than those of other individuals that were born at the same time but have not reproduced. The genes of the early reproducers then begin to spread throughout the population. Individuals whose genetic makeup allows them to reproduce earlier in life will come to dominate a population if there is no counterbalancing advantage to those individuals that delay reproduction until later in life.

Things are not always equal, especially in terms of life history trade-offs. Because of this, not all of the individuals in any population reproduce as early in life as may be biologically possible. Individual must spend their limited energy and resources on demands other than reproduction. These trade-offs between reproduction and, for example, growth or defense against disease mean that in many populations individuals who defer reproduction to later ages may have a better chance of surviving and leaving offspring than those that attempt to reproduce early.

Consider the data shown in Figure 4.6, which depicts several hominoid developmental landmarks. In comparison with living apes, human beings experience developmental delays in eruption of the first permanent molar, age at menarche, and age at first birth. However, humans have a shorter infancy and shorter birth interval, which in apes and traditional human societies are virtually coincident. Dental development is an excellent marker for life history in the primates, and it was shown above that there is a very strong correlation between age at eruption of M1 and many life history events. In general, primate mothers wean their infants about the time M1 erupts. This makes sense, since the mother must nurse her current infant until it can process and consume an adult diet, and this requires at least some of the permanent dentition. As discussed in Chapter 2, several primate and social carnivore species provide food to their young during the postweaning period. In

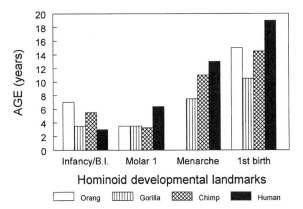

FIGURE 4.6 Hominoid developmental landmarks. Data based on observations of wild-living individuals or, for humans, healthy individuals from various cultures. Note that compared with apes, people experience developmental delays in eruption of the first permanent molar, age at menarche, and age at first birth. However, people have a shorter infancy and shorter birth interval, which in apes and traditional human societies are virtually coincident. The net result is that humans have the potential for greater lifetime fertility than any ape. Species abbreviations are: Orang, *Pongo pygmaeus*; Gorilla, *Gorilla gorilla*; Chimp, *Pan troglodytes*; Human, *Homo sapiens*, Developmental landmarks are: Infancy/B.I., period of dependency on mother for survival, usually coincident with mean age at weaning and/or a new birth (B.I. = birth interval); Molar 1, mean age at eruption of first permanent molar; Menarche, mean age at first estrus/menstrual bleeding; 1st birth, mean age of females at first offspring delivery. (From Bogin [1988, 1994], Galdikas and Wood [1990], Nishida et al. [1990], Smith [1992], and Watts and Pusey [1993].)

these species the molar and premolar teeth may erupt before the postweaning dependency period ends. These primates and carnivores are similar in that both are predatory (the primates hunt insects) and it takes the young time to learn and practice hunting skills. The effect of the postweaning dependency on the mother is delayed reproduction. In a review of reproductive behavior of the carnivores Ewer (1973) found that female lions, hyenas, the sea otter (a fish-hunter), and many bears wait two or more years between pregnancies. The same delay holds for the more carnivorous primates, such as marmosets, tamarins, and chimpanzees. From this we may conclude that reproduction in the social and predatory mammals occurs either at or well after the age at which the first permanent teeth erupt.

The human species is a striking exception to this relationship between permanent tooth eruption and birth interval. Women in traditional societies wait, on average, three years between births, not the six years expected on the basis of M1 eruption. The short birth interval gives humans a distinct advantage over other apes, as we can produce and rear two offspring through infancy in the time it takes chimpanzees or orangutans to produce and rear one offspring. The basic point I am emphasizing here is that by reducing the length of the infancy stage of life (i.e., reducing the period of lactation) and by developing the special features of the human childhood stage, humans have the potential for greater lifetime fertility than any ape. Well-adapted species are those that survive for many generations, and they do this, in large measure, by being able to adjust rates of reproduction to maintain population sizes in equilibrium with environmental resources. When population size declines, for example, after an episode of disease or starvation, a well-adapted species can increase birth rates to restore the equilibrium. With a shortened birth interval, humans can make adjustments in birth rates more quickly than any ape. The human advantage is not that our species can have more offspring, for that might lead to overpopulation. Rather, the human advantage lies in our species' ability to regulate population size more efficiently. We accomplish this by prolonging growth and development, inserting new life-cycle stages, and developing a larger, more complex brain. Each of these contribute to human biocultural adaptations to the environment. At the beginning of this chapter I quoted Allison Jolly with reference to human mental agility replacing the reproductive agility of other animals. Given the nature of human biocultural behavior, it is perhaps more accurate to conclude that human beings have both mental and reproductive agility.

The evolution of the human childhood stage gave our species a reproductive advantage but also introduced new liabilities. Children are not fed by nursing, but they still depend on older individuals for feeding and protection. Moreover, children must be given foods that are specially chosen and carefully prepared to meet their nutritional demands. The peoples of traditional societies solve the problem of child care by spreading the responsibility among many individuals. A review of the literature I conducted with Holly Smith (Bogin and Smith, 1996) found that in Hadza society (African hunters and gatherers) grandmothers and great-aunts are observed to supply a significant amount of food and care to children. In Agta society (Philippine hunter-gatherers) women hunt large game animals but still retain primary responsibility for child care. They accomplish this by living in extended family groups—two or three brothers and sisters, their spouses, children, and parents—and sharing the child care. Among the Maya of Guatemala (horticulturists and agriculturists), many people live together in extended family compounds. Women of all ages work together in food preparation, manufacture of clothing, and child care. In some societies, fathers provide significant child care, including the Agta and the Aka Pygmies, a hunting-gathering people of central Africa. Summarizing the data from many human societies, Lancaster and Lancaster (1983) call this type of child care and feeding "the hominid adaptation," for no other primate or mammal does all of this.

A stimulus to release these parental behaviors toward children may be found in the very pattern of growth of the children themselves, as discussed next.

2. The Allometry of the Growth of the Human Child Releases Nurturing and Caregiving Behaviors in Older Individuals

The central nervous system, in particular the brain, follows a growth curve that is advanced over the curve for the body as a whole (Fig. 3.7). The brain achieves adult size when body growth is only 40 percent complete, dental maturation is only 58 percent complete, and reproductive maturation is only 10 percent complete. The allometry of the growth of the human child maintains an infantile appearance (large cranium, small face and body, little sexual development) that stimulates nurturing and caregiving behaviors in older individuals. A series of ethological observations (Lorenz, 1971) and psychological experiments (Alley, 1983; Todd et al., 1980) demonstrate that these growth patterns of body, face, and brain allow the human child to maintain a superficially infantile (i.e., "cute") appearance longer than any other mammalian species (see Box 4.1). The infantile appearance of children facilitates parental investment by maintaining the potential for nurturing behavior of older individuals toward both infants and dependent children (Bogin, 1999a; McCabe, 1988).

BOX 4.1
Evolutionary Psychology of Childhood

Reproductive success is the major force behind the evolution of all species. Part of the reproductive success of the human species is due to the intense investment and care that parents and other individuals lavish on infants and children. In the course of human evolution, at least since the appearance of the genus *Homo* in the last 2 million years, patterns of growth were shaped by natural selection to promote and enhance parental investment. One way this was accomplished was by stimulating what may be called the "psychology of parenting."

Lorenz (1971) stated that the physical characteristics of mammalian infants, including small body size, a relatively large head with little mandibular or nasal prognathism, relatively large round eyes in proportion to skull size, short thick extremities, and clumsy movements, inhibit aggressive behavior by adults and encourage their caretaking and nurturing behaviors. Lorenz believed that these infantile features trigger "innate releasing mechanisms" in adult mammals, including humans, for the protection and care of dependent young. Gould (1979) questions the innateness of the human response to infantile features. Such behavior may be "learned from our immediate experience with babies and grafted upon an evolutionary predisposition for attaching ties of affection to certain learned signals" (p. 34). The important point is that whether innate or learned the resultant behavior is the same.

There seems to be a pan-human ability to perceive the five stages of human postnatal development and respond appropriately to each. An elegant series of

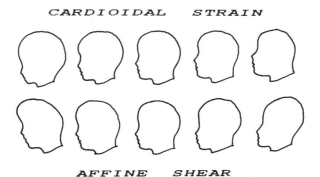

CARDIOIDAL   STRAIN

AFFINE   SHEAR

FIGURE B4.1 Two mathematical transformations of human head shape used in the experiments of Todd et al. (1980). The middle profile in each row was drawn from the photograph of a 10-year-old boy. The transformations were applied to this profile of a real child. The cardioidal strain transformation is perceived by most adults as growth. The affine shear transformation is not perceived as growth.

experiments performed by Todd et al. (1980) show that human perceptions of body shape and growth status are consistent between individuals. When adult subjects (about 40 college students, all childless) were shown a series of profiles of human skull proportions, they could easily arrange them correctly into a hierarchy spanning infancy to adulthood. The subjects could also ascribe maturity ratings to skull profiles that were geometrically transformed to imitate the actual changes that occur during growth (Fig. B4.1). This perception was selective because a variety of other types of geometrical transformations elicited no reports of growth or maturation. When the growthlike mathematical transformations were applied to

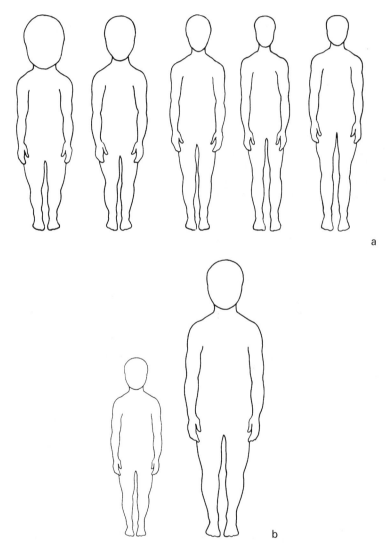

a

b

FIGURE B4.2 (*a*) Series of five shape-variant drawings used in the experiments of Alley (1983). These drawings show the typical body proportions of a male at (from left) birth, 2, 6, 12, and 25 years of age. (*b*) Example of the size-variant pairs of drawings used in the experiments of Alley (1983).

profile drawings of the heads of birds and dogs, human subjects reported identical perceptions of growth and maturation, even though in reality the development of these animals does not follow the human pattern of skull shape change. Even more surprising is that subjects reported the perception of growth when the growthlike mathematical transformations were applied to front- and side-view profiles of Volkswagen "beetles," objects that do not grow.

In another series of experiments, Alley (1983) studied the association between human body shape and size and the tendency by adults to protect and "cuddle" other individuals. In the first experiment, subjects were shown two sets of drawings. One set was based upon two-dimensional diagrams depicting changes in human body proportion during growth. Alley's version of these diagrams are called "shape-variant" drawings (Fig. B4.2a). Alley's second set of figures were called "size-variant" drawings (Fig. B4.2b). He used the middle-most, "six-year-old" profile in the shape-variant series to construct sets of figures that varied in height and width but not in shape. Note that these figures have no facial features or genitals. Perceptual differences between figures are due to body shape or size alone.

In the first experiment, the subjects were shown pairs of the shape-variant drawings (i.e., profiles of a newborn and a six-year-old, a two-year-old and a 12-year-old, etc.) or pairs of the size-variant drawings and asked to state which one of the pair they "would feel most compelled to defend should you see them being beaten." In another experiment they were asked about their feelings to "hug or cuddle" the person depicted. The results of both experiments, summarized in Table B4.1, find a fairly strong reported willingness to defend newborns and two-year-olds and a moderate willingness to defend older persons. The reported willingness to cuddle decreased with the "age" of the drawings. Placed in the context of the ethological study of parental caregiving in mammals and birds, Alley believes that his results demonstrate a general tendency to protect or cuddle others based on the perception of maturational status.

McCabe (1988) reviews the work of Alley and other similar studies. Taken together, these studies indicate that adults are more likely to protect or nurture individuals with "neotenous" facial features. McCabe defines such features as having a relatively large ratio of cranium size to lower face size. McCabe also

TABLE B4.1
Mean Reported Willingness to Defend or Cuddle Persons of Different Body Proportions

Age Portrayed (years)	Defend	Cuddle
Newborn	7.7 (1.7)	3.4 (2.3)
2	7.1 (1.7)	3.4 (2.0)
6	5.8 (1.8)	3.2 (2.2)
12	5.0 (1.9)	3.0 (1.9)
25	4.3 (1.9)	2.7 (2.2)

Note: Standard deviations are given in parentheses.
Source: From Alley (1983).

cites studies of the facial features of nursery school-aged children under court protection for abuse compared with nonabused age-matched controls. The abused children had smaller ratios of the cranium/lower face—that is, they were less neotenous or "cute"—than the nonabused controls.

These psychological experiments and case control studies provide support for the arguments developed in this chapter for the evolution of human childhood. In particular, small body size and a superficially infantile appearance promote appropriate parental behavior by older individuals toward children.

3. Children Are Relatively Inexpensive to Feed

The relatively slow rate of body growth and small body size of children reduce competition with adults for food resources, because slow-growing, small children require less food than bigger individuals. A five-year-old child of average size (the 50th centile of the NCHS reference curves for growth) and activity, for example, requires 22.7 percent less dietary energy per day for maintenance and growth than a 10-year-old juvenile on the 50th growth centile (Guthrie and Picciano, 1995; Ulijaszek and Strickland, 1993). Thus, provisioning children, though time consuming, is not as onerous a task of investment as it would be, for instance, if both brain and body growth were both progressing at the same rapid rate. Moreover, in times of food scarcity children are protected from starvation by this unique pattern of brain and body growth.

Case (1978) proposed another advantage of small body size in relation to slow growth. He describes people as having "low growth efficiency," by which he means that people have the slowest postnatal growth of virtually any mammal, but a high basal metabolic rate. For any given body size, human children require more energy for maintenance and growth than most mammals of the same body size. This is due, of course, to the relatively large brain of human children. Small body size during human infancy and childhood helps to reduce the total number of calories needed to maintain a big brain and high metabolic rate.

4. "Babysitting" is Possible

As children do not require nursing, any competent member of a social group can provide food and care for them. Early neurological maturity versus late sexual maturity allows juveniles and young adolescents to provide much of their own care and also provide care for children (Bogin, 1994). Grandmothers and other post-reproductive women also provide much child care (Bogin and Smith, 1996). Again, this frees younger adults, especially the mother, for subsistence activity, adult social behaviors, and further childbearing. This type of caretaking is rare in other primates, even for apes. Usually, an infant nonhuman primate must be cared for by its mother or it will die. Adoptions of orphaned infants by females do occur in chimpanzee social groups, but only infants older than four years and able to forage for themselves survive more than a few weeks (Goodall, 1983). Goodall noted deterioration in the health and behavior of infant chimpanzees whose mothers had died. The behavioral changes include depression, listlessness, drop in play frequency, and whimpering. Health changes such as loss of weight were seen. Goodall reported that even those older infants who survived the death of their mother were affected by delays in physical growth and maturation.

It is well known that human infants and children also show physical and behavioral pathology after the death of one or both parents (Bowlby, 1969). It seems, though, that the human infant can more easily make new attachments to other caretakers than the chimpanzee infant. The ability of a variety of human caretakers to attach to one or several human infants may also be an important factor. The psychological and social roots of this difference between human and nonhuman species in attachment behavior are not known. The flexibility in attachment behavior that hominid ancestors evolved allowed, in part, for the evolution of childhood and the reproductive efficiency of the human species.

One common pattern of child care in many traditional cultures is to have juveniles assume caretaking responsibilities for children. This occurs among two well-studied African hunting and gathering cultures, the !Kung and the Mbuti. Mothers carry their infant and nursing children (nursing a child to age four is common in these cultures) with them while foraging. Weaned children must stay "home" at the base camp, as preadolescent children have neither the strength nor the stamina to follow their parents while gathering or hunting (Draper, 1976; Konner, 1976; Turnbull, 1983a,b). At !Kung camps children of various ages play together within the camp boundaries while juveniles discharge many caretaking functions for younger children. The children seem to transfer their attachment from parents and other adults to the juveniles, behaving toward them with appropriate deference and obedience. The **age-graded play group** functions to transmit cultural behavior from older to younger generations and to facilitate the learning of adult parental behavior (Konner, 1976). Of course, the children and juveniles are never quite left on their own, as there is always one adult, or more, in camp at any time, but this person is not directly involved in child care. Rather, he or she is preparing food or tools or otherwise primarily engaged in adult activity. The Mbuti (nomadic hunters and gatherers of central African rain forests) have a similar child care arrangement. After weaning, toddlers enter the world of the *bopi*, the Mbuti term for a children's playground but also a place of age-graded child care and cultural transmission. Between the ages of two or three to eight or nine children and juveniles spend almost all of their day in the *bopi*. There they learn physical skills, cultural values, and even sexual behavior: "Little that children do in the *bopi* is not of full value in later adult life" (Turnbull, 1983b, pp. 43–44).

The age-graded play group provides for both the caretaking and enculturation of the young, freeing the adults from these tasks so that they may provide food, shelter, and other necessities for the young who may be at various stages of development. A woman may be pregnant, have a child weaned within the past year, and have one or more older offspring simultaneously. Thus, adults may be able to increase their net reproductive output during a relatively short period of time. This benefit, and the selective advantage of a greater number of surviving offspring afforded by age-graded caretaking, may in part account for the evolution of the prolonged childhood and juvenile growth periods of hominids. The play group, in the protective environment of the home base or camp, provides the children with the freedom for play, exploration, and experimentation, which Beck (1980) has shown encourages learning, socialization, and even tool using.

5. Childhood Allows for Developmental Plasticity

Following the discussion in Stearns (1992, p. 62) and Mascie-Taylor and Bogin (1995, several chapters), the term *plasticity* means a potential for change in the phenotype of the individual caused by a change in the environment. The fitness of a given phenotype varies across an environment's range of variation. When phenotypes are fixed early in development, such as in mammals that mature sexually soon after weaning (e.g., rodents), environmental change is positively correlated with high mortality are. Social mammals (carnivores, elephants, primates) prolong the developmental period by adding a juvenile stage between infancy and adulthood. Adult phenotypes develop more slowly in these mammals. They experience a wider range of environmental variation, and the result is a better conformation between the individual and the environment. In Chapters 5 and 6 the nature of human plasticity in growth and adaptation is discussed in detail. The point here is that plasticity leads to increased evolutionary fitness, meaning that more offspring can survive to reproductive age. In mammalian species without a juvenile stage, less than 10 percent of live-born offspring survive to reproductive age, while between 10 and 30 percent survive in the social mammals with a juvenile growth stage (Lancaster and Lancaster, 1983; Pereira and Fairbanks, 1993). The insertion of a childhood stage between infancy and the juvenile period in humans results in an additional four years of relatively slow physical growth and allows for behavioral experience that further enhances developmental plasticity. The combined result is increased fitness (reproductive success). Lancaster and Lancaster (1983) report that humans in traditional societies, such as hunters and gatherers and horticulturalists, rear about 50 percent of their live-born offspring to adulthood.

SUMMARY OF CHILDHOOD

These five themes of childhood—feeding, nurturing, low cost, babysitting, and plasticity—account for much of the evolution and pattern of growth of our species. Understanding these themes helps to resolve the paradox of human growth and evolution—lengthy development and low fertility. In reality, humans have greater reproductive economy than any other species since we raise a greater percentage of offspring to adulthood. These successfully reared young adults then begin their own reproduction and thus ensure some "intimation of immortality" for their parents. In the center of it all is human childhood. For the child is indeed, to paraphrase Wordsworth, parent to the reproductively successful and well-adapted adult.

WHEN AND WHY DID ADOLESCENCE EVOLVE?

The evolution of an adolescent stage is also depicted in Figure 4.5. Human adolescence is the stage of life when social, economic, and sexual maturation take place. All three are needed for successful reproduction. The case was presented in the previous chapter for the special growth and development characteristics of human adolescence. Evidence for when and why human adolescence evolved is presented here.

The single most important feature defining human adolescence is the skeletal growth spurt that is experienced by virtually all boys and girls. There is no evidence for a humanlike adolescent growth spurt in any living ape. There is no evidence for adolescence for any species of *Australopithecus*. There is some tentative evidence that early *Homo*, dating from 1.8 MYA, may have a derived pattern of growth that is leading toward the addition of an adolescent stage of development. This evidence is based on an analysis of shape change during growth of the femur (Tardieu, 1998). Modern humans have highly diagnostic shape to the femur, a shape that is absent in fossil ascribed to *Australopithecus* but present in fossils ascribed to *H. habilis, H. rudolfensis*, or early African *H. erectus*. The human shape is produced by growth changes during both the prolonged childhood stage and the adolescent stage. The more humanlike femur shape of the early *Homo* fossils could be due to the insertion of the childhood stage alone or to the combination of childhood and adolescent stages. Due to the lack of fossils of appropriate age at death, the lack of dental and skeletal material from the same individuals, and the lack of sufficient skeletal material from other parts of the body, it is not possible to draw any more definitive conclusions.

A remarkable fossil of early *H. erectus* is both of the right age at death and complete enough to allow for an analysis of possible adolescent growth. The fossil specimen is cataloged formally by the name KMN-WT 15000 but is called informally the "Turkana boy" as it was discovered along the western shores of Lake Turkana, Kenya, by Kamoya Kimeu in 1984 (Brown et al., 1985; Walker and Leakey, 1993). This fossil is 1.6 million years old, making it an early variety of *H. erectus*. The skeletal remains are almost complete, missing the hands and feet and a few other minor bones. It is the most complete known specimen of *H. erectus*. Holly Smith (1993) analyzed the skeleton and dentition of the Turkana fossil and ascertained that, indeed, it is most likely the remains of an immature male. The youth's deciduous upper canines were still in place at the time of death, and he died not long after erupting second permanent molars. These dental features place him firmly in the juvenile stage by comparison with any hominoid. The boy was 160 cm tall at the time of death, which makes him one of the tallest fossil youths or adults ever found.

Part of Smith's analysis focused on patterns of growth and development, especially the question "Did early *H. erectus* have an adolescent growth spurt?" Based on her analysis, the answer to that question is no. Judged according to modern human standards, the Turkana boy's dental age of 11 years is in some conflict with his bone age (skeletal maturation) of 13 years and his stature age of 15 years. If the Turkana boy grew along a modern human trajectory, then dental, skeletal, and stature ages should be about equivalent. By chimpanzee growth standards, however, the boy's dental and bone ages are in perfect agreement, both at seven years of age. As *H. erectus* is no chimpanzee, the Turkana boy's true age at death was probably between 7 and 11 years. What is clear is that the Turkana boy followed a pattern of growth that is neither that of a modern human nor that of a chimpanzee. Based on Smith's analysis, the boy's large stature becomes more explicable. The reason for his relatively large stature-for-age is that the distinct human pattern of moderate to slow growth prior to puberty followed by an adolescent growth spurt had not yet evolved in early *H. erectus*. Rather, the Turkana boy followed a more apelike pattern of growth in stature, making him appear to be tall in comparison with a modern human boy at the same age. At the time of puberty, the chimpanzee has usually achieved 88 percent of stature growth, while humans have achieved only 81 percent. Smith and Tompkins (1995) state that the human pattern of growth suppression up to puberty followed by a growth spurt after puberty had not evolved by early *H. erectus* times: "Because of this, any early *H. erectus* youth would seem to us to be too large" (p. 273).

Unfortunately there are no appropriate fossil materials of later *H. erectus* available to analyze for an adolescent growth spurt. There is one fossil of a Neandertal in which the associated dental and skeletal remains needed to assess adolescent growth are preserved, and this fossil is being analyzed by Jennifer Thompson and colleagues. So far, they have published a description of the skull (Thompson and Bilsborough, 1997) and abstracts of preliminary descriptions of growth and development (Thompson, 1995; Thompson and Nelson, 1997). The specimen is a juvenile, most likely a male. It is called Le Moustier 1 and was found in 1908 in Western France. The specimen is dated at between 42,000 and 37,000 years B.P. (before present). Thompson uses information on crown and root formation of the molar teeth to estimate a dental age of 15.5 ± 1.25 years. Compared with modern human standards for length of the long bones of the skeleton, Thompson and Nelson (1997) estimate that Le Moustier 1 has a stature age of about 11 years, based on the length of his femur. The dental age of 15.5 years and the stature age of 11 years are in very poor agreement and indicate that like the Turkana boy, Le Moustier 1 may not have followed a human pattern of adolescent growth. The dental age indicates that by human standards Le Moustier 1 was in late adolescence at the time of death, but the stature age indicates he was still a juvenile or had just entered adolescence. Quite unexpectedly, these differences in dental and skeletal maturity are exactly the opposite of those for the Turkana boy.

What is clear is that adolescent growth, at least the pattern of adolescent growth found in modern humans, does not seem to be present in either the Turkana boy or the Le Moustier 1 fossil. In modern humans, certain diseases, prolonged undernutrition, and unusual individual variations in growth may produce the skeletal and dental features of the fossils. While it is possible that these two fossil specimens fall into one of these categories of unusual growth, the most parsimonious conclusion that one may draw from these findings is that the adolescent growth spurt in skeletal growth evolved recently. Quite likely this would be no earlier than the appearance of archaic *H. sapiens* in Africa at about 125,000 years ago. If Neandertals are direct ancestors to modern humans, then the adolescent skeletal growth spurt may be less than 37,000 years old.

Why Did the Growth Spurt Evolve?

One often cited reason for the adolescent growth spurt is the prolonged time required to learn technology, social organization, language, and other aspects of culture during the infant, child, and juvenile stages of growth. At the end of this period, so the argument goes, our ancestors were left with proportionately less time for procreation than most mammals and therefore needed to attain adult size and sexual maturity quickly (Watts, 1985, 1990). But surely this cannot be the whole story. Consider first that there is no need to experience an adolescent growth spurt to reach adult height or fertility. Historical sources describe the *castrati*, male opera singers of the seventeenth and eighteenth centuries who were castrated as boys to preserve their soprano voices, as being unusually tall for men (Peschel and Peschel, 1987). Also, children who are born without gonads or have then removed surgically prior to puberty (due to diseases such as cancer) do not experience an adolescent growth spurt but do reach their normal expected adult height (Prader, 1984). Of course, *castrati*, whether or not opera singers, do not become reproductively successful. There are, however, normal individuals, for the most part very late maturing boys and many girls, who have virtually no growth spurt. Nevertheless, these late-maturing individuals do grow to be normal-sized adults, and they become fertile by their early twenties—not significantly later than individuals with a spurt.

Another problem with the "lost-time" argument for the adolescent growth spurt is that it does not explain the timing of the spurt. Girls experience the growth spurt before becoming fertile, but for boys the reverse is true. Why the difference? Sexual dimorphism in adult height is one obvious consequence of the timing difference and hence a possible positive value for the growth spurt itself. Adult men are, on average, 12 to 13 cm taller than adult women (Eveleth and Tanner, 1976).

Dimorphism in stature is only one of a series of sex-based differences in development that take place during adolescence. The order in which several pubertal events occur in girls and boys is illustrated in Figure 4.7 in terms of time before and after peak-height velocity (PHV) of the adolescent growth spurt. In both girls and boys puberty begins with changes in the activity of the hypothalamus and other parts of the central nervous system (CNS). These changes are labeled as "CNS puberty" in the figure. Note that the CNS events begin at the same relative age in both girls and boys, that is, three years before PHV. This is also the time when growth rates change from decelerating to accelerating. In girls, the first outward sign of puberty is the development of the breast bud (B2) and wisps of pubic hair (PH2) (see Chapter 2 for an explanation of the system of staging the breast and pubic hair development of girls and genital and pubic hair development in boys). This is followed, in order, by (1) a rise in serum levels of estradiol, which leads to the laying down of fat on the hips, buttocks, and thighs; (2) the adolescent growth spurt; (3) further growth of the breast and body hair (B3 and PH3); (4) menarche; (5) completion of breast and body hair development (B5 and PH5); and (6) attainment of adult levels of ovulation frequency.

The path of pubertal development in boys starts with a rise in serum levels of luteinizing hormone (LH) and the enlargement of the testes and then the penis (G2). This genital maturation begins, on average, only a few months after that of girls. However, the timing and order of other secondary sexual characteristics are unlike that of girls: (1) About a year after CNS puberty, there is a rise in serum testosterone levels (T) followed by the appearance of pubic hair (PH2); (2) about a year later motile spermatozoa may be detected in urine; (3) PHV follows after about another year, along with deepening of the voice and continued growth of facial and body hair; (4) the adult stages of genital and pubic hair development follow the growth spurt (G5 and PH5); and (6) near the end of adolescence boys undergo a spurt in muscular development.

The sex-specific order of pubertal events tends not to vary between early and late maturers, between well-nourished girls and boys and those who suffered from severe malnutrition in early life, between rural and urban dwellers, or between

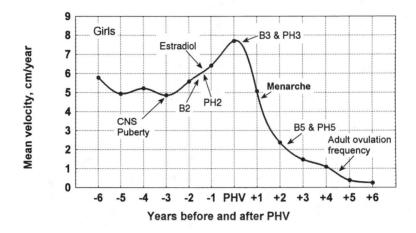

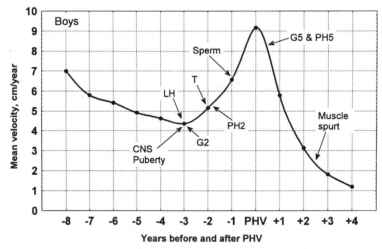

FIGURE 4.7 Ordering of several sexual maturation events for girls (top panel) and boys (bottom panel) during the adolescent growth spurt. The velocity curves are calculated using data derived from a sample of healthy, well-nourished girls and boys living in Guatemala. See text for an explanation of each labeled event.

European and African ethnic groups (Bogin et al., 1992; Cameron et al, 1988, 1990, 1993). In addition to these biological events, there are behavioral and social events that also follow a predictable course during adolescence. Indeed, the biological and cultural events are usually tightly correlated. A comparison of the biocultural timing of adolescent events in two societies is given in Figure 4.8. Girls from a London, England, sample and a Kikuyu (African) sample are compared in the upper panel and boys from the same two samples are compared in the lower panel (the data are reported by Worthman, 1993). The Kikuyu are a Bantu-speaking, agricultural society of the central highlands of Kenya. The London sample represents adolescents who are relatively well nourished and healthy. The Kikuyu sample represents adolescents who suffer from periodic food shortages and, perhaps, a higher incidence of infectious and parasitic diseases. The adolescent events for each sex are placed in chrono-

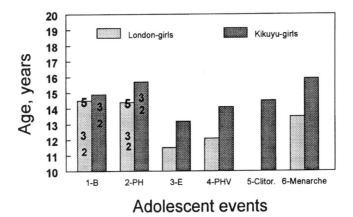

FIGURE 4.8 Comparison of biocultural events during adolescence in a sample of London and Kikuyu girls and boys. The data are abstracted from Worthman (1993), who provides references to the original studies. The events are presented in order of occurrence. The bars indicate the median age at onset of each event. Explanation of each event is given in the text. The abbreviations for the girls' events are: 1-B, breast stages; 2-PH, pubic hair stages; 3-E, first notable rise in serum estradiol concentration; 4-PHV, peak-height velocity; 5-Clitor., clitoridectomy; 6-Menarche, age at menarche. Abbreviations for the boys are: 1-G, genital stages; 2-LH, first notable rise in serum luteinizing hormone concentration; 3-T, first notable rise in serum testosterone concentration; 4-PH, pubic hair stages; 5-Sep., separation to "boys' house" for Kikuyu; 6-PHV, peak-height velocity; 7-Cir/Gr., circumcision for Kikuyu, or graduation from secondary school for London boys.

logical order, and the bars indicate the median age at which each event occurs. These comparisons show two things. The first is how differences in health and nutrition between human societies may influence the timing but not the order of adolescent events. The second is how societies as diverse as urban Londoners and rural Kikuyu adjust the timing of some social events to the timing of the biological events of human adolescence.

For both London and Kikuyu girls, the first biocultural event is breast development (bars 1-B), and the second event is pubic hair development (bars 2-PH).

The numbers on these bars indicate median age of entry to each stage of development (B2, B3, B5, etc.). The third event is a rise in serum estradiol concentration (bars 3-E). This hormonal event, and similar hormonal changes in boys, can only be detected by special tests, not by the adolescents or their parents. But, the rise of estradiol leads to biological and behavioral changes that are easily detectable in the form of fat deposits on hips, thighs, and buttocks and new levels of cognition (Piaget's formal operations stage). The fourth event is PHV (bars 4-PHV). Note that for the Kikuyu, PHV occurs about two years later than for the London girls. For many Kikuyu girls the fifth biocultural event is clitoridectomy; about 40 percent of girls underwent this operation, which removes the tip of the clitoris, at the time of Worthman's research in 1979 and 1980. Clitoridectomy takes place just after PHV, at about breast stage 3, and just before menarche. The operation is timed so that it precedes the onset of sexual activity and marriage that follow menarche (Worthman, 1993). London girls may experience some adolescent rites of passage after PHV, but these are usually less well-defined and less traumatic than clitoridectomy. The sixth event is menarche, which is taken as a sign of impending sexual maturation in all cultures. In many cultures, menarche often precipitates intensified instruction about sexual behaviors and the practice of these behaviors (Schegel and Barry, 1991).

For both London and Kikuyu boys, the first two biocultural events are enlargement of the testes, or genital stage 2 (bars 1-G), and a rise in serum concentration of LH (bars 2-LH). In fact, the order of the two events could be switched as it is the rise of LH that leads to testes enlargement. Here these two events are considered to be coterminous. The third event is a rise in the serum concentration of testosterone (bars 3-T), which precipitates a cascade of physical and behavioral changes. The fourth event is pubic hair development (bars 4-PH). For the Kikuyu, the fifth biocultural event is separation (bar 5-Sep.), which means that the adolescent boys leave their nuclear household and begin living in an age-graded adolescent male household. Worthman states that separation to the "boys' house" is closely correlated with age at first emission and that separation takes place at about the same age that girls undergo clitoridectomy. These events show that Kikuyu parents are able to recognize and respond to the sexual maturation of their adolescents. The sixth event is PHV (bars 6-PHV). The seventh biocultural event for Kikuyu adolescents is circumcision (7-Cir.), which is done to all young men and marks their entry into training for adulthood. Circumcision is timed to occur along with the spurt in muscle mass, which allows boys to perform physical labor at adult levels. London boys do not undergo a circumcision rite of passage, but within that same year they usually graduate from secondary school (7-Gr.). That event, which London girls also experience, is a rite of passage in most industrialized societies and often marks entry into the social world of adults.

More will be said about the biocultural significance of these adolescent events in the next few pages. At this point it is important to focus on two general issues. The first is that the adolescent growth spurt is a biologically and socially significant event for both sexes. The second is that the order of adolescent events is different for each sex, for example, the growth spurt occurs earlier in the sequence as well as at an earlier age in girls than in boys. Given this, the sexual dimorphism expressed in this sequence and the timing of these events may be considered species-specific characteristics. Evolutionary biologists usually find that species-specific traits evolve to enhance the survival and reproductive success. Thus, the human adolescent growth spurt must have its own intrinsic evolutionary value and is not just a by-product of slow prepubertal development.

WHY DO GIRLS HAVE ADOLESCENCE, OR WHY WAIT SO LONG TO HAVE A BABY?

Differences between boys and girls in the timing, duration, and intensity of the adolescent growth spurt require that each sex be analyzed individually if we are to understand how the separate paths of development through adolescence promote their reproductive success as adults. Moreover, the value of adolescence becomes apparent only when we consider human biology and behavior cross-culturally and historically. We need to include the role adolescence plays in contemporary Western, industrialized society, but thinking only of the present-day cultural milieu cannot reveal the evolutionary and biocultural nature of adolescence. Taking this approach from the female perspective, the human mother-to-be must acquire knowledge of (1) adult sociosexual relations, (2) pregnancy, and (3) child care. The dramatic physical changes that girls experience during adolescence serve as efficient advertisements of their sexual and social maturation—so efficient, in fact, that they stimulate adults to include adolescent girls in their social circles and encourage the girls themselves to initiate adult social interactions, such as working with and learning from adult women, social and sexual bonding with adult men, and sexual intercourse. Psychologists call this the intensification of gender-related roles (Hill and Lynch, 1983). Ethnographic research shows that gender role intensification during adolescence is a universal feature of human cultures (Schlegel and Barry, 1991; Whiting and Edwards, 1988).

In human societies, juvenile girls are often expected to provide significant amounts of child care for their younger siblings. This stands in contrast to most other social mammals, whose juveniles are often segregated from adults and infants. Whiting and Edwards (1988) surveyed information available in the Human Relation Area Files, a data base of 186 societies, concerning apprenticeships in child care. They found that "the preferred age for child nurses in many of our sample communities is between 6 and 10 years" (p. 272). Whiting and Edwards believe that the best time for girls to learn child care skills is during these juvenile years. Social and emotional bonds between the juvenile and her mother and other adults are shifting from ones of dependency to ones of interest in their family and the work of adult women. In a few years these juvenile girls enter adolescence "and become less interested in the world of their family and more interested in sex, the future, and their own children" (p. 272). These findings show how the biocultural nature of gender role intensification is associated with human life history stages.

Schlegel and Barry (1991; see also Schlegel, 1995) used the Human Relation Area Files in their cross-cultural survey of adolescence. Their interest was more in the social, emotional, and cultural roles of adolescence than in biology. Nevertheless, they took a biocultural approach and found that both a biological and a social stage of life that may be called adolescence is found universally in human cultures. This is noteworthy only because some psychologists, educators, and historians have claimed that adolescence is an "invention" of industrialized societies. Schlegel and Barry do not make a clear distinction between the juvenile and adolescent stages of life. Even so, they confirm the earlier work of Whiting and Edwards, showing that during both the juvenile and adolescent periods both learning and social restructuring take place. They state that there is a "cognitive and affective reorganization away from the behavioral modes of childhood and toward adult modes . . . The adolescent assumes greater autonomy, more peer relationships with same-sex adults, and an interest in sexual activities" (p. 8). The authors characterize the juvenile and adolescent stages as periods of "unlearning and relearning." The human capacity to makes these shifts in learned behavior, such as from childhood dependency to adolescent autonomy, attests to the biological and psychological plasticity of our species and negates the notion that adult humans are neotenous, that is, permanent children in any sense. These shifts do not support other models of human development via heterochrony, such as sequential hypermorphosis. Schlegel and Barry emphasize that with the onset of the juvenile stage, most societies segregate boys and girls socially and each sex experiences very different types of learning. Juvenile girls are included in the social and work world of the family and of older women, while boys are encouraged to form social bonds with other juvenile boys. By working closely with adult women, juvenile girls are assisted in the restructuring of their learning and acquire first-hand experience in child care and many domestic tasks.

By the time these juvenile girls enter adolescence, they have gained considerable knowledge of the needs of infants and children. To complete their restructuring and relearning for reproductive success as adult women, these girls need to gain knowledge of sexuality and reproduction. As adolescents they can do this efficiently because they look mature sexually, and are treated as such, several years before they actually become fertile. The adolescent growth spurt serves as one important signal of sexual maturation. Early in the spurt, before PHV is reached, girls develop pubic hair and fat deposits on breasts, buttocks, and thighs. By the time of PHV, girls have achieved 91 percent of their adult height. Since the adolescent spurt and PHV of girls occur about two years earlier than those of boys, the girls are, on average, taller than boys of the same age (Figs. 1–4; Tobias, 1970). In essence, all of these changes in body composition, in absolute stature, and in stature relative to boys help to make the girls look like women and to appear to be maturing sexually. About a year after PHV, girls experience menarche, an unambiguous external signal of internal reproductive system development. However, most girls experience one to three years of anovulatory menstrual cycles following menarche, meaning that they cannot become pregnant. Two studies of girls and young women living in Switzerland and Finland examined the frequency of ovulation for 4.5 years following menarche (reviewed in Worthman, 1993). Ovulation frequency varied from zero to 10 percent of menstrual cycles at six months postmenarche. The frequency increased to about 30 percent after 1.5 years, varied between 40 and 55 percent after 2.5 years, and leveled off at 60 to 65 percent after 4.5 years. Since the mature level of ovulatory frequency is about 65 percent of menstrual cycles, it appears that it takes about five years for healthy, well-nourished girls to achieve adult maturity for fertility. Adolescent girls, and the adults around them, may or may not be aware of this period of "adolescent sterility." Everyone in the social group is aware of the dramatic changes taking place in the adolescent girl, and these changes certainly stimulate both the girls, and the adults around them, to participate in adult social, sexual, and economic behavior. For the postmenarche adolescent girl this participation provides the learning and experience she will need to be a successful woman and mother, and it is "low risk" in terms of pregnancy for several years.

It is noteworthy that female chimpanzees and bonobos, like human girls, also experience up to three years of postmenarche infertility, so this time of life may be a shared hominoid trait. As with human adolescents, the postmenarchial but infertile chimpanzees and bonobos participate in a great deal of adult social and sexual behavior. Primate researches observing these apes point out that this participation, without pregnancy, allows for practicing many key behaviors that are needed to rear an infant successfully (Goodall, 1983). Although ape and human females may share a year or more of adolescent sterility, apes reach sexually mature adulthood at about 12 years of age, much sooner than humans. This limits the learning and practice period for the apes.

Full reproductive maturation in human women is not achieved until about five years after menarche. The term "full reproductive maturation" means the biological, social, and psychological maturation of the woman have reached the point where risks of pregnancy are near the minimum for both the mother and her offspring. Menarche occurs at a median age that varies from 12.1 to 13.5 years in healthy populations (the normal range in age at menarche is 8 to 17 years), which means that the average age at full sexual maturation occurs at age 17 or 18 years. Fertility may occur earlier, even as early as six months after menarche. Fertility, however, does not equal reproductive maturity. Becoming pregnant is only a part of the business of reproduction. Maintaining the pregnancy to term and raising offspring to adulthood are equally important. Girls under 17 years old have difficulty with both of these, since the risks for spontaneous abortions, complications of pregnancy, such as high blood pressure in the mother, and low-birth-weight babies are more than twice as high as those for women 20 to 24 years old. The likelihood of these risks declines, and the chance of successful pregnancy and birth increases markedly after age 18.

Another feature of human growth not found in the African apes is that female fertility tracks the growth of the pelvis. This aspect of the developmental biology of human fertility was described in Chapter 2. Recall that girls do not attain adult pelvic inlet size until 17 to 18 years. Cross-cultural studies of reproductive behavior show that human societies acknowledge (consciously or not) this special pattern of pelvic growth. The age at first marriage and childbirth clusters around 19 years for women from such diverse cultures as the Kikuyu of Kenya, Mayans of Guatemala, Copper Eskimo of Canada, and both the Colonial period and contemporary United States (Bogin, 1994). Why the pelvis follows this unusual pattern of growth is not clearly understood. Perhaps another human attribute, bipedal walking, is a factor. Bipedalism is known to have changed the shape of the human pelvis from the basic apelike shape. Apes have a "cylindrical" shaped pelvis, but humans have a "bowl-shaped" pelvis. The human shape is more efficient for bipedal locomotion but less efficient for reproduction because it restricts the size of the birth canal [Trevathan, 1987; Trevathan (1996) details the relationship between the evolution of bipedalism and human birth]. Whatever the cause, this special human pattern of pelvic growth helps explain why girls must wait for many years from the age at menarche to the age of full reproductive maturity.

That time of waiting provides the adolescent girls with many opportunities to practice and learn important adult behaviors that lead to increased reproductive fitness in later life. It seems that there was selection pressure in favor of female adolescence, because girls with the extra developmental time prior to reproduction were able to learn social, economic, and parenting skills that would help ensure greater reproductive success later in life. There is direct evidence for the reproductive value of human adolescence when the data for nonhuman primates are examined. The first-born infants of monkeys and apes are more likely to die than those of humans. Studies of yellow baboons (Altmann, 1980), toque macaques (Dittus, 1977), and chimpanzees (Teleki et al., 1976) show that between 50 and 60 percent of first-born offspring die in infancy. In hunter-gatherer human societies, such as the !Kung, about 44 percent of children die in infancy (Howell, 1979). For comparison, it may be noted that in the United States, in the year 1960, about 2.5 percent of all live, first-born children died before the age of one year (Vavra and Querec, 1973).

Studies of wild baboons by Jeanne Altmann (1980) show that while the infant mortality rate for the first born is 50 percent, mortality for the second born drops to 38 percent, and for the third and fourth born reaches only 25 percent. The difference in infant survival is, in part, due to experience and knowledge gained by the mother with each subsequent birth. Such maternal information is usually mastered by human women during adolescence, which gives the women a reproductive edge. The initial human advantage may seem small, but it means that up to 21 more people than baboons or chimpanzees survive out of every 100 first born—more than enough over the vast course of evolutionary time to make the evolution of human adolescence an overwhelmingly beneficial adaptation.

WHY DO BOYS HAVE ADOLESCENCE?

The most important difference in the pattern of adolescent development for girls and boys is that boys become fertile well before they assume adult size and the physical characteristics of men. Analysis of urine samples from healthy, well-nourished boys age 11 to 16 years old show that they begin producing sperm at a median age of 13.4 years (Muller et al., 1989). Yet the cross-cultural evidence is that few boys successfully father children until they are into their third decade of life. Traditional Kikuyu men do not marry and become fathers until about age 25, although they start seminal emissions at about 14.5 years (Fig. 4.8, age at separation) and become sexually active following their own circumcision rite at around age 16 to 18 years (Worthman, 1986, 1993). The National Center for Health Statistics of the United States reports that only 3.09 percent of all births are fathered by men under 20 years old. Another nationally representative longitudinal survey shows that only 7 percent of young men then aged 20 to 27 years old fathered a child while they were teenagers (Marsiglio, 1987). Among the Ache, who were traditionally foragers of the forests of Paraguay, adolescent boys did not become net food producers until age 17 years, and they did not marry until about age 20 years (Hill and Kaplan, 1988). In the Central Canadian Arctic, Inuit people living as traditional hunters did not even consider that an adolescent boy was ready for marriage until he was 17 to 18 years old (Condon, 1990). Even then, the adolescent man had to provide bride service to his prospective in-laws for several years before he became a father. All this delay in fatherhood occurred despite the fact that there was considerable pressure to reproduce because of "the slim margin of survival in the pre-contact period" (Condon, 1990, p. 270).

The explanation for the lag between sperm production and fatherhood is not likely to be a simple one of sperm performance, such as not having the endurance to swim to an egg cell in the woman's fallopian tubes. A more likely explanation is the fact that the average boy of 13.4 years is only beginning his adolescent growth spurt (Fig. 1.4). Growth researchers have documented that in terms of physical appearance, physiological status, psychosocial development, and economic productivity the 13-year-old boy is still more of a juvenile than an adult. Anthropologists working in many diverse cultural settings report that few women, and more importantly from a cross-cultural perspective few prospective in-laws, view the teenage boy as a biologically, economically, and socially viable husband and father.

The reason for the delay between sperm production and reproductive maturity may lie in the subtle psychophysiological effects of testosterone and other androgen hormones that are released following gonadal maturation and during early adolescence—effects that may "prime" boys to be receptive to their future roles as men. Studies on a cross section of youths in Europe, North America, Japan, and Africa establish that as blood levels of testosterone begin to increase, but before the growth spurt reaches its peak, there is an increase in psychosexual activity. Nocturnal emissions begin (Laron et al., 1980) and there is an increase in the frequency of masturbation. Sociosexual feelings, such as infatuations and "dating," intensify (Higham, 1980; Petersen and Taylor, 1980): in cross-cultural perspective dating refers to overt interest in forming social bonds with eligible sexual or marriage partners. Alternatively, it is possible that physical changes provoked by the endocrine changes provide a social stimulus toward adult behaviors (Halpern et al., 1993). Whatever the case, early in adolescence sociosexual feelings intensify, including guilt, anxiety, pleasure, and pride. At the same time, boys become more interested in adult activities, adjust their attitude to parental figures, and think and act more independently. In short, they begin to behave like men.

However, and this is where the survival advantage may lie, they still look like boys. One might say that a healthy, well-nourished 13.5-year-old human male at a median of 160 cm (5 ft, 2 in.) tall "pretends" to be more childlike than he really is. Because their adolescent growth spurt occurs late in sexual development, boys appear to be juvenile-like for much longer than girls. During the adolescent years, boys are even shorter than girls of roughly the same chronological age, furthering an immature image (Fig. 1.4). Even more to the point is that the spurt in muscle mass of adolescent males does not occur until an average age of 17 years (Malina, 1986). At PHV the typical boy has achieved 91 percent of his adult height but only 72 percent of his adult lean body mass. Since most of the lean body mass is voluntary muscle tissue, adolescent boys cannot do the work of men. This is one important reason why the Kikuyu, the Inuit, and many other cultures do not even think of younger adolescents as manlike. As Schlegel and Barry (1991) found in their cross-cultural survey, adolescent boys are usually encouraged to associate and "play" with their age mates rather than associate with adult men. During these episodes of play, these juvenile-looking adolescent males can practice behaving like adult men before they are actually perceived as adults. The activities that take place in these adolescent male peer groups include the type of productive, economic, aggressive/militaristic, and sexual behaviors that older men perform. But, the sociosexual antics of adolescent boys are often considered to be more humorous than serious. Yet, they provide the experience to fine tune their sexual and social roles before either their lives or those of their offspring depend on them. For example, competition between men for women favors the older, more experienced man. As such competition may be fatal, the juvenile-like appearance of the immature but hormonally primed adolescent male may be life saving as well as educational.

SUMMARY OF ADOLESCENCE

Adolescence became part of human life history because it conferred significant reproductive advantages to our species, in part by allowing the adolescent to learn and practice adult economic, social, and sexual behaviors before reproducing. The basic argument for the evolution and value of human adolescence is this: Girls best learn their adult social roles while they are infertile but perceived by adults as mature; whereas boys best learn their adult social roles while they are sexually mature but not yet perceived as such by adults. Without the adolescent growth spurt and the sex-specific timing of maturation events around the spurt, this unique style of social and cultural learning could not occur. Over the course of time and space, the styles of learning these behaviors have come to vary considerably cross-culturally. The evolution of human adolescence, therefore, has to be modeled in terms of both its biological and cultural ramifications for life history.

POSTREPRODUCTIVE LIFE STAGE

In addition to childhood and adolescence, there is another unusual aspect of human life history. Women in all human societies often live past an age when they are able to reproduce. Women usually experience menopause by the time they are 50 years old or sooner. One generally accepted definition of menopause is "the sudden or gradual cessation of the menstrual cycle subsequent to the loss of ovarian function" (Timiras, 1972, p. 531). Postmenopausal women then enter a nonreproductive life stage that may last for one or more decades. Men do not experience a biological cessation of reproduction as dramatic and as clear as menopause. Still, men older than 50 years of age father far fewer children than younger men. Data for the United States in the year 1993 are presented in Table 4.2. There are too few fathers older than age 55 to report. Part of the reason for the fertility decline in men may be biological. Men do experience a decline in hormone production, including serum androgen, growth hormone, melatonin, and dehydroepiandosterone, with age. This is sometimes called **andropause** (Vermeulen, 2000) or ADAM (androgen decline in the aging male; Morales et al., 2000). The decline in fatherhood after age 50 may also be partly a cultural artifact. Men in other societies may father children to later ages. There are few good studies of male fertility at older ages. One of the best is of the Turkana, a pastoral society of Kenya. Between the ages of 30 and 60 years Turkana men have consistently high rate of fatherhood, averaging two children

TABLE 4.2
Live Births by Age of the Father, United States, 1993

Age (years)	Number of Births
Under 15	487
15–17	29,696
18–19	101,749
20–24	608,003
25–29	923,142
30–34	931,586
35–39	498,080
40–44	173,263
45–49	51,280
50–54	14,725
55 and over	7,030

Source: Data from National Center for Health Statistics (NCHS). *Vital Statistics of the United States, 1993*, Vol. 1, natality. Hyattsville, MD: NCHS.

every five years. After age 60 years the rate drops to one child fathered every five years (Leslie et al., 1999).

The point I wish to emphasize here is that many women and men live for decades after the prime reproductive years. Very few other species of animals have a similar postreproductive stage of life. Further discussion of the postreproductive life stage is deferred to Chapter 8. That chapter treats aging of the human population in greater detail.

CONCLUSION

Perhaps the best summary of the importance of taking a life history perspective of human evolution—including the evolution of human growth and reproduction— was stated by Bonner (1993, p. 93): "The great lesson that comes from thinking of organisms as life cycles is that it is the life cycle, not just the adult, that evolves. In particular, it is the building period of the life cycle—the period of development— that is altered over time by natural selection. It is obvious that the only way to change the characters of an adult is to change its development." The stages of human post-natal life from birth to maturity—infancy, childhood, juvenile, and adolescence— shape the biology and behavior of adults and confer upon them greater reproductive success than any other mammalian species.

Human reproductive success is due to the biocultural adaptations of our species. These adaptations may have arisen as both a consequence of and a response to the evolution of the human life cycle. The stages of the life cycle and the growth patterns of the human body, the face, and the brain facilitate parental investment in offspring by releasing the potential for nurturing behavior of adults toward infants and older but still physically dependent children and socially dependent juveniles. Human culture, in large part, is a response to the need to nurture, protect, and teach these young people. The physical features of childhood and juvenile stages are lost during the time of the adolescent growth spurt. At the end of adolescence, boys and girls enter the social world of men and women. In physical features, interests, and behaviors these young adults are more similar to their parents than to their preadolescent selves of just a few years ago. Each new generation follows the cycle of reproduction, growth, and maturation that was set in place millions of years ago and continues to be expressed in all human populations and in the development of every human being alive today.

FIVE

FOOD, DEMOGRAPHY, AND GROWTH

In the last chapter we saw how life history theory provides the intellectual link between the study of human growth and demography. Food provides the physical link between the growth of individual people and the growth of populations, as both processes depend on the energy and other nutrients supplied by food. My purpose in this chapter is to explore the evolution of human nutrition, especially as this evolution relates to human growth and demography. In doing so, I will review human nutritional requirements and why we have so many requirements. I will investigate the development of human systems of food production, especially the transitions from foraging and horticulture social groups, to societies practicing intensive agriculture, to the rise of industrial production, and now to postindustrial societies. We will see how food production systems are part of a larger social, economic, and political environment. That environment regulates the supply and distribution of critical resources to people. This, in turn, strongly influences the dynamics of population regulation and the growth of individual human beings.

When the energy from food is in limited supply, the amount and rate of human growth decline. When energy is oversupplied, excess growth, especially in body fat, is the consequence. Growth, then, provides a sensitive indicator of the ability of social groups to acquire, produce, and distribute food. The major economic transitions of human history are often associated with the way food is produced and distributed. The most important of these were the Agricultural Revolution of the Neolithic period (10,000 B.P.), the Industrial Revolution, which began in Europe in the late-eighteenth century and continues in the poorer nations of the world today, and the Postindustrial, or Electronic, Revolution of the late-twentieth century. Demographic transitions are usually linked with these economic transitions. There are real connections between these types of transitions, but there are also spurious connections and even no connections. The real and the bogus connections are explored here.

143

FOOD FOR THE BODY AND THE SPIRIT

During a lifetime a human being will eat thousands of pounds of food. The body will use this food to grow, to repair damaged tissue, to maintain organs, such as the brain and the heart, and to reproduce and nourish a new generation. Some of these foods will be enjoyable to eat because they are perceived as looking appetizing and tasting delicious. Other foods may not be enjoyable to eat but will be consumed anyway because they are "good for the body or the spirit." Biochemically, the body does not distinguish between foods that are liked or disliked, for the human body does not use food; rather the body requires the biological nutrients contained in food. Biology, however, is not the entire story of human nutrition. Cultural variables such as the type of food eaten, its manner of preparation, and the social context in which it is consumed often determine the efficacy of that food to meet human needs for health and well-being. Although at times the biology and culture of nutrition will be treated separately, a major theme of this chapter is to view human nutrition, growth, and demography holistically as a biocultural phenomenon.

The biocultural nature of people and food is shown by the Maya story of creation in Box 5.1. The domestication of maize, or corn, and other plants occurred in Mesoamerica about 7,000 B.P. The people who first domesticated maize were small-scale farmers living in tribal or chiefdom societies. Box 5.2 reviews the nature of tribal, chiefdom, and other types of human societies. By 3,000 B.P. maize-based agricultural societies were established, and these developed into the state-level, hierarchical societies of the Olmec and, eventually, the Maya. The central place of

---

BOX 5.1
Conception of the People of the Corn

It was night, and the gods sat thinking in the darkness. Among them were the Bearer, Begetter, the Makers, Modelers named Tepeu Gucumatz, the Sovereign Plumed Serpent. Twice before they had tried to create a human being to be servant to the gods. One time the humans were made of clay and the other time of wood; but on both occasions the creatures so formed were stupid, without any intellect and without spirit. So, they were destroyed. As the dawn approached, the gods thought, "Morning has come for humankind, for the people of the face of the earth." Their great wisdom was revealed in the clear light; they discovered what was needed for human flesh—white corn and yellow corn. Four animals brought the food: fox, coyote, parrot, and crow. The animals showed the way to the citadel named Broken Place, Bitter Water Place. Here was a paradise filled with white and yellow corn and all the varieties of fruits and vegetables, including *pataxte* and *cacao*. The white and yellow corn were given to Xmucane, the divine Grandmother of the gods, and she ground the corn nine times. She washed the ground corn from her hands with water and this mixture made grease. The corn was used to make human flesh, the water made human blood, and the grease made human fat. From these staple foods were born the strength and vigor of the new beings.

SOURCE: From the *Popol Vuh: the Maya Book of the Dawn of Life and the Glories of Gods and Kings*; compiled from the translations of Tedlock (1985) and Figueroa (1986).

BOX 5.2
Classification of Human Societies

Anthropologists define four basic types of human societies based on social, economic, and political organization. *Bands* are characterized as basically egalitarian, with little overt economic or political differentiation. The amount of gender and sexual differentiation varies from one band to another. Bands often produce food by foraging, also called hunting and gathering. Bands usually number 25 to 50 people of all ages and sexes, and they are usually mobile. Classic examples of bands are the San (or !Kung) people of the Kahlahari desert and the Eskimo or Inuit of the arctic. *Tribes* are characterized as small groups of people (usually less than a few hundred living in any one community) who share common cultural values, including language and beliefs concerning their origin and history. Tribes have relative little political and economic stratification, rather being organized by kinship relations. Food production may include some foraging, but also may be by horticulture or agriculture (horticulture does not use animal labor or irrigation—agriculture may use one or both of these), by animal husbandry, or both. Classic example of tribes are the Yanomamo of South America and the Navajo of North America.

Chiefdoms have political stratification—the chief is usually the most powerful office. Chiefdoms are also comprised of relatively small social groups and may produce food by the same methods used in tribal societies. But, chiefdoms are characterized by an economic system of redistribution of goods. Gifts of food and other products are given to the chief, who redistributes these to the members of the social group. There is often competition between individuals in how much they will give to the chief and between chiefs in how much is redistributed. Well-known examples of chiefdoms are the Trobrianders of Melanesia and the Kpelle of West Africa. Finally, states are highly stratified in terms of social, economic, and political status. In states the political power is highly centralized, usually in the person of a king, high priest, or other single office. States attempt to control most aspects of the life of their citizens, which usually number in the thousands to millions. Permanent police forces and armies, which will use violent action, are needed for this control. Food production is highly centralized and organized. Usually, large labor forces are required to make and maintain massive irrigation works for agriculture. Excess production is used to pay taxes, and these taxes are used to feed and support those segments of the society not engaged in food production, including the military, artisans, and bureaucrats. Historical state-level societies are the Maya of Central America and Harappans of India. Living state societies are Japan, Germany, and the United States.

---

maize as the staple food in Maya society is emphasized in the creation story. People are corn, in both the literary and literal sense. Today, the living Maya people of Guatemala depend on maize for 80 percent of their energy intake. It is likely that the ancient Maya also consumed a large portion of their calories from maize, or more correctly from maize-based foods. Very little maize is eaten in Guatemala today. Instead people eat *tortillas, tamalitos, tamales, tacos, enchiladas, atoles* (a beverage), and many other foods and drinks made from *masa harina*. *Masa harina* is a flour made from maize that has been dried, ground, and processed by boiling in lime water (Fig. 5.1). Some of the "tortilla chips" sold in American supermarkets may be made from a flour like *masa harina*, but most brands are made from corn meal,

FIGURE 5.1 Xmucane grinding yellow and white corn to make people. The corn is processed by drying the seeds and then grinding with a *mano* (grinder) on a *matate* (grinding stone). Xmucane's behavior is a metaphor for the Maya people's dependence on agriculture and the technology required to process corn into nutritious foods.

which is ground maize without any further processing. The difference is vitally important in terms of nutrition and health, for without the processing a maize-based diet leads to death from pellagra. Later in this chapter the biochemical and nutritional properties of *masa harina* and the cause of pellagra are explained in greater detail.

The Maya, ancient and modern, do not live by *tortillas* alone. At Broken Place, Bitter Water Place (a supernatural site, located inside a mountain) all varieties of fruits and vegetables were found and given to people. A visit to any Maya marketplace today in Guatemala or Southern Mexico shows that dozens of species of fruits, vegetables, and dried mushrooms are sold, along with fresh and dried fish and meat. Archeological and ethnographic fieldwork substantiates the diversity of foods in the Maya diet over the past 1,000 years or more (Saenz de Tejada, 1988). Even *pataxte* and *cacao* were given to people by the gods (Fig. 5.2). These are fruits from which

FIGURE 5.2 Maya priest surrounded by cocoa pods. Cocoa was a sacred food, reserved for high-status Maya and for religious ritual (after Caraway, 1981).

cocoa and chocolate are made (chocoholics might recite an extra prayer of thanks to Sovereign Plumed Serpent before retiring tonight). A chocolate and hot pepper beverage used in Maya religious ritual was usually reserved for the royal family or other high status people. Thus, food is used not only to sustain the body but also to demarcate social position and as part of religious behavior.

We will return to the Maya food and nutrition later in this chapter, and we will see how these relate to Maya growth and demography. But first, we turn our attention to some of the basics of human nutrition.

NUTRIENTS VERSUS FOOD

Nutritional biochemists have determined that there are 50 essential nutrients required for growth, maintenance, and repair of the body. Essential nutrients are those substances that the body needs but cannot be manufactured by our bodies. These substances are divided into six classes: protein, carbohydrate, fat, vitamins, minerals, and water. Table 5.1 lists the essential nutrients in these categories. People do not usually eat the essential nutrients directly as pure chemicals; rather we eat food. This was certainly true for all of our animal ancestors throughout evolutionary history. Human foods come from five of the six the kingdoms of living organisms: plants, animals, fungi (e.g., mushrooms), protists (e.g., species of algae referred to as "seaweed"), and eubacteria (e.g., bacteria used in fermented foods). These organisms present us with a dazzling array of colors, flavors, odors, textures, shapes, and sizes. The sixth kingdom, Archaebacteria, are not eaten directly, but are essential in the diet of other species that people do eat. Herbivores, for example, have archaebacteria in their guts to digest the plant cellulose.

TABLE 5.1
Essential Nutrients of the Human diet

Carbohydrate: glucose

Fat or lipid: linoleic acid, linolenic acid

Protein
Amino acids: leucine, isoleucine, lysine, methionine, phenylalanine, threonine, tryptophan, valine, histidine
Nonessential amino nitrogen

Minerals
Macronutrients: calcium, phosphorus, sodium, potassium, sulfur, chlorine, magnesium
Micronutrients: iron, selenium, zinc, manganese, copper, cobalt, molybdenum, iodine, chromium, vanadium, nickel, silicon, boron, arsenic, fluorine

Vitamins
Fat soluble: A (retinol), D (cholecalciferol), E (tocopherol), and K
Water soluble: thiamin, riboflavin, niacin, biotin, folic acid, vitamin B_6 (pyridoxine), vitamin B_{12} (cobalamin), pantothenic acid, vitamin C (ascorbic acid)

Water

Source: After Guthrie and Picciano (1995).

Eating a Balanced Diet

How does a person know which foods to eat so that all of the essential nutrients are consumed in required amounts? Children learn what to eat because they are dependent on their parents, or other older individuals, to prepare their food. By tasting these foods and watching older people prepare them, children acquire patterns of food preferences, including what should not be eaten, under what social conditions a food should be eaten, and the ways to prepare foods. Thus, people learn what they like, for not all people eat all the same foods. For instance, some people in the United States eat chocolate-covered ants, but most Americans do not think of insects as food. In parts of Africa and South America, however, insects such as ants, termites, and beetle larva are food; in fact, they are considered delicacies! Yanomamo Indians of southern Venezuela cultivate certain plants in which they know beetles will lay their eggs. The Yanomamo harvest the beetle larvae and eat them raw or roasted (Chagnon, 1983). From a nutritional point of view insects are excellent sources of protein, fats, and some minerals. In fact, pound for pound grasshoppers have more protein than cattle or hogs; yet this fact is unlikely to encourage the sale of "grasshopper nuggets" at fast-food outlets in the United States.

Every group of people has developed a cuisine, that is, an assortment of foods and a style of cooking that is unique to that culture. Some examples are Italian cooking, Chinese cooking, and Mexican cooking. Even Americans have a cuisine, including foods such as corn-on-the-cob and hamburgers. Despite the differences in specific foods, the cuisine of each human culture provides all the essential nutrients. No one knows exactly how each cuisine developed to meet human biochemical requirements. One probability comes from experiments with nonhuman animals and with people. These experiments indicate that diets, or cuisines, are developed by learning to avoid foods that produce illness or feelings of malaise and seeking foods that promote feelings of well-being (Franken, 1988, p. 107). There are many other probabilities as to why each culture developed its own cuisine. Not all foods grow in all countries, for instance, maize originally comes from Central America and rice originally comes from Asia. But, most food preferences cannot be so easily explained. The isolation of many human cultures, exploration and contact between cultures, ethnic identity, and social, economic, political, and religious status are some of the reasons. Hindu culture, for example, specifies different cuisines for people of different castes. According to Burghart's (1990) analysis of Hindu dietary recommendations, not all castes can tolerate all foods. The intolerance is due to harmful reactions between the qualities of the food (such as animal meat) and the nature of the bodies of different caste members. Many other unknown factors occurring during thousands of years of human history are also responsible for the development of culture-specific cuisines.

From the foregoing, two universal observations about human nutrition can be made:

1. All people have the same basic biological requirements for nutrients.
2. Each culture has a unique cuisine that has the potential to satisfy these nutrient requirements.

Some additional universal features of human food systems, compiled by Pelto and Pelto (1983), extend this list:

3. People are extremely omnivorous, eating hundreds of different species of plants, animals, fungi, bacteria, and even algae.
4. People depend on systems of food transport from the place where foods are found or acquired to their place of consumption.
5. People make use of systems for food storage that protect the nutritional quality of foods from the time of their acquisition until the time of their consumption. That time period may last for months, even in premodern societies.
6. People expend great effort at food preparation, such as cooking, mixing, flavoring, and detoxifying natural ingredients, and depend on technology to do this preparation (e.g., the hand-axes and fire used by *Homo erectus* or the food processors and microwave ovens of *Homo sapiens*).
7. People share and exchange food regularly and have cultural rules that order such sharing and exchanges.
8. People have food taboos, that is, social proscriptions against the consumption of certain foods based on age, sex, state of health, religious beliefs, and other culturally defined reasons.

One final item must be included in this list of human food behavior.

9. People use foods for nonnutritional purposes, such as for medicine to cure or cause disease and as offerings in ritual or religious behavior (Etkin and Ross, 1997). In these contexts food may have some physiological function

(plants do contain active pharmaceutical compounds), but the foods also have symbolic meaning for the people using them.

Evidence from fossil and archaeological remains of human ancestors indicates that these nine universal features of human nutrition and food have been in existence for at least 35,000 years, and possibly more than 100,000 years. Yet, until this century, most foods were acquired locally. The most parsimonious way to account for these biological and cultural universals relating to food is to hypothesize that a common evolutionary history for all people shaped human nutritional requirements, food acquisition and processing systems, and food behavior. This is a hypothesis that can be verified or rejected by research.

SOURCES OF KNOWLEDGE

There are several kinds of data that may be considered in the study of the evolution of human nutrition. Archaeological and paleontological evidence provide the only direct data on what our ancestors ate and what effect diet may have had on our physical and behavioral evolution. However, studies of living primates and other mammals, living hunter-gatherer societies, and cross-cultural comparisons of cuisines provide indirect evidence that is useful in reconstructing human nutritional history.

Primate Studies

The living primates include prosimians, New World monkeys, Old World monkeys, Asian and African apes, and people. Fossil evidence indicates that all primates evolved from insectivore-like mammals that lived some 75 MYA. The geological context of these fossils indicates that the general habitat was tropical forest. Primate ancestors may have been those insectivores that moved into the flowering trees of these tropical forests to exploit insects and then the flowers, fruits, gums, and nectars of those trees (Cartmill, 1974; Conroy, 1990). The flowering plants and trees, called angiosperms, appear in the fossil record about 100 MYA, and their appearance opened up new habitats and ecological niches that promoted the coevolution of other species, including the primates.

The large number of essential nutrients required in the human diet is, likely, a consequence of the tropical primate diet. Tropical forests are characterized by having a high diversity of species but a low density of any given species. There are thousands of species of tropical trees, and at any one site there may be between 50 and 100 different species per hectare (Oates, 1987), but only a few trees of the same species may be growing on that hectare. With a wide variety of food resources, especially fruit, foliage, and insects, ancestral primates were able to obtain many vitamins, minerals, protein, carbohydrates, and fats from their diet. It is metabolically expensive, in terms of energy consumption, for an organism to manufacture its own nutrients (a process called autotrophism). Through mutation and selection, those early primates that reduced autotrophism and shifted to a dependency on dietary intake to meet nutrient needs would have gained an energetic advantage, one that could be put to use, for instance, to increase reproduction.

All mammals, for example, require vitamin C for maintenance and repair of body tissue, but only in some mammals, including most members of the order Primates, is vitamin C (ascorbic acid) an essential nutrient. About 25 MYA a mutation occurred in the metabolic pathway that produces vitamin C in primates ancestral to living monkeys, apes, and people. The glucose (carbohydrate energy) needed to convert biochemical precursors to ascorbic acid was released for use by other body systems (Scrimshaw and Young, 1978). The wide distribution of vitamin C sources in tropical environments and the ability of primates to utilize these sources assured that this nutrient could be supplied by the diet alone.

A Meat and Potatoes Diet

The human primate is unusual in that seeds, grasses, roots, and vertebrate meat are major components of both modern and ancient diets. Using published data, Harding (1981) divided naturally occurring tropical forest foods into eight categories and calculated the dietary frequency of each category for 131 species of primates (Table 5.2). People were not included in this analysis. The data show that variety is the rule, and most species included seven of the eight food categories in their diets ("grasses and roots" was the category most often missing). The chimpanzee, our closest living primate relative, eats foods from all eight categories. The human penchant to eat grasses and roots is so unusual that on a worldwide basis living people eat more grasses, such as wheat and maize, and roots, such as potatoes and manioc, than any other foods listed in Table 5.2. Seeds, grasses, and roots have their nutrients protected by cellulose membranes that must be mechanically broken. This can be done by mastication or by using technology. People, and our hominid ancestors dating back to *Australopithecus*, possess the anatomy (e.g., small canines, flattened molars, and enlarged pterygoid muscles—the muscles that move the lower jaw from side to side) that allows for a type of chewing called rotary grinding, which can break cellulose. People and our ancestors of the genus *Homo* are also dependent on technology (e.g., tools, fire) for food processing (Fig. 5.1).

Technology is also required for hunting at a level that makes vertebrate meat a regular part of the diet. For this reason, meat from vertebrates, either hunted or

TABLE 5.2
Dietary Frequency and Major Diet Components of 131 Primate Species

Food Category	Dietary Frequency	Major Component[a]
Fruit	90	45
Soft plant foods	79	9
Mature leaves	69	15
Invertebrates	65	23
Seeds	41	2
Hunted and scavenged vertebrates	37	0
Tree parts	34	0
Grasses and roots	13	5

[a]Percentage of species for which this category was identified as the major food.
Source: From Harding (1981).

scavenged, is not reported as major components for any nonhuman primate species. Of the 131 species surveyed, only some baboons and chimpanzees regularly hunt mammalian prey (Strum, 1981; Teleki, 1981). Vertebrate meat is nutrient dense and thus a valuable food source. How people have come to exploit meat as food is the subject of the next section of this chapter.

HUMAN DIET EVOLUTION

People have unusual dietary specializations because we have exceptional nutritional requirements compared with other primates. All primates require a relatively high quality diet, but people require a higher quality diet than any other species. Leonard and Robertson (1994) compared the diet of 5 human foraging societies (!Kung, Ache, Hiwi, Inuit, and Pygmies) to 72 nonhuman primates species and found that diet quality of the human groups was almost twice that of other primates of the same body size. The human ability to include seeds, roots, and meat in the diet increases quality, as these are nutrient-dense foods. Building on the research of Martin (1983), Leonard and Robertson (1994) show that the need for high diet quality is a consequence of the human brain being several times larger than expected for a primate our size (see Figs. 4.2, and 4.4). Using estimates of brain and body size for extinct hominids, Leonard and Robertson estimate that humanlike dietary requirements evolved with the appearance of the genus *Homo*. But, the only way to find out what our ancestors actually ate is to look at the evidence, which comes from the study of remains of hominids and their activities.

Archaeology and Fossil Studies

Archaeological methods "include the identification of edible materials, functional analyses of artifacts employed in food preparation, coprolite [fossil feces] analysis, information on paleohabitat, and analyses of [hominid] skeletal material" (Sillen and Kavanagh, 1982, p. 68). Paleontological data are derived from the kinds and percentages of fossil remains found at a site. Each type of evidence contributes some knowledge, but each has serious limitations. The association of hominid fossil remains with the skeletal remains of other fossil vertebrates may result from geological forces, such as rivers carrying dead carcasses to a central location or a volcanic eruption burying simultaneously a community of animals, rather than hominid food-gathering behavior. Early speculation by Dart (1957) that the bone accumulations at the South African cave sites of *Australopithecus* represented hominid hunting activity are now considered incorrect. Rather, Brain (1981) argues that the fossil remains, including the hominids, represent the activity of nonhominid carnivores, especially leopards, and geological forces. Brain names his book on this subject, aptly, *The Hunters or the Hunted*, and his conclusion is that the early hominids were the prey of the leopards.

Research conducted during the 1980s produced a 180 degree shift in the fossil evidence for the evolution of human hunting. In *The Descent of Man*, Charles Darwin (1871) proposed that hunting large game provided much of the selection pressure for human evolution. That view persisted through the 1960s, and the book *Man the Hunter* (Lee and DeVore, 1968) represented majority opinion that uniquely human characteristics, such as bipedalism, large brains, division of labor, sharing, intense parental investment in offspring, and reduced family size were the consequence of hunting and carnivory (see especially the chapter by Washburn and Lancaster in that volume). Implicit in this argument is the notion that the type of diet consumed by human ancestors played a significant role in the evolution of human biology and behavior. This notion is reasonable, but the explicit assumption of carnivory and hunting became less acceptable as existing evidence was reevaluated and new evidence discovered. The existing data, based on fossil and archaeological remains and the study of living hunting and gathering people, such as the !Kung and Australian Aborigines, showed that gathering and processing of plant foods were the main activities of tropical foragers. Moreover, women in living foraging societies provided most of the calories consumed by these people. These observations turned "man the hunter" into "woman the gatherer," and the hunting hypothesis was attacked for both lack of data and its male-biased implications (Zihlman, 1981).

The new evidence is based on analyses of bone and stone tool material associated with early hominids. Potts and Shipman (1981) used scanning electron microscope images of mammalian long bones dating to 1.7 MYA to show that cut marks produced by stone tools were incised above those made by carnivore teeth and the teeth of known scavengers, such as porcupines. Assuming that the order of markings reflects the order of use by hunters and scavengers, the hominids were the last to have at the bones, even after porcupines! Subsequent analysis shows that hominids may have been collecting bones for their marrow and brain tissue rather than for any meat still remaining on the surface of the bone (Binford, 1987). Marrow and brain are high in fat and protein, but few carnivores have the morphology necessary to break open large long bones. Hyenas do have the ability to exploit marrow and are formidable predators and scavengers but are most active at night (Schaller and Lowther, 1969). Hominids are most active during the day and thus could scavenge for carcasses with less threat from hyenas. The invention of stone tools, first manufactured by hominids about 2.2 MYA, may have been a dietary adaptation for extracting marrow. At Olduvai Gorge there are sites where the bones of large game animals (from gazelles to elephants) are found together with stone tools. The tools are called scrapers and choppers. Blumenschine and Cavallo (1992) report that the bones are mostly from limbs and skulls and that these are precisely the animal parts that only hyenas and tool-wielding hominids can crack open. Further, they report that one-half hour's work with a chopper can yield enough calories from the marrow and brain of a carcass the size of a wildebeest to meet an adult's daily energy requirements.

Hominids may also have scavenged for larger pieces of meat. Cavallo (1990) studied the ecology and behavior of leopards in Tanzania. Most carnivores, such as lions and hyenas, leave their prey on the ground and consume most of the internal organs and limb meat within a few hours after the kill. Leopards, in contrast, carry their kills up into trees and consume their prey over several days. The kill may even be left unattended for up to 10 hours, for other terrestrial carnivores ignore the carcasses hanging in trees. Cavallo believes that human ancestors may have scavenged these arboreal caches of meat. This speculation is supported by the South African cave evidence of Brain (1981) showing that australopithecines and leopards lived together and that the hominids were often the prey of the carnivores. Cavallo argues that by the time of the appearance of *Homo*, some hominids may have reversed the predator–prey relationship. There are reports that groups of baboons have killed leopards and confirmed observations of chimpanzees scavenging tree-cached leopard kills and taking and eating leopard cubs (Cavallo, 1990). Stone-tool-wielding hominids may have done the same on occasion.

Perhaps it was the occasional (or regular?) consumption of leopard that caused the hypervitaminosis A of a *H. erectus* individual. The skeleton is from the Koobi Fora formation, located on the eastern shore of Lake Turkana, Kenya, and is dated to 1.6 million years B.P. (Walker et al., 1982). Analysis of the skeleton indicates that it was female and has "striking pathology" in the long bones of the limbs. These bones have a deposit of abnormal coarse-woven bone, up to 7 mm thick in places, above the normal skeletal tissue on the outer surface of the bone. Walker and his colleagues consider many possible causes for this pathological bone growth and conclude that an overconsumption of vitamin A (hypervitaminosis A) is the most likely cause. Similar cases of hypervitaminosis A have occurred in arctic explorers who consumed the livers of polar bear and seal. The liver stores vitamin A and the liver of carnivores, who are at the top of the food chain, usually contain the greatest amounts of this vitamin. Walker et al. suggest that the cause of the bone pathology in this specimen of *H. erectus* was due to eating the liver of carnivorous animals.

Despite the evidence for scavenging animal carcasses and, perhaps, preying on leopards, the bulk of the hominid diet has almost always been from plants. The stone tools of the early hominids may also have been used to process hard-to-chew plant foods, such as seeds. Indeed, Walker (1981) and Kay (1985) studied the finer details of early hominid dental structure and tooth wear using the scanning electron microscope and tooth wear experiments. These researchers propose that the diet of the early hominids, including *Australopithecus* and *Homo habilis*, was largely herbivorous, including softer plant foods (leaves, fruits) as well as the tougher seeds and tubers. Given all the evidence now available, perhaps it is safest to say that the gathering of plants, insects, birds eggs, and other relatively immobile foods and the scavenging of marrow from carnivore kills typified early hominid food behavior.

The early hominid dietary pattern continues through *H. erectus* times. Binford (1987) reanalyzed fossil material from Torralba, a *H. erectus* site in Spain, and Zhoukoudian, a cave site near Bejing, China, spanning the period from *H. erectus* to *H. sapiens*. During the *H. erectus* period of occupation (250,000 to 450,000 years B.P.), both sites show evidence for the gathering of plant foods and scavenging, rather than for hunting. The animal bones at these sites appear to have been processed and consumed on the spot, rather than carried to any sort of "base camp." If this is so, then past theories about the evolution of human biology and behavior, including bipedalism, large brains, division of labor, sharing, and intense parental investment in offspring, that depended on hunting and "family style dining" at home bases have to be rejected. Binford (1984) states that convincing evidence for the regular hunting of big game does not appear in the fossil record until 90,000 years B.P. at the earliest.

Homo erectus added fire to its repertoire of technology. Fire, which may have been used as early as 1.4 MYA and was certainly controlled by 750,000 years B.P., provided warmth, light, protection, and a new way to process foods. Where and how cooking was invented is a matter for speculation. Cooking, by roasting or boiling, increases the nutritional benefit of many vegetable foods by helping to break down the cellulose of those foods that is indigestible to people. Fire may be used to open large seeds that resist even stone tools. Cooking, especially drying or smoking, helps to preserve foods for storage. Fire may also be used to get foods, especially by driving game toward a convenient killing site. All of these uses of fire did not appear simultaneously, and many appear to be the invention of *H. sapiens* rather than *H. erectus*. What is certain is that the controlled use of fire was a significant addition to hominid technology with profound consequences for nutritional status.

Fossilized Feces

Coprolite analysis might seem to provide unequivocal evidence of dietary habits, but it too is subject to misinterpretation. First, the coprolite must be identified unambiguously as being from a hominid. Second, coprolites can only verify that a particular substance was eaten. That substance may or may not have been a food item itself; it may have been ingested coincidentally along with a food, such as a seed or insect clinging to an animal or plant. Third, only indigestible substances will be found in feces, and those substances must be suitable candidates for fossilization to be preserved in a coprolite. Thus, coprolite analysis may provide a very biased picture of the true dietary intake. Even so, considerable information has been obtained about the diet of prehistoric humans and limited information about the diet of hominid species ancestral to modern people. The animal affinity of desiccated coprolites can be determined by placing the specimen in a trisodium phosphate solution for 72 hours. Human coprolites turn the solution an opaque dark brown or black color, and no other species produces this effect (Bryant and Williams-Dean, 1975). Other characteristics of human feces are inclusions of charcoal and the presence of undigested animal parts from a wide variety of species. Charcoal comes from cooking food over a wood fire. Since people cook their food and other animals do not, the presence of charcoal in feces is indirect evidence for a unique human behavior. People also have an eclectic diet compared with most other mammals, so undigested parts from a wide variety of species is another indicator of the human affinities of a coprolite.

More than 1,000 paleoindian coprolites from the American southwest have been identified and analyzed. One group of specimens was collected from Texas sites that date from 800 B.C. to A.D. 500, representing the temporary camps of hunting and gathering peoples (Bryant, 1974). By comparing the pollen content of the coprolites with that found in the adjacent soils, it was determined that the people had consumed high quantities of flowers. Because the physical characteristics of flower pollens are unique to each species, it was possible to determine that flowers of agave, sotol, yucca, prickly pear cactus, gilia, and leadtree were popular foods. Also found were remains of wild onion bulbs, bark, grasshoppers, fish, small reptiles, and snails. Although not the current cuisine of Texas, this diet is typically human in its diversity of species. The flower pollen even provides a time frame for the occupation of the sites, spring and early summer.

The oldest verified coprolites of a hominid species are from the *H. erectus* site of Terra Amata located on the French Mediterranean. These coprolites may be as old as 300,000 B.P. and they are heavily mineralized. They have only a slight reaction to trisodium phosphate rehydration (Bryant and Williams-Dean, 1975). The specimens contain sand grains, charcoal, and mollusk shell fragments. The sand and shell are expected since Terra Amata is a beach-front site, and the charcoal helps establish that foods were cooked before consumption (maybe evidence for a prehistoric clam bake!).

Trace Element and Stable Isotope Analysis

A general picture of the relative amounts of plant and animal food in the diet may be available from chemical analyses of stable isotopes and trace elements in skeletal remains. The ratio of delta ^{15}nitrogen ($\delta\ ^{15}N$) to delta ^{13}carbon ($\delta\ ^{13}C$) is one widely used method. The stable isotope of carbon, $\delta\ ^{13}C$, can determine if foods in the diet were based on plants using the C_3 or the C_4 photosynthetic pathway. The more $\delta\ ^{13}C$ in a skeleton, the more C_4 plants in the diet. The C_4 plants include the domesticated grains maize, millet, and sugarcane, while C_3 plants include virtually all those growing wild in temperate regions. The amount of the stable nitrogen isotope $\delta\ ^{15}N$ in skeletons indicates an animal's place within the food web. The amount of $\delta\ ^{15}N$ is higher as more animal protein is included in the diet. Figure 5.3 illustrates the relationship of these stable isotopes to diet in several mammalian species. This method is most useful when analyzing human skeletons during the transition to agriculture, that is, during the past 10,000 years.

Another method of diet reconstruction compares the ratio of the trace element strontium to calcium (Sr/Ca) in bone. A higher ratio indicates that more

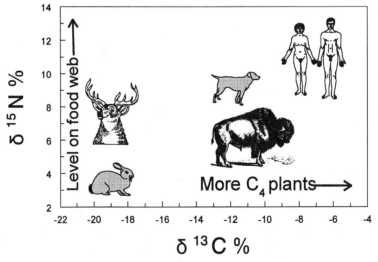

FIGURE 5.3 Delta ^{13}C and delta ^{15}N values plotted for human and other mammalian bone samples from several archaeological sites in the Sierra Blanca region of New Mexico. Sites date from A.D. 800 to A.D. 1400. Humans eat higher on the food chain and eat more C_4 plants than any other mammal in the sample. The human condition is due to both hunting other animal species and the consumption of grasses, including cultivated maize, and other C_4 plants. Based on data from Katzenberg (1992).

plant food than animal food was consumed by the animal. This method may help us understand more ancient human diets and was used to analyze fossil remains of archaic and modern *H. sapiens* from sites in Israel, dating between 70,000 and 10,000 B.P. (Schoeninger, 1982). The purpose of the study was to see if a change in diet correlates with the change in human form, from the more robust skeletons of archaic people to the more gracile skeletons of modern people. It was found that Sr/Ca ratios in bone increased with time, suggesting more plant food in the diet, but the increase occurred 20,000 years after the modern human form appears in the fossil record. It seems, then, that the morphological transition from archaic to modern *H. sapiens* was not due to the utilization of new foods. This finding attests, once again, to the ancient nature of the human diet. Rather, the morphological transition was due to improvements in the technology for both acquiring and processing existing foods. These improvements reduced human physical labor and resulted in a less muscular body and a more gracile skeleton.

Isotopes and Social Status

Although caution must be exercised in the interpretation of Sr/Ca ratios in living or fossil bone, the technique has proven useful in some cases. In archaeological samples of human skeletons from Mexico, Schoeninger (1979) found a strong negative correlation between indicators of social status and strontium in bone. Burials with greater amounts of high-status grave goods had lower Sr/Ca ratios than burial with fewer or no high-status grave goods. This suggests strongly that high-status individuals consumed more meat and lower status individuals consumed more plant foods in their diet.

Using stable isotopes preserved in human bone, a team of archaeologists and biological anthropologists found that high social status does not always lead to more meat in the diet. In highland Ecuador, in a suburb of the present capitol of Quito, there is an archeological site called La Florida. The site dates from A.D. 100 to A.D. 450 and includes well-preserved burials of 9 high-status individuals of the ruling elite and 23 low-status individuals buried along with the elites. Some of the low-status people were buried alive, and historical sources indicate they were members of a hereditary servant class, essentially slaves, who served their masters in life and, apparently, in death. Ubelaker et al. (1995) analyzed these skeletal remains for age at death, sex, and stable isotopes of carbon and nitrogen. Ubelaker and colleagues found that the skeletons ranged in age from 5 to 50 years at the time of death, with children and adolescents in both the elite and the low-status samples. Age at death has no effect on the levels of stable isotopes in these skeletons, but there is a statistically significant difference in the $\delta^{13}C$ levels between the two groups. The only C_4 plant, that is, the only domesticated plant, that ancient people of highland Ecuador consumed in quantity was maize. The elites have higher levels of $\delta^{13}C$, indicating they consumed more maize than the low-status individuals. There was no difference between the two groups for $\delta^{15}N$ levels, indicating equal amounts of animal protein in the diet. Ubelaker et al. point out that these findings contradict the conventional wisdom that elites always ate more animal protein while the low-status people ate mostly vegetable-based foods. The authors explain that the extra maize consumed by the elites was in the form of an expensive and politically restricted food called beer. Elites controlled the production and consumption of beer. Maize beer was produced by the chief's household and was doled out to the commoners at feasts in return for their labor. Chiefs also paid tribute to each other in the form of beer and offered copious amounts of beer at royal funerals. Chiefs were buried with many ceramic vessels, and at La Florida 70.5 percent of these were devoted to the brewing and serving of maize beer.

STUDIES OF LIVING HUNTERS AND GATHERERS

Today, 99.9 percent of people derive their food from some form of agriculture. However, from the time of the *Australopithecus* until about 10,000 years ago, a time period that covers 99 percent of human evolution, all hominids lived in bands and produced food by foraging—the gathering, scavenging, and, more recently, hunting of wild foods. Most human physical traits, and many behavioral propensities, evolved during the time that hominids lived as hunters and gatherers. This includes our current human dietary requirements, adaptations for food acquisition and processing, biocultural responses to food, and patterns of growth and reproduction. Studies of the few remaining cultures of hunting and gathering peoples offer an indirect view of that ancient style of life, now nearly extinct. These ethnographic and ecological studies compliment the information derived from paleontological and archaeological sources.

Foragers are a diverse group geographically and culturally, ranging from the arctic Inuit and Eskimo, to the tropical forest Ache (Paraguay), to the dry scrub San (Africa), and to the desert Australian Aborigines. Yet, the research shows some consistencies in behavior and diet. The diversity of food resources utilized is high among gathering and hunting peoples compared with agriculturalists. The !Kung San of southern Africa, for instance, eat 105 species of plants and 144 species of animals (Lee, 1984). The Australian North Queensland Aborigines exploit 240 species of plants and 120 species of animals (Gould, 1981). The Ache forage on fewer species, about 90 types of plants and animals (Hill and Hurtado, 1989). Even the Dogrib, residing in the subarctic of Canada, gather 10 species of plants and 33 species of animals (Hayden, 1981). That is a small food base for hunters and gatherers but still a large number relative to agriculturalists who, on a worldwide basis, subsist largely on four species of plants and two species of animals. Of nine species of staple plant foods, wheat, rice, potatoes, and maize together account for 1,680 of the 2,284 million metric tons consumed (sorghum, sweet potatoes, barley, millet, and cassava are the other five staples; Garine, 1994). Of the animal foods, cattle and hogs account for 80 out of every 100 metric tons of domesticated animal meat. Poultry, lamb, goat, buffalo, and horse make up the bulk of the remaining 20 metric tons (Bogin, 1985).

A second common feature is that gathered foods (e.g., plants, insects, birds eggs, and turtles) are the primary subsistence base in most foraging societies. Lee (1968) compared 58 forager groups and found that the primary subsistence source was gathering for 29, fishing for 18, and hunting for 11. Ten of the hunting groups and 16 of the fishing groups lived north or south of the 40° parallel. Thus, not only is gathering the most common subsistence pattern, it is correlated with tropical, subtropical, and low-temperate habitats. Such habitats were the home for all species of hominids until the middle to late Paleolithic period.

TABLE 5.3
Demographic Characteristics of Forager Groups

Group (Location)	Group Size	Population Density/100 mi²	Frequency of Moves
Nootka (Canada)	1,500	200	180 days
Andamanese (Asia)	45	200	60–180 days
Paliyans (India)	24	200	As needed, ~45 days?
!Kung San (Africa)	20	41	14–21 days
Hazda (Africa)	9	40	14 days
G/wi San (Africa)	55	16	21 days
Ache (South America)	48	8	daily, 0.143 day
Guayaki (South America)	16	7	3 days
Western Desert Australians	20	3	7–14 days
Mistassini (Canada)	15	1	180 days

Source: After Hayden (1981); Ache data from Hill and Hurtado (1989).

Often, the use of many species for subsistence is correlated with the high diversity, low density, or seasonality of food items in the environment. In habitats where low density is combined with the wide dispersal of foods, foragers must be mobile and live in small groups. Demographically speaking, a small mobile social group is a third typical feature of forager societies, but as shown in Table 5.3, it is not a universal feature. Leaving aside the Nootka, average group size ranges from 9 to 55 and average densities range from 1 to 200 people per 100 square miles. Mobility ranges from daily movement from camp to camp in the case of the Ache to seasonal sedentariness at one camp (e.g., a winter lodge) in the case of the Mistassini (hunters of the Canadian boreal forests).

The Ache are unusual in their daily movement, but contemporary Ache live at agricultural mission settlements and only travel on foraging trips 25 to 35 percent of the year (Hill and Hurtado, 1989). Based on foods consumed, the purpose of these trips appears to be hunting, with up to 66 percent of calories consumed while traveling coming from mammalian meat. Thus, their daily movement may be the result of intense hunting in a short period rather than a typical pattern of mobility. The Nootka are also unusual due to both large group size and density. The Nootka lived on the Pacific coast of Canada. Oceanic conditions, high rainfall, and varied terrestrial topography make this region extremely abundant in plants and animals. The Nootka had available a nearly inexhaustible supply of food, so much food that of 16 forager studied by Hayden (1981) the Nootka have the longest list of edible plants and animals that were, in fact, avoided. Their diverse and reliable food base allowed the Nootka to form large camps to exploit seasonal foods (such as salmon and whales), maintain permanent villages, and maintain relatively large populations and population density.

The high density of the Andamanese and Paliyans is due to both food availability and their being restricted to relatively small areas. The Andamanese live on an island rich in food resources from both land and sea. The Paliyans (of southern India) live in a rich habitat capable of supporting high densities and are surrounded by agriculturalists, which means they live, effectively, within an ecological island. All the other groups have much lower population densities. Even with all this culture-to-culture variability there are some general trends in this small sample of foragers; larger groups tend to be more densely populated, and larger, or more densely populated, groups tend to move less often. For the statistically minded reader, the Pearson correlation coefficients between the three variables—size, density, and moves—vary from 0.51 to 0.58, indicating a moderate association between the variables.

A fourth common feature is that all foragers depend on technology to procure, process, and store food. Technology ranges from simple to complex, both in amount and sophistication. Savanna and desert foragers, such as the !Kung and Australians, use a digging stick to get at roots and tubers that are hidden from view or not possible to extract using hands alone. The digging stick seems simple, but that tool more than doubles the calories available to the people who use it as compared with non-human primates living in similar habitats (Washburn and Moore, 1980). The !Kung also use the bow and arrow to hunt large game. The bow is lightweight and not, by itself, capable of delivering a lethal blow to prey. Rather, the shaft of the arrow carries a dose of a neurotoxin that paralyzes the animal without spoiling the meat. The toxin is derived from the larva of a beetle, which must be specially processed to be effective. The simplicity of the material culture of the !Kung belies the effectiveness and sophistication of their system of hunting. At the other extreme of material culture are the Inuit and Eskimo, who possess dozens of pieces of equipment for hunting or fishing, including hooks, spears, sleds, knives, and specialized clothing. The relative complexity of Inuit and Eskimo material culture is required to extract food from a harsh environment.

Food preparation techniques include cooking (e.g., boiling, steaming, roasting, frying), soaking, grinding and grating, pounding, drying, fermenting, and putrefying (as in "aged" meat). Many human foods are poisonous prior to preparation by one or more of these techniques. Acorns and horse chestnuts, eaten by many North American Indian foragers, are toxic when raw. Manioc, a root crop, is a dietary staple of many African societies. Manioc is poisonous until it is processed. The toxins in all these foods are removed by leaching, that is, by boiling them in water and then allowing the food to dry prior to consumption. Rhubarb and cashews, eaten by some people in modern industrial societies, are also toxic until cooked by boiling or roasting. Finally, food storage by drying, caching, and, where possible, freezing or salting is common to many forager groups. It is essential to remember that dependence on technology for food procurement, the processing of food, and food storage are all behaviors unique to the human species and found universally in all known human cultures.

Sharing and the division of labor comprise a fifth characteristic of foragers. Much has been made of both food sharing and division of labor because these two behaviors were considered as necessary consequences of the "hunting hypothesis" for human evolution (Issac, 1978; Washburn and Lancaster, 1968). The basic premise is that male hominids ranged widely to hunt large game while female hominids, encumbered by pregnancy and dependent children, gathered plant foods in a smaller area. Both sexes returned to a home base and shared the fruits (and ribs) of their labor with each other and the children. That hypothesis is out of favor currently, because there is no fossil evidence for the type of big game hunting that requires sharing and division of labor to be effective prior to the appearance of *H. sapiens*. Nevertheless, the fact that all known living hunters and gatherers share some food, even small game and vegetables in many cultures, and have some division of labor indicates that this is a universal human nutritional adaptation.

Although universal, the degree to which sharing occurs is not constant in all cultures. Some forager groups share food regularly and have cultural rules to encourage food exchange. The !Kung and Ache, for example, prohibit hunters from keeping their own kills; rather the meat must be given to others, often a respected elder, for distribution to all members of the band. Ache women who share plant food are given praise by others, and "children are taught that stinginess is the worst trait a person can have" (Hill and Hurtado, 1989, p. 439). In contrast, several Australian groups and the Paliyans share less regularly. Hayden's (1981) review of these cultures shows that Australian men usually ate all the game they hunted in the bush, rarely bringing meat back to camp for their wives and daughters. Women and children might eat more than 50 percent of their total food intake while foraging (Hayden calls this "snacking") and would bring back to camp only those foods needing processing. The Paliyans also practiced snacking while foraging and brought back little food to be shared at the camp.

Sharing and division of labor may best be viewed as behaviors that (1) reduce the effects of unpredictability and variance in food supply and (2) increase reproductive fitness, meaning increase the healthy development of the individual and her or his likelihood to reproduce. Most foragers live in social bands that are often an extended family. Arctic foragers such as the Aleut and Eskimo are examples, as these peoples lived in extended nuclear families and each "family" comprised a hunting unit (Shephard and Rode, 1996). Men would undertake the hunt for large mammalian prey. Women would dress and prepare meat for consumption. In maritime areas, adult men and women would fish together. By dividing the social band into working groups based on sex and age, more of the necessary subsistence tasks may be accomplished in a shorter period of time. In tropical and temperate regions, adults may gather plant foods, honey, insects, and other small animal foods and hunt larger animal prey. Children may remain at the camp in age-graded play groups, with older children caring for younger children, or may accompany their parents so as to learn foraging techniques (Bogin, 1999a). In extreme environments children may provide significant amounts of foraged food, as they do in Hadza society (Blurton-Jones, 1993). Men often range over larger areas in search of food and hunt larger prey than do women, and this serves to further increase the total supply and diversity of food. Using statistical analysis and mathematical models of food behavior among the Ache, Hill and Hurtado (1989) find that division of labor and sharing results in an 80 percent increase in nutritional status and nearly a three-fold increase in the predictability and regularity of daily food intake.

Reproductive fitness, measured by the number of offspring that survive to reproductive age, is increased by division of labor and sharing. Most animals must acquire all their own food. A few primates, including baboons and chimpanzees, are known to share some food, but only in a limited way compared with people. Chimpanzees are more like people in terms of reproductive biology; that is, both species take a relatively long time to reach sexual maturity and typically bear one offspring at a time. As shown in the previous chapter, this places a tremendous reproductive constraint, which I called a demographic dilemma, upon the chimpanzee. People living in traditional hunting and gathering societies delay repro-ductive age even longer than chimpanzees but do not wait as long between successful births. It was shown that the !Kung of southern Africa average 3.6 years between successful birth and average 4.7 live births per woman. Women in another hunter-gatherer society, the Hadza (Blurton-Jones et al., 1992), have even shorter intervals between successful births, stop nursing about one year earlier, and average 6.15 births per woman. The Ache, foragers of a tropical rainforest and living part time on mission settlements, average only 3.1 years between births and 7.2 births per woman (Hill and Hurtado, 1989). Compared with all other primates, people are the reproductive champions. The evolution of the special human characteristics of childhood are part of this reproductive advantage. But childhood is beneficial only because human parents, male and female, regularly share food with their offspring.

This must be viewed ecologically as both a feeding and reproductive strategy, for human adults are able to achieve relatively high reproductive outputs in a rel-atively short period of time. Food sharing is a central part of human reproduction as it leads to greater reliability and predictability of food intake, better growth of individuals, improved nutritional status, and increased reproduction and survival of the young. Given these benefits, it is easy to see how food sharing evolved by natural selection during the course of human history. But as is often the case in evolution-ary biology, there is no such thing as a "free lunch."[1] Every evolutionary change involves a balance of positive and negative trade-offs. One trade-off faced by nearly all foragers is high mortality for infants and children. Russian observers noted the age at death between the years 1822 and 1836 for one Aleut population living on Fox Island in the eastern Aleutian Islands. The average population size during this period was 225 women and 266 men. About 100 deaths occurred to girls and boys between the ages of one to four years, which is about 20 percent of all mortality (Laughlin, 1972). Other studies found that up to 40 percent of all deaths occurred before age five years (Shephard and Rode, 1996). This high mortality rate at such young ages kept the total population size stable and small, even though women aver-aged six pregnancies. The high infant and childhood mortality also resulted in a more stable population pyramid, that is, with as many people at older ages as at young ages. After World War II, the introduction of western medical care, especially anti-biotics, reduced much of this infant and child mortality. Women also reduced the lactation period, from up to 36 months to less than 18 months. This increased fer-tility rates—up to 7.9 pregnancies per women in some groups are reported—and with fewer early deaths, population size rapidly increased. Population pyramids also changed, becoming "bottom heavy," as in the case of many poorer nations. After 1970, fertility rates declined, so that by the 1990s women averaged between 2.3 and 4.0 births (Shephard and Rode, 1996).

The experience of arctic foragers is typical of many other groups that made the transition from traditional to western lifestyles. Changes in values and behavior concerning fertility are just one of the trade-offs associated with this transition.

---

[1] The so-called free lunch was offered at saloons in nineteenth-century United States. The lunch, consisting of a small sandwich, was "free" with the purchase of a beer or other alcoholic beverage. The phrase "there is no such thing as a free lunch" is an expression meaning that any current benefit requires some payment, or other trade-off, currently or in the future.

Later in this chapter we will see that the reproductive benefits of the evolution of human nutrition also led to less desirable consequences of excessively short birth intervals and too many births in some agricultural and industrial populations. These groups had to decide between several trade-offs in order to maintain demographic and social stability.

SUMMARY OF EVIDENCE FOR THE EVOLUTION OF HUMAN NUTRITION

The human place in nature as primates explains our broad requirements of essential nutrients. Fossil and archaeological evidence accounts for the development of cuisines and the technology for food acquisition, preparation, and storage. The study of living hunting and gathering peoples compliments and supports these other sources of evidence. Six features of food, behavior, and demography are typically found in hunting and gathering societies: (1) a high diversity of food types, (2) greater dependence on gathering rather than hunting, (3) small mobile social groups, (4) dependence on technology for acquiring and processing foods, (5) division of labor and sharing, and (6) stable population size with high infant and childhood mortality balancing fertility.

DIET, AGRICULTURAL DEVELOPMENT, AND DEMOGRAPHY

As stated earlier in this chapter, very few people still live as foragers (less than 0.01 percent). Most people alive today either grow their own food and raise their own domesticated animals or derive their food from people who do so. The initial shift from foraging to horticulture and agriculture is very recent, certainly not more than 12,000 years old. The change to growing food spread slowly, and for the vast majority of humanity the dependence on agriculture is less than 5,000 years old. In an evolutionary sense, this is a very short period of time. Our bodies and our social behavior were shaped by millions of years of hunting and gathering, and we remain adapted for the life and times of foragers. Not surprisingly, the shift to growing our own food resulted in some problems. Some of the nutritional problems of societies in today's world are (1) a narrow food base, leading to deficiencies for some essential nutrients; (2) an inadequate supply of food (i.e., undernutrition) for about 60 percent of the world's population, especially the poor in the least developed countries; and (3) an oversupply of energy, leading to obesity and related diseases in the rich nations and, increasingly, among the more affluent segments of the population in the poor nations. The immediate causes of these problems include a host of social problems, such as poverty and other economic inequalities, political unrest (such as civil and ethnic wars), inadequate water management, and unregulated population growth. Although these are significant proximate causes for the world's current nutritional crisis, there is a more fundamental explanation that had its origin at the end of the Paleolithic period.

Agriculture and the Decline of Human Nutrition and Health

The major culprit of the nutritional and demographic dilemma is agriculture. More recently, industrialization and urbanization have compounded the effects of agriculture on the nutritional status, demography, and health of human populations. Agriculture, industrialization, and urbanization are often stated to be the hallmarks of "progress" of the human species. Though progressive in a technological sense, each of these achievements had negative consequences for human nutrition and health. There were also consequences for human populations in terms of demography and growth.

There is much evidence from the poorer nations of the world that the food production systems of rural people correlate strongly with their nutritional status. In a classic study of Indonesian food production, Geertz (1963) shows that simple horticulturalists living on the outer islands, such as the Moluccas, have the most abundant variety and amount of foods. In contrast, food shortages and frank malnutrition are most common on the inner islands, such as Java, especially in the areas of intensive rice agriculture. The inner islands produce more total food but also have more people and more malnutrition. Whyte (1974) extended these findings to much of tropical Asia. Whyte's analysis shows that foragers, horticulturalists, and fishing societies have diversified diets but often inadequate calorie intakes. These societies are better nourished, however, than peoples practicing mixed agriculture-pastoralism and intensive irrigation agriculture, especially of rice. The agriculturalists suffer marginal to serious malnutrition for total calories and many vitamins, minerals, and protein.

The dilemma of modern agricultural societies has deep historical roots. Studies of archaeological populations show that several indicators of biological stress increase with the transition from foraging to horticulture and agriculture (Cohen and Armelagos, 1984). These stress indicators include bone lesions due to anemia (called porotic hyperostosis), deficits in enamel formation in teeth (hypoplasias), loss of bone tissue from the skeleton, bone lesions due to infectious disease, such as tuberculosis (called periosteal reaction), and reduced skeletal growth in children and adults (Goodman et al., 1988). The Dickson Mounds site of the Illinois River Valley provides a classic example. From A.D. 950 to A.D. 1300 the human population of that area changed from mobile foragers to sedentary intensive agriculturalists. During this short time period, "the shift in subsistence led to a fourfold increase in iron deficiency anemia (porotic hyperostosis) and a threefold increase in infectious disease (periosteal reaction). The frequency of individuals with both iron deficiency and infectious lesions increased from 6% to 40% (Goodman et al., 1988, p. 180).

The incidence of **enamel hypoplasias** (malformations of the tooth crown, which include pitting, linear furrowing, or complete lack of enamel) also increases from the forager to the agricultural period. These dental deficiencies occur when malnutrition or disease disrupt the secretion of enamel-forming material. For the permanent teeth, that process takes place during infancy and childhood. Thus, enamel hypoplasias leave a permanent record in the teeth of nutritional or disease stress that people experienced in early life. In the Dickson Mound skeletal material the prevalence of hypoplasia increases with time, going from 45 to 80 percent of individuals affected. Furthermore, the number of hypoplasias is correlated with demographic indicators, such as mortality. Individuals with one hypoplasia died, on average, five years earlier than people with no hypoplasias. With two or more hypoplasias age at death was reduced by nine years. Since people's teeth form in a fixed pattern that is virtually the same in all human beings, it is possible to correlate the frequency of hypoplasias found on different teeth with the age of the individual when the disease stress occurred. At the Dickson Mound that correlation indicates that infants and young children were especially subject to health stress at the age of weaning (about two to four years old). Deficiencies in the weaning diet, combined with increased exposure to infections and other diseases at the time of weaning, were very likely the cause of the hypoplasias (Goodman et al., 1988).

With the development of agriculture the Dickson Mound people shifted from a diverse food base to one dependent on maize. The emphasis on monoculture reduced the supply of essential nutrients, especially amino acids and vitamins not found in maize, and this compromised the health of the people. Compounding these nutritional problems was rapid population growth. Despite a lowering in the average age at death at the Dickson mound site, population sizes increased due to a shorter interval between births (about two years as compared with four years in forager populations). Larger populations and sedentarism gave rise to the conditions favorable for the spread of infectious disease, and the poor nutritional state of the people made them more susceptible to these diseases.

Political Economy, Food, and Health

There are other archaeological examples of decline in human health with the spread of agriculture, including sites in Africa, the Middle East, Latin America, and Asia. But, not all people living in agricultural societies suffered health problems. The social organization and political economy of each society played a major role in the distribution of resources, especially food and health care. One example comes from nearly three decades of research on ancient and medieval Nubia (Van Gerven et al., 1995). Nubia is a region of the Nile River valley from southern Egypt to northern Sudan, bounded by the First Cataract at Asswan to about the Fourth Cataract in modern Sudan. For the past 5,000 years the people of Nubia lived by the agricultural production of "sorghum, millet (locally known as *dura*), barley, beans, lentils, peas, dates, and wheat. In addition, a few cattle, sheep, and pigs were kept, but animal products appear to have been a minor part of the Nubian diet" (Van Gerven et al., 1995, p. 469). While the dietary base remained stable for millennia, the political base of Nubia changed many times. From about 350 B.C. to A.D. 350, called the Meroitic period, there was political unification of all Nubia under a centralized, militaristic state society. The Meroitic state had great wealth, great urban centers, but also great social stratification. The following Ballana period (ca. A.D. 350 to A.D. 550) was politically decentralized, with people living in smaller, but more self-sufficient settlements. Overall, health status, as revealed from skeletal and dental indicators, was better in the Ballana period than in Meroitic times. People also lived longer during the Ballana period.

By the end of the sixth century A.D. Nubia was again unified under a series of Christian kingdoms. The Christian period ended in A.D. 1365, following the ascension of a Moslem prince to the throne in A.D. 1323. Van Gerven and colleagues analyzed skeletons from a Christian period cemetery located in the town of Kulubnarti, near the Dal Cataract. The early Christian period was highly central- ized and socially stratified, and the people of Kulubnarti "were but a small and con- tributing satellite to a centralized and distant authority" (Van Gerven et al., 1995, p. 478). The people contributed taxes in the form of food surplus and labor. By the late Christian period, the central state authority was in decline and satellite com- munities like Kulubnarti were essentially ignored and independent. The population of Kulubnarti reverted to subsistence agriculture and local political control and were free of taxation. The skeletons from the cemetery show that infant and child mor- tality was greatest during the early Christian period. Enamel hypoplasias occurred at earlier ages and were more frequent, and there was more evidence of anemia during early Christian times. Late Christian period people suffered from all of these indicators of poor health too, but less so. All of this shows, again, that the political economy of a society interacts with the food base to shape the pattern of health of the people.

CONQUEST, FOOD, AND HEALTH

Colonization of the New World, Africa, and Asia by the Spanish and other Euro- peans introduced new plants, animals, foods, and diseases. Europeans also intro- duced a new political economy. Generally, the diet and health of native people suffered [Larsen and Milner (1994) provide reviews of the biological effects of New World conquest]. The colonizers, however, also suffered from the introduction of new foods to their diets. **Pellagra** is a nutritional disease caused by a lack of niacin (vitamin B_3). The word pellagra is Italian, meaning rough or painful skin, and was used to describe that disease when it first appeared in the eighteenth century in that country. In Spain the same disease also appeared at that time but was called *mal del sol* ("sun disease"). Pellagra's classic symptoms are the four D's—dermatitis, diarrhea, depression, and dementia. The early symptom of light-sensitive dermati- tis gave the condition its Spanish name. However, sunlight only aggravated the real cause, a diet based on the consumption of highly refined maize. Maize was domesticated in the New World and exported to Europe after contact with native American people. Maize grew well in Europe and quickly became an abundant and inexpensive food that replaced many traditional grains. This was true especially in the diet of the poor of southern Europe, which, by the 1700s, was predominantly based on maize, molasses (derived from sugarcane, which is of Asian origin), and salt pork.

Maize is naturally low in the amino acids lysine, tryptophan, and cystine and in the vitamin niacin. Molasses and salt pork are also deficient in these same nutri- ents. Milling the maize removes the husk and germ, further reducing the niacin content, from 2.4 to 1.4 mg per cup. The minimum daily need for niacin in adults is set at 13 mg per day by the World Health Organization. For cultural reason, Europeans preferred the bleached white appearance of the highly milled maize, as it imitated the more expensive wheat flour consumed by the wealthy. For the poor, who followed a monotonous diet based on maize flour, pellagra was the result. Pellagra spread to the United States as European people, and diets, became the dominant cultural force. It was confined to cotton-producing and cotton-milling areas in the southern states were the maize, molasses, and salt pork diet was common. Even as late as 1918 an estimated 10,000 deaths from pellagra occurred in the United States, and 100,000 cases were reported.

Hospitals and mental institutions treated the disease as an endemic condition (endemic diseases are peculiar to a people or a region). At that time the cause of pellagra was blamed on heredity, unsanitary living conditions, or an infectious agent in spoiled maize (Guthrie and Picciano, 1995). In an experiment conducted in 1917, inmates in a U.S. prison were asked to switch from the normal prison diet to the maize, molasses, and salt pork diet in exchange for reprieve. After five months the prisoners developed pellagra, and the nutritional cause of the disease was established. Not until 1937, however, was the specific cause, niacin deficiency, discovered.

People of the Corn

In the Americas, where maize was first domesticated, some populations received 80 percent of their total caloric intake from maize. The living Maya, the people of the corn, still consume this amount of maize. Yet, pellagra was unknown in the New World prior to European contact. The reason for this is that New World people used the whole grain of the maize, including the germ, and prepared the maize in a manner that enhanced the tryptophan content and the available niacin. Throughout Central America, Mexico, and those regions of the United States where maize was (or is) the dietary staple, the following method of preparation is commonly used. Ears of maize are dried and the kernels removed from the cob. The kernels are ground by hand (minimal milling, see Fig. 5.1) and placed in a pot of water. Ground limestone (calcium carbonate) is added to the pot and the contents are boiled. The mixture is removed and dried until it forms a malleable dough (called *masa* in Latin American Spanish) that can be shaped into foods such as *tortillas* and *tamales*. The limestone is an alkali and reacts chemically with the maize and the water to increase the tryptophan content of the maize by hydrolysis (Katz et al., 1974). In turn, tryptophan is a precursor for niacin, that is, in the human body tryptophan can be converted into niacin by metabolic processes. The rate of conversion is about 60 mg of tryptophan for 1.0 mg of niacin (Guthrie and Picciano, 1995). The limestone used to make *masa* also adds calcium to the diet. A cup of dry corn meal (unenriched) provides 1.4 mg of niacin and 8 mg of calcium, while a cup of dry *masa* flour contains 4.8 mg of niacin and 211.6 mg of calcium. Thus, a diet in which 80 percent of the calories are derived from *masa*-based foods provides sufficient niacin and calcium.

Maya Diet and Demography

The Maya provide an example of the interactions between systems of food production, diet, health, and demography. Archaeological research indicates that Maya agriculture developed from small-scale gardening practiced by tribal peoples. These people, who lived prior to A.D. 250, inhabited villages numbering less than 100 people. Their gardens were probably like those of the Lacandon Maya, a contemporary tribal people of southern Mexico and Guatemala. The Lacandon practice **swidden horticulture**, in which garden plots are cut from the forest and the vegetation is burned. Sometimes, swidden horticulture is called "slash-and-burn" farming. That name has negative connotations, as if the people are destroying the forest, when in fact the swidden technique conserves the tropical forest. Tropical soils are poor in quality, as most of the nutrients are locked up in the growing vegetation. To release the nutrients, the people burn the cut vegetation and plant in the ash. A mix of many crops are planted, including underground root crops, low bushy plants (such as beans and squashes), taller crops (such as maize), and fruit trees. This multilayered garden imitates the natural tropical forest and by so doing enhances the growth of all crops and the diversity of the diet. The gardens produce well for about two years. Then, new gardens must be cut and burned, while the old gardens lie fallow for a number of years until the vegetation recovers. Swidden horticulture is a very efficient method of food production but is limited in that it can support villages with only a couple of hundred people at best. Even with hundreds of villages spread across what is now southern Mexico, Guatemala, and parts of Honduras and El Salvador, the population size of the pre-Maya horticulturalists numbered less than 200,000.

The rise of the Maya state society began about A.D. 250 and lasted until about A.D. 900—often called the Classic period of Maya history. This is a period of political conquest and warfare that consolidated the scattered tribal settlements into cohesive and highly stratified social groups. At its height, the total Maya population lived in more than 40 cities, ranging in size from 5,000 to 50,000 people each. Each city was ruled by a local leader, usually a king. Each city was semi-independent, trading with other cities at times and making war with them at other times. Surrounding the cities were rural settlements where even more people lived. Maya population size may have exceeded 2 million people. The rural population provided the food that fueled the military and political ambitions of Maya kings and their followers.

To provide food for the city dwellers and the military, the rural peoples converted the swidden horticulture system into an irrigation agriculture system. The type of agriculture was a shrewd intensification of the old garden plots. Instead of planting in the ashes of temporary swidden gardens, the new agriculture planted in modified wetlands. The farmers would pile up mud from swamps or lakes to create agricultural plots called **chinampas**, or what are sometimes erroneously called "floating gardens." In fact, these were a type of hydroponic field with a mix of water canals and ponds between raised irrigated beds. Dozens of species of water plants, fish, shellfish, and traditional dry-land vegetables and fruits could be grown. People also raised birds and small mammals for food. *Chinampas* were later used by the Aztecs who, in the Valley of Mexico, were able to produce about 300 tons of food per square kilometer. This is about 10 times as much as produced by swidden horticulture and 100 times as much as produced by foragers (Webster et al., 1993).

The abundance provided by this innovative and intensive agricultural method not only supported 2 million Maya but allowed them to enjoy a relatively good level of health, at least during the first half of the Classic period. Evidence of good health comes from estimates of stature from skeletons of the time. This is illustrated in Figure 5.4 for male skeletons recovered from Tikal, a major Maya city-state and center of cultural life (agriculture, trade, religion, etc.) during the Classic period. During the early Classic period skeletons from tomb burials average about 170 cm. The tomb burials are those of high-status individuals, often Maya royalty. These individuals would have enjoyed the best possible conditions for life that Maya

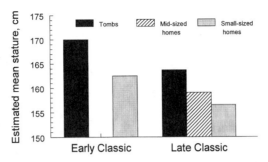

FIGURE 5.4 Mean stature of skeletons recovered from tombs, midsized houses, or small-sized houses at Tikal during the Early Classic or Late Classic Periods (redrawn from Haviland and Moholy-Nagy, 1992).

society could have provided. Just for comparison, the average stature of Mexican-American men 18 to 24 years old living in the United States was 171.2 cm in 1984. The Classic Maya buried lower ranking people under the floor of their homes. The size of homes is an indication of the wealth and social status of both the occupants and the burials. Individuals buried in small-sized Maya homes averaged 163 cm in stature. The difference between the elites and the lower social class is an indication of a lower quality environment for growth for the general population. Clearly, the elites reserved the best diet, indeed the best of everything, for themselves.

By the late Classic period the quality of life declined for all segments of Maya state society. The mean stature of both tomb and nontomb burials declines by about 5.0 cm. In late Classic times we have comparisons for both mid-size and small-size homes, which shows how closely stature follows social rank. The decline in stature occurs during a time of increasing warfare between Maya city-states, increased investment in militarization (larger armies, weapons production, construction of fortifications, etc.), and declines in food production and public building (Webster et al., 1993). The "material and moral condition of that society" (Tanner, 1986) were directed away from the environmental factors that would promote growth and toward those factors that would inhibit growth [see Bogin (1999a) for a review of the negative effects of a war time environment on human growth]. The population size of Tikal was probably also in decline in the late Classic period. In addition to the constraints imposed by the ever-increasing warfare between Maya kings, it seems that lower productivity of the *chinampas* system, an increase in infectious disease, and the disruption of trade networks "pushed" people out of Maya cities and into the rural hinterlands. By the time of the Spanish conquest in 1520, the Maya culture area still had a population of about 2 million, and these people were more widely dispersed into chiefdom and tribal societies (Lovell and Lutz, 1994).

"MAN OR MAIZE": WHICH CAME FIRST?

Demographers, anthropologists, and others debate the reasons for the expansion of Maya population with the advent of agriculture and the formation of state society. There are two opposing hypotheses about human population growth. The first is that the discovery or invention of a means to produce more food leads to increased fertility and population growth. This is, essentially, the "principle of population" of Malthus. Prior to the discovery of agriculture there had to be a balance between births and deaths in order to maintain a stable population that could be fed by foraging or swidden horticulture. Once people "discovered" agriculture, they could produce more food and, consequently, produce more people.

The opposing hypothesis is that as population increases there is an inexorable need to develop more intensive means to feed the increasing number of mouths. In this view, population was growing during foraging and horticulture times, and more people were accommodated by intensifying existing food production techniques. Eventually, increasing population pressure led to the adoption of more intensive food production technology, as the old ways could not cope. This is an idea that Boserup (1965) developed in detail. Her point is that agriculture was not "discovered" or "invented"; rather people knew about agriculture for a long time. They did not use it because it requires more work, and people will not work any harder than they need to. Agriculture requires people to prepare and maintain fields and irrigation works. These technologies do produce more total calories than foraging or horticulture, but they also consume more of people's time and energy. The number of calories produced does increase with agriculture, but the cost per calorie in terms of human labor also increases. The net result is that farmers produce fewer calories per hour than foragers, but farmers produce more total food.

The Mayan creation story holds that people come from maize, which we may interpret as support for the hypothesis that agriculture leads to population growth. But, we also know from the archaeological record that the formation of Mayan militaristic states goes hand in hand with the development of *chinampas* and other intensive food production technologies. We may interpret this as evidence that increased population growth, or increased population density due to political consolidation, led to agriculture. It is certainly true that after the collapse of Mayan state societies the people dispersed into smaller political units and reverted to less intensive food production strategies (Webster et al., 1993). As discussed above, a similar pattern occurred in ancient Nubia when centralized political control reverted to local control of the economy and food production. The Boserup model is supported by these cases and others in the historical record, such as the collapse of the ancient Roman empire and the return to less intensive methods of food production by the former Roman subjects.

A fairly simple model of the proposed demographic changes that coincided with the transition from foraging to agriculture is shown in Figure 5.5. The model was published by Livi-Bacci (1997) and is a useful summary. Here I offer just a few caveats to consider when interpreting the model. In Figure 5.5, the factors influencing fertility are limited to nutrition, disease, predation, length of the birth interval, and cost of child rearing. The transition involves a decline in quality and variety of foods eaten. The narrow food base of agriculture leads to greater instability of the supply of essential nutrients. But, agriculture also opens the possibility of storing large surpluses of the foods grown. The classic demographic transition model focuses on the surpluses and predicts lower mortality and increased fertility. The revised transition model focuses on the quality, variety, and stability of the diet and predicts higher mortality, especially infant and child deaths, and possibly higher fertility to cope with the loss of life. The disease load would increase due to larger,

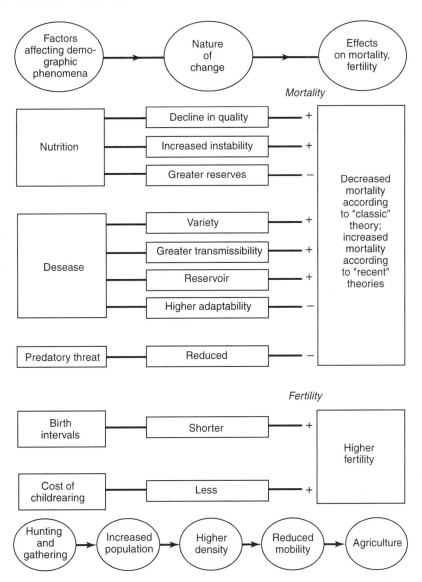

FIGURE 5.5 Presumed demographic effects accompanying the transition from foraging to agriculture. From Livi-Bacci (1997, Figure 2.2, p. 46).

sedentary groups of people offering a host population for new infectious diseases. This would increase mortality; indeed, the higher disease load often works synergistically with the decline in diet quality to exacerbate mortality. But, larger populations also may allow for more rapid and effective adaptation to the new diseases. Larger populations have more genetic and immunological variability, and natural selection will use this variation to find biological disease resistance. Larger, settled populations also may develop new behavioral strategies and social knowledge to combat and resist disease. These changes would reduce mortality, at least until a new disease comes along. The threat from predators may be reduced by agriculture, especially when the expansion of agricultural lands comes at the expense of natural forest and displaces predators to remote locals. But, some predators adapt to human agriculture and pastoralism and remain a minor threat to human life. Birth intervals decrease with agriculture, and this increases the birth rate. Shorter birth intervals do not always lead to more living people. As we will see in the next chapter, short birth intervals can increase infant mortality since a mother with two infants may not have sufficient resources to care for both. Finally, the model in Figure 5.5 indicates that the cost of child rearing decreases with agriculture and this leads to increased fertility.

Figure 5.5 shows that the Malthusian and Boserup models are not mutually exclusive and, in fact, demographers believe that some elements of each hypothesis were at work in the past. The consensus seems to be that population growth prior to about 12,000 B.P. was slow. An estimate of 5 million people alive at 10,000 B.P. was given in Chapter 1. Other estimates range up to 10 million people. Most of these people lived in small mobile foraging groups or swidden-based villages. We tend to consider these people as "primitive" and suffering from many diseases due to unsanitary living conditions. But, mobile foragers and shifting swidden farmers may have enjoyed a higher standard of living. By moving periodically from place to place, they left behind their unsanitary wastes. Living in small groups, they did suffer from the infectious diseases familiar to later peoples, including colds, influenza, measles, as well as the plague! To maintain themselves and spread these infectious diseases need a much larger host population. Preagricultural people suffered from parasitic diseases and trauma (broken bones, injuries from violence). Infant and child mortality may have been high at times, such as during food shortages, or it may have been relatively low when food and other resources were plentiful. People could have adjusted fertility rates to match, or slightly exceed, mortality, resulting in stable or very gradually growing population size (Armelagos et al., 1991). Studies of living foragers reveal that their lives are relatively affluent in terms of free time, since many foragers can produce sufficient food with only three days of work per week. Foragers such as the !Kung use this free time to socialize, sing and dance, practice religious, and sleep. !Kung women space births (about every four years) so that they only have to contend with one infant at a time. This provides more free time for food production and recreation. At the risk of sounding Pollyanish, life was good. Agriculture changed this way of life, and whether this was due to more food leading to more people or the other way around does not really matter. Agriculture changed the way people worked, the size of their settlements, their diseases, their political organization, and even their religions (monotheism is a product of agricultural state societies). The advent and spread of agriculture in the last 10,000 years was sudden in terms of the preceding 100,000 plus years of human history. But this was gradual in comparison with the next major revolution of technology and social change.

INDUSTRIALIZATION, URBANIZATION, AND THE FURTHER DECLINE OF HUMAN HEALTH

Industrialization, and its concomitant urbanization, compounded the problems started with the introduction of agriculture. Industrial peoples are removed yet another step from their food sources and often become more dependent on a limited variety and quality of food. Industries and cities divert vast amounts of water away from agriculture and food production, to be used instead for power generation and more recently for materials processing and cooling. Industrial processes cause pollution of the environment, that is, they concentrate naturally occurring but widely dispersed substances that are toxic to people, such as lead, coal dust, and hydrocarbons, into small areas. Industrial processes also create new substances that are toxic to people, such as polychlorinated biphenyls (PCBs) and dioxin. Industrialization further concentrates people in smaller areas, increasing the opportunity for contact with pollutants and the transmission of infectious disease. Industrialization increases sedentarism, restricts outdoor activity, breaks up traditional kinship-based societies, and increases socioeconomic stratification. The sharing of food and other goods and services decreases. Finally, patterns of food consumption are regimented in industrial societies. Foragers and subsistence farmers tend to eat smaller amounts more frequently throughout the day (snacking). Industrial workers tend to eat fewer meals, for example, "three meals per day," rather than spacing food and increasing food variety intake by snacking. Each of these changes in behavior and social organization has the potential to impact negatively on human nutrition and health.

Historical records for the population of the Connecticut River Valley during the eighteenth and nineteenth centuries show that as a market economy and industrialization increased so did the incidence of tuberculosis and diarrheal infections (Meindl and Swedlund, 1977; Swedlund et al., 1980). Infectious disease can impair nutritional status by curtailing appetite and food intake, impairing the absorption of nutrients by the digestive system, and, at the same time, increasing the body's need for nutrients, especially protein (Scrimshaw and Young, 1976). Poor nutrition may make a person more susceptible to disease by depressing the body's immune responses (Chandra, 1990). This synergism between malnutrition and infection shows up clearly in records of physical growth in the height and weight of individuals or populations. Since human growth is dependent on an adequate supply of all essential nutrients, both malnutrition and infection work against optimal growth. We have already seen that agricultural intensification during the late Classic period resulted in a decline in average Mayan stature. Industrialism only made things worse.

During the years 1750 to 1900, the time of the Industrial Revolution in the western world, the growth in height of people living in industrialized areas was less than that of people living in agricultural areas (Bogin, 1988). In a historical study of eighteenth-century British military recruits, Steegmann (1985) found that men from rural areas averaged 168.6 cm while the average height of men born in urban areas was 167.5 cm, a small but statistically significant difference. Steegmann notes that during the eighteenth century Britain was a developing nation. Industrializing urban regions were becoming increasingly dependent on food supply from rural areas. Crop failures, unreliable transportation, lack of food storage and preservation techniques, and demand from higher paying external markets resulted in periodic food shortages in cities. Figure 5.6 illustrates the relationship of food availability and the stature of military recruits, based on the year of birth of those men, for all of England and Ireland between 1750 and 1778. The average heights of men born in "bad" years (food shortages) are significantly less than those of men born in "good" years (food adequacy). Industrializing areas were particularly hard pressed in bad years, and in 1753 and 1757 there were food riots in some

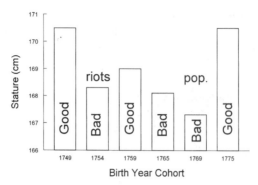

FIGURE 5.6 Adult stature of eighteenth-century military recruits from England and Ireland born in different years. The dates of each birth-year cohort begin with the year indicated and continue until the next birth cohort, for example, the earliest cohort was born between 1749 and 1753, the next cohort was born between 1754 to 1758. "Good" and "bad" are relative terms that refer to historical estimates of food availability in England. "Riots" refers to years of food shortages so severe as to cause riots and "pop." indicates a period of rapid population growth (after Steegmann, 1985).

cities. Research with modern populations shows that severe malnutrition during infancy and childhood has a permanent stunting effect on human growth in height (Bogin, 1999a). Steegmann's British data for the 1700s conforms with undernutrition as the cause for the reduced height of men born during periods of food shortages.

A recent example of the effects of industrialization and pollution on human growth and well-being is the work of Paigen and colleagues (1987) at Love Canal. The site of the research was a residential neighborhood in Niagara Falls, New York, that was constructed above a 3,000-meter-long unfinished canal. Prior to building homes and a school at the site in the 1950s, the canal, "was used as a burial site for 19,000 metric tons of organic solvents, chlorinated hydrocarbons, acids, and other hazardous waste during the 1940's" (Paigen et al., 1987, p. 490). By 1977, the presence of unsafe levels of chemicals in the ground water, the soil of the school playground, and the indoor air of homes was established. In 1978, due to an excess of miscarriages by women from Love Canal, the State of New York evacuated 235 families. In 1980 the federal government of the United States evacuated the remaining 800 families.

Prior to the 1980 evacuation, Paigen and colleagues measured the height and weight of 921 children between the ages of 1.5 and 16.99 years from 424 households of Love Canal. A second control sample of 428 children from Niagara Falls were also measured. The children of the control sample were from homes in noncontaminated neighborhoods but similar to the Love Canal sample in terms of socioeconomic and ethnic background. No difference in weight was found between the Love Canal and control samples. However, children born and residing in Love Canal for at least 75 percent of their lives were significantly shorter than the children from Niagara Falls. That difference could not be accounted for by statistically controlling the effect of parental height, socioeconomic status, nutritional status, birth weight, or history of chronic illness. The authors of the report conclude that chronic exposure to the toxic industrial wastes is a likely cause of the growth retardation of Love Canal residents.

DEMOGRAPHIC TRANSITION

The curious thing about industrialization is that even as its pernicious effects reduced human health and physical growth there seems to have been a burst of population growth that followed the industrial revolution of the nineteenth century. The demographic consequence of industrialization is traditionally called the **demographic transition**. Demographers tried to explain the population surge with a fairly simple model (Davis, 1945; Thompson, 1929). In its most succinct form the model holds that as a society becomes more economically developed there will be a reduction in mortality and, at some time later, there will be a reduction in fertility. Figure 5.7 shows the basic elements of the model. The lag between the drop in mortality and fertility results in a population surge, and that is the demographic transition. Two concrete examples of the transition are shown in Figure 5.8. The case of Sweden is an example of the transition in Europe associated with the Industrial Revolution. The case of Mexico illustrates the transition in a poor nation in the twentieth century.

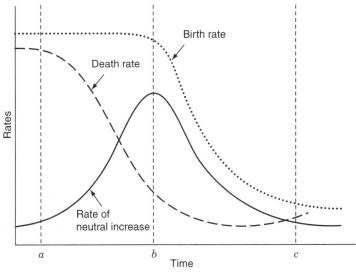

a = Beginning of transition
b = Greatest difference between birth and death rates
c = End of transition

FIGURE 5.7 Model of the demographic transition (from Levi-Bacci, 1997).

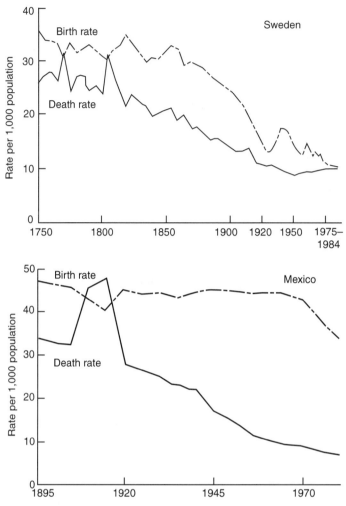

FIGURE 5.8 Examples of the demographic transition in Sweden and Mexico. (*Source*: Department of Meteorology, University of Maryland College Park. Copyright © 1996 at web site *http://www.meto.umd.edu/~owen/CHPI/IMAGES/demog.html*).

Historically, demographers defined three stages of the transition. Stage 1 defines an "undeveloped" society, which according to demographers means that the society is preindustrial. Demographers assumed that there would be a natural progression from a preindustrial to an industrial stage in all societies. Anthropologists do not accept this notion of progress and do not consider nonindustrial societies to be undeveloped. More will be said about notions of progress in the next section of this chapter. Stage 1 societies have high fertility and mortality. The population is balanced and remains stable in size. The age and sex structure of a stage 1 society takes the form a true population pyramid, with a broad base of infants and children who will not survive to adulthood. Stage 2 societies are in the initial phases of development. Mortality rates decline, it was alleged, due to improvements in sanitation, health care, and medical technology. Since fertility rates remain high during stage 2, the population size rapidly expands. The older ages of the population pyramid expand as more infants and children live to adulthood. In stage 3 fertility rates decline so as to match mortality rates. This is the hallmark of a fully developed society. The population growth again approaches zero (stable population size) and the population pyramid becomes rectangular or even inverted as there are more elderly than new infants and children.

Problems with the Model

There are many problems with this model and with demographic transition theory. The major problem is that at its core the demographic transition model is really a "grand unification theory." The model tries to explain most, if not everything, that happened to the human population in the last two to three hundred years. The models of population and individual growth of Pearl (1925) and Brody (1945), discussed in Chapter 1, are also grand unification theories. Just as Pearl and Brody tried to show that one curve of growth could be applied to the growth of all species of living things, the demographic transition theorists initially tried to show that their three-stage model would explain population dynamics at all times and in all places. The empirical research, however, shows that the model cannot be applied so broadly. The model does not explain why fertility and mortality changed, and even worse, the model does not account for the way in which demographic change actually took place (Friedlander et al., 1999).

First, mortality and fertility are continuous variables, and their values do not organize into just "high" and "low" categories. Take another look at Figure 5.8. There are peaks and troughs in both the change of fertility and mortality with time. This is most clear for Mexico during the Revolution of 1910 to 1920. Baby booms, such as the post–World War II boom in Sweden and in most of the other rich nations, show that fertility rates are fluctuating and variable. So, one basic premise of the traditional demographic transition model is not correct—fertility and mortality do not move so smoothly from stage 1 to stage 3.

Second, another problem with the traditional model may also be seen in Figure 5.8. The population explosion occurred in very different ways in what are now the rich and the poor countries of the world. In eighteenth and nineteenth-century Europe, the introduction of public health changes, especially relating to sanitation and water quality, occurred slowly and changes in mortality also occurred slowly. In the poor nation of the mid to late twentieth century, the benefits of advances in public health and medicine were felt immediately and life expectancy rose very rapidly. This may be seen in the sharp drop in mortality for Mexico after the Revolution. But, these advances came at a different stage of development from what applied in earlier decades in Western Europe and North America. In those nations the public health improvements came along with industrialization and urbanization. These economic and social changes, which preceded the public health initiatives, had already begun to change fertility attitudes and behaviors. As I will explain below, for Europeans and North Americans, children had less economic value and large families were less desired. In the poor nations, the introduction of life-saving technology and sanitary practices came when the majority of the population was still agrarian in nature. On the farm, children were still deemed an economic asset, and as a result, birth rates in these countries did not typically fall in concert with death rates. Population growth rates climbed to unheard-of heights of 3 to 4 percent per year—a pace sufficient to double a country's population in about 20 years. The growth rate in Europe during the "demographic transition" of the nineteenth century was on the order of only 1.5 to 1.7 percent.

As originally developed, the demographic transition model held that the Industrial Revolution and urbanization were the causes of first mortality decline and later fertility decline. Industrialization was supposed to have increased literacy and knowledge of "modern" ways of living. Industrial employment was also supposed to have increased real wages, giving people the money to buy more and better food, housing, health care, and everything else that would lower mortality, especially infant and child mortality. After some time, it was argued, parents would want to limit family size, not only because more of their infants survived, but also because of a decline in "child utility." On the farm, large families are economically useful, as more workers lead to higher productivity. In an urban, industrial setting large families are an economic drag, as children are expensive to care for and require years of education before they are economically useful. Along with knowledge of contraception, the lower utility of children leads to lower fertility—or so the traditional argument goes.

This is a logical scenario, but in practice it did not play out this way. Demographers now know that the demographic transition in Europe started in France in the eighteenth century, many years before the Industrial Revolution in that country. To make matters worse for the traditional model, there was a simultaneous decline in both mortality and fertility, and these rates declined equally in both urban and rural areas (Coleman and Salt, 1992; Livi-Bacci, 1997). Some research even shows that the fertility decline in France preceded the mortality decline (van de Walle, 1986), just the opposite of the prediction of the traditional demographic transition model! It seems that French knowledge of contraception and favorable attitudes toward its use are responsible for the fertility decline. A similar demographic change took place in the Scandinavian countries, that is, no lag between the mortality and fertility decline and no association of population change with industrialization.

PROGRESS?

The original idea that the demographic transition was tied to industrialization and urbanization seems to have come from the population history of England and the English idea of "progress." The Industrial Revolution took place first in England, and it is associated with demographic change in that nation. The correlation between industrialization and population change led some demographers to think that the first was causal to the second. The notion of progress also contributed to this causal interpretation. Progress is a European philosophical position that posits an inevitable gradual betterment of humankind. The idea has roots that go back to St. Augustine but was most strongly articulated by eighteenth-century philosophers such as Turgot and the Marquise de Condorcet in France and by members of the school of British empiricism and positivism. The idea of progress was part of the Enlightenment period of European philosophy. To prove their "Doctrine of Progress," Turgot and Condorcet compiled an encyclopedia of intellectual improvement from the Greeks to the eighteenth-century French. With the rise of industrialization, the British were able to "prove" the inevitability of progress via economic and social change.

The correlation between industrialization, demographic change, and philosophical notions of progress is spurious. Industrialization just happened to occur in England as the decline in mortality was also taking place. Fertility was actually on the rise in eighteenth-century England, and it stayed high in the early-nineteenth century (Fig. 5.9). Birth intervals were generally declining since the year 1650 and, possibly the number of stillbirths were also in decline (Wrigley, 1998). These trends, beginning long before industrialization, significantly increased the fertility of English women and the growth of the population. The population explosion became such a problem that many infants were abandoned in the streets. Disgusted by the accumulation of infant corpses in the gutters, social reformers in England established foundling homes for the abandoned 1741. But, inadequate care in these homes led to death of most of the infants and children housed in them (Coleman and Salt, 1992). From our perspective today, we would hardly describe as progress the rise of industrialization and the rise of infant mortality in the late-eighteenth century. Offspring of the poor who survived faced more of the terrors of progress. Abysmal working conditions in factories, forced child labor, the crowding and unsanitary conditions of urban areas all led to a decline in the quality of life for most of the working class.

Coleman and Salt (1992) show in a detailed analysis of the so-called demographic transition of England and other European countries that reasons for the decline in mortality and later the decline in fertility are not so easily explained. They

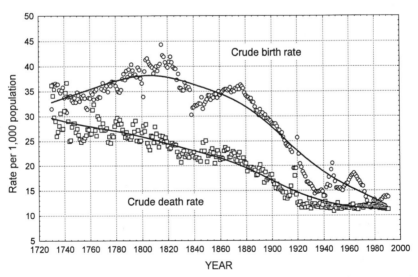

FIGURE 5.9 Birth and death data for England, 1733–1991. The data are for crude birth rate and crude death rate. The solid lines running through the data are least-squares regressions, which indicate the average trend of the data points. Note that there is considerable variation around the regression lines, especially for the crude birth rate. (Data provided by David Coleman, Oxford University.)

find that some combination of "widespread education, rising incomes, sanitary reform, and effective government" may be parts of the answer, but, "a specifically formulated general explanation which meets all of these circumstances is still awaited" (p. 61). Friedlander et al. (1999) review 50 years of progress in the study of demographic transitions. They too conclude that the original grand unification theory, with its rigid three-stage model of the demographic transition, does not hold up under the scrutiny of empirical research. Friedlander et al. suggest that explanations of fertility and mortality transitions require the following five types of data: (1) an understanding of the specific historical context of each case; (2) the use of appropriate fertility concepts rather than vague notions of "natural fertility" versus constrained fertility (they show that people have always regulated fertility); (3) a careful analysis of patterns of marriage and of marital fertility; (4) the inclusion of many proximate determinants of fertility, including socioeconomic, political, and cultural variables, as well as the diffusion of information and values across social groups; and (5) the evaluation of factors regulating fertility both before and after the transition, which may reveal historical continuities that are ignored by the standard demographic transition model.

PLAGUES AND PROGRESS

Any explanation will also have to take account of other biological changes occurring in the population. Europe was racked by wave after wave of infectious diseases for several hundred years prior to industrialization. The plague is the most well known example. Plague entered Europe via Sicily in 1347. The plague was so virulent that by 1400 it had spread so far and fast that the population of Europe declined by about one-third. Whole villages and regions were depopulated. People lived in absolute fear, and explanations and cures for the plague centered on Jews, witches, and other totally ineffective means of controlling the disease.

This type of **epidemic** (the term used for a disease that spreads quickly and widely, almost without control, in a population) is typical of a disease that is both highly lethal and for which the host population, in this case human beings, have no biological or behavioral defense. Over time, both the host and the pathogen change. Through natural selection the pathogen, in this case the bacillus *Yersinia pestis*, becomes less virulent and lethal, since in this form it is able to infect more people than it would if every contact killed the host. The host may also develop biological defenses, such as antibodies against the disease. The host also learns how to cope with the disease, how to treat and care for victims, and how to take preventative measures against infection. The net result is that the epidemic conditions wane. In Europe last great epidemics of plague hit the region between England and the Rhine Valley between 1663 and 1670. By 1720 there were only sporadic outbreaks elsewhere (Livi-Bacci, 1997). This type of disease cycle is typical for the other epidemics that broke out in Europe in the eighteenth, nineteenth, and early-twentieth centuries. During the epidemic phase mortality is high, especially for the young, who have the least defenses. High fertility may be a strategy used to replace infants and children lost to the disease. Perhaps this explains, in part, the ever-rising crude birth rate in England from the early sixteenth century to the late-nineteenth century. Or people may decide that it is a hopeless waste to bring more children into the world only to watch them die of epidemic disease, which may explain the decline in fertility in France in the eighteenth century. A further complication is that a new epidemic disease would appear just as the old ones were waning. The effects on population growth are, then, anything but predictable.

Physical growth is an important variable to consider. The progress model of demographic transition predicts that quality of life was improving with industrialization and urbanization, which we know is not true for most of the people. Data for the height of military conscripts, prisoners, indentured servants, slaves, and children in foundling homes quantify a decline in the quality of life. Average stature was rising in the late-eighteenth century in much of preindustrial Europe, but stature dropped in the first decades of the nineteenth century (Komlos, 1994). The decline in average stature coincides with a similar decline in real wages and increases in the cost of food. Industrialization was progressive only for those who controlled production, not for those employed in the factories or the families of workers living in the cities. There did not yet exist reliable and sanitary systems of food transport and distribution. Just as occurred during the agricultural revolution, the quality and diversity of the diet decreased during the Industrial Revolution. How diet, disease, and physical growth will fit into a satisfactory model of demographic change at the time of industrialization remains to be seen. In the next chapter I will return to a further consideration of disease, demography, and growth in relation to migration. I will offer a biocultural model of interaction between many of these variables that may add some clarity to the debate surrounding the demographic transition.

DIET AND THE DISEASES OF MODERN LIFE

After the year 1900, the affluent people of industrial areas in Britain and other western nations begin to achieve adult heights greater than those of people in rural areas. The technology of the western nations, including efficient transport of regional and nonnative foods, refrigeration, nutritional supplementation, treated water, and public sanitation, allowed their people to overcome some of the nutritional and health deficits of agriculture, industrialization, and urbanization (Bogin, 1988). Other evidence for the improving conditions of life in the rich nations comes from mortality statistics. Prior to 1850, deaths from epidemic diseases were a leading cause of mortality in the cities of Europe and North America. Death rates were so high that urban populations required massive migration from rural areas just to maintain constant numbers (McNeill, 1979; see also Chapter 6). Between 1850 and 1900 death rates in urban and rural areas began to equalize, and since 1900 urban mortality rates, at all ages, have been lower, generally, than rural mortality rates. The processes of change in the rich counties that resulted in better physical growth and lower rates of mortality for urban populations are now taking place in the poor nations. However, conditions for life in many cities of the poorer nations are still abominable.

Improved physical growth and longer life do not mean that modern urban populations are free of the specter of malnutrition and disease. Rather, as the threat of undernutrition and infectious disease was relaxed, a suite of new diseases related to diet and lifestyle of industrialized/urbanized people developed to burden modern affluent people. Data from end of the twentieth century show that cardiovascular disease and cancer are the two leading causes of death in the United States. They are followed by cerebrovascular disease (e.g., strokes), accidents (mostly motor vehicle and firearm accidents), pulmonary diseases, and diabetes. The literature on the relationship of diet to heart disease, cancer, and diabetes is abundant and controversial. Alcohol, a dietary component as well as a drug, contributes substantially to accidents and many of the other leading causes of death.

The increase of cardiovascular disease in the rich nations in this century can be linked to diet, human growth, and, even, demographic change in several ways. An intriguing hypothesis to account for the epidemic of heart disease that occurred after World War II is proposed by Barker (1992). Using both geographical analysis and the health history of thousands of individual people, Barker and his colleagues show that babies with some indication of growth retardation (low birth weight, small, but normal, size, or small head circumference) have a higher risk for cardiovascular disease as adults. Growth retardation at birth is very often a nutritional problem. Either the mother is poorly nourished, or despite adequate maternal nutrition, not enough nutrients cross the placenta to the fetus.

Poor nutrition during childhood may add to the risk for heart disease. Fellague-Ariouat and Barker (1993) interviewed women, from England and Wales, aged 80 years or older about their food habits when they were 10 to 15 years old (spanning the years 1899 to 1924). All of the women grew up in families of lower economic status. The women who lived in areas that today have low cardiovascular mortality tended to be rural, "to eat four meals a day rather than three, to live in households which had gardens, kept hens or livestock, and to go into domestic service, where diets were generally good. Those who grew up in areas which have high cardiovascular mortality tended to eat less red meat, live in houses without gardens, to enter industrial occupations and have higher fertility rates" (p. 15). The high mortality areas were more industrialized, mainly cotton mills, when the women were young. The families of these women had migrated from rural areas, shifting demographic pressures from the countryside to the industrial-urban regions. These industrial regions seem to have decreased the quality of the diet and the frequency of food consumption of young people, leading to poorer health in adulthood. Combined with higher fertility, poor diet during the years of physical growth and industrial occupations may have led to the high incidence of cardiovascular disease in adulthood.

Other research links heart disease to adult behaviors that included high calorie intakes and a sedentary lifestyle, which lead to obesity. Long-term studies find that since World War II, as industrialization, sedentary lifestyles, and sugar and fat consumption increased in Japan, Israel, many African countries, Polynesia, and Micronesia and among Native Americans and Eskimos, so did the incidence of obesity and cardiovascular disease (Hamilton et al., 1988; Weiss et al., 1984). Of course, these associations are only correlations and do not prove that sugar and fat are among the causes of heart diseases. Indeed, other populations have not responded to increased sugar and fat consumption in the same manner. What seems clear, however, is that in susceptible populations there is a synergistic interaction between industrial/urban lifestyles, diet, and metabolic diseases (Weiss et al., 1984).

Dental decay and gum disease are linked with a high consumption of sugar. The average American consumes 154 g of sugar per day, or about 124 lb per year! At the turn of this century the average sugar intake was about 20 lb per year, mostly from whole-food sources. About half of the sugar in the modern diet comes from refined white sugar (sucrose) and the other half from corn syrup (fructose), both of which are added to virtually all processed foods as sweeteners and preservatives.

Other disease risks of obesity are type II diabetes, a disease of glucose regulation, and certain cancers. Glucose is one of the major sources of energy used by the body to maintain metabolism. Normally, the amount of glucose in the bloodstream and in body cells is regulated by food intake and insulin. The carbohydrates in food are converted by the body into glucose, and insulin, secreted by cells in the pancreas, triggers body cells to absorb the glucose. Type I diabetes, which occurs in about 20 percent of people with the disease, is due to the lack of insulin production. In type II diabetes, the type found in about 80 percent of diabetes sufferers, the body cells become resistant to insulin and blood levels of glucose stay too high. This leads to hypertension, kidney disease, general circulatory disease, blindness, and death. Sugar does not cause diabetes, but obesity and lack of exercise play an important role. Much type II diabetes can be controlled or cured with a diet lower in fats and sugars and an increase in exercise, behaviors that are more in line with our forager ancestors.

A relationship between diet to cancer is well founded, but as with diabetes and heart disease, the exact causes are unclear. What is clear is that evidence for cancer is rare in the prehistoric times and the historic period prior to the Industrial Revolution. Less than 200 cases of cancer are known from all of the skeletons so far examined by paleopathologists (E. Strouhal, personal communication). No tumors have been found in any Egyptian or Nubian mummy (D. Moerman, personal communication). A carcinogen (cancer-causing substance) is usually needed to provoke a cancer. Many carcinogens are industrial products, but some are found naturally in foods. Cancer rates for modern people change as food preferences change. Takasaki and colleagues (1987) studied the rates for different types of digestive system cancer in the Japanese population during the period 1950 to 1983. The researchers argue that between 40 to 60 percent of the incidence of cancer may be attributable to diet, especially in those cases where carcinogens come into direct contact with the gastrointestinal tract. In the earlier years, the typical Japanese cuisine was based on rice seasoned with highly salted condiments, some green and yellow vegetables, and very little milk or dairy products. Takasaki et al. report that this type of diet is linked with stomach cancer, and stomach cancer is the most frequent type of digestive system cancer in Japan. During the 1960s, the postwar industrialization and economic recovery of Japan proceeded rapidly. One of the consequences of that expansion was a shift from the traditional cuisine to one that included significantly more dairy products and fat. Between 1965 and 1983 rice consumption dropped from about 300 to about 200 g per person per day. Milk and dairy products increased from about 75 to 150 g per person per day. Diets high in fats are associated with cancers of the intestine and colon. In Japan, mortality rates (age adjusted) per 100,000 population for stomach cancers dropped from about 37 to 22, while the same rates for intestinal cancer increased from about 2 to 4.5.

Epidemiological studies, such as Takasaki and colleague's (1987) Japanese research, show many links between cancer and specific foods or cuisines. The same holds true for heart disease, diabetes, and the other diseases of modern life. This research negates the belief that these diseases are the natural consequence of aging. Rather, these diseases are potential indicators of the environmental quality of life and the well-being of human populations. The fact that heart disease, cancers, and diabetes are the major causes of death in the rich nations belies the notion of progress that is a central belief of European and American culture. While it is true that the average age at death has increased steadily in the rich nations this century, most of the increase is due to the control of infant and child mortality from infectious disease. Adults suffer as much, or more, disease than 100 years ago and may suffer these diseases from an earlier age.

Food is safer today than 100 years ago, in that processing, refrigeration, and other technologies prevent spoilage and food poisoning. However, the processing that increases short-term safety also adds salt, sugar or artificial sweeteners, and, often, fats (both natural and artificial) to our diet, which may lead to long-term health risks. Advances in food technology also permit producers and consumers to eat more preferred foods. Preferred foods may be "good or bad" for people depending on the scientific, philosophical, and moral code of a society. The ability to produce virtually unlimited quantities of preferred foods may be one reason why people in the rich nations, especially the United States, tend to eat more food than ever before. In addition to the technological advances in food production, there are social and ideological reasons for this as well. In the wealthier nations, food production and consumption have become part of the industrial and commercial social structure of the society (Lieberman, 1991). Food is part of "big business," that is, the economic, social, and political organizations that structure social organization in the industrial nations. Consider the social impact of the fast-food industry, McDonald's Corporation for example. In the United States, the industrialization of food production has reached the point where far more energy is expended by the machines that harvest, process, and transport food than is returned as food calories. Listed in Table 5.4 are several processed foods, the amount of energy it takes to manufacture them, the energy return from the foods themselves, and the energy cost of the container used to package the food. To manufacture 1 kg of instant coffee, for example, requires 18,948 kcal. Drinking all that as coffee, slightly more than 529 6-oz cups, provides 2,645 kcal. The metal and plastic container that the coffee is packaged into costs an additional 2,213 kcal to manufacture. Chocolate, breakfast cereals, table sugar from beets and sugar cane, frozen fruits and vegetables, and frozen fish also require more, or as much, energy to produce and package than they return as food energy. Hamburgers, the bread they are sandwiched into, and ice cream provide relatively high energy returns for the cost of processing these foods. But, people do not live by hamburgers and ice cream alone, not even Americans. Less processed foods, such as fruits, vegetables, flour, and milk, provide as much or more energy than they cost to process. This energy profit is countered by relatively high energy losses for manufacturing the container that holds these foods. The figures in Table 5.4 do not include the costs to grow, harvest, and transport the foods or the cost of operating factories and stores that process and sell the foods. From an ecological perspective, one that measures energy flow through a society, industrial food production systems operate at an energy loss. Every other species of living thing would go extinct under these conditions. People living in industrial societies manage to survive because industrial and business activities are able to generate substantial financial profits, which can be used to offset food production costs. Unfortunately,

TABLE 5.4
Energy Inputs for Processing Common Food Items of Industrial Societies, Energy Provided by Eating These Foods, and Energy Cost to Produce Containers for These Foods

Processed Food	Energy Input (kcal/kg)	Energy Return (kcal/kg)	Container Energy Cost (kcal)
Instant coffee	18,948	2,645	2,213
Chocolate	18,591	5,104	722
Breakfast cereal (corn flakes)	15,675	3,877	722
Beet sugar (~17% sugar in beets)	5,660	4,000	~400
Cane sugar (~20% sugar in cane)	3,380	4,000	~400
Fruits and vegetables (frozen)	1,815	~500	722
Fish (frozen)	1,815	1,058	~400
Baked goods (white bread)	1,485	2,680	559
Meat (hamburger)	1,206	2,714	~400
Ice cream (vanilla)	880	2,015	722
Fruit and vegetables (canned)	575	~500	2,213
Flour (enriched, sifted)	484	3,643	~400
Milk (3.7% fat)	354	643	2,159

Source: Energy inputs and containers—Harris, 1993; energy returns—Guthrie and Picciano, 1995, Appendix K.

these financial profits often come at the expense of the biologically evolved nutrition needs of the people. The industrial societies of the western world are also at historically low levels of population growth—some nations are even in population decline. Amazingly, huge quantities of food are both consumed and wasted in these rich nations with dwindling populations.

Evidence of the commercialism of food and diet is easy to find. Print and electronic media bombard people with the message that food promotes pleasure. This is especially true of foods that are high in fats and sugars. Garine (1987), a French anthropologist of food, observes that the style of food consumption today in the wealthy nations reflects a quest for pleasure and increased social status, more than a desire to fulfill human biological necessity. Of course, this has been the case at least since the time of the ancient Maya and Romans. Only recently, however, are people able to eat any food, in any quantity, as often as they wish, if they can afford the price. This may make people happier, and even more productive, in some sense, but there are biological consequences of this sensual and socioeconomic pursuit for satisfaction. There is an increasing body of research that shows that in addition to the body fat that accumulates from overeating, the chemical by-products of excessive food digestion are themselves harmful. This includes the digestion of any food, including low-fat foods, sugar-free foods, and any other so-called health food. These digestive by-products may cause cellular damage that induces metabolic disease, such as diabetes, and accelerates aging (Weindruch, 1996). Maybe today is a good time to go on that diet, that is, restrict food and begin an exercise program, that you have been thinking about!

ELECTRONIC REVOLUTION

The late-twentieth century experienced the third great economic transition in human history—the electronic revolution. The rich industrial nations of the western world have given way to postindustrial societies increasingly dependent on information and its manipulation. The electronic computer ushered in this new age, and the creation of the Internet and the World Wide Web are fueling its rapid expansion. People now make a living in a virtual world, without the production of any tangible product. Of course, people still need to eat real food; a virtual diet is not yet possible. People also need to reproduce the "old fashioned way," and physical growth cannot be performed by a computer program. However, electronic media are having an impact on human diet, demography, and growth.

Will the electronic transition lead to some new version of the demographic transition? No one knows, but let me offer a few possibilities. In both the richer and poorer nations computer technology is becoming interface between people and food, from food design, to packaging, and distribution. Brazil is an example from the poorer nations. Brazil is the eighth largest industrial economy in the world, with a population of almost 171 million people. Brazil accounts for one-half of Latin America's population. Because of its population size and the strong demand for computer technology, Brazil is the leading point of entry into Latin America for U.S. technology companies (Saba, 1999). Brazil is one of the fastest growing nations for online users. Overall, Latin America has a predicted compound annual growth rate for new users from (from 1998 to 2003 of 19 percent, eclipsing Western Europe (0 percent) and North America (–8 percent). Brazil contributes at least one-third to the Latin American demand. Other poor nations will likely follow Brazil's example.

Computer technology is already the biggest factor in the marketing of food in the richer nations (Hollingsworth, 1998). With expansion of the electronic market to the poor nations, which have 80 percent of the world population, computer technology will dominate all marketing. This trend will surely shape the nature of the human diet for a large segment of the world population. Computer simulations may be used to concoct and test new recipes and types of food. Those found acceptable, both to human tastes and business profits, can be presented to a world market in short order. Massive advertising may convince people across the planet to desire these new foods. One outcome of this may be the further narrowing of diversity in cuisines. So long as all human nutritional requirements are satisfied, and people can afford these newly desired foods, all may be well. Some observers of this trend worry that all may not be well. The use of computer prototyping software can dramatically reduce the time and costs required to develop a new food product. Computer applications can also increase the efficiency of food processing. But, the computer is not a substitute for knowledge of the underlying fundamentals of food engineering (Datta, 1998).

At its most basic level, food is biochemistry and there are limits to the biological and chemical manipulations possible with food. The agricultural revolution produced more food but less variety. Diseases such as pellagra were one outcome, and as discussed above, these diseases had widespread negative impacts on human growth and population biology. The Industrial Revolution ushered in new levels of food processing, such as the milling of whole grains. Large-scale mechanical milling provided almost unlimited quantities of white wheat flour and white rice, that is, flour and rice from which the seed coat and the germ were removed. The white flour and rice had previously been eaten mainly by the higher socioeconomic classes of Europe and Asia, as it was too expensive for the lower SES groups. Its expense made it a prestigious and desirable food. With the new milling methods the white varieties became affordable to high- and low-SES groups, and the poor began to abandon use of the brown varieties of wheat and rice. The problem is that highly milled grains lose much of their nutritional value because the bulk of the minerals and vitamins are in the germ. Richer people did not miss these nutrients as they could afford to buy a wide variety of fruits, vegetables, and meats that provided them. As white flour and rice spread to the poorer segments of societies, new diseases appeared, such as beri-beri in Asia (caused by a niacin deficency). Tens of thousands of people died, and more were growth retarded and disabled by this disease. The misuse of computer technology to create the new human diet may induce new nutritional diseases with even more spectacular consequences.

Computers and electronic information may also lead to new levels of food safety. The U.S. Department of Agriculture (USDA) is now using Pulse Net for food safety. Pulse Net is a multistate computer network of public health laboratories. One of its benefits is that Pulse Net enables USDA personnel to recognize cases of food-borne illness linked to specific food items and to particular bacterial strains. International travel, migration, and international food trade also present threats of food-borne illness. It is estimated that 80 to 90 percent of cases of salmonella in Scandinavian countries is due to international travel (Käferstein et al., 1997). In the United States, increased consumption of fresh fruits and vegetables, viewed as a "healthy choice," means that up to 75 percent of these fresh foods are imported. These fresh food are susceptible to contamination both before and after importation. The health data indicate that as consumption of fresh fruits and vegetables increased in the last decade, the number of food-borne disease outbreaks doubled (Käferstein et al., 1997). Käferstein et al. describe the use of Hazard Analysis and Critical Control Points, a computer-based system to identify food-handling practices that may be hazardous to health and modify them to curtail these outbreaks.

There are electronic benefits to the poorer nations. In much of Africa, Asia, and Latin America there is limited access to electricity and, hence, refrigeration. Taylor (1999) asks how appropriate are food preservation techniques such as freezing and chilling in an African context? He suggests that it is time for an African renaissance in food preservation. Taylor suggests that poorer nations need to make use of alternative technologies, possible due to computer-aided design and manufacture, to produce freshlike foods with extended shelf life at room temperature. This may produce safe and more abundant food supplies, reduce mortality and morbidity, enhance human productivity, and, if the traditional demographic transition model has any validity, lower fertility and help stabilize African population growth.

CONCLUSION

This chapter offers one perspective on the evolution of human nutrition in relation to demography and growth. The mammalian and primate background for human nutrition, the hominid fossil and archaeological evidence, the behavior and diet of human foraging societies, and the development of modern foods and lifestyles are treated in some depth. Other aspects of human evolution related to food and nutrition are neglected here, such as a detailed discussion of food taboos, ritual and profane foods, and effect of seasonal periods of food shortage and abundance on human biology and behavior. Also neglected are connections between food production systems diseases that are not directly caused by food or diet. Malaria, for example, spread to human populations following the introduction of agriculture in Africa (Livingstone, 1958). Malaria kills and debilitates more people, even today, than any other infectious disease and, consequently, is a potent agent of natural selection and human evolution. There is evidence that some African societies have developed biocultural systems to produce and consume food, especially cassava, that reduces the threat of malaria (Jackson, 1990). But, the consequences of malaria on human demography and physical growth have barely been explored.

The most pressing nutrition problem of the twentieth century is also barely mentioned. This is the undernutrition and starvation that afflict three-fourths of the world's children—nearly 2 billion people. The toll that this suffering takes on human health, demography, growth, productivity, and happiness is virtually immeasurable. The cause of this suffering lies with the social, economic, and political inequalities between rich and poor; inequalities that the affluent populations have not been willing to change (Foster, 1992; Shields, 1995). As mentioned above, the electronic revolution may give the poorer nations the ability to change this situation without help from the rich.

The primary message of this chapter is that food is central to human life. From a biological perspective food is central because of the essential nutrients needed for growth, repair, and maintenance of the body. From a sociocultural perspective food is central because of the behaviors and beliefs that have evolved around foods and their use. From a medical perspective food is central because of the consequences of diet and food behavior for human health. Each of these impacts the demography of human populations and the physical growth of their members.

SIX

MIGRATION AND HUMAN HEALTH

As mentioned in the previous chapter, the Maya culture area had a population of about 2 million people at the time of the Spanish conquest in 1520. By then, the great Maya cities of Tikal, Palenque, Copan, and others had already been abandoned and the Maya people were widely dispersed into chiefdom and tribal societies (Lovell and Lutz, 1994). One Maya site was Iximche, an economic, political, and religious center in the central highlands of Guatemala. Iximche was the capital of the Kaqchikel Maya. The name Kaqchikel refers to both the language spoken and the political entity of this chiefdomship. The Kaqchikel people had been part of the larger Quiche political domain until about 1670, when the Kaqchikel seceded from Quiche domination and founded their own realm. Fifty years after its founding of Iximche, the Spanish conquistador Pedro de Alvarado arrived in Guatemala. At that time approximately 10,000 people lived in and around Iximche (Norton, 1997). Alvarado did not have the military strength to conquer Guatemala on his own. He needed help from the Maya themselves, and he used the enmities between rival tribal and chiefdom groups for this purpose. Alvarado arrived in Iximche in 1524 and quickly used the ongoing feud between Kaqchikel and Quiche Maya. With Kaqchikel help, Alvarado's army attacked and subdued the Quiche. Iximche was declared the first Spanish capital of Guatemala. The alliance between Alvarado and the Kaqchikel people did not last long. The ever-increasing demands of the Spanish for labor, food, and other goods and for Maya women led to Maya resistance. Alvarado responded with military attacks against his former allies and in 1526 destroyed Iximche by burning it to the ground. The Kaqchikel people were forced to flee to the hinterlands.

This story was repeated over and over again in Guatemala. The armed attacks and the forced migrations disrupted social life and resulted in population decline. Exacerbating these events was something even more devastating—epidemic disease. The Spanish brought with them diseases that were common in Europe, but unknown in the New World. These were the diseases of smallpox, measles, typhus, and plague. The Maya, and other American peoples, were unprepared at every level to deal with these diseases. The people had no biological resistance to the diseases, nor did they have either medical or public health knowledge of how to deal with the sick. Americans had no social strategies to support or care for the stricken. Moreover, the disease attacked everyone, young and old, adults in their prime, political leaders, commoners at the same time. With large portions of the Maya population disabled by disease, and racked with the fear of these epidemics and Spanish military attacks, everyday life collapsed. Food production stopped, and the sick died of hunger and thirst because there was no one to care for them. Families fell apart and the economic, social, and political system was in chaos. Lovell and Lutz (1996) report that eight epidemics swept Guatemala between 1519 and 1632. They occurred singly, or in even more lethal combinations. Faced with these epidemics, and the legacy of conquest, which included . . . "warfare, culture shock, ruthless exploitation, slavery, forced migration, and resettlement" (ibid, p. 399), the Maya population spiraled downward. By 1625 it hit its lowest point of only 128,000 people, a decline of almost 94% from the population size of only 100 years earlier. During the following centuries the Maya population increased. The increase was noted in every official census, and by 1994 the Maya population of Guatemala was estimated to be between four million (Guatemala News Watch, 1995) and six million (Tzian, 1994).

The decline and recovery of the Maya in Guatemala attests to the resilience of human populations in the face of demographic catastrophe. For the Maya, the catastrophe came in the form of Spanish conquistadors migrating from Europe to the New World. The Spanish came with the hope of finding riches in the form of gold and other material wealth. They also came with the desire to flee from the sickness and death due to epidemic disease that periodically swept Europe. The quest for wealth is a **pull factor** that encourages migration. The escape from disease is a **push factor**. Other factors, such as servitude, marriage, and mayhem (natural disasters and warfare), also push and pull people from place to place. Migrants may move from place to place within a region or nation, or between regions. Migrants may move once or repeatedly. They may oscillate repeatedly between their place of origin and one or more temporary residences, they may go through a period of oscillations and then reside permanently in a new place, or they may move once and live until death at a new residence. Because of the variety of these patterns of migration it is often difficult to define and identify migrants.

The literature on migration is very large and quite diverse. Most of the literature treats the social, economic, and political causes and consequences of migration. Some treats the emotional and psychological aspects of migration. The biology of migration is a separate literature. The movement of people from place to place is a major determinant of the biological structure of human populations. Such movement injects new genetic, physiological, and morphological variability into the recipient populations. It also may deplete these sources of biological variation from the non-migrating donor population. Migrants carry diseases from their home to their new places of residence; they are also exposed to new diseases en route and once they arrive at their destination. Migrants also develop new diseases due to the special circumstances of their life and behavior. All of these social and biological factors make the study of human migration difficult, intellectually exciting, and of much practical importance for human welfare.

RURAL-TO-URBAN MIGRATION

To make sense out of all the possibilities offered by human migration, I focus on the effects of rural-to-urban migration for the growth of individuals and the human population. The study of rural-to-urban migration is fraught with all of the uncertainties and difficulties inherent in other types of migration research. But, there are compelling reasons to emphasize rural-to-urban migration in this book. Rural-to-urban migration is one of the most prevalent types of human movement. The extent of this type of migration in today's world is enormous. In 1800, there were about 25 million people living in urban areas. In 1980, there were about 1.8 billion (Rogers and Williamson, 1982), and in 1995 there were 2.6 billion urban dwellers. By the year 2050, it is estimated that this number will double to 5.2 billion (OECD, 1999). This is a 208-fold increase in two and one-half centuries. In contrast, the natural increase in total world population will only be 9.3-fold in the same 250 years [one billion people in 1800 to 9.3 billion in the year 2050 (U.S. Bureau of Census, 1999)].

The study of the process of rural-to-urban migration and its effects on demography, human growth, and health is important for four reasons. First, it entails movement into a habitat and an ecological niche, the city, that is evolutionarily novel for our species. Second, it is the most common type of migration that has occurred in all periods of recorded history (Smith, 1984). Third, it is occurring more rapidly today than ever before, especially in the least developed nations of the world (OECD, 1999). Fourth, we understand relatively little about the long-term effects of this migration on human biology. Indeed, the effect of rural-to-urban migration may be one of the "missing" components of the traditional demographic transition model. What does seem clear at this point in time, is that rural-to-urban migration lowers both fertility and mortality. Rural-to-urban migration also impacts human growth. Urban populations today are usually taller, heavier, and differently shaped than rural populations (e.g., narrower bodies with relatively longer legs). But this was not always the case, as cities of the past had detrimental effects on human health, longevity, and growth. How the change came about is explained in the sections that follow.

The Extent of Urbanization

Let us first consider the extent of rural-to-urban migration throughout the historic period and even back to its archaeological context. It is logical to assume that urban migration began at the time when cities came into existence, but this is not true. Sometime before 5,000 BP, urban centers appear in ancient Sumer. These "cities" developed from villages, which in turn had grown from small agricultural settlements. Though these cities represented "a new magnitude in human settlement" (Childe, 1942, p. 94), their growth was slow and they were still considered as an extension of the agricultural settlement. The Sumerian language makes no distinction between village, city, or "any permanent cluster of houses made of sun-dried mud bricks" (Tuan, 1978, p. 2). Farming areas around the city were called *uru.bar.ra*, the "outer-city" (Oppenheim, 1974). Though people may have moved from the outer-city to the inner-city, such movement cannot properly be called rural-to-urban migration by today's definition of this term.

Ancient and medieval cities of Europe and Asia continued the practice of mixing settlements of houses, government buildings, and religious edifices with orchards, vineyards, and gardens. Urbanites in these cities still practiced a rural lifestyle on a daily basis (Tuan, 1978). A clear distinction between city and countryside and a clear conception of rural-to-urban migration is not apparent in historical records or in literature up through the 17th century.

Population size of the medieval city was small by modern standards. The typical size of the city ranged from 2,000 to 20,000 inhabitants until the end of the 16th century (Mumford, 1956). Two factors, disease and rural in-migration may have determined limited urban population growth. McNeill (1976, 1979) takes a novel approach to history and migration studies. He views much of history and most of migration as driven by disease. McNeill states that the concentration of a large and dense human population in an urban area establishes the conditions for the communication of infectious disease from one person to another. Settled village life had set up the conditions for the infection of anthrax, brucellosis, and tuberculosis in human populations. Urban life increased the chances for the spread of more devastating epidemic diseases like cholera, smallpox, and plague (Cockburn, 1967; Armelagos and Dewey, 1970).

McNeill argues that epidemic die-off in the urban centers of the world prior to about 1750 did not allow cities to sustain their own populations. Archaeological evidence supports this. Storey (1985) estimated the birth rate and the age at death for a skeletal sample from the pre-Columbian urban center at Teotihuacan, located in central Mexico. The sample was excavated from the trash midden burials of an "apartment compound" occupied by low socioeconomic status residents of the archaeological city. The estimate of mortality prior to age 15 is relatively high at 50%, and one-third of these deaths occurred during the first year of life. Life expectancy was low; most adults only lived to their late thirties (87% were estimated to have died by age 40). Storey shows that this rate of mortality is similar to that of pre-industrial Old World cities such as Rome and London. Storey adds that excavations at the apartment complex site indicate that the poor sanitation, high population density, and problematic food supply of the Old World cities seem to have been characteristic of New World cities too. These estimates of mortality for the low socioeconomic class of Teotihuacan belie previous claims for greater longevity for pre-Columbian urban populations compared with the Old World. Those earlier claims were based on skeletal remains of the ruling class, and are clearly not applicable to the majority of the population. Storey's research at Teotihuacan supports McNeill's model of in-migration to maintain urban populations. Based upon the skeletal sample she and others studied, population increased in the early period of the city, but remained constant during the middle and later periods. More deaths than births occurred, and in-migration was needed to make up the difference.

Kennedy (1973) presents data showing that even as late as 1850, English and American cities had mortality rates higher than their rural areas. More recent analyses indicate that urban mortality rates, especially infant and child mortality, remained higher than rural rates in the large cities of England and Wales until at least 1900 (Szreter and Mooney, 1998). Until the last century, then, rural in-migration was necessary to maintain urban population growth. Why people would want to move into an urban death trap is unclear. McNeill (1979) states that urban growth depended on "moral and property systems, family practices, and biological/

technological balances in the countryside that allowed and encouraged raising more children than were needed" (p. 96). Thus, the rural "push" of overpopulation and socioeconomic limitations were major factors. This was the case for much of the emigration from the Irish countryside in the eighteenth and early-nineteenth centuries. Large families, exclusion of all but the first-born son from inheritance of land, and the lack of rural opportunities for wage-earning employment resulted in massive urban migration prior 1845. With the failure of the potato crop and the ensuing famines of 1845 to 1848, the rate of migration only increased (Kennedy, 1973). Even today, in the least developed countries, these reasons, plus the urban "pull" of an expected higher standard of living in the city, are sufficient to explain rural-to-urban migration. When asked, today's urban migrants often say life will be better, even as they move into an urban shantytown with high rates of unemployment and poverty (Rogers and Williamson, 1982). There is some historical evidence that the pull of an expected higher standard of living operated in the eighteenth and nineteenth centuries of Europe as well. The Industrial Revolution opened job markets in the industrializing cities. The promise of real wages (i.e., money) and the desire to spend that money on the ever-increasing market of industrially produced goods were powerful economic and emotional incentives to move to the city. But, as will be discussed later in this chapter, the historical data also show that life for the vast majority of city residents was in fact of lower quality, at least in terms of physical growth and mortality.

BIOLOGY OF THE CITY

Given this history, it is probable that the phenomenon of rural-to-urban migration, as we understand it today, began when people realized that rural-versus-urban life presented the individual with different opportunities. Some of these opportunities directly influenced human biology, especially in terms of fertility, disease, and mortality. Scholars debate the extent to which people understood these biological impacts. It is clear, however, that cities, as we know them today, came into existence at the end of the sixteenth century. By the time of Shakespeare, London was a city of some 100,000 people living within an area of 1 square mile. Massive urban in-migration from rural areas was one consequence of this degree of population concentration. Due to epidemic deaths within the city, London required an annual average rate of in-migration totaling about 5,000 people in order to sustain its population (McNeill, 1979). While this is an impressive number, it pales before the rates of movement to some cities in the twentieth century. During the 1970s and 1980s, for example, Mexico City received about 5,000 immigrants per day from rural areas of Mexico!

By about 1750 the rate of urban mortality due to epidemic disease was sharply reduced. The term "sharply reduced" requires some explanation. Death rates decreased sufficiently so that urban populations no longer required in-migration from the countryside to be sustained. The decrease in epidemic disease mortality may have been due to the dual effects of biological adaptation of the human host and pathogen toward each other as well as improved sanitation, water treatment, and other public health measures (Dubos, 1965). Nevertheless, relatively high rates of death from **endemic** disease were still part of urban ecology. An endemic disease is one that is maintained at high rates in a population but no longer spreads uncontrollably and is not as lethal as when it was an epidemic. Smallpox is an example (Szreter and Mooney, 1998). Smallpox was once an epidemic disease, striking young and old alike and killing all ages with equal ferocity. By the eighteenth century smallpox became an endemic disease, and mostly a disease of childhood, much like measles was considered an endemic disease of childhood by the early-twentieth century. An unusually detailed record of "bills of mortality" was maintained in the city of Glasgow, Scotland, during the period 1783 to 1840. These "bills" listed cause of death, age at death, and several other demographic variables. Few cities of the world maintained such records prior to this time. During the period 1783 to 1800 smallpox was the principal cause of death to people under age 10 years old, accounting for 20 percent of all such deaths. Only with the introduction of Jenner's vaccine, discovered in 1798, did death rates begin to fall—to 4 percent by 1812.

But, smallpox deaths in Glasgow rose again after 1835, to 8 percent, as the health conditions in the city deteriorated. One reason for this deterioration was the unabated flow of rural-to-urban migrants to the city. Figure 6.1 is based on estimates of population and expectation of life at birth in Glasgow from 1821 to 1861. The population grows by 2.6 times in this period of 40 years (from 161,000 to 420,000 people), which is far greater than is possible by natural increase (that is, due to births of city residents). Migration explains most of this population increase. The political, economic, and social practices of mill owners in the cities and landowners in the countryside were still pushing people from the country and pulling them into the city. To what extent the "allure" of Glasgow was also pulling people is difficult to ascertain. With a growing population of low-paid factory workers, along with marginally employed and unemployed people, living in squalid housing, the allure must have been a thin veneer at best. Still, the people arrived, and at a steadily increasing rate. The decline in expectation of life until 1837 is strong evidence that the

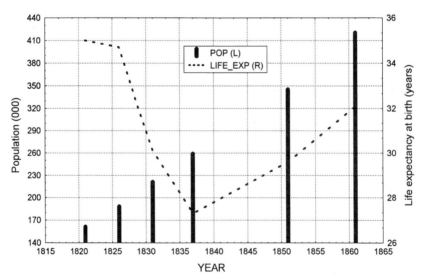

FIGURE 6.1 Estimates of population size and expectation of life at birth for the city of Glasgow, 1821–1861 (Szreter and Mooney, 1998).

biological and social conditions of the city deteriorated. The young were most affected, as 50 percent of all deaths occurred to infants, children, and juveniles between birth and age 10 (Szreter and Mooney, 1998). The rise in life expectancy after 1837 indicates that health and social conditions improved. Indeed, a number of laws were enacted to ameliorate the dreadful conditions in the slums and in the factories. I will have more to say about these laws in relation to the physical growth of children later.

The situation in Glasgow was typical of cities throughout England and Wales. Szreter and Mooney (1998) use empirical data and statistical estimates to calculate expectation of life at birth for British cities with populations of 100,000 or more people. They compare these estimates with national averages for expectation of life at birth for all of England and Wales and also with estimates published by Woods (1985). Woods's estimates are based on the assumption that life expectancy would steadily increase as industrialization proceeded and city size grew. Szreter and Mooney describe Woods's estimates as conjecture and based on the notion of "progress" derived from the classic demographic transition model. These three estimates of life expectancy are shown in Figure 6.2.

Between 1750 and 1950, the bulk of rural-to-urban migration took place in what are now the rich developed nations. There was also a great deal of international migration, especially from the Old World to the Americas. Many of these migrants moved from the rural villages of the "Old Country" to the cities of the New World. By 1950, 53 percent of the population of the rich nations were urbanites, compared to only 16.7 percent of the population of the poor, less developed countries. By the year 2015 the percentage for all poor countries is estimated to reach 49 percent, but the rich nation figure will be about 80 percent (OECD, 1999).

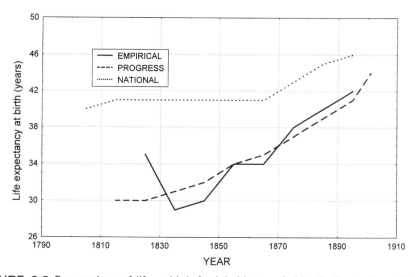

FIGURE 6.2 Expectations of life at birth for inhabitants of cities in England and Wales of 100,000+ population. The curve labeled "Empirical" gives the empirically based estimates of Szreter and Mooney (1998). The curve labeled "Progress" gives the estimates of Woods (1985), based on the classic demographic transition model. The curve labeled "National" gives the estimates for all England and Wales (from Szreter and Mooney, 1998).

Therefore, the demographic, growth, and health consequences of living in cities, as we know them today, may be more readily observable in the populations of the rich countries. We can also use the past experience of the rich nations to construct explanations and hypotheses about present-day urban migration that may be tested with the more recent data from the poor countries.

BOX 6.1
Cape Verde: Migration and *Morabeza*

Maria Inês Varela-Silva

This is one of three text boxes in this chapter that tell something about the Cape Verde islands and its people. Cape Verde is an archipelago of 10 islands and 5 islets, located 650 km off the northwest coast of Senegal (Fig. B6.1). The islands

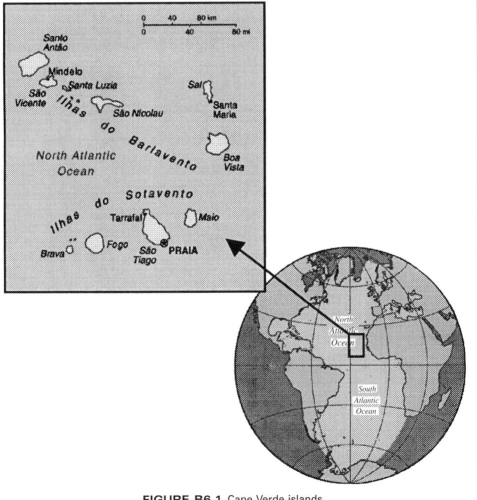

FIGURE B6.1 Cape Verde islands.

are divided into windward and leeward groups. The windward, or Barlavento, group on the north includes Santo Antão, São Vicente, São Nicolau, Santa Luzia, Sal, and Boavista; the leeward, or Sotavento, group on the south includes Santiago, Brava, Fogo, and Maio. Cape Verde has a total area of 4,033 km² (1,557 mi², slightly larger than the state of Rhode Island).

Located on the route between Africa and the Americas, these uninhabited islands were discovered by the Portuguese in the fifteenth century. Senegalese fishermen had used the islands as a staging site before the first Europeans arrived, but the Senegalese never settled. In the early years the islands were used for slave storage. In 1495 the archipelago was declared a crown possession of Portugal, and Portuguese migrants began to settle there, along with African slaves. The Portuguese maintained dominance over the Africans through the system of slavery. When the slave trade (for which the islands had served as a port of call) was abolished in 1876, their importance dwindled.

There was a good deal of "blood mixing"—especially births to African women fathered by Portuguese men, but also many other combinations—and this explains the biological heterogeneity of the Cape Verdean population today. More than two-thirds of the people of Cape Verde are of mixed African and European ancestry and are known as Creoles, or *mestiços*. Nearly all of the remainder are of African ancestry.

At the time of its independence, on July 5, 1975, Cape Verde had accumulated all the symptoms of underdevelopment: high levels of fertility and malnutrition of infants and children, virtually nonexistent health and education systems, a precarious agricultural economy totally dependent on uncertain rainfalls, fishing, and manufacturing industry in an embryonic state (Filho, 1981; Silvestre, 1994). Only 11 percent of the land is arable, none of it supports forests or woodland, and about 6 percent is suitable to pasture. The natural resources are meager, consisting of salt, basalt rock, pozzuolana (used to produce hydraulic cement), limestone, and kaolin. A fledgling tourism business is, gradually, helping the economic development of the country.

The estimated population in 1999 was 405,748, giving the country an overall density of 100.6 persons per square kilometer (260.6 per square mile). The population growth rate in 1998 was 1.5 percent annually. Life expectancy at birth was 74 years for women and 67 years for men. According to the United Nations Educational, Scientific and Cultural Organization the estimated adult (+15 years old) illiteracy rate was, in 1995, 19.3 percent for men and 39.4 percent for women. The economy depends extensively on remittances from Cape Verdeans living overseas, which help to offset the country's large trade deficit. Because Cape Verde is poor in natural resources and suffers from frequent droughts, it has experienced large emigration for many years. More people with a Cape Verdean ancestry live outside the country than inside.

The culture of Cape Verde reflects a symbiosis of the five centuries of relationship between European and African influences (Varela-Silva, 1996). The Portuguese government, generally, showed a lack of interest, and even disdain, for the Cape Verdean population. These attitudes persisted until the independence in 1975 and left the Cape Verdean population to its own resources. This allowed a strong and idiosyncratic culture to surface. One example of Cape Verdean culture is expressed in the word *morabeza*. The official language is Portuguese. The national language, however, is Crioulo, which is an amalgam of archaic Portuguese combined with many African words, syntax, and grammar that is a unique and complete language unto itself. *Morabeza* connotes a feeling of kindness, tenderness, hospitality, and sense of helping the others, among others. The concept of this term, *morabeza*, includes all the good feelings that a human being can show: They are proud of being known as the "people of *morabeza*." The Cape Verdeans do not consider themselves "violent by their own nature" being, in opposition, kind, nice, showing solidarity to the others, in other words, having *morabeza* (Varela-Silva, 1996).

One of Cape Verde's emigrants is the renowned singer Cesária Évora. One of her songs is titled "*Morabeza*." She sings it to the people of Mindelo, the second largest city of the islands (47,109 people in 1990, located on São Vicente, the largest city is Praia, population, 1998 estimate, 95,000), located on Santiago. The words of the song, first in Crioulo and then in English, are (on the CD "Cesaria Evora—Miss Perfumado, 1992, RCA/BMG):

Morabeza

Sol disponta—The sun rises
Num leque radioso—in a radious halo
Ceu di Mindelo infeita—and adorns Mindelo's sky
Cu se vistido luminoso—with its luminous dress

Ceu visti de azul—Sky dressed blue
Bordado di oro—embroidered in gold
Mindelo de norte a sul—Mindelo from north to south
Visti di gala e flor—dressed with gala and flowers

Gente di Mindelo—People of Mindelo
No abri nos broce—We open our arms
No po coraçon na mon—We put our hearts in our hands
Pa no bem da'l um abraço—To give you all a strong embrace
Um abraço de morabeza—An embrace of Morabeza
Dess povo de São Vicente—From the people of São Vicente
Ess home de alma grande—From that Man with a big spirit
Di rostro sabe e contente—With a wise and content (happy) visage.

The culture of Cape Verde is a culture of migration and of migrants. In another song, Cesária Évora expresses the feeling of "*Sodade*"—a feeling of nostalgia and hopeful longing to be with loved ones who are so far away. She sings (on the CD "Cesaria Evora—Miss Perfumado, 1992, RCA/BMG):

Sôdade

Quem mostra bô—Who shows to you
Ess caminho longe—This far road (or way)?
Quem mostra bô—Who shows to you
Ess caminho longe—This far road (or way)?

Ess caminho—this road (or way)
Pa São Tomé—to São Tomé

Sôdade, sôdade
Dess nha terra São Nicolau—from my homeland São Nicolau

Si bô'screve me—If you write to me
Mi ta 'screve be—I will write to you
Si bô 'squece me—If you forget me
Mi ta 'squece be—I will forget you

Ate dia—Until the day
Qui bô volta—You return here

Sôdade, sôdade
Dess nha terra São Nicolau—from my homeland São Nicolau

URBAN MIGRATION SINCE WORLD WAR II

Most of the post–World War II increase in rural-to-urban migration has occurred in the poor countries of Third World. Since 1975, for the first time in history, the majority of the world's urban population lives in the cities of Third World nations. The distribution of urban population is shown in Figure 6.3. Of the 1.543 billion urban dwellers of 1975, 859 million of them lived in these cities. This number represented about 56 percent of the total world urban at that time. Twenty years later, the total urban population had increased by more than 1 billion and 71 percent of the total lived in the cities of the poor nations. It is estimated that by 2015, nearly 84 percent of an urban population totaling almost 4 billion people will be living in the poor nations (OECD, 1999). By that time, migration and natural increase will result in a total of 26 so-called megacities, that is, cities with over 10 million inhabitants (Fig. 6.4). With the exception of New York, Los Angeles, Paris (with "only" 9.7 million people), Tokyo, and Osaka, the other 21 megacities will be located in the poor nations. Another 10 cities in the poor nations will have at least 8 million inhabitants. The concentration of the world's urban population into cities of developing nations is due to many economic, social, and historical factors. One analysis by Puga (1998) compares urbanization patterns in Europe versus the less developed nations. Puga notes that in both the rich and poor nations the initial growth of cities may be attributed to three major factors: (1) transportation costs, (2) economies of scale, and (3) labor migration across regions and sectors. Cities concentrate not only people, but also goods and services, and this lowers transportation costs. Economies of scale refers to the fact that with greater concentrations of producers and consumers, the scale of cities brings economic efficiencies that cannot be had by equally populous but more disperse populations. Cities also provide possibilities for employment, because people can both

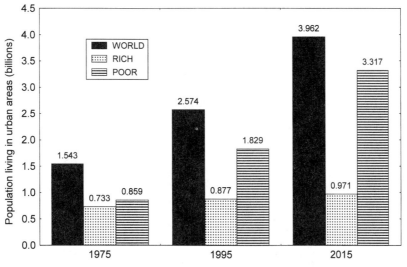

FIGURE 6.3 Population living in urban areas of the world in three time periods. The data are presented for the total world population, the number living in cities of the richer nations, and the number living in cities of the poorer nations (OECD, 1999).

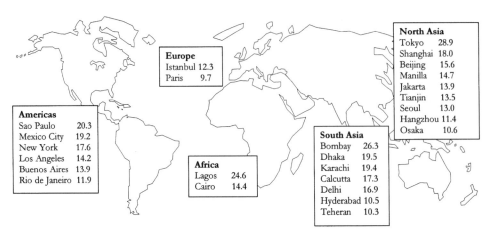

FIGURE 6.4 Megacities (10 million or more inhabitants) of the world in the year 2015 (after OECD, 1999).

move from employer to employer within the same job area (labor migration across regions) or move from one job type to another (labor migration across sectors).

Puga then notes the important differences between the richer and poorer nations. European urbanization took place mainly in the nineteenth century. Relative to today, there were higher costs of transportation but also weaker economies of scale. Furthermore, with greater dependence on rural agriculture in the nineteenth century there was a less-elastic supply of labor to the urban sector. These factors allowed for a more disperse network of small urban centers, a historical tradition that continues today in much of Europe. The Netherlands, for example, has many cities, but none tops 1 million inhabitants. In contrast, during the twentieth century the poorer nations were faced with the overwhelming power of economies of scale, which pulls social, economic, and political institutions into ever-larger urban agglomerations. Combined with large rural populations and little gainful rural employment, people were pushed off the land and into the cities. These factors could help explain why megacities have come to dominate in the poor nations, whereas a comparatively small share of urban population lives in Europe's largest cities.

Large populations, dense populations, and high rates of in-migration are the most important characteristics of cities today. These characteristics lead to several types of problems for humans. These include the "technological problems of water supply, pollution, waste management; socioeconomic problems of poverty, unemployment, and social conflict; and biological problems of disease and ill health" (Harrison and Jeffries, 1977, p. 65). It is to these biological problems, which are especially acute in the poor nations, that we now turn our attention.

ARE CITIES GOOD OR BAD FOR PEOPLE?

In most nations today, "cities generate a majority of the economic activity, ultimately consume most of the natural resources, and produce most of the pollution and waste" (World Bank, 1996). Depending upon where one's interests lie, these characteristics of contemporary cities are wonderful or disastrous for human well-being.

The historical evidence certainly shows that people living in cities have suffered in terms of health. But is this an inevitable property of cities, or is it due to biocultural factors that are only correlated with certain types of urban lifestyles, but not really caused by cities per se? There are several different lines of reasoning that lead us to suspect, a priori, that urban living should be deleterious to human biology and culture. This evidence includes a consideration of the following:

1. **Evolution.** Humans evolved as nomadic hunters and gatherers, living in small band populations. Cities are composed of sedentary, industrially and technologically employed peoples living in large groups. Humans are capable of a great range of adaptive responses to new environmental stress, but the genetic limits of this range are determined by the nature of adaptation to past environments (Harrison and Jeffries, 1977). The newness of the urban environment in evolutionary time is, therefore, a potential threat to human physical well-being.

2. **Growth and Development.** People develop phenotypic adaptations to their local environments. These include the irreversible changes in growth that occur during childhood and adolescence as well as the development of disease immunities that occur even in adulthood (Weissman et al., 1978). Adaptation to local diets and activity patterns also shape human physiological adaptations. Migration to an urban environment following long-term residence in a rural area may well present a significant stress to human physiology.

3. **Demographic.** Following from McNeill's (1979) model and empirical research, urban populations were faced with high rates of mortality. In addition to massive levels of in-migration, this may have stimulated high rates of fertility to maintain urban population size. Or, excessive deaths to people of childbearing age may have reduced fertility. These demographic stresses may result in both biological and social disorder.

4. **Biocultural Adaptation.** Band, tribal, and chiefdom societies were the basis of human social organization for the 99 percent of our evolutionary history that preceded the appearance of the first cities. These social groups are characterized by kinship (biological and fictive) as the organizing principle of society. However, kinship is less of a determinant of urban population structure. The large, densely populated conglomerates of cities require different patterns of social organization. These patterns have been analyzed in the social science literature dealing with urbanization (Butterworth and Chance, 1981; Hauser and Schnore, 1965; Michelson, 1970). Suffice it to state here that rural-living peoples continue to organize their lives along the lines of our preurban ancestors. When these rural peoples migrate to the city, they may be forced into rapid social change. This may lead to considerable psychological stress, and precipitate physical and mental illness (Carlstram and Levi, 1971; Clegg and Garlick, 1980).

Thus, rural-to-urban migration may lead to a considerable reduction in the "fitness" of human populations, as reflected in reduced fertility, poor growth and development, poor health, and greater mortality at all ages.

The prevalence of disease and mortality in the premodern city has already been discussed. But, what of the modern city? In an essay on the historical development of the modern city, Tuan (1978) explores "the idea that cities are artifacts and worlds of artifice placed at varying distances from human conditions close to nature." It is Tuan's opinion that the natural human condition is that "bound to food production and . . . the natural rhythms of day and night and of the seasons (P. 1)." To Tuan, the development of contemporary cities, such as New York, Tokyo, Bombay, and Lagos, is not inevitable, natural, or desirable. Life in the cities of the poorer nations is viewed with even greater disdain by O'Dell (1984). In her opinion, the urban poor of the less developed countries live in "crowded, squalid, often temporary dwellings [that] sprawl along mud paths littered with garbage, human refuse, and pests of every variety . . . Urban mortality rates, especially for small children, are higher than those in rural areas."

The opinion of other writers is that the evils of the city even extend back into the rural areas. Lipton (1977) perceives an urban bias in public policy. Keyfitz (1982) describes this bias as "the perversity of urbanization." By this he means that urban centers prosper at the expense of rural social and economic development. Keyfitz notes that as the standard of living in the countryside deteriorates, this pushes people into the city. The result is overurbanization, a force of unknown magnitude and significance for human survival.

To counteract the pernicious effects of overurbanization, some researchers write about "optimal city size" and place that size at 250,000 to 500,000 people (Rogers and Williamson, 1982). But, there is little hard evidence that larger cities are, in themselves, harmful to people. These "optimal" numbers are calculated in terms of economic factors, not in terms of social or biological realities. The reality is that "life in the city implies first and foremost a regular supply of goods and services, and the existence of institutions associated with this provision" (Eveleth and Tanner, 1976 p. 145). In the countryside of the less developed countries, the rhythm of nature means that prior to the harvest people may go without adequate food. Water may be contaminated by disease organisms, especially in the rainy season. Workloads are heavy, even for children and pregnant or lactating mothers. Social, economic, and health support services are rare. In the cities of these developing nations, food storage and distribution services provide a supply of food throughout the year. Treated water is available. The physical demands of labor are often less than those of rural agriculture. The largest health, educational, and welfare facilities are in the city. In short, the city may not be such a bad place.

Of course, not all of the people of the city share equally in these services and benefits. But, the slums and suffering that exist in the city are not the fault of urbanization per se; they are the fault of the larger society. Perhaps at this point it is best to counter the view that cities are bad for people with the notion that the city "is the product of human society and arises from human social nature" (Briggs, 1983, p. 371). The city is not artificial. As we will see in the sections to follow, the biological consequences of living in the city are not always, or even often, deleterious. Most empirical studies of rural-to-urban migration in the latter part of the twentieth century find that the health of migrants is better, their mortality is lower, their children grow taller, and their fertility is closer to optimal than for rural **sedentes** (people who remain in their place of birth). These indicators show that by evolutionary, developmental, and biosocial criteria, people usually adapt success-fully to the urban environment.

BIOCULTURAL RESEARCH ON URBAN ADAPTATION

The human sciences were slow to appreciate the importance of the phenomenon of rural-to-urban migration. It was not until 1885 that Ravenstein published his famous "laws of migration." This was a list of eight common characteristics of migrants and migration including: 1, most migrants move only a short distance; 2, there is a process of absorption, whereby people immediately surrounding a rapidly growing town move into it and the gaps they leave are filled by migrants from more distant areas, and so on until the attractive force (pull factor) is spent; 3, there is a process of dispersion, which is the inverse of absorption; 4, each migration flow produces a compensating counter-flow; 5, long-distance migrants go to one of the great centers of commerce and industry; 6, natives of towns are less migratory than those from rural areas; 7, females are more migratory than males; and 8, economic factors are the main cause of migration. Most of these "laws" are now outmoded because newer research finds too many exceptions of contradictions. It is best to consider the list as findings based on Ravenstein's research of the migration situation in Europe in the nineteenth century.

Interest in the biological effects of urban migration followed with Livi's (1896) study of the growth of Italian migrants and Ammon's (1899) work on the growth of rural-born Germans in Baden (both cited in Boas, 1922). Migration studies were of sporadic interest through the 1960s. In the late 1960s the International Biological Program was established, and one of its aims was to consider human biology in various environments. Soon after, edited works by Boyden (1970), Harrison and Gibson (1976), and Baker (1977a) appeared that addressed the issues related to the human urban environment. The remainder of this chapter reviews the findings on the biological consequences of rural-to-urban migration.

GROWTH AND DEVELOPMENT

The earliest studies of the biology of urban migrants deal with physical growth. So, it is appropriate to begin the discussion of the biological effects of turban migration with these works. Today it is common for anthropologists, public health workers, physicians, economists, historians, and others to use measures of physical growth and development in their research. This is so because the physical growth of an individual, and the aggregate growth of the population of which they are members, is highly sensitive to the overall quality of the environment (Schell, 1997; Tanner, 1986; Waterlow et al., 1977). That environment includes the conditions for health and disease, nutritional status, and educational, social, and emotional support (Bogin, 1999a). The tradition of measuring human growth to assess the quality of the environment has roots that extend far back in history (Boyd, 1980; Tanner, 1981), but it is most well developed by the founders of modern public health. Medical hygienists in the nineteenth century established the decline of health associated with urbanization and industrialization by measuring the height and weight of people. In

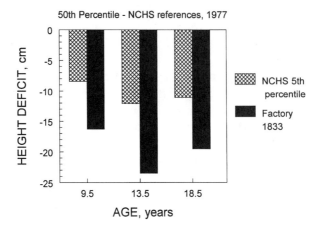

FIGURE 6.5 Height of English factory children in 1833 compared with the National Center for Health Statistics (NCHS) references. The heights of the factory children are shown as deficits, in centimeters, to both the 50th percentile and the 5th percentile of the NCHS references.

France, Louie-René Villermé (1782–1863) found in 1829 that military conscripts from mill or factory areas were too short and suffered too many disabilities to make them fit for military service. Edwin Chadwick (1800–1890) published data on growth and health of factory children in his *Report of the Commissioners on the Employment of Children in Factories* (1833). Some of these data are reproduced in Figure 6.5, which compares the average height deficit of the English factory children (as reported by Tanner, 1981) against the international reference data for stature published by the United States National Center for Health Statistics (NCHS) (Hamill et al., 1977). In this figure, the "0" line represents the 50th percentile height of the reference population. The factory children are 16.3 to 23.5 cm shorter than the NCHS 50th percentile and 7.9 to 11.4 cm below the NCHS 5th percentile. In a group of children an average height below the 5th percentile is an indication of major growth delay and stunting. This magnitude of stunting is usually seen only in children with serious pathology. Even children growing up under conditions of poverty in the least developed nations of the world today have average heights above the 5th percentile of the NCHS references. At 18.5 years of age only the Pygmy populations of central Africa have smaller average heights—about 150 cm for Pygmies versus 158 cm for the factory children.

Children were employed in factories because they were less costly than adults and more easily persuaded and coerced than adults into performing onerous tasks. Of course, children had long worked on farms in rural areas, but they usually worked as part of a family system of production. The possibility of using child workers as independent, wage-earning laborers was a direct consequence of the Industrial Revolution. Between the years 1765 and 1782, James Watt (1736–1819) developed a commercially viable steam engine, which forever changed the nature of human labor. The factory system ushered in under steam power reduced the need for the muscle power of adults and allowed children to be employed for many tasks. Industrial employment became a powerful technological and social force working against the welfare of children. One survivor of childhood labor described his life to a British Parliamentary investigation in 1832 (Sommerville, 1982, pp. 161–162):

> Have you ever been employed in a factory?—Yes.
> At what age did you first go to work?—Eight.
> Will you state the hours of labour at the period when you first went to the factory, in ordinary time?—From 6 in the morning to 8 at night.
> When trade was brisk what were your hours?—From 5 in the morning to 9 in the evening.
> With what intervals at dinner?—An hour [once per day].
> During those long hours of labour could you be punctual; how did you awake?—I seldom did awake spontaneously; I was more generally awoke, or lifted from bed, sometimes asleep, by my parents.
> Were you always on time?—No.
> What was the consequence if you had been too late?—I was most commonly beaten.
> Severely?—Very severely, I thought.

The testimony continues at some length and describes a life in the factories of fatigue and hunger punctuated by beatings.

In response to these findings, Friedrich Engels (1820–1895) campaigned extensively against the employment of children in English factories. Engels cited evidence of stunted growth, spine and bone deformities, and the physical and sexual abuse of child workers. Some physicians, Engels proclaimed, said that the factory districts would produce "a race of pigmies" (Sommerville, 1982, p. 146) by a kind of evolutionary decline. Engels may have misunderstood the workings of evolutionary biology, but his social approach to growth stunting was correct. Chadwick's *Report* included Engels's concerns and that report, along with personal testimonies, led to the passing of the Factories Regulation Act (1833) in England. The Act prohibited the employment of children under the age of nine and stipulated that periods for eating and rest must be provided for older children during the workday.

Age was determined by the state of dental maturation as assessed by the eruption of permanent teeth. Sir Edwin Saunders published, in 1837, an extensive survey that verified the relationship between tooth eruption and chronological age. Saunders assessed the state of permanent molar eruption in English school children at ages 9 and 13 years and showed that dental eruption was a better indicator of chronological age than height. By this work Saunders helped establish that development of the dentition is less influenced by the environment, while height, and therefore skeletal development, is more affected. In later years an appreciation of these differences would lead to the crucial concept of "biological versus chronological age" and research leading to the production of atlases of dental and skeletal development as well as tables of normal growth in height, weight, and other dimensions. These atlas and tables are the basic tools used by public health workers today to assess the well-being of individuals and populations [see Bogin (1999a) for more details of this history and for examples of the use of growth tables and developmental atlases]. In a very direct way, then, research on the well-being of rural-to-urban migrants led to many basic discoveries about human physical growth and development. The application of these discoveries in public health and medicine led to the betterment of health for young people and adults.

More careful research of the differences in growth between people living in the countryside and the city began toward the end of the nineteenth century. Meredith (1979) and Malina et al. (1981) review studies from the period 1880 to 1920 that show rural-living children in the United States and Europe were taller than their urban peers. A historical study by Steegmann (1985) found that this was true even a century earlier. Eighteenth-century British military records show that the stature of rural-born recruits averaged 168.6 cm and the urban-born recruits averaged 167.5 cm, a statistically significant difference. The rural height advantage persisted until about 1930, after which urban children are consistently taller and heavier than rural children. These studies give us some ideas about changes in the rural and urban environment at the turn of the century. Rural versus urban differences in growth (height, weight, body proportions), body composition (lean and fat body mass), and maturation (skeletal age, menarche) have been summarized by Eveleth and Tanner (1976), Meredith (1979), and Susanne (1984). But, despite dozens of studies on urban versus rural populations, there are only a few that treat rural-to-urban migrants.

Studies by Livi (1896) and Ammon (1899) (both cited in Boas, 1922) treat urban migrants. Livi found that the children of urban migrants in Italy were taller than rural sedentes. He believed the reason for this was heterosis, the marriage of urban migrants from different rural regions leading to "genetic vitality" in their offspring. Ammon also found the children of migrants to be taller than rural sedentes, but he argued for the action of natural selection to explain this. It is not clear exactly what he meant by this. Perhaps he believed that when faced with the rigors of the urban environment only the "fittest" (the tallest?) would survive.

Livi's and Ammon's speculations that heterosis or natural selection were at work stem directly from their erroneous belief that human types were genetically fixed and that types would not change when exposed to different environments. That belief was shattered by the publication of Boas's (1912) study of the changes in the bodily form of descendants of immigrants. Boas found that the children of immigrants to the United States were taller and differently shaped than their parents and the nonmigrating populations from which their parents came. He stated that neither natural selection nor heterosis could adequately account for these changes. Rather, modifications in the process of growth and development as a response to environmental change were responsible. Boas was vigorously attacked for this position. In a series of papers he whittled away at his attackers (see Boas, 1940). His evidence against the fixity of types was that (1) the physical differences between parents and children appear early in the life of the child and persist until adulthood; (2) the longer the childhood exposure to the American urban environment, the greater the physical difference; (3) children from large families are shorter than children from smaller families of the same "racial type"; and (4) differences between parents and children are greater when both were foreign born, meaning that only the children would have been exposed to the new environment during the developmental years, than when the child was American born, meaning that the parents may have spent some of their growth years in the United States.

The classic studies by Shapiro (1939) on the growth of Japanese children in Japan and Hawaii and of Goldstein (1943) and Lasker (1946, 1952) on the growth of Mexicans in Mexico and the United States confirmed the nature of human developmental plasticity. Today, human developmental plasticity is taken for granted, but it was the migration data of Boas that established the validity of this phenomenon.

Shapiro's Japanese migrant study compared the growth of Hawaiian-born Japanese of Japanese immigrant parentage, Japan-born Japanese who migrated to Hawaii, and Japanese sedentes living in the same villages from which the migrants originated. The sedentes were mostly farmers and laborers in rural villages. The exact location of the migrants is not given, but 65 percent of the recent immigrants were employed in sedentary occupations (store clerks), and 76 percent of the Hawaiian-born were either students or sedentary workers. The immigrants appeared to have been developing an urban lifestyle. The sedentes and the recent immigrants differed in a few anthropometric measurements, some increasing and some decreasing with migration. The largest differences were between the immigrants and the Hawaiian born. The latter are taller and more linear in body build than their parents or the sedentes. Shapiro argues that with migration there were improvements in diet, health care, and socioeconomic status and that these conditions, associated with an urban lifestyle, are responsible for the growth changes.

A nearly ideal study of rural-to-urban migration and growth was carried out in Poland. The results were published in Polish by Panek and Piasecki (1971) and were summarized in English by Eveleth and Tanner (1976). A new industrial town was created on the outskirts of Cracow in 1949. In 1965 the population reached 1,599 persons per square kilometer, similar to many European cities. Most of the population growth was due to migration from rural villages. The children and youth measured for the study had been born in the "new city" or had lived there at least 10 years. The children living in the new city were, on average, 5 to 6 cm taller and 1 to 2 kg heavier than the rural sedentes. The urban children matured earlier, both for tooth eruption and age of menarche. Thus, even in the post–World War II period, the children of urban migrants experienced significant improvements in growth.

Children living in the cities of the less developed countries are usually taller and mature earlier than their rural age peers. But, migrants to urban slums in these countries do not usually experience the benefits of the urban environment. In Asia, Africa, and Latin America these slums are often on the outskirts of the cities. As squatter settlements they have no official access to city services and facilities. Not surprisingly, the growth of migrant children living in these slums is not significantly different from that of children living in the impoverished rural areas (Davies et al., 1974; Graham et al., 1979; Johnson, 1970; Morley et al., 1968; Villarijos et al., 1971). In at least one case, the urban slum children of Oaxaca, Mexico, are significantly shorter and lighter than nearby rural children from a reasonably prosperous town (Malina et al., 1981).

In contrast to these cases, Bogin and MacVean (1981c) studied the growth of three groups of children living in Guatemala City: (1) children of two city-born parents, (2) children of two rural-born migrant parents, and (3) children of one city-born and one rural-born migrant parent. All of the children were of low socioeconomic status and attended a public school. Most lived in impoverished areas of the city, but none were from the types of urban slums discussed above. All of these children were taller and heavier than rural-living children of the same age. Also, as expected, children of city-born parents were significantly taller than children of rural-born parents. Unexpectedly, children with one city-born and one rural-born parent were the tallest. This was true for families in which the mother or the father was the migrant. The families of the rural-born parents were of significantly lower socioeconomic status than the families of the two other kinds of parents. This difference probably correlated with factors responsible for the growth differences, but other important information, such as age of the mothers and age at migration to the city, was not known.

A possible reason for taller children in this Guatemalan study is the biological selection of individuals for migration and for marriage. Such selection may explain the biological correlates of migration in some of the other studies already discussed. By biological selection it is meant that migrants may not be a random sample of the rural population. Migrants may be genetically taller, mature more rapidly, or differ in other physical aspects from rural sedentes. Positive assortative mating between such people may further differentiate migrants from sedentes.

Several studies provide tentative support for biological selection. In Shapiro's (1939) study, the recent Japanese immigrants to Hawaii were taller than the Japan sedentes. However, age at migration, length of time in Hawaii, and premigration living conditions were not known. Though Shapiro suggested that biological selection was possible, he argued more strongly for the plasticity of human growth in the new environment. By this he meant that migrant children grew more than sedentes, but only after they migrated to Hawaii. Steegmann's (1985) historical study of eighteenth-century British military recruits found that conscript who migrated from their county of birth were significantly taller (169.1 cm) than recruits living in the county of their birth (167.6 cm). Recall, though, that he also found that urban-born recruits were shorter than rural-born men. Steegmann points out that eighteenth-century Britain was a developing country and that food shortages and unhygienic living conditions characterized urban areas. Thus migration to the city was probably not responsible for an increase in stature; rather taller men living in rural counties were more likely to migrate than shorter men. Whether these were genetically taller men or individuals who had experienced better living conditions prior to migration is not known.

In the United Kingdom, Martin (1949) found that, among men inducted into the army, (1) migrants (men living in a county other than their county of birth) were taller and heavier than the national average and (2) migrants were taller and heavier than the natives of the recipient counties. However, Martin also found that the sedentes of the recipient areas were taller and heavier than the sedentes of the exporting counties and that migrants to "tall" counties were taller than migrants to "short" counties. These two facts suggested that the receiving counties in general, and the tall counties in particular, had better living conditions than the exporting, or short, areas, but data for this and age at migration were not known.

Based on a retrospective study of 14 different ethnic groups, Kaplan (1954) found that migration was selective for physical type. Growth differences between migrants and sedentes were found too soon after migration to be due to an environmental change. However, no account of age of migration or the premigration environment was given. Illsley et al. (1963) studied migrants into and out of

Aberdeen, Scotland. They found that all migrants were taller than rural or urban sedentes. Migrants had generally better health than sedentes. Migrant women had lower rates of low birth weight and perinatal death for their children. Finally, migrants were generally of higher socioeconomic status than sedentes. The Illsley et al. study suggests what the true meaning of migrant selection may be; it is more likely to be selection for socioeconomic status than biological selection per se. More recent studies confirm this. Kobyliansky and Arensburg (1977) studied migrants from Russia and Poland to Israel. The migrants were of higher socioeconomic status and were taller than the Eastern European sedentes. Mascie-Taylor (1984) reviewed geographic and social mobility in England and found that the effects of selection are additive; migrants tended to be the taller individuals of any geographic area and the taller individuals within any social class. However, the higher social classes were also more mobile. Which is more important, stature or social class? Higher socioeconomic status can, by itself, lead to increased body size and rate of maturation. As MacBeth (1984) concluded in her review of this issue, the socioeconomic status difference confounds any unique biological difference between migrants and sedentes. Further confounding the issue is the fact that there is greater mobility to higher social classes for the tall [a review of this topic is presented in Bogin 1999a)]. However, the predominant selection of migrants seems to be for socioeconomic status rather than for tallness. This is supported by migration research from the social and economic literature (Rogers and Williamson, 1982) as well as the biological literature cited above.

Indeed, the most well controlled, prospective studies found no evidence for biological selection. These studies identified and measured individuals before migration. Lasker (1952) and Lasker and Evans (1961) found that age of migration and length of time in the new environment were responsible for growth differences between migrants from Mexico to United States and Mexican sedentes. Similarly, no growth differences were found between eventual urban migrants and rural sedentes in South Africa (De Villiers, 1971), Switzerland (Hulse, 1969), and Oaxaca, Mexico (Malina et al., 1982).

It seems, then, that the classic research by Boas (1912), Shapiro (1939), Goldstein (1943), and Lasker (1952) on the human growth response to migration came to the correct conclusion. Environment, as mediated by such factors as socioeconomic status, is the primary determinant of biological change in growth and development following rural-to-urban migration. The most recent studies support this conclusion. Asian migrants to the city of Glasgow, Scotland, have been getting taller with each generation born in the city (Shams and Williams, 1997). The same has happened to urban-dwelling people of Portugal in the past century (Padez and Johnston, 1999). There is no evidence of migrant selection for height in either Glasgow or Portugal, but there is every indication that improved nutrition and public health are the causes for greater growth in height. As the benefits of the urban environment filter back to rural settings, even the rural sedentes show greater growth in stature (Rousham and Gracey, 1998). Perhaps the most powerful replication and confirmation of the classic research is my own research on Maya immigrants to the United States, which was presented in Box 1.2. These Maya immigrants show the largest increase in growth in height so far recorded in the research literature (see also Bogin and Loucky, 1997).

BOX 6.2
Migrations Caused by Droughts and Consequent Floods of Famine: Case of the Cape Verde Islands

Maria Inês Varela Silva

Cape Verde experiences meager and unpredictable rains. The islands are also subjected to *harmattan* winds from the Sahara, which bring much dust and sand. These conditions result in periodic droughts that have devastated the islands, causing massive famine and suffering (Carreira, 1982, pp. 15–16):

> The inevitable irregularity of the rains, witnessed by so many droughts over the years, causes a grave lack of basic subsistence foods—maize, beans, manioc, sweet potato—and of fodder for cattle. Hence, there is endemic, or at least latent, famine. When it breaks out, it brings catastrophic mortality of men and domestic animals, from lack of food and water. "Crisis years," as they are called when 10–30 percent of the population have sometimes died, and livestock been reduced to derisory numbers, have succeeded one another at regular intervals.

One consequence of these natural disasters is migration of the human population away from the islands. According to Carreira (1984), the first recorded drought happened between 1580 and 1583. The number of human deaths is not known, but many people moved to the wet African coast trying to escape from the famine and disease that followed the drought. The drought of 1610 to 1611 caused a similar situation and was followed by several other social catastrophes, such as robberies of all sorts and a great increase of women who sacrificed their "honour" to rich men in order to get some food and protection. To add to all of this, a plague of flies swept the entire island of Santiago killing the cattle and, as a final disaster, an epidemic of chicken pox killed a large number of the population. Data for the seventeenth to the nineteenth centuries are rare, but there is some information about the famine that occurred in 1809 to 1811. In a report to the King of Portugal, dated August 24, 1811, the people from Boavista Island asked for help stating that, in addition to the large number of human deaths, the proportions of livestock deaths were incredibly high and the herds were reduced to the following proportions:

- 1,200 alive goats out of 50,000,
- 200 donkeys alive out of 20,000,
- 42 cows alive out of 6,000, and
- 4 horses alive out of 4,000.

The demographic data shown in Table B6.2, which covers the period 1870 to 1970, reveals fluctuations in the number of births and death, most of which is caused by death as a consequence of famine. The population size, by sex, is given for each of the leeward and windward island groups. The declines in population size noted in the census of 1905, 1929, and 1949 reflect the mortality caused by famine: 14,480 deaths in 1903 to 1904, 5,192 deaths in 1919 to 1920, 17,575 deaths in 1921, 24,463 in 1941 to 1943, and 20,813 deaths in 1947 to 1948—a total of 82,523 deaths. These numbers were calculated after the deduction of the normal general mortality, according to the annual averages in each period before each crisis. Despite the droughts, famines, and death, the Cape Verdean population has increased in size with time (Carreira, 1982, p. 17):

> Famines cut down thousands, but the human resources were reconstructed within a few years, merely by natural increase, at a rate of between 2.5 and 3.5 percent.

TABLE B6.1
Population of Cape Verde Islands, by Island Group, and Gender Proportions (Number of Women per 100 Men)

Years	Leeward Islands		Windward Islands		Total (Men and Women)	Gender Proportions (Women/Men)
	Men	Women	Men	Women		
1870	20,897	25,157	13,733	16,216	76,003	119.5
1882	30,456	38,109	16,588	18,608	103,761	120.5
1888	36,937	43,890	18,567	21,723	121,127	118.2
1891	39,252	46,060	20,220	22,300	127,832	114.9
1898	42,711	50,694	23,396	25,736	142,537	115.0
1900	43,917	49,785	24,876	28,846	147,424	114.3
1905	37,390	44,548	23,859	28,396	134,193	119.1
1909	40,152	48,595	24,775	28,821	142,343	119.2
1919	45,670	51,438	28,999	33,800	159,907	114.2
1929	40,532	50,186	28,682	34,347	153,738	122.1
1939	48,299	57,270	31,949	32,803	174,403	117.3
1949	33,980	43,440	28,943	32,808	139,171	121.2
1950	38,772	47,422	28,530	33,607	148,331	105.5
1960	58,249	67,512	35,778	40,010	201,549	114.4
1970	*	*	*	*	272,072	*

This last figure was reached between 1950–60 and 1960–70, precisely during periods when there was neither famine nor heavy death toll nor even significant immigration to influence the demographic movement. Thus, the high fertility of the archipelago population has brought on, over the years, a true "population explosion" . . . The most concrete evidence lies in the rapid rebuilding of population reserves after heavy losses by famine, and in the huge positive demographic balances that appear when one considers general birth and death statistics.

Also shown in Table B6.1 are the numbers of adult women per 100 men. This gender proportion gives, in a certain way, an indication of the influences of the preferential male migration. Migratory floods away from the Cape Verdean islands during the twentieth century are due in part to the periods of drought and famine. But, the migratory flow is also due, according to Mattos (1994), to the following phenomena:

(a) *Push factors*—economical difficulties of the population and high birth rate, which only makes resources and employment more difficult.

(b) *Pull factors*—the need of unskilled, or poorly skilled, laborers in developed countries, offer of better standards of living, and sense of adventure (facilitated by the demographic pressure).

(c) *Values and communication*—the historical tradition of emigration (since the days of whaling in the eighteenth century), information about the "new worlds" transmitted by the former emigrants, the stories (told by other emigrants) about the higher standard of living, and the ease with which it is obtained in the new worlds.

The Cape Verdean emigration has focused on several destinations, depending on the internal and external situation of the country. Being a very strong tradition, even nowadays, it is rare to find a family in Cape Verde that does not have, at least, one of its members living and working abroad (França, 1992; Silvestre, 1994). The distribution of emigration is as shown in Table B6.2, according to the Cape Verdean Census of 1985.

The motives for emigration to these destinations are not all the same. The main ones are summarized, below according to regions of the world.

(a) To the United States and the Americas

The beginning of the emigration had its origin in the eighteenth century, mainly related with the American whaling industry that expanded into the Sea of Azores and around the Cape Verdean Islands. This reinforced the contact between Americans and Cape Verdeans and opened opportunities for the latter to become part of the whaling crews. Many of these Cape Verdean crew members eventually settled in the home ports of the ships along the New England coast of the United States.

Apart from whaling, the people from the islands began to travel by their own initiative, but the data are not reliable about the exact number of emigrants to the United States. Several laws were enacted in the United States to avoid the massive

TABLE B6.2
Estimations of Main Destinations of Cape Verdean Emigrants

Continent	Destination	Number of Emigrants
America	United States	250,000
	Brazil	3,000
	Argentina	2,000
	Subtotal	255,000
Europe	Portugal	50,000
	The Netherlands	10,000
	Italy	10,000
	France	8,000
	Luxembourg	3,000
	Spain	2,000
	Switzerland	1,500
	Belgium	800
	Sweden	700
	Germany	500
	Norway	200
	Subtotal	86,700
Africa	Angola	35,000
	Senegal	23,000
	S. Tomé e Príncipe	8,000
	Guinea-Bissau	2,000
	Subtotal	68,000
Total		409,700

Source: From Census (1985).

entrance of foreigners, but clandestine ways were found to reach their purposes of living in the United States. Nevertheless, this increasing difficulty to enter the United States initiated a migratory flow to Argentina and Brazil, which continued until the middle 1930s.

(b) To Africa

The migratory flows to Africa were due in large part to the fact that, by going to the other Portuguese colonies, the Cape Verdeans did not have to face the problems of language as well as the problems of the legalization of their entrance. All subjects of Portugal had free access to immigrate to all colonies.

(c) To Europe

Anti-immigrant laws in the United States also promoted emigration to several countries in Europe. There are not precise data about the reasons for choosing a particular country, and for this reason, I will focus only on the migration flow to Portugal. The Cape Verdean community in Portugal has been the oldest and the biggest of Europe. Even so, the Cape Verdean emigrants have faced serious difficulties, especially after the independence of Cape Verde, when they came to be considered as a foreigners (Silvestre, 1994).

According to França (1992), there were three major migrations to Portugal, which were coincident with specific historical and economical periods:

1. The first one occurred during the 1960s, motivated by some governmental entities in order to fill the gap left in some economical sectors by the Portuguese who were emigrating out of the country. Cape Verdeans also filled jobs vacated by young adult Portuguese men who were mobilized to fight in the colonial wars in Angola and Mozambique.

2. The second migration arrived immediately after the Portuguese political revolution, which took place in April 1974. Included within this group of immigrants were also people returning from the other colonies (Angola, Mozambique, Sao Tomé e Príncipe, and Portuguese Guinea). These immigrants included European colonists as well as political refugees. Many of these people were escaping the political instability and violence in the former colonies caused by the beginning of the process of independence. Cape Verde and Sao Tomé e Príncipe were the only former Portuguese colonies that reached independence without civil war. Today, Cape Verde maintains a democratic and peaceful regimen—they are the people of *morabeza*.

3. The third migration occurred during 1980s and became the most problematic one as the immigrants were caught by an economical crisis in Portugal. Due to this fact, these people constitute the most professionally unqualified level of the population. Moreover, the integration of the people from this last flow has not succeeded as well as the two previous flows, as they have yet not built their own social identification abroad (Mattos, 1994).

The Cape Verdean community in Portugal from the third migration brought with them several ways of living and traditions that clashed with the rules of Portuguese society, creating many conflicts (Varela-Silva, 1996). These conflicts led the Cape Verdean people to find defensive mechanisms against the majority society in order to re-create and preserve their original realities. Nevertheless, the facts of the past and the present reality forge permanent links between the Portuguese and the Cape Verdean communities. The Cape Verdean immigrants conscientiously assume the difficult conditions of living in Portugal. In kind, the Portuguese people and the government have been trying to find ways to integrate these new groups of people.

The different cultural values and behaviors of Cape Verdeans and Portuguese constitute a means of enrichment of both groups. But, only a "good marriage" between them will be able to maximize the positive interactions. The glorious Portuguese "Age of Discoveries" is long gone, and there are no more new worlds, in a geographic sense, for the taking. However, there are many new sociocultural worlds to discover and without invasion. Cooperation between these worlds will allow the fusion of the Portuguese soul with the Cape Verdean fate and vice versa, in the way that, since the beginning, should have been done.

FERTILITY AND DEMOGRAPHY

Demographers focus on two issues relating to urban migration: (1) the rate of migration and (2) the age patterns of migration. In contrast, anthropologists often focus on other questions, such as (1) what is the most important reason for the phenomenal growth of urban populations and (2) how are rural lifestyles and values, including marriage and kinship, altered by urban migration? Both demographers and anthropologists share one research question: Who are the more fertile, urban natives or the urban migrants? In the discussion that follows I place emphasis on the anthropological questions but make reference to the demographic issues as required.

Rural-to-urban migration is certainly an important contributor to the growth of cities, but the rate of migration sets only the level of urbanization. It cannot account for all of urban population growth. Reclassification of rural lands, and peoples, surrounding metropolitan areas also increases the urban population, but this has only a minimal effect (Rogers, 1982). **Natural increase**, that is, the fertility of the urban population, seems to be the key factor. Natural increase sets the rate and the limit of urban population growth (Rogers, 1982). This brings us to the second question, that is, who contribute the most to the rate of natural increase, rural-to-urban migrants or the city born? Most research finds that migrant women have lower fertility than rural sedentes (Brockerhoff and Yang, 1994; Coleman, 1994; Meyers and Morris, 1966; Orlansky and Dubrovsky, 1978; Rogers, 1982; Umezaki and Ohtsuka, 1998; Zarate and Zarate, 1975; Zavattaro et al., 1997). Some studies find that migrants have lower fertility than urban natives (Brockerhoff and Yang, 1994; Orlansky and Dubrovsky, 1978; Rogers, 1982). Other research finds migrants have higher fertility than the urban born (Baker, 1977b; Liberty et al., 1976a,b; Hutchinson, 1961; Robinson, 1963; Zarate and Zarate, 1975). Contradictory findings are not surprising since "fertility" is the outcome of many biological, socioeconomic, and cultural forces.

Overall, the data are consistent with regard to rural-versus-urban differences. Urban fertility rates (and mortality rates) are lower than rural rates everywhere in the world today. Several factors are associated with cities that have been cited for lowering women's fertility:

1. higher socioeconomic status (Orlansky and Dubrovsky, 1978);
2. increased education (Chaundhury, 1978; Hinday, 1978; Ketkar, 1979; Kumudini, 1965; Lee and Farber, 1984; Macisco et al., 1969; Zavattaro et al., 1997);

3. low infant and childhood mortality (Frisancho et al., 1976; Ketkar, 1979; Robinson, 1963; Scrimshaw, 1978; Stinson, 1982);

4. age at migration and marriage (Hinday, 1978; Macisco et al., 1969; Robinson, 1963);

5. greater labor force participation (Freedman et al., 1959; Hinday, 1978; Ketkar, 1979; Lee and Farber, 1984; United Nations, 1975; Zavattaro et al., 1997);

6. modernization and political liberalization (Goldscheider, 1971; Sabagh and Yim, 1980; Scholl et al., 1976);

7. a high personal achievement orientation and value system (Benedict, 1972; Bogin and Loucky, 1997; Bogin and MacVean, 1981; Macisco et al., 1970); and

8. greater and use of birth control in the city (Umezaki and Ohtsuka, 1998).

All of these factors are associated with urban living. However, some studies find that even after these factors (such as age, education, occupation) and other influences on fertility (such as parity) are controlled, urban living itself still accounts for a significant reduction in fertility (Hinday, 1978; Lee and Farber, 1984; Mcyers and Morris, 1966; Rindfuss, 1976). Brockerhoff and Yang (1994) review the data for six sub-Saharan African countries—Ghana, Kenya, Malai, Senegal, Togo, and Uganda—and conclude that the decline in migrant fertility is due to "the rapid and pronounced improvement in the standard of living experienced by migrants after settling in the urban area" (p. 19).

Even though fertility in urban areas is lower than that in rural areas, there are a number of theoretical reasons why the fertility of rural-to-urban migrants might increase. The most important reasons relate to the opportunities for better health care, nutrition, and social services in the city. Healthier women and men are likely to be either more fertile or better able to carry a pregnancy to term and support an infant. Also, as shown in the previous section, the urban environment promotes faster growth and earlier maturation. All recent studies of rural-versus-urban physical maturation show that city-living girls reach menarche earlier than rural-living girls (Eveleth and Tanner, 1976). Presumably, the city folk also achieve functional fertility earlier. Finally, in some regions of the world more women than men migrate from rural areas to the city, and most of these are young women. This is the case for the recent migrations in the less developed countries of Asia and Latin America (Orlansky and Dubrovsky, 1978) and was true for migrations in northern Europe during the last century (Ravenstein, 1885). In contrast, just the opposite is true for much of Africa and Portugal (Brettell, 1986). Most of the initial migrants are men, who go to the city and try to settle there. Any women and children left in the rural areas are sent for after the man finds work and a place to live.

Thus, the potential for high migrant fertility is always present, but this potential is strongly countered by each of the factors listed above. Especially important are an average later age at first marriage, socioeconomic and cultural values that tend to delay births, and increased awareness and availability of contraceptive techniques, which all tend to reduce fertility among urban migrant women (Boyden, 1972).

THREE CASE STUDIES OF MIGRANT FERTILITY

The following case studies are offered to illustrate some of the factors that act simultaneously to influence fertility, especially in rural-to-urban migrants. These cases help to show why it is necessary to take a biocultural approach to the study of human fertility.

Case 1

Bogin and MacVean (1981c) studied three groups of families living in Guatemala City. There were (1) families with two city-born parents, (2) families with two rural-born migrant parents, and (3) families with one migrant and one city-born parent. Family size (number of children ever born to the parents) was assessed by a questionnaire. Mean family size for the group with two rural-to-urban migrant parents was 4.8 children, for the group with two city-born parents it was 4.5 children, and for the group with one migrant and one city-born parent it was 4.2 children. The first and last means are significantly different. The reason for the difference in fertility between families of different migration status was not clear. Some important variables, such as age of the mother, her age at marriage, and length of time in the city, were not known.

Even so, the fact that the families with one migrant and one city-born parent had the fewest children is unusual but not without precedent. Zarate and Zarate (1975) reviewed the research findings for migrant versus nonmigrant fertility differentials. Their review included studies from the United States, Puerto Rico, Latin America, Asia, and Africa (only one African and three Asian studies were published at that time). They found that the fertility of migrant women was generally higher than that of urban natives but lower than that of rural sedentes. An exception to the general trend was that younger migrant women, those under 35 years old, often had fertility rates lower than or equal to urban natives. Zarate and Zarate referred to studies from Puerto Rico by Macisco et al. (1969, 1970) and research in Thailand by Goldstein (1973) that may account for the age cross-over in fertility. These researchers speculated that the "innovative character" and "high achievement motivation" of the younger or more recent urban migrant may account for the decision to delay births. In a similar vein, Bogin and MacVean argue that compared with the other family types, the families with one migrant and one city-born parent had a combination of rural and urban experiences, values, and motivations that may have given them a wider range of adaptive strategies to urban life. A more recent study of Italian migrants to Belgium also finds that "mixed" marriages have the lowest fertility (Zavattaro et al., 1997). The migrants came from rural areas of southern Italy between the late 1940s to the 1960s. Their marriage and fertility patterns were analyzed, and it was found that over time the fertility of succeeding generations of migrants declined. The mean family size of the first generation, the original migrants, was 6.34 children. Mean family size of the second generation declined to 3.77, and further declined in the third generation to 1.96 children. Homogamous marriages (both Italians) of the third generation averaged 2.14 children, while heterogamous marriages ("mixed" marriages of one Italian and one Belgian spouse) averaged 1.79 children. Italians of higher education levels were more likely to be married with a Belgian. So, perhaps the lower fertility of the mixed marriages is an education and socioeconomic status effect.

Case 2

Most studies find migrant fertility to be lower than that of rural sedentes. In contrast, the fertility of women migrating from highland areas in the Andes Mountains to lowland rural or urban areas increases (Abelson, 1976; Foxman et al., 1984; Hoff and Abelson, 1976). One reason for decreased fertility and fecundity at high altitude may be **hypoxia**. The reduced partial pressure of oxygen at high altitude makes many physiological processes difficult for nonpregnant people. Pregnancy exacerbates this shortage of oxygen, which compromises the viability of the fetus (Moore et al., 1998). Infant mortality is also higher in the mountains than in lowland rural or urban areas. Undernutrition, infectious disease, cold, and other factors besides hypoxia contribute to low fertility and infant mortality. To compensate for prenatal and postnatal reproductive losses, high-altitude peoples may have cultural values and practices that maximize fertility and child survival in their native environment. These values and practices may be carried over to the new lowland environments and result in very high fertility rates in the first-generation migrants. Longitudinal studies of fertility adjustment in these migrants are needed to clarify the factors involved in this process.

Case 3

China is the world's most populous nation. In an attempt to control population growth, China imposed a one-child-per-couple family planning policy in the 1970s. Despite the policy, the nation experienced a slight rise in the birth rate in the mid-1980s. Many observers attributed this rise to the heightened fertility of those rural-to-urban migrants who moved without a change in registration. That is, these people were temporary migrants who retained their permanent residence in their place of origin. Some demographers presume that these people migrated in order to have two or more children by avoiding the surveillance of family planning programs at their town of origin and their destination. Goldstein et al. (1997) investigated the accuracy of this presumption. They used life history data from a 1988 survey of Hubei Province, and they compared nonmigrants, permanent migrants, and temporary migrants. They found that family planning policies have a strong impact on timing of first birth and on the likelihood of higher order births, meaning that most people have only one child. They also found that migrants generally do not have more children than nonmigrants. In fact, migration tends to lower the propensity to have a child. More to the point, the fertility of temporary migrants did not differ significantly from that of other women. The slight rise in the mid-1980 birth rate must be due to other, as yet unknown, causes.

MIGRANT SELECTION?

The question of migrant selection comes up in several of the studies cited above. For instance, people who delay marriage and births should find it easier to migrate, as they are more independent. The fact that in much of the world young, unmarried women predominate in the migration flow is evidence for such selection. Lee and Farber (1984) looked at this question of selection in detail for a group of married migrant women. The authors proposed three reasons for the common finding of fertility decline in rural women migrating to the city: (1) selection—migrants are a special group as regards, for example, demographics and socioeconomic status; (2) disruption—the act of migration interferes (e.g., economically and psychologically) with fertility goals for a time; and (3) adaptation—migrants assimilate the values of the urban social environment, which may occur even prior to migration and results in lowering of fertility with time. Lee and Farber found no evidence for disruption, for migrant women's fertility did not increase in the years following migration. To examine the effects of selection and adaptation, Lee and Farber analyzed the data of the Korean World Fertility Survey of 1974—5,000 women aged 20 to 49, married only once, with at least one live birth. Matching migrants and rural sedentes for socioeconomic status, education, and stated preferences for family size controlled the effect of selection. The migrants, living in the cities at the time of the survey, had significantly lower fertility than sedentes. Fertility decline persisted as the length of time in the city increased. The results negated selection and supported the adaptation explanation. In this case adaptation was interpreted as a shift from agricultural to wage-earning labor, greater labor force participation for women, and a revision of fertility goals as greater knowledge and experience in the city was obtained.

An important corollary of the Lee and Farber study is that rural-to-urban migration is lowering the overall fertility of populations in the poor, developing nations. Holmes (1976) predicted that rural fertility would increase with time as the low-fertility individuals selectively migrated to the city, but the Korean data show that rural-to-urban migration is reducing the fertility rate of that nation as a whole. This was also shown to be true for Latin America (Rogers, 1982) and is now the case for the whole world according to the most recent data for Africa and the rest of Asia (U.S. Census Bureau, *http://www.census.gov/icp/www/wp98.html*). The massive flow of rural-to-urban migrants initially increases the urban population, but as the migrants adapt to the urban environment, fertility decreases. This is exactly what happened in the United States during the last 100 years. In 1940, internal migrants from rural areas in the United States still had higher fertility than urban natives, though the youngest migrants were already achieving lower fertility than even the urban born. By 1960, only the oldest group of rural born had higher fertility than the urban born and even they decreased fertility by 20 percent (Zarate and Zarate, 1975). Because the United States is so highly urbanized, and the urban influence extends into rural areas, fertility has decreased dramatically. It is likely that the experience of the developed nations applies to the less developed countries as well. That is, the overall decline in world fertility and population growth is due in large part to rural-to-urban migration. Since the urban population of the entire planet, both rich and poor nations alike, will soon exceed the rural population, world fertility should continue to decline for the foreseeable future.

HEALTH STATUS AND MORTALITY

Migrants are susceptible to the diseases of both their place of origin and their new environments. Migration from the countryside to the city represents a drastic change in the physical, social, and cultural environment. It was noted long ago by Hippocrates that "it is changes that are chiefly responsible for disease, especially the violent alteration." Thus, it is not surprising that some studies find that rural-to-urban migrants have higher rates of disease than urban natives (Baker, 1984; Velimirovic, 1979; Way, 1976). It has been noted that urban migrants have increased risks for the development of certain infectious diseases (e.g., tuberculosis), hypertension, coronary heart disease, Type 2 diabetes (diabetes mellitus), gout, and obesity (see review by Bogin, 1988). But these diseases develop after the act of migration, and usually after the immigrants have lived in the city for several decades. Most research shows that the initial health of rural-to-urban migrants is better than that of the nonmigrating rural population (Baker, 1977a; Hajat et al., 2000; Hollsteiner and Tacon, 1982; Swanbrow, 2000). One sociologist commenting on the health of immigrants to the United States notes that "the relatively good health profile of Hispanics and especially Asians reflects in part the effects of immigration . . . Seventy percent of Asians are foreign-born, and immigrants of all racial groups tend to have better health than their native-born counterparts. Unfortunately, the health of immigrants also declines as length of stay in the United States increases" (David R. Williams, as quoted in Swanbrow, 2000 p. 13; see also Hajat et al., 2000). Finally, the research shows that since 1950 urban migrants have lower mortality at all ages than rural sedentes (Baker, 1977a; Rogers, 1982).

The migrants did not always have this health and mortality advantage. Placed in an evolutionary and historical context, rural-to-urban migration can be seen to have a changing pattern of impact on human health and mortality. As discussed above, the evolution of human infectious disease is coincident with the development of cities. The low-socioeconomic segments of the urban population were (and still are) also at risk for malnutrition and physically debilitating working conditions, especially for children. As a consequence, until the early part of this century city populations suffered higher infant, childhood, and adult mortality than rural populations. For instance, between 1871 and 1880 infant mortality in Sweden was 193/1,000 in urban areas and 119/1,000 in rural areas. Swedish life expectancy at that time was 43.4 years in the city versus 51.6 years in rural areas (Preston et al., 1981). Total life expectancy in England and Wales in 1841 was 40.2 years but only 35 years in London and 24 years in Manchester. Similar statistics hold for Norway and France. The census of England and Wales of 1911 shows that childhood mortality prior to age five was 20 percent of live-born children in urban areas and 14 percent in rural areas (Preston et al., 1981). Jorde and Durbize (1986) analyzed death certificates for Utah Mormons and found that prior to 1890 mortality rates were generally higher in urban areas than in rural areas. After 1890 the relative frequency of mortality of the two areas is reversed. The 1900 census of the United States shows the same pattern. Expressed as a ratio of actual deaths to statistically expected deaths, urban areas had a ratio of 1.14 (i.e., higher than expected) and rural areas a ratio of only 0.92 (Preston et al., 1981). Even controlling for the effects of socioeconomic status, working status of the mother, presence or absence of the father, or migrant versus sedente status shows that it was healthier to live in the countryside than in the city. Living conditions for most people in the urban areas of Europe and the United States at that time were like conditions in the urban slums of the less developed countries today.

Today, adaptations to the diseases of urbanization, including physiological changes, public health programs, child labor and education laws, medical treatment, and, possibly, genetic change, result in generally better health in the urban versus rural areas of the developed and developing world. Rural poverty, malnutrition, and high rates of infectious disease interact synergistically and result in higher rates of morbidity and mortality than in the city (Haines and Avery, 1982; Preston, 1975; 1980; Scrimshaw, 1978). This is true even for disadvantaged urban-living children, but the urban effect is complicated by several factors. In a survey of 17 poor nations, Brockerhoff (1994) found that the children of rural-to-urban "migrant women had similar or slightly higher mortality risks than children of women who remained in the village" (p. 127). The data for this survey are mothers and their infants under two years old examined in the late 1970s and the 1980s. Brockerhoff notes that during the two-year period before and after the women migrated to the city, their infants' "chances of dying increased sharply as a result of accompanying their mothers or being left behind, to levels well above those of rural and urban non-migrant children. Children born after migrants had settled in the urban area, however, gradually experienced much better survival chances than children of rural non-migrants, as well as lower mortality risks than migrants' children born in rural areas before migration" (p. 127). Brokerhoff concludes that despite the initial decline in child survival with mothers' migration to the city, the majority of disadvantaged urban children would be "much worse off had their mothers remained in the village, and that millions of children's lives may have been saved in the 1980s as a result of mothers moving to urban areas" (p. 127).

THE U-CURVE MODEL

What general conclusions can be made from all of these studies? The first conclusion is that most of the research on health and migration is retrospective and basically limited to census-type data. These studies demonstrate that migration and health changes are correlated, but they cannot be used to determine true cause-and-effect relationships (Loue and Bunce, 1999).

A second conclusion is that, over time, the health status of rural-to-urban migrants changes. It is often high at the time of migration, then declines as the migrants try to adjust to the city, but finally rises as the children of the migrants make successful adjustments to urban life. The pattern of migration and health change may be represented by a **U-shaped curve**. One of the first uses of the U-curve response was by Gullahorn and Gullahorn (1963), who used the U-model to described the emotional adjustment of voluntary migrants. First there is an emotional "high" of excitement prior to the move, then a period of evaluation of the new surroundings, then a period of depression as problems mount and solutions seem unattainable, and finally a return to emotional balance as the migrant adapts to his new surroundings.

The U-curve hypothesis seems to also predict the course of change in the physical health of rural-to-urban migrants. The available few studies of a prospective, longitudinal, and/or multidisciplinary nature do show that health usually deteriorates following migration but then improves as the length of residence in the new urban environment increases. There are exceptions for specific diseases like coronary heart disease, obesity, and some cancers, which increase in incidence with time following migration. Support for the U-curve hypothesis comes from a study of Filipino migrants living on Oahu, Hawaii (Brown, 1982). General stress levels were evaluated by measuring 24-hour excretion rates of urinary catecholamines. Excretion rates increased in direct response to levels of physiological stress. Migrants with either low or high degrees of contact with urban Hawaiian society had lower levels of catecholamine excretion than migrants with intermediate degrees of contact. Increased stress may predispose an individual to both infectious and noninfectious disease (Carlstram and Livi, 1971; Dubos, 1965). Thus, migrants attempting to adapt and acculturate themselves to a new urban environment should experience an increase in morbidity, and they generally do. Eventually these migrants seem to adapt, in that their health status improves, and they live longer than their rural nonmigrating peers. Their psychosocial adjustment no doubt lowers stress levels, but we must not forget that the greater availability of public health facilities, medical services, social services, and education and the more reliable supply and greater variety of food in the city correlate with the eventual improvement in health and longevity that most migrants can expect to enjoy.

South Pacific migrants to urban areas are eventually able to adapt to the change in lifestyle. One research group used a biosocial approach to study changes in blood pressure due to migration and modernization in Samoa and Hawaii. McGarvey and Baker (1979) compared Samoans from traditional rural areas and more modern areas in Samoa to Samoan migrants to Hawaii. Sedente blood pressure was higher in modern areas. Among migrants, those from the traditional areas of Samoa had higher blood pressure than their sedente counterparts. Migrants from modernized areas of Samoa had blood pressure equal to that of their nonmigrant peers. When all the migrants were compared, those most in contact with modern life had blood pressures lower than migrants with intermediate contact. Hanna and Baker (1979) repeated this finding in a study of Samoan migrants living in Honolulu. These urban-living Samoans had lower blood pressure than Samoan migrants living in rural, traditional areas of Hawaii. In both studies, blood pressure was also positively correlated with fatness. Though fatness tended to increase with migration and age, the relationships were not linear. Rather, fatness continued to increase with greater time in the urban environment, while blood pressure at first rose with fatness and then fell with further time in the city.

Bindon and Baker (1985) examined the relationship of modernization, migration, and obesity among Samoan sedentes and migrants to Hawaii. They found that migration, per se, did not affect the frequency of obesity, even when adjustments were made for length of time in Hawaii or the fraction of a subject's lifetime spent in Hawaii. Living in a modern society did lead to a rapid increase in the frequency of obesity for Samoan sedentes in American Samoa and migrants to Hawaii. American Samoan women developed the greatest incidence of obesity of all groups. These women retained their traditional rural occupational activities but lived in households that depended on wage labor for subsistence. Thus, the women were excluded from significant cash earning roles in these households. Migrant men developed the highest incidence of obesity when they lived in the total cash economy of Hawaii. Education was negatively correlated with obesity, especially for young women. So, as was the case with blood pressure, acculturation to Western society via education and other means may eventually lead to a return of more desirable levels of fatness and health.

EFFECTS OF MIGRATION ON
THE REMAINING POPULATION

The rural-to-urban migration literature is replete with studies of the biological effects of migration on migrants after they have reached their destination. Some studies also consider the effects of immigration on the recipient population. Few studies examine the biological changes that occur in the nonmigrating rural population. It is important to consider the remaining population. The social and economic literature on migration may serve as a starting point. Rural-to-urban migrants are generally better educated, of higher socioeconomic status, younger, and less traditional in cultural values than rural sedentes (Butterworth, 1977; Butterworth and Chance, 1981; Dubisch, 1977; Illsley et al., 1963; Jenkins, 1977; Kennedy, 1973). It is well known that these social characteristics correlate positively with physical size, fertility, health, and mortality. Due to this social selection, rural sedentes tend to be shorter and lighter (Mascie-Taylor, 1984), are more fertile (Zarate and Zarate, 1975), suffer more from the diseases of poverty (malnutrition, preventable infectious diseases, and parasitic diseases; Baker, 1977a), and experience higher mortality at all ages compared with urban migrants (Rogers, 1982). But, as noted in previous sections of this chapter, the migrant advantages occur only after the migrants arrive and adapt to the lifestyle of the city. There are few biological differences between eventual migrants and sedentes before the act of migration takes place.

While there does not seem to be biological selection for migrants, there is selective migration for age and sex. This selection has effects on rural demographics. The urban flow of the young, especially young women, results in overall rural depopulation despite the higher fertility of the sedentes. This has happened in the richer, developed nations, where natural increase in the cities is greater than in the rural areas. It is now occurring in the poorer, less developed countries as well (United Nations, 1980; Rogers, 1982). An extreme case of this demographic effect occurred in Ireland (Kennedy, 1973). The natural rate of increase in the rural counties during the last 150 years would have produced a total national population of over 20 million people by the year 1970. Massive rural emigration to the cities

---

BOX 6.3
Changing Family Structure in Cape Verde: Some Effects
of Emigration on the Remaining Population

Maria Inês Varela-Silva

Emigration from Cape Verde leaves an impact on the remaining population. One effect is on family structure and desired family size. In Cape Verde, the family is the center of the social structure. However, the Cape Verdean concept of the family may be difficult to understand by European and North American standards. For the Cape Verdeans, the main link that joins people and constitutes the basis of the family is the "blood-link." A cousin who is related by descent might be considered a stronger member of the family than other people related by marriage, even one's wife. Cape Verdeans feel this way because, as one man said, "we do not change the blood, but we can change our wife." In addition to family linked by blood, an enlarged concept of family is also prevalent, one that includes some close friends.

These links cause strong social pressures, giving to the Cape Verdeans a sense of responsibility and solidarity with all the members of the "*family*," no matter where they live or how far they are apart. This solidarity is seen as a moral obligation to support (not only economically) all the members, no matter if they are in the home islands or abroad. Family links between people who are widely separated geographically is essential to Cape Verdeans. This notion of "family distance" is understandable considering that the phenomenon of emigration is deeply rooted in the Cape Verdean culture. In 1990, about 340,000 of the Cape Verdeans were living in the home islands, while between 400,000 and 700,000 were living abroad. Emigration from Cape Verde has a deep historical tradition, extending back to the days of the slave trade. Even so, family members abroad maintain close ties with their homeland. The lack of family support, no matter the distance between people, is considered socially incorrect, constituting a sign of a bad personality.

In a general way, the Cape Verdean families have a large number of siblings. The motives for this occurrence are as follows:

The number of siblings is, both for men and women, a sign of prosperity and wealth.

For men, the fact of having his wife pregnant is a sign of her faithfulness and his virility.

For women, the pregnancies show the interest that their men still have for them.

A larger family may easily provide support, help, and care during the old age of the parents.

The Cape Verdean proverb "The one who has one child does not have any; the one who has two children has only one" reflects the social importance of a large number of siblings to the maintenance of a good social image and family functioning.

Since the independence, Cape Verde has become (World Bank Group Countries, *www.worldbank.org*)

> one of the top performers in Sub-Saharan Africa in several aspects. Commendable records of transparency and good governance have helped in shaping the country's economy and social development. Cape Verde has also used public resources to good effect in its efforts to fight poverty and protect the environment, and the Government's new National Development Plan (1997–2000) has been endorsed by the donor community . . . Policy reform effort were accelerated in late 1997 with the support of International Development Association (IDA) for the Economic Reform Support Operation . . . On the political front, Cape Verde is a functioning democracy, which has made impressive political and legal reforms and entrenched the rule of law.

But the concept of the family remains untouched no matter these changes. A large family is still the basis of the social structure. In recent years this has caused some conflicts, as the social role of women has started to change. A case history of one Cape Verdean woman illustrates this.

Ana Semedo (a pseudonym) is a professionally trained high-school teacher living on the Island of Santiago. She is married with an engineer and they have a 10-year-old boy named João. By choice, they decided not to have any more children, considering the professional responsibilities of both and also because they could provide one child better care in terms of education and health, leading to higher quality of life and the chance of a better future.

During the first two years, they were considered a happy family, but after a while they started to be questioned about *when* would they give a brother or a sister to little João. In the beginning they tried to explain their decision not to have more children. But the more they tried to justify their choice, the greater was the social pressure to change their minds. Their family, including all of their blood relatives and their close friends, as well as colleagues at work and, in general, everyone who was informed by their option expressed feelings of some pity, desolation, and moral condemnation. The parents were not supposed to behave in this way.

The couple managed to resist the people's reactions, understanding their point of view and never reacting in a negative way to the general criticisms. It was, after all, a matter of family—their small family with three members, but a family anyway.

The most alarming signs appeared when their son came home from school one day and asked his parents, "How will my life be in the future, when I will come to a point that I have to justify to my own children the reasons why they do not have aunts, uncles, and cousins?"

Ana Semedo and her husband are now facing a conflict between their personal decision and their right of having free will to decide about their family and the frustration they caused their family, their friends, and their society.

of England and the United States, however, resulted in a total national population of just over 2 million at that time.

The social selection of urban migrants does have a limit in terms of its effect on the biology of rural sedentes. The rural nonmigrants of the developed nations have not become a homogeneous group for stature, fertility, or total health characteristics. Pronounced variation at the genetic and phenotypic levels are still measurable, even in rural Ireland (Boyce, 1984; Clegg, 1979; Relethford et al., 1980). Much of this variation is due to the movement of people between rural areas, a topic that deserves its own treatment. It is also due to the spread of modernization, urban values, and some aspects of urban lifestyle into the countryside. As this occurs and the rural environment changes, especially in terms of diet and activity patterns for children, human biology changes as a result of our species capacity for developmental plasticity. This process of change is occurring today in the less developed countries, as evidenced by the continuation of secular trends in growth and maturation (Bogin, 1999a). In the most developed nations, such as the United States and England, secular trends appear to have ceased and there are no longer any rural-urban differences in stature, fertility, and mortality when socioeconomic differences are controlled. That is, the urban poor and the rural poor suffer equally. On a more positive note, the country folk usually come to adopt many of the city ways of life and enjoy the benefits and liabilities of urbanization without experiencing the trauma of migration.

In sum, rural sedentes can be differentiated both socially and biologically from urban-living migrants. By our current criteria for biological "well-being," rural sedentes in all but the most developed nations are at a disadvantage. However, variability within each group is so great that it is not possible to characterize biologically neither the typical rural sedente nor the "average" urban migrant. Moreover, social variation accounts for most of the biological differences. This means that any group rural sedentes can be made to look like urban migrants in terms of growth, health, fertility, and mortality—all that need occur is the fact of migration, or the urbanization of the formally rural areas.

SUMMARY: MIGRATION AND ADAPTATION TO THE CITY

Figure 6.6 is a summary of the process and the biocultural consequences of rural-to-urban migration. This figure applies to the migration process now taking place within the poorer, less developed countries, from the poorer to the richer nations, and the process that took place in the more developed countries between 1750 and 1940. The leftmost column begins with the rural-living individual. Moving down this column, the next box characterizes the social profile of likely sedentes. Some major rural environmental variables that influence human biology are listed in the next box. The last box in the first column lists the biocultural correlates of sedentism. The social profile of likely rural-to-urban migrants is given in the upper box of the second column. The complex series of events that culminates in the permanent movement of people from the countryside to the city is not considered in the figure. Instead the box labeled "migration" implies this process. The biocultural consequences of recent migration are given in the last box of this column. The downward movement of the arrows in the second column indicate that, initially, rural-to-urban migrants are generally healthy, even healthier than the city-born population. But, these immigrants are on the down slope side of the U-shaped curve that characterizes the social and physiological responses to migration. Column 3 summarizes the biocultural status of migrants after long-term residence in the city. The arrow connecting the second and third columns curves upward to indicate that the long-term migrant eventually moves along the upward slope of the U-curve response, making social and physiological adjustments to the urban environment.

The rightmost column lists the psychosocial, biological, and technological variables common to the urban environment. These variables directly influence the biology of the rural-to-urban migrant. The thicker arrow indicates that these variables influence the biology of long-term migrants more than recent migrants (connected by the thinner arrow). This is due to the process of adaptation and adjustment required before migrants become fully exposed to the advantages and liabilities of the city.

The process of migrant adaptation and adjustment to the city is not completely understood. Butterworth and Chance (1981) review the social anthropology literature relating to Latin American migration research. They conclude that "most migrants adapt more or less successfully and without trauma to city life, [but] we have as yet no satisfactory theoretical model that can explain this adaptation and its variations" (p. 103). Today, two decades later, the situation is not much better. As late as 1999, the U.S. National Center for Health Statistics concluded that, "In general, research relating to immigrants and their health has not attended to the

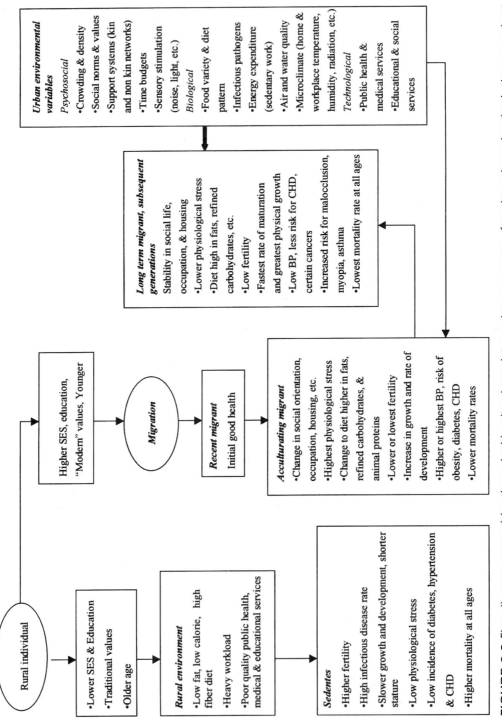

FIGURE 6.6 Flow diagram summarizing the major biocultural correlates and consequences of rural-to-urban migration in the poorer, least developed nations today and in the richer, more developed nations prior to 1940. Abbreviations: BP, blood pressure; CHD, coronary heart disease (from Bogin, 1988).

methodological issues . . . most notably, the definition of an immigrant, . . . changes in health or access to health care concurrent with changes in immigration status, . . . [or] random samples of individuals" (Loue and Bunce, 1999 p. 1). It is known that rural-to-urban migration and international migration are primarily social and behavioral processes that have consequences for human biology. There is no evidence for genetic selection, or, indeed, any type of biological selection of migrants.

The standard model for migration research starts with the collection of social data and then tries to correlate these with biological outcomes. This research approach may not be able to provide the "satisfactory theoretical model" that Butterworth and Chance (1981), and all researchers, hope for. Since the social, behavioral, and biological aspects of migration are so closely related, a biocultural perspective is needed to understand the process of urban adaptation. Such a perspective is taken throughout this chapter.

BIOCULTURAL VIEW OF MIGRATION

A tentative biocultural explanation for migrant adaptability may be offered here, based on the work of Macisco et al. (1970) in Puerto Rico, Bogin and MacVean (1981c) in Guatemala, and the synthesis of literature discussed in this review. Macisco and colleagues (1970), working in Puerto Rico, argued against the view that migrants are at a disadvantage in the urban environment. They cited the generally higher educational status of migrants versus nonmigrants and the migrants' initiative to migrate as evidence that the migrants were able and willing to make the necessary adjustments to urban life. These researchers speculated that migrants may have possessed a greater repertoire of adaptive strategies to the stress of the city than the city born, due to the migrants' combined rural and urban experience. Bogin and MacVean (1981c) found that many migrants from rural Guatemala to Guatemala City married urban natives. These "mixed" families appeared to adapt more successfully than either families with two migrant parents or two city-born parents. The mixed-parent families had fewer children and taller children than either rural sedentes or the city born and a socioeconomic status at least equal to the city-born families. All of the families in this Guatemalan study were of low SES and lived under difficult conditions. Mixed families may have the best of both worlds—the rural and the urban social strategies for survival and adaptation to the rigors of the city. Based on both of these studies, plus more recent research, we may conclude that factors such as personal initiative, higher than average educational attainment, initially good health, relatively young age, and the ability to draw upon rural and urban experience are part of the reason for the adaptability of rural-to-urban migrants.

The demographic changes and modification in growth and development that occur in people following migration, and in their descendants, are a result of their social selection, their social and behavioral flexibility, and the basic plasticity in human biology to respond to environmental change. Rural-to-urban migrants, both within a single nation and between nations, do adapt socially and biologically. With time, the descendants of the immigrants become biologically, and often culturally, indistinguishable from the host population. The potential nightmare of a world of impoverished cities overrun by ill-adapted immigrants can be tempered by the real-ization of this fact. An anonymous observer offers the following view of the future of humanity in the city (OECD, 1999 p. 33):

> Man's love-hate relationship with the city will continue in the 21st century. Love, because cities will remain a vital part of growth and development, and a vibrant part of creative human culture; and hate, because they will continue to deliver their litany of management problems in pollution, over-crowding, congestion, and crime. These costs will probably rise, but so will the advantages.

SEVEN

GROWTH OF HUMANITY

The natural price of labour is that price which is necessary to enable labourers, one with another, to subsist and to perpetuate their race, without increase or diminution.

DAVID RICARDO (1772–1823), AN ENGLISHMAN AND
ONE OF THE FOUNDERS OF POLITICAL ECONOMY

Scholars have searched for centuries to try to understand why populations grow or shrink. The above quote is just one example, albeit a rather famous one, of a possible relationship between demography and economics. More recently, the theoretical economist Partha Dasgupta (1993) explored this relationship in an insightful and compassionate book. Dasgupta observes that Ricardo's statement suggests a simple demographic principle: "population growth is dependent on the wage rate, and there is a critical wage at which population growth is nil" (1993, p. 11). Below the critical wage population growth should be negative. If this were true, then restraining wages to that critical rate would stop population growth in any country, at least in those groups that depend on wages. Ricardo's simple principle is, of course, not true. Once economists understood this, they were spurred to search for a better economic model of population growth. Dasgupta reviews much of that literature and finds that many of the proposed relationships between economics and demography are little better than was Ricardo's. They are at once too simple and, worse yet, dangerous and misleading. They are dangerous because they lead some governments to manipulate wages, and by extension food, housing, health services, and other commodities, in the hope of controlling population growth. At one extreme, this practice may only produce poverty and misery for those affected. They are misleading because they do not "say anything about a person's capacities for work and reflection and play" (1993, p. 11).

My goal in this chapter is to bring together the diverse lines of research and scholarship discussed in previous chapters. I want to show how a consideration of "a person's capacities for work and reflection and play"—in other words, a person's well-being—provides us with a far more satisfactory approach to demography. Dasgupta argues that a consideration of human growth and well-being are the key ingredients missing in the traditional economic approaches to demography. I agree, and I wish to show the power of a transdisciplinary approach to the study of the human populations by presenting a few examples of the integration of human demography and human physical growth.

This chapter begins with an overview of human body size variation in contemporary human populations. The discussion then moves to a consideration of how variation in body size reflects variation in the social conditions, including demographic regime, under which groups of people live. This lesson is applied to changes in body size over the past 1.6 million years—since the time of our fossil ancestor *Homo erectus*. Our ancient ancestors, living in demographically small foraging groups, were, on average, as tall or taller and more massive than human beings alive today. Understanding the ancestral condition sets the stage for a consideration of when, why, and how evolutionary changes occurred in the growth of both the human body and the human population.

This background on the social and biological history of the growth of humanity can take us only so far. A more complete account of the history of the human population will come from an integrated biocultural approach. Toward this end, the discussion turns to an overview of the new and exciting field of "anthropometric history"—a transdisciplinary field combining history, economics, anthropology, demography, and more. Anthropologists, historians, and economists are using past records of human growth and population dynamics to reconstruct the physical, social, and political well-being of people. Until the twentieth century, social, economic, and political data that are commonly used today were generally unavailable. For example, there are few records of educational attainment for the vast majority of the population as well as scant records of real wages or gross national production. There are, however, many excellent sources of data on human physical growth and some good sources of census data. To show how these growth and demographic data may be used to understand the growth of humanity, I will present three examples. The first is an analysis of human growth, demography, and economic history in Latin America during the past 8,000 years. The second is a biocultural analysis of growth and population structure of the Irish just before and after the great famine of the mid-nineteenth century. The third example is an analysis of population depletion of rural Portugal during the twentieth century, and its effects on physical growth of the Portuguese population. These examples illustrate the strength of the biocultural and transdisciplinary approach to understand the growth of humanity.

POPULATION VARIATION IN BODY SIZE

People come in all sizes and shapes. Some individuals are tall or short because their parents were that size, that is, the stature of an individual man or woman is often due to his or her genetic inheritance. But, we also know that people change size from generation to generation. As discussed in the previous chapter, rural-to-urban migrants in the poor nations of the world often give birth to offspring who are destined to be taller than their parents. An improved environment for health and nutrition, among other things, results in the greater stature and weight. When the environment for physical growth changes a great deal, as is the case for rural-to-urban migration, then the genetic influences on body size often take a back

TABLE 7.1
Growth Data for Average Height (cm), Weight (kg), and Weight/Height in Several Populations of Young Adult Men and Women

Population	Age, Years	Height		Weight		Weight/Height	
		Men	Women	Men	Women	Men	Women
Netherlands national sample, 1980 medians	20	182.0	168.3	70.8	58.6	0.39	0.35
United States national sample, 1977 medians	20–21	177.4	163.2	71.9	57.2	0.41	0.35
Kenya Turkana pastoralists, 1970s means	20	174.3	161.6	49.8	47.4	0.29	0.29
Japan University of Tokyo students, 1995 means	~20	171.6	159.1	63.3	50.7	0.37	0.32
Bolivia Aymara Indians, 1980s means	20–29	162.0	149.0	58.1	52.4	0.36	0.35
Guatemala Maya Indians, 1980s means	17–18	158.7	146.9	52.2	49.3	0.33	0.34
Congo Efe Pygmy, 1980s means	19–29	144.9	136.1	43.3	40.6	0.30	0.30

Sources: Netherlands, Roede and van Wieringen (1985); United States, Hamill et al. (1977); Africa, Turkana, Little et al. (1983); Japan, T. Satake (personal communication); Guatemala, Bogin et al. 1992; Bolivia, Mueller et al. (1980); Africa, Efe, Dietz et al. (1989).

seat. Indeed, when we compare the average height, weight, or other body dimensions of populations living in different nations, the environmental differences are paramount.

Consider the data in Table 7.1 for the average height, weight, and weight-to-height ratio (a simple measure of body proportion) for several human populations. The data are listed in descending order according to the average height, and both the men and the women in each population follow that order. Young adults in the Netherlands may be, on average, the tallest people in the world. Their tallness can be seen most vividly when we compare some of the shortest young Dutch men with the average stature of Aymara men in Bolivia and Mayan men in Guatemala. Dutch men at the third percentile (the bottom 3 percent for height) have a height of 169.3 cm and, thus, are taller than the mean stature for Aymara or Maya. Young adults in the United States are, on average, shorter than the Dutch but, relative to the other populations, are a "tall" group of people.

Why are the mean statures for the United States less than those for the Netherlands? There is no evidence that the Dutch have "taller" genes than do Americans. Consider these statistics: in 1850 European-Americans were the second tallest people in the world, with American men averaging 167.6 cm (5 feet 6 inches)—the tallest people in the world in 1850 are discussed in Box 7.1. About 150 years later, American men now average 177.4 cm (5 feet 10 inches), but have fallen in the standings and are now, on average, shorter than the Dutch and several other north European populations. Back in 1850 the Dutch averaged only 162.6 cm (5 feet 4 inches) and were then the shortest men in Europe (for both Americans and Dutch, and just about everyone else, women average about 12 cm less than men at all times). Stature increased in both populations because the quality of life improved, but more so for the Dutch. We know this is true due in part to studies on how height is determined. It is the product of plasticity in our childhood and in our mothers' childhood as well. If a girl is undernourished and suffers poor health, the growth of her body, including her reproductive system, is usually reduced. With a shortage of raw materials, she cannot build more cells to construct a bigger body; at the same time, she has to invest what materials she can get into repairing already existing cells and tissues from the damage caused by disease. Her shorter stature as an adult is the result of a compromise her body makes while growing up.

BOX 7.1
Giants in the Americas?

When Europeans arrived in North and South America in the sixteenth Century, they encountered some tall people. At least, these people were tall relative to the size of the European explorers, sailors, and soldiers who made first contact. Europeans were of relatively short stature due to centuries of feudal political organization, which kept the bulk of the rural population in poverty, and the incipient rise of cities, which subjected the urbanites to inadequate nutrition and unsanitary living conditions (see Chapter 6). In addition, the entire European region had been wracked by episodes of epidemic disease since the twelfth century. Like the Europeans, some Native Americans lived in large-scale state societies, which meant that the majority of the population was of shorter stature than the elite leaders. Other American people, however, lived in band, tribal, and chiefdom societies and some of these groups occupied regions with abundant food resources and low levels of disease. With much food, good health, low population density, and fairly egalitarian social organization, these Americans were relatively tall.

Indeed, there are stories of giants from both North and South America. Patagonia is a region in southern Argentina. The surface of Patagonia descends from the Andes Mountains and flows east in a series of broad, flat steps extending to the Atlantic coast. Much of the region is composed of gigantic landforms and coastal terraces. These were created by the same tectonic forces that formed the Andes. In all, the Patagonian region is characterized by great size in both breadth and height. Ferdinand Magellan arrived there in 1520 with the first contingent of Europeans. Magellan gave Patagonia its name, possibly after a story by Francisco Vasquez published in 1512 and called *Primaleon*. This is the tale of the fantastic adventures of the knight Primaleon, who sailed to an island populated by wild "patagonians" and gigantic beasts. Magellan met the flesh-and-blood inhabitants of the real Patagonia and estimated their height to be 12 to 13 palms (about 252 to 273 cm, or 8.3 to 9.0 feet).

Other explores followed Magellan. In 1579 Sarmiento measured the Patagonians and reported a mean height of three "varas" (249 cm). In 1615 they were measured at 10 to 11 feet tall, but subsequent visitors found them to shrink, so that by 1767 the tallest Patagonians were "7 English feet and more" (Hermanusen, 1998). There may be some errors of conversion from the old measurement units to modern metric or English units, but the consensus is that the Patagonians were very tall. The problem with that consensus is that the skeletal remains available of Patagonians from the eighteenth and nineteenth centuries indicate a mean male stature of only 173 cm and a mean female stature of 162 cm, although a few individual men may have been as tall as 192 cm. In 1949, the Argentine anthropologist Imbelloni (1949) measured 11 living Tehuelche men. Tehuelches are the descendants of Magellan's Patagonians. Imbelloni reports a mean male stature of 176.6. Based on a health survey of living Tehuelches conducted in the 1990s, Oyhenart et al. (in press) find that the mean heights of 12 men and 11 women between the ages of 21 and 60 years are 163.9 and 147.7 cm, respectively.

The Patagonians of colonial times may have been very tall. They had abundant food resources, a sparse population, and little or no disease, all the ingredients for good growth. But they were not giants. The reports of early explorers were most likely exaggerations, sometimes done knowingly so as to impress friends and bene-factors back in Europe. The exaggerations may also have been based on the fact that the Europeans were short, with many men under 160 cm. If some of the Patagonias were as tall as 192 cm, then it is easy to imagine the relatively tiny Europeans strain-ing their necks to look up and embellishing their estimations of height. Even the mea-sured heights may have been "embellished" by poor technique, prior expectation, or outright misrepresentation. It is important to note that from the nineteenth to the twentieth centuries the mean stature of Tehuelches declines almost 13 cm for men. The decline seems to be due to the deterioration of living conditions for these people. In the past, the Tehuelches were independent, but during the twentieth century they were forced to live on reservations. Food availabilty, population density, and infec-tious diseases all worsened, and stature declined.

Stories of giants also circulated in North America. As European colonists spread across the continent, they encountered earthen mounds. Some of these mounds were of enormous size. In fact, the largest structure built in all of the Americas prior to the late-nineteenth century is Monk's Mound, found at Cahokia, an archaeological site in southern Illinois. Between the years 1050 and 1250, Cahokia was the largest prehistoric Native American city north of Mexico. This city, covering 16 km^2 (6 mi^2), may have been inhabited by as many as 20,000 people. The Cahokians, members of Mississippian culture, developed a complex agricultural system, including an advanced system of irrigation canals and water storage areas. To do this required the excavation of more than 1.4 million cubic meters (50 million cubic feet) of earth. The excavated earth was used to create ceremonial mounds. The largest of these is Monks Mound, site of the principal temple, which covers 6 hectares (14 acres) and rises in four terraces to a height of 30 m (100 ft).

At the time of contact there were a few Mississippian societies still active in Louisiana, and French colonists describe mound-building activity. However, Cohokia, and most of the other sites with massive mounds, were abandoned before Euro-peans arrived in North America. When Europeans first saw these huge mounds and the remains of complex agricultural activity, they would not believe that the ances-tors of Native Americans constructed them. To Europeans, the Indians were savages, without the intellectual or moral skills needed to build such works. To explain the mounds, Europeans invented a "race" of giants who had once lived in the area. Even the amateur archaeologist Thomas Jefferson (also third president of the United States) wrote about this extinct race of giants. These giants were not only great architects but also totally peaceful. The giants were exterminated by the Indian savages, and the great mounds and agricultural works were left to disintegrate. This story was, of course, based on racism and hatred against Native Americans. The story helped to spread fear of Native Americans and allowed Europeans to justify brutality against Indians as retribution for alleged past atrocities. European-Americans so believed in these giants that a small fortune was made by a New York State farmer who "discovered" and displayed the Cardiff Giant—alleged to be the petrified remains of one of these peaceful leviathans. In fact, George Hull created this giant in 1869. Hull purchased a block of Iowa gypsum and had the giant carved as a hoax. He had the carving transported to his Binghamton, New York, farm. The carving was displayed there and attracted crowds of up to 3,000 people per day, paying 25 cents apiece. None other than P. T. Barnum tried to buy the carving, but was refused. Undaunted, Barnum made his own Cardiff Giant—a copy of the fraud—and placed it on display! Eventually, scientific "authorities" inspected the evidence and declared the Cardiff Giant to be a fraud (Feder, 1996). Mark Twain wrote a tale, called "A Ghost Story," that pokes fun at the whole affair.

A more tempered case of tall stature in the Americas comes from the tribes of the Great Plains of North America. Between 1888 and 1903, Franz Boas supervised the collection of anthropometric and demographic data on several thousand Native Americans and Siberians. Prince and Steckel (1998) analyzed Boas's data and found that during the nineteenth century the Indians of the Great Plains were the tallest population in the world. A map of the Great Plains and the distribution of the major Native American culture groups is given in Figure B7.1. There is variation in stature

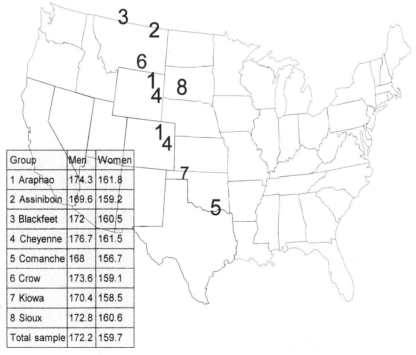

Group	Men	Women
1 Araphao	174.3	161.8
2 Assiniboin	169.6	159.2
3 Blackfeet	172	160.5
4 Cheyenne	176.7	161.5
5 Comanche	168	156.7
6 Crow	173.6	159.1
7 Kiowa	170.4	158.5
8 Sioux	172.8	160.6
Total sample	172.2	159.7

FIGURE B7.1 Map of the United States showing the location of several Native American Plains culture groups. The names of the groups are listed in the table along with the mean height in centimeters, for men and women. The data are from Prince and Steckel (1998).

from tribe to tribe, but the overall mean height of men is 172.2 cm, and for women the mean is 159.7. This makes the Plains Indians taller than any of the Latin American groups shown in Figure 7.5. It also makes the Plains Indians between 1.0 and 2.0 cm taller than European-Americans, who, in turn, were 5.0 to 10.0 cm taller than Europeans. This means that the Plains Indians were the tallest people in the world in the mid-nineteenth century.

The Plains were sparsely settled during the nineteenth century, and the Native American population was probably under 100,000 people. The people appear to have eaten a rich and varied diet, including much meat from the hunting of deer and buffalo and a wide variety of vegetables and fruits. Prince and Steckel also show that the Plains Indians lived under a modest disease load. There were periodic epidemic diseases, many of these introduced by Europeans, but the native American populations were able to reorganize demographically after each epidemic. Most of tribes were nomadic, meaning that they could move away from disease areas. They could also move away from their own wastes, another source of disease. Moreover, the Indians lived in egalitarian societies, in which the health and well-being of all members of the society were protected.

This contrasts sharply with the conditions for life of the European-American population of North America at that time. European-Americans ate a better diet than that available in Europe but the diet was less varied than that of the Plains hunter-gatherers. European-Americans also lived in permanent settlements, and in the larger towns and cities this meant exposure to many sources of disease. Epidemics were bad for the Indians and for the Europeans, but the ecology of American cities allowed for a chronic exposure to many diseases. Work loads may also have been heavier for the European-Americans, or at least the work was more constant. Also, children were often forced to do quite demanding physical labor. All of this took a toll on the possibilities for growth of the European-Americans.

Such a woman can pass on her short stature to her child, but genes have nothing to do with it for either of them. If she becomes pregnant, her small reproductive system probably will not be able to supply a normal level of nutrients and oxygen to her fetus. This harsh environment reprograms the fetus to grow more slowly than it would if the woman was healthier, so she is more likely to give birth to a smaller baby. Low-birth-weight babies, those weighing less than 2,500 g (5.5 lb) after a full pregnancy, tend to continue their prenatal program of slow growth through childhood. By the time they are teenagers, they are usually significantly shorter than people of normal birth weight. Some particularly striking evidence of this reprogramming comes from studies on monozygotic twins, which develop from a single fertilized egg cell and are therefore identical genetically. But in certain cases, monozygotic twins end up being nourished by unequal portions of the placenta. The twin with the smaller fraction of the placenta is often born with low birth weight, while the other one is normal. Follow-up studies show that this difference between the twins can last throughout their lives.

As such research suggests, we can use the average height of any group of people as a barometer of the health of their society. After the turn of the century both the United States and the Netherlands began to protect the health of their citizens by purifying drinking water, installing sewer systems, regulating the safety of food, and, most important, providing better health care and diets to children. The children responded to their changed environment by growing taller. But the differences in Dutch and American societies determined their differing heights today. The Dutch decided to provide public health benefits to all the public, including the poor. In the United States, meanwhile, improved health is enjoyed most by those who can afford it. The poor often lack adequate housing, sanitation, and health care. The difference in our two societies can be seen at birth: in 1990 only 4 percent of Dutch babies were born at low birth weight, compared with 7 percent in the United States. For white Americans the rate was 5.7 percent, and for black Americans the rate was a whopping 13.3 percent. People of "color" in the United States (e.g., African-Americans, Latin Americans, and some Asians) tend to be overrepresented in lower social strata. The American growth data reported here are for people of European and African descent. The disparity between rich and poor in the United States carries through to adulthood: Poor Americans are shorter than the better-off by about 1 inch. Thus, despite great affluence in the United States, the average height of Americans is below that of the Dutch.

Returning to the data of Table 7.1, note that the Turkana, who are nomadic, animal-herding pastoralists living in rural Kenya, are one of the tallest populations of Africa. The Tutsi of Rwanda, who have a mean male stature of 176.5 cm, are about 2 cm taller, on average, than the Turkana. It is a myth that Tutsi (sometimes called the Watutsi) are the tallest people in the world, averaging more than 213 cm (7 feet) tall (Bogin, 1998a). A relatively low **standard of living** in Rwanda, including chronic food shortages, high levels of childhood diseases, and recurrent warfare in the past 20 years, severely curtails the possibility of good growth. Similar situations occur in much of Africa, and one result is that the tallest "Africans" in the world today are not to be found anywhere in Africa. African-Americans of the United States are the tallest African-derived population in the world (Cameron, 1991). When socioeconomic differences between ethnic groups are controlled, African-Americans are as tall, on average, as European-Americans, and both of these groups are taller than any other ethnic group living in the United States (Frisancho, 1990; Fullwood, 1981). The sample of Japanese shown in Table 7.1 represent reasonably affluent university students. They are the tallest and heaviest, on average, of any group of young Japanese adults measured in the twentieth century, but they are considerably shorter and lighter, on average, than the Dutch or the Americans.

The Aymara of Bolivia and the Maya of Guatemala are Native American peoples. Both groups are of very low socioeconomic status (SES). Both live in rural areas, and as infants and children, many individuals suffer from mild to moderate malnutrition, along with repeated bouts of infections of the gastrointestinal and respiratory systems. Undernutrition and infectious disease are associated with growth retardation, and these are likely to be factors that account for the relative short stature of the Maya and Aymara. We have already seen in Chapter 1 that when Maya migrate to the United States and experience better health care and diet, their children are significantly taller and heavier. The African Efe pygmies may be, on average, the shortest people in the world, and their short stature appears to have a strong genetic component (reviewed in Bogin, 1999a). However, there is a wide range of variation in the stature of individual pygmies. When the distribution of male stature of the pygmies is compared with the Tutsi, the tallest pygmy men are found to be larger than the shortest Tutsi men (Barnicot, 1977). This analysis shows that average figures may be quite misleading for individuals within a population—the individual differences in stature are likely due to genetic effects. Such differences in stature between individuals may be found within and between all human populations. But, these differences tend to cancel each other, leaving the much larger between-population differences, which are due mostly to the impact of the environment for growth, as the most important for study.

The rank order of mean weights in Table 7.1 does not follow the same order as stature. On average, U.S. men are the heaviest and Efe women are the lightest of all the populations listed. The relatively tall Turkana men have a lower average weight than that of any other samples, save the Efe. Turkana women have a lower average weight than all samples, except the Efe and the Maya women. The ratios of weight for height show that the Turkana and the Efe have the lowest values, reflecting their linear body build. The Turkana, Efe, and many other sub-Saharan African peoples have arms and legs that are relatively long in proportion to their total stature (Eveleth and Tanner, 1976, 1990). The Turkana and the Efe are also absolutely lean, meaning that their bodies have less fat tissue than other human populations. Together, body proportions and body composition give these two groups a linear body build. The similarity in the proportion of height to weight between these African samples is striking, since the Turkana are, on average, 25.5 cm (about 10 inches) taller than the Efe pygmy sample.

Dutch and American men have the highest average ratios of weight for height. Body weight is the total mass of all body tissues, including muscle, bone, organs, and fat. For the comparisons presented in Table 7.1, however, the major differences in weight-for-height ratio are due to fatness. For example, Little et al. (1983) compared the Turkana with the U.S. reference population of Table 7.1 and found the greater weight-for-height ratio of the Americans was due to both more fat and more lean tissue (e.g., muscle), but especially more fat. Since the year 1977, when the U.S. data were published, Americans have not changed in stature but have increased in mean weight. Today, Americans are the fattest population of all the industrialized countries (IBNMRR, 1995). Japanese university students, both men and, especially, women, have lower average weight-for-height ratios than similarly aged Dutch or Americans. Why this is so is not known exactly. The Japanese sample represents a highly educated group, while the Dutch and American data are based on national samples. More highly educated people tend to be less fat than the population at large, at least in many industrialized nations.

Aymara and Maya men have weight-for-height ratios that are lower than for Japanese men, but the women have ratios that are higher than for Japanese women and virtually equal to the ratios for U.S. women. One factor influencing these ratios is that relative to the Dutch, Americans, and Japanese, the Aymara and Maya have short arms and legs in proportion to total stature (Eveleth and Tanner, 1976; Gurri and Dickinson, 1990). This means that the head and trunk of the body contribute disproportionately more to total weight. The Maya, and probably the Aymara as well, have less total body fat, on average, than Europeans or Americans, but they have more of it concentrated on their trunks (Bogin and MacVean, 1981b; Johnston et al., 1984). This results in what is sometimes called a "short and plump" physique, which elevates the weight-for-height ratio. Adult Maya and Aymara living in their native countries develop this physique as a result of malnutrition and growth retardation in early life. Maya children living in the United States are not only significantly taller but also have significantly longer legs than the Maya in Guatemala (Fig. 7.1 and Fig. 7.2). The Maya living in the United States also become much fatter, on average, which maintains their plump physique (Fig. 7.3).

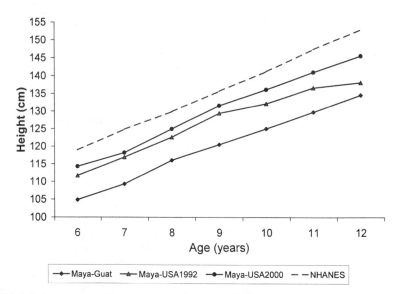

FIGURE 7.1 Comparison of mean stature between Maya children living in Guatemala and in the United States. Based on more recent data than those used for Figure B1.1 in Chapter 1. The Maya living in Guatemala (Maya-Guat) were measured in 1998 by Luis Rios and Isabel Fernandez Abad of the Universidad Autónoma de Madrid. The Maya in the United States (Maya–USA1992 and Maya–USA2000) were measured by Bogin and Loucky (1997) and by Bogin et al. (2000). The differences in stature between the two locations have become even larger than was seen in the data depicted in Figure B1.1 in Chapter 1.

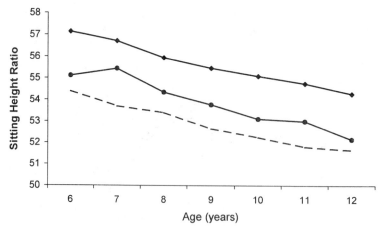

FIGURE 7.2 Comparison of mean sitting height ratio between Maya children living in Guatemala and the United States (based on the same samples as for Fig. 7.1). The Maya–USA2000 study also measured sitting height. When total stature is divided into sitting height ([stature/sitting height] × 100), we get a ratio that estimates the proportion of stature that is due to growth of the legs versus growth of the head and trunk of the body. This figure shows that Maya living in the United States have significantly smaller sitting height ratios at all ages, meaning that they have significantly longer legs, than Maya living in Guatemala.

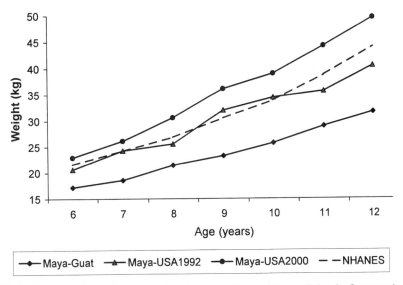

FIGURE 7.3 Comparison of mean weight between Maya children living in Guatemala and in the United States (based on the same samples as for Fig. 7.1). The Maya in the United States are significantly heavier than the Maya living in Guatemala. The Maya in the United States have become heavier since measured in 1992.

POPULATION VARIATION IN DEMOGRAPHY

Human populations also come in a variety of sizes and shapes. Recall the presentation of population pyramids in Chapter 2. These pyramids show the size and shape of a population in terms of the number of males and females alive in different age groups. Readers may view population pyramids for the nations listed in Table 7.1 at the web site of the U.S. Census Bureau (*http://www.census.gov/ipc/www/ idbnew.html*). Once at this page, click on the "Population Pyramids" link and follow the instructions to select the country and the year for a population pyramid. These pyramids are for entire nations, which works well for the Netherlands, the United States, and Japan. There are no pyramids for the Turkana, Aymara, Maya, or Efe at this web site. There are demographic studies of the Turkana (Little and Leslie, 1999) and sketchy information for the Efe (Bailey et al., 1992). Even so, the population pyramids for their respective nations—Kenya, Bolivia, Guatemala, and Congo—provide some indication of the demographic conditions for this region of the world.

   Table 7.2 presents some other demographic indicators for the nations represented in Table 7.1. The indicators are the "vital rates," which are births per 1,000 population, deaths per 1,000 population, net migration per 1,000 population, rate of natural increase, and net growth rate. These vital rates summarize the demographic indicators discussed in previous chapters. The Netherlands, the United States, and Japan are low-growth-rate nations (growth rates below 1 percent). This is due mostly to low birth rates and, for Japan, a net migration of zero. The Netherlands and the United States have positive migration values, meaning that there is more immigration than emigration. Kenya and Bolivia are middle-growth-rate nations (growth rate between 1 and 2 percent). Birth rates are higher than for the previous nations, and for Kenya death rates are also noticeably higher. Net migration for Kenya is zero,

TABLE 7.2
Vital Rates for Countries Listed in Table 7.1

Country	Births per 1,000	Deaths per 1,000	Migrants per 1,000	Rate of Natural Increase (%)	Net Growth Rate (%)
Netherlands	12.12	8.72	2.30	0.340	0.569
United States	14.20	8.70	3.50	0.550	0.910
Kenya	29.35	14.08	0.00	1.527	1.526
Japan	9.96	8.15	0.00	0.181	0.180
Bolivia	28.15	8.36	−1.47	1.979	1.832
Guatemala	35.05	6.92	−1.89	2.813	2.625
Congo (Kinshasa)	46.44	15.38	0.82	3.106	3.188

Source: From the U.S. Bureau of the Census, International Data Base.

and there is a net emigration from Bolivia (much of it to Chile and Argentina). Finally, Guatemala and Congo are high-birth-rate nations (above 2 percent). For Congo the data are only for the city of Kinshasa. Birth rates are the highest of all the nations listed. Emigration out of Guatemala tempers some of the population growth, while immigration into Congo exacerbates the rate of natural increase.

The data presented in Tables 7.1 and 7.2 provide some information about the "growth and shape of humanity." It is not possible to make any direct statistical analysis of the combined growth and demographic data of these tables. However, we can begin to tease out some patterns of association between physical growth and population biology. To do so, we need a model of the way in which the world works that will guide our observations and our analysis. All scientists and scholars use a world model, although the model is not always stated explicitly. Here I use a model based on a biocultural and life history approach to human growth and population structure.

MIRROR OF SOCIETY

Variations in physical growth and population structure are sensitive indicators of the quality of the environment. Chapter 1 used the metaphor developed by Tanner (1986) that human growth is a mirror for society, reflecting the material and moral conditions under which people live and grow. In her novel *The Bluest Eye*, Toni Morrison (1970) details some of the pernicious effects of racism against African-Americans in the United States. In one passage, Morrison mirrors the effects of racism in the loss of a tooth to Pauline. As a young couple, Pauline and her husband, named Cholly, migrate from the south of the United States to a northern industrial town. Note how at the end of this passage, Morrison speaks of "the conditions"—meaning the material and moral conditions of life for African-Americans that result from racism—that are the cause of this tooth loss (p. 116):

> Young, loving, and full of energy, they came to Lorain, Ohio. Cholly found work in the steel mills right away, and Pauline started keeping house.
> And then she lost her front tooth. But there must have been a speck, a brown speck easily mistaken for food but which did not leave, which sat on the enamel for months, and grew, until it cut into the surface and then to the brown putty underneath, finally

eating away to the root, but avoiding the nerves, so its presence was not noticeable or uncomfortable. Then the weakened roots, having grown accustomed to the poison, responded one day to severe pressure, and the tooth fell free, leaving a ragged stump behind. But even before the little brown speck, there must have been the conditions, the setting that would allow it to exist in the first place.

The "conditions" and the "setting" that Morrison mentions here refer to the social, economic, and political environment of the United States during most of the twentieth century that fostered inequality between African-Americans and the majority white population. This refers to inequality in housing (including both official segregation and unofficial "redlining"), in diet, in health care, in employment, and in education. The inequality begins with a social bias called racism, and this social bias results in biological consequences, including differences in growth, birth rates, mortality, and migration between whites and blacks. Racism has a cumulative effect, meaning that the social and biological differences between blacks and whites become greater from one life history stage to the next.

Morrison does not cite data on human physical growth or on the demographic structure of the United States, but such data are available. Growth differences begin at birth. The median birth weight for a full-term (40-week) delivery is 3,540 g for white boys and 3,400 g for white girls, but only 3,355 and 3,230 g for black boys and girls, respectively. These are median values for primiparous (first-time) mothers (Zhang and Bowes, 1995). The differences are more acute when expressed in terms of low-birth-weight infants, that is, a birth weight below 2,500 g for a normal gestation length of 37 to 42 weeks. In 1997, the percentage of low birth weight for whites was 6.4 percent, but was 13.0 percent for blacks (Anderson et al., 1998). Researchers debate the causes for this difference in birth weight. In my book *Patterns of Human Growth* (Bogin, 1999a, pp. 58–63) I review the data and interpretations and conclude that the difference is the result of several generations of racism and its effects on the reproductive biology of African-American women. Differences in growth between whites and blacks continue to adulthood. I noted earlier in this chapter that when matched for SES, there are no differences between black and white adults in average stature. As a group, however, African-Americans are of lower SES than whites. The differences are especially evident in educational attainment. White men with 13 or more years of schooling average 177 cm (69.7 inches), while black men with less than 9 years of schooling average only 172.5 cm (67.9 inches). The 4.5-cm difference is typically seen between populations of the rich and poor nations of the world. The height differences between women are not as great, but they are in the same direction (Fulwood, 1981).

The mortality rate for black infants is higher than for white infants during the neonatal period (first 28 days after birth) and the postneonatal period (from day 29 until the end of the first year after birth). Since the year 1950 the rate of mortality for black and white infants has declined, but more so for whites. In relative terms, the mortality differences between the two groups are greater today than ever before. In 1991 the infant mortality rate for whites was 7.5 per 1,000 live births, and the rate for blacks was 16.5. The authors of this mortality study (Singh and Yu, 1995) note that educational disparities between whites and blacks also increased since 1950, and this SES disparity is one likely cause of the mortality difference. A study of adult mortality shows that black Americans have consistently higher death for heart disease, cancers, and other major causes than for white Americans. Worse yet, the data indicate that there has been no change in magnitude of this difference since 1950 (SoRelle, 2000).

By this point, the value of biocultural and life history models of human growth and demography should be clear. Racism is a cultural practice that has several biological effects. Racism operates across the life span and expresses its biological effects on all stages of life history. The examples above relate to such growth variables as fetal growth (birth weight) and adult stature. Demographic impacts of racism are shown to affect infant and adult mortality. Other examples available from the literature include effects on fertility, patterns of migration, and rates of maturation. The remainder of this chapter uses the biocultural and life history model to understand variation in the average height of human populations and variation in their demographic structure.

EVOLUTIONARY BACKGROUND TO GROWTH AND POPULATION STRUCTURE

One popular but incorrect notion is that the average height and skeletal mass of modern humans are greater than those of any of our ancestors. The fossil of the "Turkana boy," the early *H. erectus* specimen described in Chapter 4, provides evidence that modern statures may have been achieved a long time ago. The boy was about 160 cm (5 feet 2 inches) tall at the time of death, which makes him one of the tallest fossil youths or adults ever found. If this boy followed anything like a human pattern of growth, he may have been about 185 cm (6 feet 1 inch), as tall as an adult (Ruff and Walker, 1993). If so, this is a stature greater than the average for any population alive today. However, Smith concludes that *H. erectus* did not have an adolescent growth spurt and ended growth in stature at a relatively earlier age than is the case for living people. Indeed, the average stature estimate for six adult specimens of *H. erectus*, dating from 1.7 to 0.7 MYA, is 170 cm. This sample includes both male and female skeletons, which means that the average statures is a bit above the average for European people alive today (168 cm).

Based on several studies of more than 200 individual skeletons of early to late Pleistocene age (1.8 MYA to 10,000 years B.P.), it seems that our ancestors, from *H. erectus* to modern *H. sapiens*, were on average about 10 percent taller and 30 percent heavier than living humans (Mathers and Henneberg, 1995; Ruff et al., 1993). Figure 7.4 shows the trend in average stature for the past 40,000 years (based on data in Henneberg, 1988). While some researchers argue for a genetic explanation for the recent decline in body size, Ruff et al. (1993) explain that the difference is to be found in the way of life of ancient and modern humans and is not due to any genetic change. The review of the foraging way of life presented in Chapter 5 shows that our ancestors were required to do more heavy labor, and this imposed more mechanical loading (i.e., physical stress) on the skeleton. The increased mechanical stress seems to have occurred from an early age, and the skeleton responded by growing larger and more massive during the years of development. In related research, Styne and McHenry (1993) find that skeletal evidence "from recent prehistory and the last 2,000 years also reveal adult height in many groups to be equal to modern humans of the same region" (p. 3).

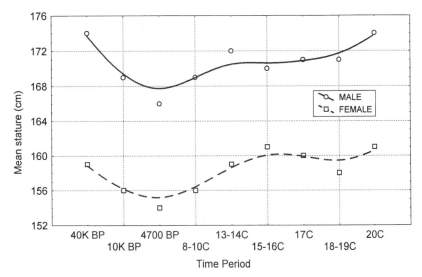

FIGURE 7.4 Average stature estimates (in centimeters) for European populations during the past 40,000 years (Henneberg, 1988). The time periods begin with 40,000 years B.P. This is the time of the Cro-Magnon peoples of the Upper Paleolithic of western Europe. The next period is 10,000 years B.P., the time of the Mesolithic. The ice ages had ended and the ecology of Europe was rapidly changing, especially in terms of food availability. The large mammal populations of the Paleolithic declined due to climate change and human hunting. The beginnings of horti-culture and settled life appear in the Mesolithic. By the Neolithic, 4,700 B.P., intensive agricul-ture is spreading across Europe. Mean stature declines steadily during these three periods. By the Medieval period of the eighth to the tenth centuries (8–10C), a recovery of mean stature begins. This trend continues to the twentieth century (20C), when mean stature again equals that for the Upper Paleolithic. The symbols ("□" for females and "○" for males) are the mean estimated heights for each sample. The curves are the distance-weighted least-squares regres-sion for the series of means for each sex. This statistical procedure fits a curve that, basically, passes through or near the mean height for each sample and provides a more continuous visu-alization of the trends in stature.

As human beings alive today, we retain the capacity to grow to the sizes and shapes that were best suited for the way of life of our ancestors. That is our bio-logical inheritance from the past. However, the ancestral conditions for life do not prevail today, and the size of living peoples reflect contemporary conditions. The advent of agriculture and permanent human settlements during the past 10,000 years (reviewed in Chapter 5) significantly changed ways of life. In addition to the reduction in physical labor, the settled farming life style introduced a new human demography. Foragers generally live in small groups, roughly 30 to 50 individuals, composed of all ages and sexes. These groups tend to be mobile and in demographic balance, with fertility about equal to mortality. Migration of individuals between groups also helps to maintain demographic balance. Archaeological research shows that the advent of horticulture, and then agriculture, led to a decline in nutritional status, an increase in nutrient deficiency diseases and infectious diseases, and an increase in local population size. As agriculture spread across the planet, an expo-nential increase in worldwide population size followed. Each of these changes con-tributes to a decline in the quality of life, often leading to poverty, which is often reflected in reduced growth in height.

SMALLER BODY SIZE IS NOT A GENETIC ADAPTATION

It is sometimes claimed that the small size of children and adults living in **poverty** (defined as a scarcity of the necessities required for normal and adequate human physical and emotional growth, development, and maintenance) may be a genetic adaptation, acquired from generations of malnutrition. The most ardent presentation of this notion was presented by Seckler (1980, 1982). Seckler, an economist, argues that smaller bodies need less total food to survive than larger bodies. For example, the Maya of Guatemala have suffered from undernutrition, heavy workloads, and disease for the 450 years since the conquest. Guatemala Maya are also a relatively short-stature population. Did they accommodate to poor living conditions by evolving a smaller and less energy-demanding body? In Seckler's own words, are the Maya of Guatemala "small but healthy?" According to recent data, the answer is no. As already noted earlier in this chapter, the children of Mayan immigrants growing up in the United States are significantly taller than Mayan children of the same age living in Guatemala, and the immigrants are continuing to grow taller and heavier (Figs. 7.1 and 7.3). Clearly, if Mayan short stature were a genetic adaptation, fashioned over centuries, such a biologically and statistically significant difference in height could not occur in less than one generation. In our most recent studies, we show that most of the increase in stature is explained by growth of the legs (Fig. 7.2). It is now fairly well established that retardation of leg growth during infancy and childhood is a clear indication of undernutrition and disease (Bogin, 1999a).

The assertion that growth retardation associated with poverty is a genetic adaptation, without functional consequence, is an abuse of the concept of biological adaptation. The consensus of research with undernourished peoples of the poor nations shows that the consequences of childhood undernutrition are (1) reduced adult body size, (2) impaired work capacity throughout life, (3) delays and permanent deficits in cognitive development, and (4) impaired school performance (Pelto and Pelto, 1989). These are all indicators of the poor biological adaptation of populations living in poverty. Amounts and rates of growth are usually reduced as an adjustment to the nutritional and health constraints of poverty, but smaller size does not overcome poverty. Indeed, an environment of poverty in early life usually results in diminished opportunities for educational, economic, and sociopolitical advancement in later life. Research also shows that poverty leading to reduced physical growth, cognitive development, and work capacity does not limit fertility (reviewed in Ellison and O'Rourke, 2000). Indeed, with few opportunities for education and gainful employment and without knowledge of or access to contraception, women living in poverty may begin to reproduce at earlier ages than women living under better circumstances. Of course, the probabilities for low birth weight, leading to higher rates of infant and child mortality, are increased by a life of poverty. These conditions for impaired growth, development, and demography recycle poverty into future generations (Garn et al., 1984).

PLASTICITY IN GROWTH AND DEMOGRAPHY

Poverty is associated with just a few of the harmful stressors to which human beings are subjected. Even in the face of fairly severe undernutrition and high disease loads people are able to survive and, even, strive to make improvements for future generations. An important component of survival is due to the biological plasticity of the human phenotype (Lasker, 1969, and Chapter 3). Human plasticity allows the individual to adjust to a very wide range of stressful environmental conditions and gives the human species an adaptive advantage not found in those species obligated to develop according to a rigid and predetermined genetic plan. Plasticity also means that when environmental conditions improve, individuals can recover quickly and return to a more optimal size and shape. The capacity for biological and psychological plasticity is the true genetic adaptation that should be our focus. Plasticity explains why human biology and behavior may serve as a mirror for society. Plasticity in human growth and demography is the focus of the remainder of this chapter.

8,000 YEARS OF HUMAN GROWTH IN LATIN AMERICA

The study of recent Maya immigrants to the United States shows that human growth is dynamic and highly plastic. Both the size and shape of the body are very responsive to the quality of the environment for growth. The data presented in Figure 7.4 also show, in a simple way, how physical and demographic growth interact over time. To better understand the relationship between the environment and the physical and demographic growth of human populations, I present the following example of 8,000 years of human growth in Latin America. The data come from a survey of the literature on the average stature of Latin American populations (Bogin and Keep, 1999). Several analysis of the height of children and adults were conducted in the original study, but here the focus is on the analysis of adult stature for Native Latin Americans. "Native Latin American" has two connotations. First, it means those people identified as the descendants of pre-Colombian forager, tribal, chiefdom, and state societies—such people are also referred to in the literature as American Indians or Amerindians. Second, Native Latin Americans may also be people of social groups that formed after European contact but came to identify themselves culturally (for example by language, dress style, and kinship organization) as Latin American. These groups include both Amerindian societies that formed postcontact as well as groups of rural *mestizos*, that is, people of mixed Spanish and Native American heritage. People of primarily European, Asian, and African biocultural descent living in the Americas are excluded from our analysis.

In total, 322 samples of adult height for men, representing 20,808 individual measurements, and 219 samples of adult height for women, representing 9,651 individual measurements, examined between the years 1873 and 1989 were found in the literature. In all samples, adult height refers to the stature of people who are reported to be 18 years old or older at the time of measurement. In addition to these data for people measured in life, Bogin and Keep also assembled some estimates of stature for archaeological samples of pre-Conquest and early post-Conquest populations from the present-day Latin American region. These estimates are based on the measurement of skeletal remains of individuals of higher social status (burials from tombs) and lower social status (nontomb burials). There are 29 samples for men and 27 samples for women, representing 1,305 and 1,158 individual measurements, respectively. The pre-Conquest data are used to provide a deeper historical perspective on the dynamics of stature variation for Native Latin Americans.

The adult height data were analyzed by plotting the data points for each sample and then fitting a distance-weighted least-squares regression to the data. This

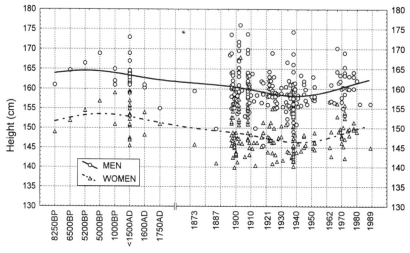

FIGURE 7.5 Mean statures of Latin American men and women during the past 8,250 years. Prior to 1873 the data are estimates of adult stature based on skeletal remains. From 1973 onward statures are based on measurements of the living. The fitted curves are trends in mean stature estimated by distance-weighted least-squares regression (see text for details). From Bogin and Keep (1998).

is the same statistical method as used to produce the curves in Figure 7.4. Separate regression equations were fit to the data for men and for women. The data for entire series of adult statures and the regressions estimated by distance-weighted least squares are presented in Figure 7.5. For the archaeological samples (i.e., A.D. 1750 and earlier), these regressions were calculated to present an idea of trends in "average" stature over time. Because intervals between archaeological data points are not equidistant, and since sample sizes are often small and certainly not representative of all people alive at those times, it is not possible to perform formal statistical analyses. Nevertheless, a descriptive analysis reveals several important associations between estimated stature and the biological and sociocultural conditions for life.

The oldest data are for skeletal remains from the Vegas culture, a foraging people living along the southwest coast of Ecuador from 8250 to 6600 B.P. (the dates given in Fig. 7.5 for the skeletal samples are always for the earlier point of a time range). These ancient foragers were relatively tall. The average stature for the entire sample presented in Figure 7.5 is 159.2 cm for men and 147.6 cm for women, and the Vegas men (161 cm) and women (149 cm) exceed this overall average. These foragers are known to have eaten a wide variety of foods, including abundant fish and shellfish (Ubelaker, 1994). As is typical of foragers, the Vegas people lived in relatively small social groups, with low population density. Life expectancy at birth is estimated at only 25 years, owing to high levels of infant mortality. But maximum longevity of those who lived past infancy is estimated at 60 years. The Vegas skeletal remains also have the lowest incidence of pathological indicators, such as periosteal lesions (indicator of infections), carious teeth, tooth loss prior to death, and enamel hypoplasias (poor formation of tooth enamel). Ubelaker summarizes all of this paleodemographic information for the Vegas people by stating that "the lowest levels of skeletal indicators of morbidity and, presumably, the healthiest time period for ancient Ecuadoreans was nearly 9,000 years ago during the preceramic, preagricultural occupation on the coast" (p. 158).

The next three archaeological samples are from the Paloma site of coastal Peru. This is a pre-Ceramic period site with many indications that it was permanently settled from 6500 B.P. to 4500 B.P. (Benfer, 1984, 1990). The inhabitants of Paloma were horticulturists, producing a wide variety of garden foods, and also hunted and gathered wild animal and plant foods. The density of the population at Paloma was low to moderate relative to archaeological sites from later time periods. Socially, the Paloma people seem to have been organized into tribal-type political groups, with minimal social stratification. They were economically and politically autonomous from any other social groups in the region. Mean estimated stature increases from the earliest period (6500 to 5300 B.P.) to the middle period (5200 to 5000 B.P.) and finally to the latest period (5000 to 450 B.P.). Benfer (1990) points out that the increases in stature occur along with declines in skeletal and dental indicators of stress, such as bone loss or enamel hypoplasias. Benfer interprets these biological changes as evidence of increasing adaptation to sedentary life and improvement of the nutrition and health of the Paloma people. Indeed, by the latest period, the mean stature of Paloma men and women would be considered as tall, even by modern Latin American reference values.

The samples dated 1000 B.P. are from several coastal and montane sites in Ecuador, spanning the time from 1000 B.P. to A.D. 190. Archaeological remains indicate that the people at these sites subsisted mainly from intensive agriculture. Ubelaker (1994) states, "By this time, agriculture was well established in both the highlands and the coast, a shift toward increased sedentism had occurred, and population densities were higher" (p. 148). Life expectancy was no better than it was for the preagricultural Vegas people. In fact, Ubelaker estimates that maximum longevity declined from 60 to 54 years. This seems to be due to an increase in the load of infectious diseases as evidenced by more pathological indicators on the bones and teeth.

Several lines of evidence indicate that the reduction in stature, longevity, and health of these samples, compared with the earlier pre-ceramic period Paloma samples, is the result of economic, social, and political changes associated with intensive agriculture. Agriculture may have produced a decrease in diet quality for the majority of people. In addition to dietary restriction, the social and political control necessary to efficiently organize agricultural labor almost invariably leads to an increase in social stratification (i.e., workers versus ruling elites) and then to economic and political inequality (Cohen and Armelagos, 1984). Further exacerbating the plight of the lower social classes are the effects of warfare and military conquest, which were common in the Andean area at this time (Webster et al., 1993). Along with the demographic pressures, these nutritional and social factors may have brought about a decline in health for the lower social classes, a decline preserved in skeletons of shorter stature.

The next group of data (marked as <A.D. 1500) are for several pre-Conquest sites in Mexico, Guatemala, and Ecuador spanning the time from about 200 B.C. to the time of the European conquest at about A.D. 1500. All are from complex, state-level societies (e.g., Toltec, Aztec, Maya) with dense populations. It is noteworthy

that by this late pre-Conquest period the variability in mean stature is almost as great as for the twentieth century. This variability is due to at least two factors: (1) the social status of the individuals within any sample and (2) social, economic, and political changes over time between samples. Because these skeletons were recovered from state-level societies, there are marked social status differences between individuals within samples. High social status is indicated when individuals were buried in tombs. Lower social status is indicated when individuals were recovered from nontomb graves. For all of the archaeological samples, the tomb burials are taller, on average, than the nontomb burials.

The second source of variation in stature is due to changes in the conditions for growth over time. This effect was illustrated in Chapter 5, Figure 5.4, for skeletons recovered from the Maya city-state of Tikal. Over time, the mean stature of both tomb and nontomb burials declines by about 5.0 cm. The decline in stature occurs during a time of increasing population growth (population growth for the ancient Maya was also described in Chapter 5), increasing warfare between Maya city-states, increased investment in militarization (larger armies, weapons production, construction of fortifications, etc.), and declines in food production and public building (Webster et al., 1993). The "material and moral condition of that society" (Tanner, 1986) were directed away from the environmental factors that would promote growth and toward those factors that would inhibit growth (see Chapter 6 for a review of the negative effects of a war time environment on human growth).

The samples dated at A.D. 1600 are from the Tipu site, located in Belize, and post-Conquest cemeteries in Ecuador. Cohen et al. (1994) report that Tipu was a mission site periodically visited by a Spanish priest but otherwise entirely inhabited by Maya. The cemetery at Tipu was in use from 1567 to 1638. The Ecuadorian cemetery samples come from two historic churches in Quito. The remains date from 1500 to 1725 and include Indian, Mestizo, European, and some Africa slave remains (Ubelaker, 1994). Tipu males are slightly taller than the Ecuadorian males, but Ecuadorian females are noticeably taller than Tipu females. Given the mixture of ethnic and social groups represented by these samples, it may be best to note only that, on average, all of these skeletal samples are shorter than the majority of the pre-Conquest samples.

The trend for a decline in average stature continues with the samples dated at A.D. 1750, which are actually burials dating from A.D. 1750 to A.D. 1940 from the same two Ecuadorian cemeteries just discussed. Indeed, it is clear that estimates of the statures of pre-Conquest Latin Americans (prior to 1500) are significantly greater than stature anytime after the Conquest [pre-Conquest mean is 163.4 cm (standard deviation, sd = 3.4 cm) for men and 152.9 (sd = 3.8) cm for women; A.D. 1600 to A.D. 1989 mean is 159.5 (sd = 4.7) cm for men and 148.6 (sd = 4.8) cm for women].

Stature of the Living

When the analysis is restricted to only the sample of people measured in life (after 1873), it is possible to analyze upward and downward trends in the regression curve for statistical significance. This is allowed because the data are graphed by equidistant time intervals and are representative of the larger native Latin American population. The overall change in mean height from 1873 to 1989 is negligible, and the linear regression coefficient for this entire time period is not significantly different from zero. However, mean statures decrease between the years 1898 to 1939 and then increase from 1940 to 1989 (the data from 1873 to 1897 are excluded as there are only four samples). For men and women, the decline from 1898 to 1939 amounts to about 4.5 cm and 3.0 cm, respectively. From 1940 to 1980 the increase is about 5.0 cm for men and 4.0 cm for women. These positive and negative secular trends are biologically significant. Separate linear regression coefficients for these two time periods also show that these trends are statistically significant.

The pattern of average change in stature is virtually identical for men and for women, and the difference in height between the sexes is almost constant. At the year 1900 the difference is 12.0 cm, at 1939 the difference is 11.5 cm, and at 1980 the sex difference is 12.5 cm. The similarity in growth patterns may also be seen in Figure 7.4.

What Do These Trends in Growth Mean?

The trends in mean stature for the Latin American populations over the past 8,000 years provide strong support for the "quality of the environment" hypothesis. This is especially evident for the post-Conquest period, a time of enormous change in the social, economic, and biological environments of Latin America. The Conquest had devastating effects on the demographic structure of Native American populations. The growth of the Maya population prior to the Conquest was described in Chapter 5. By the year 1520 that population numbered about 2 million people. In 1625, just over 100 years after European contact, the Maya population fell to 128,000 (Lovell and Lutz, 1996). Similar precipitous declines are recorded throughout Latin America. Although the population size recovered over the next 450 years, the native peoples continued to suffer. Eltis (1982, p. 473) writes, "at once decimated by European disease, subjected to intense European cultural pressures, and largely insulated from the nutritional benefits of the industrialization process, the Indians were denied access to the land which had previously saved them from malnourishment." Cook and Borah (1979) add that European imposition of forced labor, including slavery, placed additional biological and social demands on the Indians. To the extent that changes in mean stature for human populations reflect the "material and moral condition of that society" (Tanner, 1986), the decline in adult stature after the year A.D. 1500 is likely due to the effects of the Conquest on native Latin Americans. Corroborating evidence for this interpretation comes from the pre-Conquest archaeological data. These skeletal remains show that socioeconomic disparity within Native American societies, such as the Classic period Maya, are associated with a decline in stature for the lower social classes. The highland Ecuador samples of A.D. 1000 also show that stature declines are associated with a restricted diet, increased social stratification, and, possibly, military subjugation by emerging state-level societies.

The social and economic history of each Latin American nation following the Conquest is somewhat different. However, the general tendency was to have a political system of local dictatorship, with economic exploitation by European and North American nations. The health and nutrition of Amerindians and rural *mestizos* suffered under this system. These conditions remained in place up through the first half of the twentieth century in much of Latin America. The worldwide economic depression of the 1930s intensified these already deleterious conditions for the biological, economic, and social well-being of Native Latin Americans. The negative trend in stature until 1939 may be a consequence of these environmental conditions.

The positive trend in stature from 1940 to 1989 is associated with the worldwide economic recovery sparked by World War II. Latin America benefited from this recovery and did not suffer the ravages of the war in Europe, Asia, and the Pacific. Postwar economic growth continued, especially with investment from the United States. That investment had both monetary and political (i.e., cold war, anti-Communism) goals. Regardless of the motivation, the foreign investment expanded the economy and helped to increase the rate of urbanization and the redistribution of the population via rural-to-urban migration in Latin America. The positive trend for stature may be an outcome of these changes in the standard of living and demographic structure.

ANTHROPOMETRIC HISTORY

The rise in the standard of living in Latin America during the twentieth century is relatively easy to measure. Economists use statistics such as real wages (the quantity of consumables that money earnings will buy) and the gross national product, or GNP (the annual total value of goods produced and services provided in a country). Social scientists use data on education, such as years of schooling per person. Demographers and public health workers use data on morbidity and mortality, especially for infants and children. Prior to the twentieth century these types of data are difficult to find or totally absent. How, then, does one measure the standard of living, say, for the eighteenth- or nineteenth-century peasant populations of Latin America, Europe, or Asia? The answer is, analyze records of human growth (Komlos, 1991 p. 353):

> Anthropometric history was born in the mid-1970s, in conjunction with efforts by economists to quantify changes in the standard of living during the course of the last two hundred years in economics for which more conventional measures of welfare such as GNP per capita were either not available, or were controversial. In contrast to real wages, anthropometric data are plentiful, and has the additional advantage of being available for groups such as children, housewives, subsistence peasants, aristocrats, and slaves, for whom conventional economic concepts do not always apply.

Everyone has a height, and heights were measured for military conscripts, prisoners, school children, the identification of immigrants and slaves, and many other people. We have already seen how the variation in the average height of a population may be used to assess the quality of life. Human biologists started the practice of using height to estimate the quality of life. Anthropometric historians further refined the use of anthropometric data to develop a new method to assess the standard of living (Steckel, 1998).

Anthropometric history is a transdisciplinary field that blends human biology, demography, history, anthropology, and economics (Steckel, 1998). Anthropometric history is strongly linked with demographic history. Komlos (1991) and Steckel (1998) review the intellectual development of anthropometric history. In their own

research, they show that the average height of Europeans declined in second half of the eighteenth century, as did the average height of Americans in the first half of the nineteenth century. Both periods were also times of rapid population growth—1 percent per year in Europe and 3 percent per year in the United States. There was also a concomitant increase in urbanization, rural-to-urban migration, increased industrialization, social class division, and a decline in life expectancy for lower income groups due to a rise in mortality at young ages (Komlos, 1998). These and many subsequent analyses removed all doubt that average height could serve as general measure for the quality of life, a quantitative economic indicator of the standard of living, and a summary measure of human welfare.

IRISH FAMINE

In Ireland, the period of time from the winter of 1845 to 1851 is called the great famine. In the most simple and direct sense, the famine may be described as a disastrous food shortage caused by the failure of the potato crop. A more satisfactory understanding of the causes of the great famine requires a transdisciplinary and biocultural consideration of social, economic, and political conditions of Irish life in the centuries before and after the 1845. The analysis of human growth and demography of the Irish occupies a prominent place in this story. More has been published about the Irish and the great famine than can fit in any single book, let alone a book chapter. Hence, the following account is a selection of some classic works and some fairly recent research that presents the great famine in a biocultural perspective of anthropometric history.

Demographic Picture

From 1700 to 1845 Irish population quadrupled from 2 million people to over 8 million—8.5 million is a recent estimate (Froggatt, 1999). The great famine killed at least 1 million, through nutritional deficiencies, including outright starvation, and "famine fevers." From the start of the famine in late 1845 until 1848, these "fevers" were mainly typhus and relapsing fever (an infectious disease characterized by recurring fever symptoms, caused by spirochetes transmitted from one person to another by lice and from animals to humans by ticks).

In 1849 a cholera pandemic swept Ireland, further exacerbating the rate of mortality (Froggatt, 1999). Mortality accounts for only part of the rapid depopulation of Ireland after 1846. During the famine about 1.5 million people emigrated, mostly to England and America. Some were transported to Canada (see below for more details about the reasons for this transport). The end of the famine did not stop this migration. From 1850 to 1910, 4.2 million officially emigrated, and more were unofficial. The annual rate of emigration was about 1 percent per year (Guinnane, 1994), which is greater than the population growth rate in many European countries during that period. Changes in marital behavior and fertility also altered the demographic structure of Ireland. In 1851 only 10 percent of adults never married—typical of Europe. By 1911, 25 percent never married, and marital age rose (Guinnane, 1994). Fertility declined overall, but within married families a large number of offspring was typical. Large families, however, could not stop the depopulation trend. Guinnanne (1994) states that "the proximate causes of Ireland's depopulation was thus heavy emigration combined with unremarkable overall birthrates" (p. 305). These factors were in operation until 1951, when the population bottomed out at just under 3 million people.

It is tempting to view the famine as a classic case in support of the Malthusian hypothesis, and some writers have done so in the past century. More recent analysis shows, however, that none of this is Malthusian. Rather, the famine brought social, economic, and political changes that altered drastically the quality of life and standard of living of the Irish. Perhaps the best of the economic histories of Ireland is that published by Mokyr (1983). By the nineteenth century the Irish economy was decidedly agrarian, with farming, especially potato farming, the mainstay. Mokyr's analysis shows that the prefamine economy of Ireland was characterized by a low rate of monitarization, meaning that many transactions of goods and services took the form of barter rather than of payment in cash or other forms of money. So, despite the fact that income per capita in the year 1841 is estimated to be about £15.22 (English pounds) in Ireland versus £24.43 in Great Britain, the total value of goods and services in Ireland was actually much closer to that of Great Britain. There was also a low level of commercialization of business, at least as compared with the rest of Europe. Mokyr says that these factors do not make Ireland poorer, in the sense of lower personal incomes, but it does make prefamine Ireland susceptible to disaster.

The disaster came in the form of potato blight, which is a plant disease caused by the fungus *Phytophthora infestans*. A technical description of the biology of potato blight is given in Box 7.2. Potato blight is a devastating plant disease. All parts of the plant, including leaves, stems, and tubers, are attacked by the disease (Fry and Goodwin, 1997). The disease thrives under environmental conditions of high moisture and moderate temperatures (15–25°C). When infected tubers are stored in warm, wet conditions, soft-rot bacteria may become a secondary source of crop destruction. These are, of course, the environmental conditions that characterize the farm fields and storage areas of much of Ireland. Much of the agricultural land in Ireland is wet, boggy, and rocky. With only minimal modification, this type of land may be converted for highly productive potato farming. An anthropologist who lived in a West Ireland village in the 1960s describes the farming technique: "Potatoes can be grown in 'lazy-beds'—rows of earth piled into regular mounds with seaweed or sods as a fertile and substantial base—which allow a crop in the poorest land in the wettest regions. Further, lazy-beds can be worked on steep hillsides in shallow top soil, in ground where no plow could ever be used" (Brody, 1974, p. 50).

With the introduction of this farming technique potato cultivation spread, and the human population grew. Malthus himself commented on this: "in a widely cited letter to Ricardo, Malthus wrote in 1817 that, 'the land in Ireland is infinitely more peopled than in England; and to give full effect to the natural resources of the country a great part of the population should be swept from the soil' " (Mokyr, 1983, p. 38). This view certainly represents the general anti-Irish sentiments of the English, and official circles in England quickly adopted it. By 1836 Malthus changed his mind and believed that given economic investment and property security, Ireland could become as rich, or richer, than England. But, the damage was done by then. Ireland received no foreign investment, especially from England. English landlords owned most of the agricultural land. Irish farmers had to pay those rents in cash.

BOX 7.2
Biology of Potato Blight

The plant disease known as potato (and tomato) late blight is caused by the fila-mentous fungal-like oomycete *Phytophthora infestans*. Oomycetes differ from true fungi by having motile zoospores, diploid vegetative cells, and cellulose cell walls—none of which are found in the fungi. Oomycetes are sometimes called "water molds" because their growth (and disease development) is favored by wet condi-tions. Oomycetes may reproduce sexually or asexually. Late blight epidemics are a type of population explosion resulting from rapid asexual reproduction of *P. infes-tans* in susceptible host tissue. In the potato, these tissues include the foliage, stems, and tubers. During asexual reproduction, *P. infestans* is a parasite and lives from the host tissue.

"Late blight can be a remarkably rapid and destructive disease: Fields that appear healthy, but contain low incidence of disease, can be devastated within days. Some infected tubers may be destroyed before harvest, but others become visibly diseased in storage" (p. 364). This means that an apparently healthy crop may become useless after the harvest. "Bacteria that cause soft-rot diseases often invade potato tubers infected with *P. infestans*, resulting in the 'meltdown' of stored tubers. Under severe infection, entire storages must be discarded, sometimes producing huge piles of unusable potatoes. This is a serious problem because infected tubers that survive the winter in large piles can be sources of the fungus to infect the crop in the succeeding year. Thus, an important component of late blight management is the destruction of piles of cull potatoes" (p. 364–365).

SOURCE: Paraphrased and quoted from Fry and Goodwin (1997).

The low levels of monitarization in Ireland meant that after the payment of rent the local economy had to depend on barter. In a very real sense, the economic system kept the vast majority of the Irish poor, but the ever-growing population never reached a Malthusian threshold.

The Irish diet changed in the century before the great famine. Nichols and Steckel (1997) note that by about 1750 the subsistence diet of the Irish farm family consisted of dairy products, oatmeal, eggs, meats, potatoes, and in some areas, fish. Berries, wild fruit, nettles, rabbits, hedgehogs, and other game meats must have been eaten as well. The diet at this time was better in Ireland than for English workers laboring in factories and urban areas. With time, an increase in the commercializa-tion of subsistence agriculture meant that more farm products were sold and there was less for farm family consumption. Oats, wheat, dairy products—especially butter—and pork were raised for sale. By 1800 the Irish diet was narrowing and potatoes became the key component. During the Napoleonic War there was a boom in farm sales, as English investors could make huge profits from the sale of agri-cultural commodities both for the war and to feed the ever-growing urban popula-tions of England. The increase in Irish farm commercialization meant that the diet diversity of the farm families declined even further. The grain, cereals, and livestock produced on Irish farms were exported to England. The poor rural farmers were left to survive on potatoes and buttermilk, the two products with no commercial appeal. Milk products may have been highly valued but could not be transported long distances prior to the advent of refrigeration. Potatoes had little appeal for the English, who viewed both the Irish and their potato diet as biologically inferior. Disdain for the potato was widespread in Europe. Many feared that it was poisonous, a misconception based on the fact that the potato is a member of the Solanaceae family of plants. Solanaceae include food plants such as potato, eggplant, tomato, and capsicum pepper. The family also includes tobacco, deadly nightshade, the source of belladonna, and the poisonous jimsonweed. Rudolf Steiner (1861–1925) condemned the potato. Steiner, an Austrian scientist and writer, was founder of the Waldorf School and of anthroposophy, a movement based on the notion that there is a real spiritual world that may be accessed by the highest faculty of mental comprehension, namely pure thought. Steiner believed that the Irish mental faculties were deficient due to excessive consumption of potatoes. This view reflected popular fear of potatoes and anti-Irish bias throughout Europe.

The potato became both the basic food and the essential crop to maintain soil fertility in the face of increased demands for commercial products and higher rents from the Irish farmers. Potato production easily kept pace with population growth. By 1845, potato production occupied about 2.1 million stature acres, producing 12.6 million pounds of potatoes. Estimating that 47 percent of the crop was consumed by people, the rest eaten by farm animals, meant that each person in Ireland at that time had 4.5 pounds, or 1,400 kilocalories (kcal) of energy available per day just from potatoes (Mokyr, 1983). O'Grada (1989) estimates that the average per-capita consumption of the poorest third of the Irish was 12 pounds per day, or 3,733 kcal. Nichols and Steckel (1997) say this is "remarkably high," but several anthropological sources indicate that an average consumption of 10 pounds of potatoes, along with one pint of buttermilk, was typical (Brody, 1974). Potatoes are rich in protein, calcium, iron, thiamin, niacin, and vitamin C. Table 7.3 compares modern dietary recommendations with an Irish diet of 10 pounds of boiled potatoes plus 1 pint of buttermilk. Even this limited diet is more than adequate, as the data show that this combination of foods was calorically dense and nutritious. With the occasional chicken, cow, vegetables, or fish added to the plate, the Irish diet was very good.

TABLE 7.3
Nutritional Value of Traditional Irish[a] diet compared with modern recommendation for the United States[b]

	kcals	Protein, g	Calcium, mg	Iron, mg	Vitamin A, IU	Thiamin, mg	Riboflavin, mg	Niacin, mg	Vitamin C, mg	Vitamin D, IU
Irish 1845[c]	3,852	64	2,630	21.75	3,990	45.06	1.60	22.67	1,741	280–1,764[e]
United States 1989[d]	2,900	63	800	10.00	1,000	1.50	1.70	19.00	60	200

[a] From Brody, 1974.
[b] From National Academy of Sciences, 1989.
[c] Diet of 10 pounds potatoes, peeled. The Irish did not peel potatoes before boiling, so nutrient content may be higher than indicated.
[d] Recommended diet for men in the United States, 25–50 years of age.
[e] Average of winter and summer values. Considerable vitamin D is synthesized by the body when exposed to ultraviolet light.

Poor but Tall

The quality of the Irish peasant diet stands in sharp contrast to the diet of the English poor of industrial towns. The English diet averaged 2,823 kcal in the north of the country to only 2,109 kcal in the south (Nichols and Steckel, 1997). Wheat bread was the staple in the south. Oatmeal, some milk, eggs, and vegetables were the diet in the north. The more urban the population, the less varied and the less quantity of diet. The diet of English urban women suffered by their being house bound. English men worked in factories, earned the money, and both demanded and received more food. On an Irish farm, women worked to produce farm outputs. The value of their labor meant that Irish women could eat better than the English housewife.

All of these diet and economic differences between the Irish and English can be seen in sharp relief in terms of stature. Nichols and Steckel (1997) analyzed a sample of 5,005 Irish-born men transported to the New South Wales penal colony in Australia between 1817 and 1840. For identification purposes, the height of all convicts was measured. These Irish convicts were compared with 11,030 English-born male convicts. Differences in height are shown in Figure 7.6. Irish men from rural areas are 0.4 cm taller than English rural men, and the urban difference amounts to 1.0 cm. These are not big differences; moreover, one may argue that comparisons of height for convicts tell us little about the stature of the general population. To be sure, the average stature of nonconvicts is likely to be greater than that of the convicts. Other evidence shows that these are not valid criticisms. First, similar height differences between Irish and English men of the time are found consistently in other studies. Irish recruits in the British army were up to 1.5 cm taller than English recruits during the 1830s (Floud et al., 1990; Komlos, 1993). Second, indicators of the quality of life for the lowest social strata of a society tell us more about the general standard of living than would indicators based on higher status social groups. This is because the lower social strata are more vulnerable to any adverse conditions for life that exist within a society. The height evidence tells us that the typical Irishman grew up under slightly better conditions than did the typical Englishman. The height data for women shows that, in general, Irish girls also experienced better conditions for growth than English girls.

Figure 7.6 shows that rural men are taller than urban men. This is typical for the time, as urban environments were far more unhealthy than rural environments (see discussion in Chapter 5). It is important to note that the Irish–English difference in stature is not due to the greater rurality of the Irish, for the urban contrast is greater than the rural difference. English cities, it seems, were less healthy than Irish cities. The authors of this study present good evidence that the data are representative of working-class Irish and English of the time. Per-capita income and other standard economic indicators available for the general population were used to measure "wealth" for these convict samples. These measures indicate that, on average, the Irish were only half as wealthy as the English. Why, then, were the Irish slightly taller than the relatively wealthier English? The reason, according to Nicholds and Steckel, is that compared with the English, the Irish lived in a low-disease environment and ate a monotonous but nutritious diet. The English, especially those in cities, lived in more densely populated areas. We have already discussed how dense urban environments set up the conditions for the spread of infectious disease. The English also lived under the worst conditions of the Industrial Revolution, which took a toll on health and

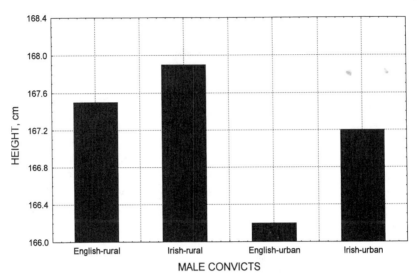

FIGURE 7.6 Mean stature of English and Irish convicts transported to Australia, according to urban or rural residency (data from Nichols and Steckel, 1997).

nutritional status. Infant feeding practices of the Industrial Revolution are at work as well. Compared with the less industrialized, low-monetarized Irish, the industrial English were less likely to breast feed their infants. Moreover, the English were more likely to neglect infants and children, who were left at home while adults worked at grueling factory jobs. Finally, repeated bouts of war with other nations, associated with naval blockades that slowed the flow of material in and out of England, made the English diet even worse.

A Reversal of Misfortune

The slight Irish advantage in quality of life came to an end with the great famine. Irish dependence on a diet of potatoes and buttermilk made them susceptible to disaster should one of these foods fail. With the great famine, both failed, as the shortage of potatoes meant starvation for livestock as well as people. The potato blight disease that destroyed the crop of 1845 to 1846 was common in Ireland before the great famine. Brody (1974) reports that blights occurred in winter of 1728, 1739, 1770, 1800, 1836 to 1837, and 1839. These earlier blights caused substantial hunger and suffering until the next spring. What made the great famine so much worse is that blight reoccurred year after year, and in all parts of the country, until 1851. This turned a seasonal hunger into a protracted famine. People ate everything available, including chicken, cows, and pigs. Without milk or eggs the hunger deepened. People ate domestic pets and denuded the countryside of "berries, nettles, roots, weeds" (Brody, 1974, p. 57).

English Response: A Biocultural Tragedy

The great famine was not a Malthusian tragedy. Ireland was not overpopulated, indeed even during the famine there was food production in Ireland. This food consisted of grain, cereals, and livestock produced on Irish farms. But these were export crops, controlled by English landlords, and almost all of this was exported to England. John Mitchel wrote "how starving wretches were transported [arrested and sent to penal colonies] for stealing vegetables by night . . . and how every one of these years, 46, 47 and '48 Ireland was exporting to England, food to the value of fifteen million pounds sterling" (Newsinger, 1996). Mitchel was a militant Irish nationalist and became one of the inspirations for modern Irish republicanism. He was arrested, jailed, and transported to America for preaching revolt against the English landlords. According to Mitchel, it was not the failure of the potato crop that killed the Irish, but the political economy of England. Mitchel cited the mass evictions of landless peasants from the land. Whole villages were depopulated by these evictions. The reason for these actions, according to Mitchel, was the desire of the English to convert Ireland and the Irish economy from a peasant society to a nineteenth-century capitalist society.

Mitchel's estimates of the amount of food available in Ireland—enough to feed double the population—were incorrect. There was a food shortage during the great famine. But, he was correct in that export crops were carried out of Ireland. Newsinger (1996) estimates that enough food to save up to 200,000 lives was exported. Mitchel was correct in his indictment of British government policy toward Ireland (Eagleton, 1995; Newsinger, 1996). The British did mount a relief campaign to help the starving in Ireland. In all, some £7 million were spent on relief. But, £70 million was spent on the Crimean War, meaning that much more could have been spent to help Ireland. The Sultan of Turkey wanted to donate £10,000 to help the Irish but was convinced by British diplomats to reduce that to only £1,000 because Queen Victoria was only willing to donate £1,000, although she eventually increased her donation to £2,000. Even the impoverished Choctaw Indians of America did more for the Irish, in a relative sense, than did the Queen (Fitzpatrick, 1998). The Choctaw had suffered on the Long March, when they were forced to leave their Mississippi homelands and walk 500 miles west to Oklahoma, during the winter, in the 1830s. Half of the people, mostly children and elderly, died on this march. Still, upon learning of the desperate conditions of the Irish, the Choctaw sent money for famine relief.

Much of the English largess toward the Irish came in the form of "public works" projects. The idea was to provide work for the poor. The work consisted of breaking stones and building roads, hardly the sort of activity that sick and starving people should be asked to perform. Worse still, the workers were often paid less than subsistence wages (O'Grada, 1999): "The British relief campaign during the Great Irish Famine of the late 1840s was not primarily to save lives. The famine was used as a way of restructuring the Irish economy along modern capitalist lines and driving out the landless laborers" (Eagleton, 1995, p. 22). Supporting this view is the fact that huge sums of money were spent on the transport of Irish convicts and "voluntary" émigrés to Australia and Canada. Free passage to Canada was offered, with the promise of money and other support upon arrival. No such support was provided, and the Canadian government was forced to provide for the Irish. Lord Palmerson, one of the English landlords, evicted all of the tenants on his lands. Many of these people, enough to fill nine ships, accepted the offer of transport to Canada (Newsinger, 1996, p. 14):

> On one of the nine ships, the Lord Ashburton that arrived on October 30, 107 of Palmerson's tenants had died of fever on the voyage and of the 477 who had survived,

174 were almost naked. They had to be provided with clothing before they could dis-embark. The Canadian Legislative Council protested to London that Palmerston had dispatched these unfortunate people "without regard to humanity or even to common decency" in conditions that were as bad as the slave trade. Palmerston's Irish brutal-ities were to be no hindrance to his later political career; he was to go on to be Prime Minister for over eight years between 1855 and 1865, making himself a byword for British chauvinism and armed aggression.

The great famine was a natural disaster compounded by social, economic, and political policies that make the potato blight seem benign by comparison. British social bias was expressed in contempt for the potato and Irish peasants. To the British the famine, "signified . . . a divine displeasure with the potato and an effort on the part of the Almighty to catapult a barbarous and desperately backward Ireland into the modern epoch" (Eagleton, 1995, p. 22). This bias was accepted at all levels of British society. No less than Thomas Malthus wrote, if "greed, sloth, dirt, idleness and perversion" should fail to accomplish the work of depopulation, then Nature "in her wisdom is at hand to step in with pestilence, epidemic and plague" (Eagleton, 1995, p. 22). British economic and political policy was based on a funda-mentalist capitalism that believed no interference with "natural" processes, includ-ing the great famine, should be attempted.

These social, economic, and political policies altered the standard of living in Ireland. The population size crashed from mortality, emigration, and reduced fer-tility: "The economic and health problems associated with the Great Famine con-tinued in many parts of Ireland for several decades, with death rates reaching a maximum in western Ireland around 1880" (Relethford, 1995, p. 249). Due to death and emigration the population structure was altered. Numbers of marriages declined, and age at marriage rose. It has been said that the Irish acquired "an appar-ent aversion to marriage" (Connell, 1968, 113). The total population of Ireland in the year 2000 is estimated at 3,797,000 people. Had the great famine not occurred, and had population growth continued as before the famine, then the population today would be over 25 million (Kennedy, 1973).

It is likely that the average stature of the population declined during and immediately following the famine, but height data are not as numerous then as before the famine. One study of changes in height over time finds that the height of Irish men and women born in 1851 to 1855 averages 170.5 and 157.6 cm, respec-tively (Relethford, 1995). Average heights of both men and women born in subse-quent five-year birth cohorts (1856 to 1860, 1861 to 1865, etc.) increases at a rate of 0.35 to 0.40 cm per decade. For Irish men and women born in 1896 to 1900 the average height is 173.6 and 158.9 cm, respectively. The most recent data I can find are for 18-year-old Irish men and women, measured in the mid-1980s (Hoey et al., 1987). The men average 175.5 cm and the women average 163.0 cm. Based on these data, the rate of increase in Irish stature slowed in the twentieth century to 0.24 cm per decade for men but increased to 0.51 cm for women. It seems that living condi-tions for girls improved in the last century, while conditions for boys did not improve. Compared with 16 European populations, the Irish men are the fourth shortest and Irish women are fifth shortest (tied with French 18-year-olds; Eveleth and Tanner, 1990). As discussed in the previous chapter, it is possible that the taller Irish migrate out of the country, and this depresses the average heights of those who remain. From a biocultural perspective, however, the average height of the remaining Irish population is a marker for the quality of life. As such, it seems that the great famine of the nineteenth century had lasting effects for the demographic and biological growth of the Irish.

DESERTIFICATION OF RURAL PORTUGAL

Portugal today is a nation of about 10 million people (this number includes the Azores and Madeira Islands), with an overall population density of 108 persons per square kilometer (278 per square mile). At least another 2 million people of Portuguese origin live in other countries. In other words, 20 percent of all people who may claim Portuguese ancestry are international migrants. Internal migrants, from rural towns to the few major cities of Portugal, constitute an even greater proportion of migrants. Lisbon, the capital city, has an official population of 831,000 (1987 estimate), but more than 1 million live and work in the metropolitan area. Porto is the next largest city, with less than 300,000 inhabitants. Some migrants return periodically to their home villages and towns, but many of the international, and even the internal, migrants have deserted their old villages. Recall from Chapter 2 that Portugal has one of the lowest fertility rates in the world today, and the national population is in decline. Combined with external and rural-to-urban migration, low fertility has depopulated much of the countryside.

The rate of external migration has been high since the colonial period, and the rate stayed high into the twentieth century. In the period 1901 to 1930, 876,941 people emigrated officially from Portugal, an average of 29,231 per year. Between 1961 and 1970, the official emigration was 571,702 people, or 57,170 per year (Brettell, 1986). From 1991 to 1998 the rate averaged about 29,000 per year (*Estatisticas Demográficas*, 1998). Scholars and the Portuguese themselves debate reasons for the high rate of migration. I have visited Portugal several times, discussed migration with Portuguese colleagues, and witnessed the return visits of migrants working in other countries of Europe. Among the reasons offered are (1) the search for sources of income, (2) a means to reduce population pressure, and (3) an outlet for the "modern-oriented" and ambitious person. An excellent discussion of the history of, the reasons for, and the consequences of Portuguese migration may be found in book *Men Who Migrate, Women Who Wait* (Brettell, 1986). The author approaches the issue as a problem of anthropological demography.

I do not discuss the reasons for migration here, rather my focus is on the effect of migration on the population structure and the physical growth of the remaining population. These effects must be considered in light of the socioeconomic status of the Portuguese. During the colonial period of 1500 to 1800 Portugal was a wealthy and powerful nation, but since the independence of Brazil in the 1820s the economic and political fates of Portugal declined. The discussion in Chapter 2 cites the poverty of Portugal in the twentieth Century. Even today, Portugal is in some ways the poorest nation of Europe. Wages for unskilled laborers are the lowest of the European Union countries. Still, a declining population within the country might allow for greater economic opportunity for the majority of Portuguese. Remittances from external migrants and a strong tourist industry might further spur the economy. Portugal's entry into the European Union should also improve the standard of living.

What are the effects of migration and economics on demography and physical growth?

For the period 1991 to 1998, 85 percent of the migrants were between 15 and 44 years of age, and 69 percent were men (all demographic data come from *Estatísticas Demográficas*, 1998). About 50 percent of migrants are married. In absolute numbers, more migrants originate from the northern region of the country (north of Porto) than any other region. Finally, 83 percent of the migrants have at least a primary school education. Perhaps the most important statistic here is that Portugal is losing its population of young men and, to a lesser extent, its population of women of childbearing age. That about half of the migrants are already married means that any children produced by these unions will grow up in another country, perhaps even become citizens of that country. The loss of young men and women and the loss of families contribute to Portugal's low rate of total population growth—essentially zero for the year 2000.

Migration is also depopulating the rural areas. The northern region of Portugal (Trás-os-Montes), where many migrants originate, is mostly rural in nature. During the period 1995 to 2000, the annual rate of change in Portugal's rural population was −4.03 percent. The annual rate of urban population change during the same period was only 2.70 percent. This indicates that some of the rural migrants may move to Portugal's cities. Urban growth is also due to natural increase and migration from other countries, for example, from the former colonies of Cape Verde, Angola, Mozambique, and Brazil into Portugal. But, relatively more of the Portuguese migrants are migrating out of their country. The net effect is that the rural landscape of Portugal is dotted with abandoned villages. Many existing villages have only elderly residents—no children, no schools, no hope for a future. A few villages use tourism to survive. An example is Piódão, a village in the central region of Portugal. Piódão is a historically and architecturally important village located in a remote valley. The population of this village was declining rapidly and the village was in danger of abandonment, which would likely result in destruction of many of its buildings. In 1994 the European Union promoted a tourism and cultural events program to save historical villages in Portugal, including Piódão, from depopulation. At present, the program is having equivocal success. One measure of population size of Portuguese villages is the number of registered voters. In 1995 there were 335 voters in Piódão of which 193 voted. In 1999 there were 321 registered and 165 voted (data from the Portuguese Ministry of Justice, election information, found at the web site *http://legislativas.iscte.pt/06/01/11/indexHist.html*). By either measure, there was a decline in the registered or the voting population. One hope for Piódão is that there are some children living in the village (there were about five living there when I visited in 1999), and a tourist hotel was recently built there. With children and work at the hotel, the population may stabilize.

Shortest Men in Europe

What relationship might migration have with the physical growth of the Portuguese? Padez and Johnston (1999) investigated this by examining the records of height of 22,841 18-year-old Portuguese males. These are, essentially, all the males born in 1978 from the central and southern regions of Portugal and measured in 1996 as part of mandatory military registration. Padez (2000) further analyzed this sample and added height data for the rest of Portugal, including Madeira and the Azores. The newer data were obtained from the records of the medical examination at the District Recruiting Centers of Portugal. The sample includes all the Portuguese 18-year-old males born between 1966 and 1979 and examined between 1985 and 1998 ($N = 882,725$). The sample represents all social strata, and as part of the registration procedure each young man was asked to provide information on their parents' educational level. Statistically significant differences in height were found between regions, with men from the most industrially developed regions being the tallest (about 173 cm on average) and those from more rural and less economically developed regions being the shortest (about 171 cm on average). Even at 173 cm, Portuguese young men are the shortest population in Europe (compared with the data in Eveleth and Tanner, 1990).

Since 1904, there has been a positive trend in height for Portuguese young men. The average increase during the 92-year period is 8.99 cm, or a rate of 0.99 cm per decade. This is about the same as for other countries of Europe, so the general improvement in living conditions in Europe as a whole also occurred in Portugal. The reason for the short average stature of contemporary Portuguese men is due to the very low base from which those improvements were made. During the period 1904 to 1998 there was a general decline in the postneonatal mortality rate in Portugal, which is one of the most sensitive indicators of the overall quality of life for any population. The drop was especially striking after 1960, when the rate was 77.5 deaths per 1,000 live born, to 1990, when the rate was 10.9 per 1,000 live born. Since then the rate declined a bit more, to 6.0. The 1960 figure is very high when compared with data from other European countries for the same year. Another indicator of the quality of life is life expectancy at birth. For Portuguese men this increased from 44.8 years in 1920 to 71.2 years in 1994. For women life expectancy increased from 49.2 years in 1920 to 78.2 years in 1994. The 1920 figures are about equal to life expectancy in many of the very poor nations today of Africa and Asia. Food intake for the Portuguese also increased in the past few decades. Total energy intake was 2,671 calories in 1963 and 3,577 calories in 1997 (Padez, 2000). Most of the increased calories come in the form of animal products, especially meat and milk, sugar, and fat. School-age children, in particular, experienced the increase in consumption of milk, and this seems to be a major reason for the increase in stature (Bogin, 1998b, 1999a). The average educational level of the population also increased markedly during the twentieth century. Educational level of the parents is strongly related to stature of their sons. The gap in average height between the two extremes of parents' educational level in 1998 is almost 4 cm. When the educational level of the 18-year-old males is considered, the difference in mean height between those with primary school only (167.37 cm) and those with some university-level education (173.27 cm) is 5.9 cm. This is a huge difference and indicates the strong socioeconomic divisions that still exist within Portugal.

As discussed above for the contemporary Irish, one reason for the average short stature of the Portuguese is the selective migration of the tallest people out of the country. A more compelling reason is that the poor living standard for the country as a whole during much of the twentieth century held back growth. Poor living conditions for the lower SES groups continue to hold back growth even today. Massive migration from Portugal was both a consequence and a cause of the low standard of living. People fled the country to find better opportunities, and in doing so depleted Portugal of its demographic energy and hope for social, economic, and political improvement. With the peaceful political revolution of the mid-1970s and the entry of Portugal into the European Community in the early 1990s, the biocultural conditions of the country rapidly improved. Moreover, depopulation of the rural areas helped to concentrate the remaining population in urban areas where human services are more readily available. In this way, the desertification of rural Portugal may have helped to improve the standard of living. If current demographic trends persist, then Portugal will continue its population decline through at least the year 2050. The analysis of the trends in physical growth presented here indicate that average increases in height will continue for the Portuguese population in the future. In sum, the population of Portugal is growing smaller but taller.

Oldest Portuguese

The Portuguese population is aging. Since 1960, the number of men and women 65 years old or older more than doubled. In 1981, 11.4 percent of the population was 65 or older, and in 1998 that figure grew to 15.2 percent. It is estimated that by the year 2015, the number of people over 65 years will be greater than the number of people under 15 years of age. This is a typical pattern for most of Europe and the other industrialized nations of the world. While typical, this pattern has serious demographic and health consequences, which in turn impact the economic, social, and political structure of society. In Portugal, and elsewhere, the over-65 population tends to be less productive in terms of traditional employment. This means lower wage earning and tax payment. At the same time, the elderly make greater demands on social and health services. At the end of the twentieth century, Portugal was spending 8.3 percent of its gross domestic product on health care (both public and private), a greater percentage than all other industrialized nations except the United States (Bonturi, 1998). Given Portugal's relatively low economic status in Europe, this level of health expenditure is a significant burden for the country.

The relatively high level of expenditure for health care, especially for the elderly, may not be helpful. The life expectancy for 65-year-old Portuguese men is an additional 14.4 years. For women it is an additional 17.9 years. Portugal is about tied with Ireland for having the lowest values for all European Union nations (Instituto Nacional de Estatística, 1999). Why Ireland and Portugal have these lowest values is not understood completely. It is known that the quality of life from conception to adulthood—the growing years—correlates with health and longevity in the later years of life. Taller populations tend to have lower mortality at all ages and be longer lived than shorter populations. Given this relationship, and given the discussion of Irish and Portuguese anthropometric history in this chapter, it is not surprising that Ireland and Portugal have lowest life expectancies for people 65 years of age.

The aging of the Portuguese population, and the aging of the human population in general, is a significant demographic trend and concern. It is also a pattern that arises from an unusual feature of human life history, namely the menopause and the postreproductive stage of life for women. The next, and final, chapter of this book returns to a discussion of life history, the evolution of human aging, and the bicultural consequences of population aging.

EIGHT

THE AGING OF HUMANITY

The first thing I do after waking up in the morning is to read the obituaries in the newspaper. If my name is not there, then I get dressed.

AN OLD JOKE TOLD BY OLD COMEDIANS.

It is often said that a good sense of humor will help a person live longer. If this is true, then the human population must be laughing a great deal. Record numbers of people now live to old age. Or, people may be praying more. A health survey of 28,000 people was conducted in 1987. A follow-up investigated the 2,000 people who died since the survey and found a religious influence on the probability of death. The faithful, those who attend a religious service once a week, starting at age 20 years, can expect to live to a mean age of 82 years. Those who eschew religious services have a life expectancy of only 75 years (Whitworh, 1999).

The aging of humanity started about 100 years ago in the richer nations, and today it has spread to all nations. In the year 1900, less than 17 million people in all the world were 65 years of age or older. This was less than 1.0 percent of all the people alive then. By the year 2050, there may be as many as 2.5 billion people 65 years old or older, which will be 20 percent of the projected population. If we look at individual nations we see the same trends. In the United States, as of the year 1998, 12.7 percent of the population was 65 years old or older, and 1.5 percent were 85 years old or older (based on a population of 270,561,000 in 1998). Those percentages are expected to increase to 18.5 and 2.2, respectively, by the year 2025. The year 2000 figures for China are 7.1 percent for 65+ and 0.3 percent for 85+. By the year 2025, these percentages are expected to rise to 13.5 and 1.0, respectively. In the year 2000 there are 87,774,000 people over 65 in China. That number of elderly exceeds the total population size of all but 11 of the 227 nations listed in the U.S. Census database. India, currently the second most populous nation, will become number one by 2036. The percentage of elderly in India will surpass China by that time.

These are predictions based on current demographic trends. In 1935, demographers working for the Social Security Administration of the United States predicted that the number of 65+ year old people would never exceed 18 million. Unforeseeable developments in public health, medicine, and technology trashed that prediction. These developments all but eliminated many infectious and parasitic diseases, which drastically lowered infant and childhood mortality. They also lowered mortality of young women associated with childbirth and reduced mortality from cardiovascular disease, cancer, and diabetes. Also unforeseen was the post–World War II "baby boom." This surge in births, which lasted for more than a decade, added more people to the U.S. population just as the health advances mentioned began to have their greatest impact. The net effect was a large number of healthier infants and children who are now living to old age in unprecedented numbers. The Social Security system of the United States provides retirement income and health insurance to America's elderly. The population prediction of 1935 meant that America's elderly would be well provided for centuries. The population facts of 2000 place the solvency of the Social Security system for the next 50 years in some doubt.

The demographic patterns for the elderly population of the United States and China are typical of the world's richer developed nations versus the poorer developing nations. That is, the richer nations have a greater proportion of their population in the 65+ age range, but the developing nations have a greater absolute number of elderly people. The numbers since 1960 are illustrated in Figure 8.1. Note that the rate of increase of the elderly population in the developing regions is expected to increase rapidly in the next 20 years. The reason for this seems to be due to the fact that the improvements in living conditions and health care that allow people to live well past age 65 are impacting the poorer nations more rapidly than occurred in the richer nations. It took Belgium, for example, 100 years to double its percentage of elderly from 9 to 18 percent of the total population. Using the year 1998 as a base, it will take Venezuela only 22 years to do the same (Shrestha, 2000).

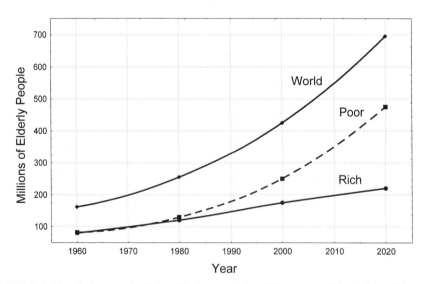

FIGURE 8.1 Trends in growth of the elderly population (65 years or older) of the rich nation, the poor nations, and the world. Rich nations include the United States, Canada, Japan, Europe, Australia, and New Zealand. Poor nations are all those of Africa, Latin America, and the Caribbean; Asia (excluding Japan); Melanesia; Micronesia; and Polynesia (redrawn from Shrestha, 2000; based on United Nations data).

JAPAN: THE AGING SUN

There is no debate among demographers and human biologists that the human population is aging. The reason is twofold: (1) fertility rates are declining and (2) people are living longer. The fertility decline was discussed in previous chapters. It is worth reiterating that as of the year 2000, the United Nations reports that 61 nations have negative birth rates, and many more are at barely replacement levels. Fewer newborns means that the existing population will "age" even if people did not live longer. But, people are living to record ages. The most long-lived appear to be the people of Andorra, with life expectancies for men at 80.56 years and for women at 86.56 years (*www.census.gov*). In second and third places are the people of Macao (men, 78.80; women, 84.55 years) and San Marino (men, 77.57; women, 85.02 years). The Japanese are in fourth place, with life expectancies at birth of 84.05 years for women and 77.51 years for men. This contrasts with sub-Saharan Africa, where the combined life expectancy at birth is about 48 years. The nation of Zambia has the lowest life expectancy at about 37 years for both men and women. War and social unrest, an inadequate food supply, contaminated drinking water, and disease take a heavy toll in Africa. The impact of the HIV/AIDS epidemic is, perhaps, the single most important factor lowing life expectancy (see Chapter 1).

The longevity of the Japanese (and the people of Andorra, Macao, and San Marino) cannot be explained simply as due to the absence of these factors. The quality of life, at least as measured by food availability, sanitation, and disease rates, is very good in Japan, and just as good in several other of the rich nations. If we look at how some of the rich nations spend money on health care, then Japanese longevity begins to make sense. In Table 8.1 are some data for eight rich nations, including Australia, Canada, France, Germany, Japan, New Zealand, the United Kingdom, and the United States. The data for this table, and the following discussion, come from Anderson and Hussey (2000). The United States spends far more on health per person than any of the other countries. This is so for both the total amount of money spent and the percent of the gross domestic product (GDP). Just

TABLE 8.1
Health Spending for the Elderly (65 Years and Older) in Eight Rich Nations

Country	Health Spending per Capita, 1997 (U.S. dollars)	Percent of Gross Domestic Product Spent on Health	Percent of Total Health Spending on the Elderly
Australia	$5,348	8.3	35
Canada	$6,764	9.3	40
France	$4,717	9.6	35
Germany	$4,993	10.4	34
Japan	$5,258	7.3	47
New Zealand	$3,870	7.6	34
United Kingdom	$3,612	6.7	43
United States	$12,090	13.6	38

Source: From Anderson and Hussey (2000).

"throwing" money at health is not an explanation for the longevity. The United States has the highest infant mortality rate (6.82/1,000 live born) and lowest life expectancy at birth (77.12 years) of all the nations listed. How money is allocated between public and private health care, and between social groups, strongly influences its effects in the population. The United States has the most privatized health care of all these nations. About 30 percent of Americans have no form of health insurance. The United States is the only nation of this group without universal drug coverage for the elderly. Only 65 percent of elderly Americans have some coverage for drug expenses, while 100 percent of the elderly have such coverage in the other seven nations. In contrast, Japan is in fourth place in terms of per-capita health spending, seventh place in terms of percent of GDP spent on health, but first place in terms of percent spent on the elderly.

Cultural values may play as big, or bigger, role in population longevity. The Japanese include their elderly in everyday social life to a greater extent than any of the other nations. The retirement age in Japan is 66.5 years, the highest of all eight nations. In Japan, 12.8 percent of the labor force is 60 years old or older, which is more than twice the level of any of the other seven nations. Japan has the smallest percentage of elderly living alone and, along with Canada, a small percentage of elderly living in relative poverty (about 1 in 10). In the United States and the United Kingdom, more than one in five elderly live in relative poverty.

Japan's Aging Crisis

The Chairman of the Mitsubishi Research Institute, Makino Noboru (1999), writes of four crises confronting Japan. Intellectual creativity, a shortage of sustainable energy, and environmental pollution are three of the crises. The fourth is "a halving of the population" (Noboru, 1999, p. 13). The Japanese population of 127 million may increase a small amount until the year 2007. Then, given present and predicted fertility rates and longevity, the population will decline to 100 million by 2050 and 67 million by 2100 (Kristof, 1999). The crisis in all this is the link of demography to economic and political power. Kristof (1999, p. 4) quotes Kaoru Yosano, Minister of International Trade and Industry for Japan, as saying, "Former Prime Minister Takeshita once told me that in the year 2500, Japan's population will be down to one person . . . When that happens, I suppose Japan's global influence inevitably will have declined." Long before that singular day, fewer births and an aging population will reduce the Japanese workforce below its critical mass. Some say this may already be a fact. Japan has suffered two recessions in less than a decade. The immediate causes are related to real estate speculation and bad banking practices. But, demography has a place. There are not only fewer children, but also fewer marriages. The average age at marriage is 26.3 for women and 28.5 for men, the highest in Japanese history. Many single adults, including about 70 percent of single women in their thirties, are choosing to live with aging parents. The children spend their money on entertainment, eating out, clothing, and travel (Butler, 1998). They do not buy homes and durable goods for those homes.

The family as a social structure is also moribund. Many Japanese families consist of a wife who stays at home to raise the 1.39 children (the mean fertility rate of Japan), while the workaholic husband rarely comes home before 10 PM and then spends less than six minutes per day with the child (Butler, 1998). Even though it costs between U.S. $140,000 to $150,000 to raise a middle-class child, with so few children there is less total spending. All of Japan's economy related with homes, marriages, and families is on a downward spiral. To help stop this trend, local governments are offering financial incentives. One town offers U.S. $700 for the first child, with increases to $6,300 for a couple's fourth child. But, birth costs $2,100 and a good nursery school—required to eventually get into the proper educational track for maximum social and financial advancement—costs at least $350 per month. None of these costs are paid for by health insurance or the government (Amaha, 1998). Children, then, are still a cost. Children might be viewed, in the long term, as an asset if they were responsible for care of elderly parents. This is the case in many other nations; however, the Japanese government tends to take care of the elderly. Five elderly people live on the tiny island of Akashima in the Sea of Japan. The government provides $490,000 annually to maintain twice-per-day ferry service to the island. The government paid to have two undersea electrical cables installed for the island; the second serves as a backup for the first. The port of Akashina is undergoing a $2.5 million renovation. Telephone service, postal delivery, and a weekly visit by a public health service doctor add to the fixed costs of maintaining this islands of five retired people. With a government generosity of this magnitude, there is no need for the "social security" provided by loving children. The children learn to expect this type of care. The neighboring island of Oshima has three children and nine teachers in the school (Kristof, 1999). These are but two cases of a pattern of government expenditure that is repeated in small islands and villages throughout Japan.

For Noboru (1999), this is part of the crisis of population facing Japan. He, and many others, wonder how long this can go on. With a declining workforce, who will pay for these government expenditures? Noboru suggests three possible remedies for this demographic dilemma. The first is the "Scandinavian method," which means to provide equal treatment to children born from marriages and out of wedlock. Noboru states that half the children born in Scandinavia are to single mothers. The birth rate to unmarried women is very low in Japan—women feel they need to marry in order to have children. Assuring single women of generous support for any child birth might encourage more births. The second remedy is the "Irish method," which is to ban abortion. About 50 percent of all pregnancies in Japan are aborted. A ban might increase the number of children born, but even Noboru states that there is no possibility that such a law could be enacted in Japan. The third remedy is the "American method," which would allow immigrants into Japan. The immediate benefit of greater immigration would be a swelling of the workforce. Noboru suggests longer term benefits: "Allowing immigrants into the country and promoting racial mixing would certainly increase the number of children. A melting pot has demerits, but it also has merits; the study of eugenics advises that too much blood purity works against the betterment of human capabilities (Noboru, 1999, p. 13).

Japanese society is obsessed with its peculiar notion of "racial purity." The above quote is just one example from a prominent individual. Noboru's notion about fertility and migration is dead wrong. As shown in Chapter 6, migrants may have lower fertility than either the originating or host population, or at least their fertility converges to that of the host. Noboru's references to eugenics and "blood purity" come off as anachronistic at best and outright dangerous at worst in a world that still deals with neo-Nazism. Japan prides itself on "ethnic homogeneity." Less than 1.5 percent of the population is non-Japanese (Lamar, 2000). Koreans and other Asians are considered to be "racially" distinct from Japanese. This is an attitude expressed by the educated public (Kristof, 1999) and also by many Japanese biologists. Two recent scientific examples are Maki et al. (1999) and Inoue et al. (2000). These researchers consider the Japanese to be a "biological race" and distinct from "Caucasians" and other "races" named in their articles. Investigation of the genetic diversity of Japanese and Koreans belie this social belief, as the Japanese, Koreans, and people of Eastern China are very closely related at the genetic level (Cavalli-Sforza et al., 1994). Studies of the biological origins of the Japanese find abundant evidence of genetic hybridization. People migrated from both northeast and southeast Asia to Japan and once there readily mixed their genes (Hammer and Horai, 1995; Sokal and Thomson, 1998). Biological reality has little effect on Japanese social attitudes. In January 2000 the Center for Strategic and International Studies of the United States hosted a conference on global aging. Representatives from Europe and the United States suggested that immigration from less developed nations would help ease the aging problem. The Japanese representatives were generally opposed to this (Anonymous, 2000). A few months later, however, Japan began planning to change immigration rules for a few types of foreign workers. One group consists of nurses who can care for Japan's elderly. The other groups are agricultural and fishery workers (Lamar, 2000). Some say that demography is destiny. Even the insular and xenophobic Japanese may be forced to open their doors to ethnic diversity in order to maintain their economy and their cuisine.

BIOCULTURAL AGING

The previous section was focused on aging in Japan to show how human longevity is a biocultural phenomenon. The biology of aging is inextricably intertwined with cultural values about the elderly, the family, marriage, and work. The case of Japan illustrates how social attitudes toward aging intermingle with attitudes toward racism. Japan is not special in this regard, as biases relating to "ageism" and racism may be found in all nations. Ageism and sexism also are bedfellows. More women than men survive to 65, and especially to 85 when the sex ratio is about 5 men for every 10 women (Anderson and Hussey, 2000). Women, then, are more likely to benefit from retirement programs, health care investment for the elderly, and similar programs, but only if such support programs exist. Shortfalls in support for the elderly could be due to a bias against women. In the United States, the Census Bureau finds that women earn only 74 percent of what men are paid, even when both are doing similar jobs with similar skills. Women also tend to leave the workforce more frequently than men to care for children or elderly relatives. Since retirement benefits are often based on lifetime earnings, women retirees may be at a significant disadvantage. Many women who survive past age 65 suffer from diseases that tend to be sex specific, such as osteoporosis. The sexism in this is that until the 1990s there was much more medical and public health concern for heart disease, typically more common among men younger than 65, than for osteoporosis in older women.

MENOPAUSE, AGING, AND SEXISM

Another form of sexism may be found in hypotheses about the nature of human aging. Hypotheses about the biology of senescence were presented in Chapter 3. Menopause was mentioned briefly there, with the promise of greater discussion in the present chapter. Here I present menopause in a biological, evolutionary, life history, and social perspective. I turn first to an overview of the process of menopause. Then I turn to some hypotheses of human aging and menopause that might be considered sexist, as these hypotheses posit little value for postmenopausal women.

The process of menopause is closely associated with the adult female postreproductive stage of life, but menopause is distinct from the postreproductive stage. Reproduction usually ends before menopause. In traditional societies, such as the !Kung (Howell, 1979), the Dogon of Mali (Strassman, 1998), and the rural-living Maya of Guatemala (Ministerio de Salud Publica, 1989), women rarely give birth after age 40 years and almost never give birth after age 44. Menopause, however, occurs after age 45 in these three societies. In the United States, between the years 1960 and 1990, data for all births show that women 45 to 49 years gave birth to fewer than 1 out of every 1,000 live-born infants. In contrast, there were 16.1/1,000 live births to women aged 40 to 44 years old (National Center for Health Statistics, 1994). Similar patterns of birth are found for the Old Order Amish, a high-fertility, noncontracepting population residing primarily in the states of Pennsylvania, Ohio, and Indiana. Amish women aged 45 to 49 years old born before 1918 gave birth to an average of 13 infants per 1,000 married women, while those women between 40 and 44 years of age gave birth to an average of 118 infants per 1,000 married women (Ericksen et al., 1979). Thus, even in the United States of 1960 to 1990, with modern health care, good nutrition, and low levels of hard physical labor, and even among social groups attempting to maximize lifetime fertility, women rarely gave birth after age 45 years. As for the !Kung, Dogon, and Maya, menopause occurs well after this fertility decline, at a mean age of 49 years for U.S. living women (Pavelka and Fedigan, 1991). After age 50 births are so rare that they are not reported in the data of the National Center for Health Statistics or for the Amish (but are sensationalized in the tabloids sold at supermarket checkouts).

It is vitally important to make a distinction between the age of onset for the human female postreproductive life versus the age at menopause. Some scholars incorrectly equate menopause with the beginning of the postreproductive stage, so one must read the literature carefully to interpret in what sense the term "menopause" is used. Another reason to make the distinction is that menopause and a significant period of life after menopause are claimed by some scholars to be mere artifact of a recent extension of life past 50 years. Olshansky et al. (1998) express this view by stating, "nobody knows with certainty what the life expectancy of human beings was even a few thousand years ago. However, reports of death tolls from infectious and parasitic diseases that occurred prior to the modern era of antibiotics strongly suggest that very few people lived much beyond age 50" (pp. 58–59). These authors then posit that extension of life beyond age 50 is the product of recent developments in medical technology and changes in lifestyle. They call this life extension "manufactured time."

Here is where the sexism lies. The implication is that there is no "natural" or biological reason to live past age 50 because reproduction is over by then. This is especially true for women. Life after 50, then, must be unnatural, or "manufactured." Some people may interpret this to mean that the role of women, and men, is primarily linked to reproduction. If so, then the postreproductive years of women offer little added value to life. I feel there are problems with both the estimates of past longevity and the concept of manufactured time. It may be true that the average age at death was 50 years or less prior to the twentieth century. Average age at death, however, may be the least likely age at which individuals die (my thanks to Maciej Henneberg for that observation). Average age at death is more influenced by infant and child mortality than it is by adult mortality. In the past, death rates for people under age five years were very high, and this brought down the average age at death. But, if one lived past childhood, it may have been possible to live well beyond age 50 (Gage, 2000; Koningsberg and Frankenberg, 1994). A study of five skeletal samples from Ecuador spanning more than 8,000 years B.P. finds that maximum age at death varied from 54 years to 68 years of age. The sample dated at 8,000 B.P. yielded an estimate of 60 years (Ubelaker, 1994). The nation of Zambia offers a contemporary example. Even with the world's lowest life expectancy at birth (37 years), there are an estimated 694,000 Zambians 50 years old or older. This amounts to 7.2 percent of the total population of 9,582,000.

These facts make the notion of manufactured time problematic. Large numbers of people today living under fairly terrible conditions do survive past age 50. During much of human prehistory, when our ancestors lived as hunters and gatherers, the quality of life was better than it is today in much of the developing world. We know this from the evidence of physical growth, as discussed in Chapter 7. Given this, there is every reason to assume that significant numbers of people lived past age 50 in those prehistoric times as well. There is no biological or cultural reason, then, to refer to these older ages as manufactured time. True enough that more people than ever are living past age 50, but the capacity to do so is not an artificial product of industrialization or modern medical technology.

THE VALUABLE GRANDMOTHER, OR COULD MENOPAUSE EVOLVE?

The point I wish to emphasize most strongly is that a postreproductive stage of life for women may have ancient biocultural roots, and it may be a very important stage of life history for our species. Some scholars suggest that the menopause is a uniquely human characteristic. Other scholars assert that menopause is a shared trait with other mammals. In a review of menopause from a comparative primate and evolutionary perspective, Pavelka and Fedigan (1991) find that menopause is a virtually universal human female characteristic and that menopause occurs at approximately the age of 50 years in all human populations. In contrast, Pavelka and Fedigan note that wild-living nonhuman primate females do not share the universality of human menopause, and human males have no comparable life history event. In a review of the data for all mammals Austad (1994, p. 255) finds that no wild-living species, except, possibly, pilot whales, "are known to commonly exhibit reproductive cessation." Female primates studied in captivity, including langurs, baboons, rhesus macaques, pigtailed macaques, and chimpanzees, usually continue estrus cycling until death, although there are fertility declines with age (Fedigan and Pavelka, 1994). These declines are best interpreted as a normal part of aging. Fedigan and Pavelka's review of the literature finds that one captive bonobo over 40 years old and one captive pigtail macaque over 20 years old ceased estrus cycling. These two very old animals showed changes in hormonal profiles similar to human menopause and upon autopsy were found to have depleted all oocytes. Finally, Pavelka and Fedigan (1991) point out that in contrast to the senescent decline in fertility of other female primates, the human female reproductive system is abruptly "shut down" well before other systems of the body, which usually experience a gradually decline toward senescence. Moreover, human women may live for decades after oocyte depletion (menopause), but other female primates die before or just after oocyte depletion (these events are correlated but not necessarily causal to each other).

Figure 8.2 illustrates the timing of the onset of the adult female postreproductive stage and menopause in the context of the evolution of human life history. The data for fossil hominids are speculative, extrapolated, in part, from evidence provided by extant chimpanzees and human beings. Nishida et al. (1990) report that wild-living female chimpanzees give birth to their last offspring in their late thirties or early forties. They may then experience between 2.5 and 9.5 years (median 3.9 years) of postreproductive life, but most of these females continue estrus cycles until death. Based on these findings, a median age of 40 years for the onset of the chimpanzee postreproductive stage is used for Figure 8.2. For human females, the data available from the industrialized nations, and a few traditional societies, provide mean ages of menopause from 48 to 51 years (Pavelka and Fedigan, 1991), and as discussed above virtually no women over age 50 give birth. Accordingly, 50 years is used as a representative age for menopause and also the maximum age for onset of

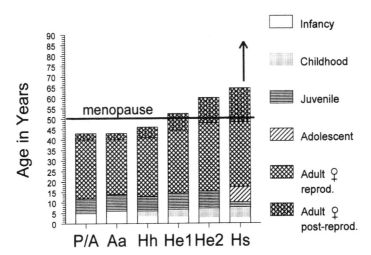

FIGURE 8.2 Evolution of human female life history emphasizing the postreproductive stage. Life expectancy estimated by the formula of Smith (1991b). The arrow above the *H. sapiens* column represents Sacher's (1975) estimate of maximum longevity to 89 years. Increased human longevity extends the postreproductive stage, not earlier stages of the life cycle. Abbreviations as in Fig. 4.9.

the human female postreproductive stage. It is also possible to propose that 50 years is the effective upper limit for the age at menopause (oocyte depletion) of hominoids in general, based upon the human condition and the one known bonobo to experience menopause.

The estimates of life expectancy depicted in Figure 8.2 are based on a regression formula developed by Smith (1991b). The formula predicts life expectancy using data for body weight and brain weight. Smith's estimate for the chimpanzee (43 years) and for *Homo sapiens* (66 years) accord well with data for wild chimpanzees (the maximum life span of captive chimpanzees is 50 years) and traditional human societies [e.g., Nishida et al. (1990) for chimps; Neel and Weiss (1975); Howell (1979) for humans]. The *H. sapiens* column also includes an extension of predicted life expectancy to 89 years. This estimate is based on the formula of Sacher (1975) for maximum longevity and is being approached by populations of the most highly industrialized nations. Smith's formula is also used for predictions of life expectancy for the fossil species. The predictions are hypothetical and based on the best available estimates of body weight and brain weight.

Age at onset of the postreproductive stage for female fossil hominids is based on an extrapolation between the known mean ages for chimpanzees and humans as given above. A linear interpolation was used to calculate the ages for the fossils. A curvilinear fit, a step function, or some other discontinuous function may better represent the true nature of change in the age of onset of a postreproductive life stage. Empirical research is needed to determine the best model. It is possible that empirical evidence for the evolution of the postreproductive stage for women will be recoverable from the fossil record because of the biology of menopause. The hormonal changes associated with the menopause process have profound effects on bone mass and the histology of tubular bones, for example, the humerus and the metacarpals (hand bones). As defined by Garn (1970), there is a gain of bone mass and an increase in deposition on the endosteal surface (the inner surface) of tubular bones during the "steroid mediation phase" of life (e.g., during adolescence and reproductive adulthood). The gain in bone mass results in a narrowing of the medulla (the marrow cavity) or maintaining a fairly constant medullary width (Fig. 8.3). Moreover, the endosteal gain is greater in women than in men. By the fourth or fifth decade of life the apposition of endosteal bone stops and resorption begins. This results in a widening of the medulla. Data for women living in the United States of European, African, Mexican, and Puerto Rican origin are illustrated in Figure 8.3. The process is found in all populations so far investigated, although there are apparent differences in the absolute amount of bone remodeling.

Skeletal changes of this sort can be detected in both archeological samples, for example, archaic/precontact Native American burials (Carlson et al., 1976; Ruff, 1991), and paleontological collections (Ruff et al., 1993; Trinkhaus et al., 1994). Based upon the predictable relationship of these skeletal changes in the bone remodeling of women to menopause, a postreproductive life history stage should be detectable in the fossil record.

Recovering these data may help settle the question of why human women have considerable longevity beyond menopause. Basically, there are two models for the evolution of menopause and a postreproductive life stage. One model posits that a postreproductive life stage could evolve if there are major risks to reproduction

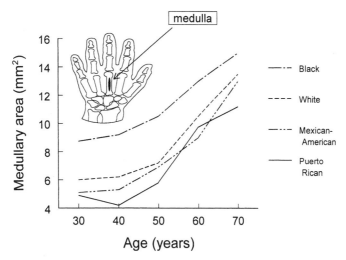

FIGURE 8.3 Age changes in medullary area for several nationally representative samples of populations of women residing in the United States. Medullary area increases after the third decade of life in all populations and the rate of bone loss increases after age 50, that is, at the time of menopause (data kindly provided by S. M. Garn).

for an older female and if the old female can benefit her younger kin. The extraordinary duration of the human female postreproductive life stage correlates with cross-cultural ethnographic research showing the crucial importance of grandparents as repositories of ecological and cultural information and the value of grandmothers for child care. Hamilton (1966) formalized the "grandmother model" into a hypothesis based on his models of kin selection theory, but until recently the hypothesis was not tested scientifically. Nishida et al. (1990) demonstrate that a few wild chimpanzee females have a postreproductive stage. They point out that the kin selection hypothesis does not correlate well with chimpanzee behavior; "the evolutionary advantage of menopause [sic] in female chimpanzees is puzzling, since they rarely, if ever, care for younger relatives . . . aged females typically live a lonely life" (p. 95). In an attempt to test the kin selection hypothesis with human data, Hill and Hurtado (1991) were unable to show that it would ever be advantageous to stop reproducing altogether. The authors used several hypothetical models that covered the range of reasonable estimates of maternal cost versus grandmother benefits. They also tested their predictions against objective ethnographic data derived from their work with the Ache, hunter-gatherers of South America. The Ache data show that offspring with grandmothers survive at somewhat higher rates than those without grandmothers, but the effect is not nearly enough to account for menopause. In a recent review of the Ache data and other cases derived from hunting-gathering and agricultural societies, Austad (1994, p. 255) finds no evidence "that humans can assist their descendants sufficiently to offset the evolutionary cost of ceasing reproduction."

The second model for menopause is the "pleiotropy hypothesis," which was described in Chapter 3. Pavelka and Fedigan (1991) apply this line of reasoning to menopause. According to their application of the pleiotropy hypothesis, menopause is a secondary consequence of the female mammalian reproduction system. This system has a physiological limit of about 50 years because of limitations on egg supply or on the maintenance of healthy eggs. Female mammals produce their egg supply during prenatal development but suspend the meiotic division of the eggs in anaphase. Approximately 1 million of these primary oocytes may be produced but most degenerate, so that in the case of female humans only about 400 are available for reproduction. During human adolescence and adulthood the remaining primary oocytes complete their maturation and are released in series during menstrual cycles. By about age 50 all of these eggs are depleted. If the woman lives beyond the age of depletion she will experience menopause. The physiological connection between oocyte depletion and the hormonal changes of menopause have yet to be elucidated. However, the pleiotropy hypothesis does account for the observation that few female mammals reproduce after 40 to 50 years of age, even though some species, such as humans, may live another 25 or 50 years.

Menopause and the postreproductive life stage of women are, then, inevitable consequences of the age-limited reproductive capacities of all female mammals. However, even if menopause is a pleiotropic consequence of mammalian repro-duction, grandmotherhood may still be an important biological and sociocultural stage in the human female life cycle. The universality of human menopause makes it possible to develop biocultural models to support a combination of the pleiotropy and grandmother hypotheses. Basically, if a 50-year age barrier exists to female fer-tility, then the only reproductive strategy open to women living past that age is to provide increasing amounts of aid to their children and their grandchildren. This strategy is compatible with Hamilton's kin selection hypothesis. The analyses cited above show that kin selection alone cannot account for the evolution of menopause or grandmotherhood. Holly Smith and I (Bogin and Smith, 1996) proposed a bio-cultural model for the evolution of grandmotherhood that combines the pleiotropy and kin selection hypotheses. In favor of this biocultural model is ethnographic evidence showing that significant numbers of women in virtually every society, traditional or industrial, live for many years after menopause. Moreover, the ethnographic evidence also shows that grandmothers and other postreproductive women are beneficial to the survival of children in many human societies (Wolankski and Bogin, 1996). Old women control important cultural information and experience that are of value to the entire society. In past times, this may be espe-cially the case during periods of food scarcity, epidemic disease, and other threats to the society that may occur infrequently during the lifetime of any individual.

Little comparative mammalian data on the value of grandmotherhood exist because the females of the wild-living species of primates, and other social mammals, only rarely survive to a postreproductive stage. There are some excep-tional species, for example, hyenas. Grandmother caretaking occurs in this species, including the nursing of grandoffspring. Indeed, when both are still fertile, mother and daughter hyenas take turns nursing each other's young (Mills, 1990). It is not known if this practice is widespread in other social carnivores. Nevertheless, the point is that when females do survive regularly past their reproductive stage of life, the basis for affliative behaviors, including some grandmother interaction and care of young, exists in social mammals.

During hominid evolution, a postreproductive life stage of significant dura-tion, and menopause, became commonplace as life expectancy increased beyond 50 years. Whether a post-50 year life stage occurred before or only after the evolution of modern *H. sapiens* is not known, but this may be investigated as described above. The regular occurrence of a postreproductive female hominid life stage would select for the females (and males?) of the species to develop biocultural strategies to take greatest advantage of this situation. Viewed in this context, human grandmother-hood may be added to human childhood and adolescence as distinctive stages of the human life cycle.

WITHER HUMANITY?

How big can the human population grow? How big, and how fast, can people grow? Do people need to voluntarily regulate the growth of individuals and populations? Will Mother Nature do it for us? These questions guide a final discussion of the interactions of the growth of populations and of individuals.

How Big Humanity?

During the last third of the twentieth century, popular opinion in the industrialized world held that the human population was growing too rapidly. Exponential population growth, it was argued, would outstrip the capacity of the earth to provide food, water, and other resources. Popular culture events of the 1970s, such as Earth Day, urged fertility restraint. Scholars and intellectuals also joined this campaign for population control. The Club of Rome published its oft-quoted book, *The Limits of Growth*, during this time (Meadows et al., 1972). The Club of Rome is a global think tank that brings together scientists, economists, businessmen, civil servants, and politicians from all nations. The goal of this nongovernmental organization is to plan for and contribute to the improvement of human societies. The Club's 1972 report considered five global trends, "accelerating industrialization, rapid population growth, widespread malnutrition, depletion of nonrenewable resources, and a deteriorating environment" (p. 21). Using mathematical models, the Club predicted that if the present trends continued unabated, then the world would be overpopulated, deplete its natural resources, and be mired in deadly industrial pollutants in the early twenty-first century. Other scholars offered even more dire assessments. According to Hern (1993), human population growth has become carcinogenic to the planet. His article presents photomicrographs of a malignant melanoma of the human brain and compares this to aerial views of several cities. There is a superficial similarity between the cancer and the sprawl of the cities.

The simplest response against the predictions of the Club of Rome and the "population growth is cancer" comparison is that they are not correct. The world has not run out of basic resources and is not close to depleting them. Cancers do not grow by the same processes that control the growth of cities. It is the twenty-first century and we are still here, the global ecosystem has not collapsed. These days, the Club of Rome devotes itself to reducing poverty and other social inequities. This is much safer, and productive, than trying to predict the future population and ecological trends. Still, the Club's concerns about the future are well founded. We will deplete the supply of fossil fuels in the next century or so. Global warming, caused in part by ever-higher atmospheric concentrations of carbon dioxide from industrial process, is a serious concern to scientists and politicians. Malnutrition and poverty are still with us, and the gap between rich and poor has increased since 1972. The Club of Rome focused on unchecked population growth as the main culprit in all of this. In 1999, some groups were still trying to do so. A report of the International Futures Programme of the Organization for Economic Cooperation and Development was issued with the title, "Population Growth: Facing the Challenge" (Andrieu, 1999). The challenges listed include (1) the rapid increase in world population, (2) aging in the developed countries, (3) the demographic transition in developing countries, and (4) social upheavals due to the first three challenges. China is highlighted and described as "a demographic time bomb" (p. 31).

At about the same time, some other groups were beginning to worry more about population decline than expansion. Indeed, as early as 1997 reports began to appear that challenged notions that the world population would double in the foreseeable future. One prediction is that population will increase, from about 6 billion today to fewer than 10 billion by 2050. By the end of the twenty-first century the size of the human population will be in decline (Lutz et al., 1997). By early 2000, both the United Nations and the World Bank issued reports on population decline in the rich nations and international migration. These reports state that the rich countries will have to attract immigrants from the poorer nations, which tend to still have high fertility, in order to have a stable and productive work force. The real population issue today, according to the reports, is not the absolute size of humanity, but rather its distribution between rich and poor nations (Rodriguez et al., 2000). In this view, China is no longer a time bomb; it is a labor force resource!

How Will People Grow?

If we accept the notion that there are not too many people, just a poor distribution, then we are still left with concerns about their healthy growth and development. Malnutrition and food insecurity are now major problems in the poorer nations. These will continue to be problems for some time. The World Bank reports that in 1990 a total of 780 million people, of the 4 billion in the developing world, were malnourished (these data, and the following information, are based on a report by Marito Garcia, which may be found at *http://www.cgiar.org/ifpri/2020/briefs/number06.htm*). The United Nations finds that protein-energy malnutrition (PEM), measured by the proportion of children falling below the accepted weight standards, affects 34 percent of all preschool children, some 184 million children, in the poorer, developing countries. Malnutrition not only stunts growth, it has a powerful impact on child mortality. Malnutrition interacts with infectious diseases, such as severe diarrheal infections, acute respiratory infections, malaria, and measles to produce a synergistic effect that exacerbates morbidity and mortality. A study by Pelletier et al. (1995) of child deaths in 53 developing nations finds that even mild-to-moderate PEM contributes to 56 percent of these deaths to infants and children in developing nations.

Insufficient food consumption leads to other problems, such as iron-deficiency anemia, vitamin A deficiency, and iodine deficiency. Anemia affects at least 370 million women between 15 and 49 years of age, and this condition contributes to

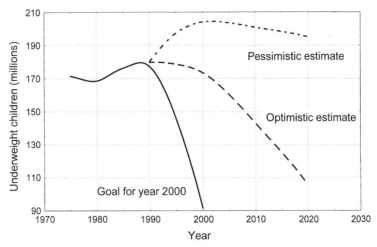

FIGURE 8.4 Estimate of malnourished preschool children in the year 2020 (World Bank, *http://www.cgiar.org/ifpri/2020/briefs/number06.htm*).

high maternal mortality rates. Every year, 250,000 to 500,000 children go blind due to vitamin A deficiency. A recent assessment by WHO indicates that some 655 million people in the developing world are affected by goiter, which is due to iodine deficiency. This figure is nearly three times the previous estimates. Many more people have less visible forms of iodine deficiency, but all forms retard both physical and mental development.

If current trends persist, the number of children with PEM will increase to about 200 million by the year 2020 (Fig. 8.4, pessimistic scenario). Breakthroughs in food production and social equality could lower this to about 100 million (optimistic scenario). Disasters, including the AIDS pandemic, may make for an even worse scenario. The goals of the World Summit for Children (held in 1990) and the International Conference on Nutrition (held in 1992) of reducing child malnutrition prevalence by half the 1990 value will not be attained by 2020 even using the best-case scenario. A concerted effort by the poor nations and funded by the rich nations to reduce child malnutrition can help. Several countries, including Thailand, Zimbabwe, Indonesia, Costa Rica, Chile, and India, have implemented successful programs to attack PEM. Garcia writes (from the International Food Policy Research Institute [IFPRI] web page cited above):

In Thailand, the prevalence of underweight children was reduced from 36 percent to 13 percent over a period of eight years, through a national program and policy that both attacked poverty and promoted explicit nutrition programs... Increase in incomes and reduction in poverty are important, but experiences in several countries indicate that even where there is no rapid improvement in incomes, malnutrition can be reduced by explicit programs and policies that aim at improving household access to food and health services and improving child care practices such as breastfeeding and proper weaning of infants. A concerted effort to follow the examples of successful countries is needed to reduce the numbers of malnourished children in the future.

Alleviating malnutrition and ill health in the poorer nations is in the selfish interest of the rich nations. With populations that are both declining and aging, the richer nations must import workers to sustain economic and social stability. The immigrants may be concentrated in manual labor and service profession today, but soon they will be needed in greater numbers in skilled trades and technical professions. Malnutrition and poor health severely curtail human development, in every sense of the word development. Unless the rich nations act now, there may not be enough qualified workers for their economies. The plight of the former "second world" nations—those nations that were under domination by the Soviet Union—illustrates this point. From the mid-1960s to the late 1980s, the people living in Central and Eastern Europe experienced declines in health status. In Hungary, Eiben (1998a) reports that mortality increased for infants, children, juveniles, adolescents, and young adults. Life expectancy at birth declined 3.5 years between 1965 and 1985. Family structure destabilized as the rate of divorce and suicide increased and the rate of alcohol abuse increased. The birth rate declined and since 1980 Hungary has been in negative population growth (−3.0 percent as of 1994). Since 1985 the gross domestic product (GDP) of Hungary has declined, so that by 1993 the GDP was only 84.5 percent of its 1985 value. The effect of all of these demographic, social, and economic problems may be seen in the physical growth of Hungary's young people in comparison with the Dutch. Comparison is made with the Netherlands as this nation enjoyed prosperity relative to Hungary throughout the last 40 years. Average heights for men and women in two time periods, 1971 and 1985, are shown in Table 8.2. From 1971 to 1985, Hungarian women increased by 1.5 cm on average, but male height hardly changed. In contrast, Dutch men increased 3.3 cm and Dutch women increased by an average of 1.9 cm. The difference between Hungarian and Dutch men is particularly telling of the difficult times experienced in Hungary.

In many other parts of the world, physical growth of children and youth has been in decline. This process is often called the **negative secular trend**. In growth research, the term "secular trend" refers to a change in the average amount of growth of a population over time. The increase of stature of the Dutch over time is an example of a positive secular trend. The landmark publication about the negative secular trend is by Tobias (1985). He presents a worldwide review of growth data for stature from the twentieth century for succeeding generations of people living under deteriorating conditions of low-SES and/or under political repression. For each of the cases Tobias examines, he finds either no secular change in stature

TABLE 8.2

Average Heights of 18-Year-Old Men and Women in Hungary and the Netherlands in 1971 and 1985

Year	Hungary		Netherlands	
	Men	Women	Men	Women
1971	175.9	160.8	177.6	166.3
1985	175.3	162.3	180.9	168.2

Source: From Eveleth and Tanner (1976, 1990).

or negative secular change. His own data from South Africa demonstrate a clear decline in mean stature for Blacks from the late-nineteenth century to the present day. These stature declines are linked to the deterioration of the social, economic, and political environment for Blacks both prior to and during the apartheid era in South Africa.

In follow-up studies, it has been shown that between the years 1880 and 1970, South African Whites had an increase in mean height of 4.5 mm per decade and South African Blacks had a mean increase of 2.4 mm per decade (Henneberg and Van Den Berg, 1990). The Whites are predominantly of Dutch ancestry, and quite unexpectedly the increase in stature of the South African Whites was significantly less than that for the Dutch living in the Netherlands—15 mm per decade—and measured in the same years. This finding is unexpected because the purpose of the apartheid policies was to guarantee political and social domination by the country's white minority over the nonwhite population. One expectation of apartheid was that it would ensure that South African Whites would live and grow up under socio-economic conditions equal to or superior to those of the industrialized nations of Europe and North America. But, the superior secular increase in stature of the Dutch in the Netherlands shows that the policy failed to do this.

My explanation for this failure is that the deterioration of living conditions for the Black population caused by the apartheid policies could not be confined to only that ethnic group. Blacks are the majority population of South Africa. Of the almost 39 million inhabitants in 1991, 75.2 percent of the population were classified as Black Africans, 13.6 percent were Whites, 8.6 percent were known as Coloureds, and 2.6 percent were Asians. When that many people live under poverty, the economic and social development of the country as a whole is likely to be arrested, and even the privileged social classes will be affected. The most meaningful single statistic in this regard is the infant mortality rate. In 1985, the infant mortality rate for South African Blacks was 68 per 1,000 live births, and for South African Whites it was 13 per 1,000 (Cameron, 1997). By comparison, the infant mortality rate in 1987 for the Netherlands, for all ethnic groups, was only 7 per 1,000.

An even clearer case of the negative secular trend comes from Guatemala during the period from 1974 to 1983, a time of intense civil war and political repression. Economic decline and political unrest due to the war are associated with a significant decline in the mean stature of cross-sectional samples of 10- and 11-year-old boys and girls (Bogin and Keep, 1998). Boys and girls from families from very high, moderate, and very low SES were measured, and all three SES groups show the decline in stature. A general deterioration of the quality of life in Guatemala, especially the quality of nutrition and health of the entire Guatemalan population, seems to be the cause of the negative secular trend. Even the very wealthy were not spared, as the environmental decline affected municipal water supply systems and led to the outbreak of cholera and other epidemic diseases.

HEALTHY PEOPLE, HEALTHY POPULATIONS

To assure the quality of the growth of humanity, programs to promote health and healthy development are needed in all nations. The United States promotes one program, titled "Healthy People 2010" (U.S. Department of Health and Human

Services, 2000). The purpose of the program is to achieve two overarching goals: (1) help individuals of all ages to increase life expectancy and improve their quality of life and (2) eliminate health disparities among different segments of the population. One specific concern is to reduce the proportion of adults who are obese. As of 2000, 23 percent of adult Americans aged 20 years and older were identified as obese. The target for 2010 is 15 percent. Another concern is to reduce the proportion of children and adolescents who are overweight or obese. Presently, about 11 percent of young people fall into these categories. The target is no more than 5 percent. Eight percent of low-income children under age 5 years were growth retarded in 1997. The 2010 target is a reduction to only 5 percent. Another goal is to increase the proportion of adolescents who engage in moderate physical activity for at least 30 minutes on five or more days per week. As of 1997, 20 percent of students in grades 9 through 12 met this goal. The target is 30 percent compliance. The program also seeks to increase the proportion of adults who perform physical activities two or more days per week that enhance and maintain muscular strength and endurance. The target is 30 percent, but as of 1997 only 19 percent of adults aged 18 years and older performed such physical activities. Finally, there are nutrition goals. Surveys conducted from 1994 to 1996 found that 28 percent of persons aged 2 years and older consumed at least two daily servings of fruit. Worse still, only 3 percent of persons aged 2 years and older consumed at least three daily servings of vegetables, with at least one-third of these servings being dark green or deep yellow vegetables. The goal is to increase adequate fruit consumption to 75 percent and adequate vegetable consumption to 50 percent.

There are many other goals of program. Virtually all of these goals are applicable to human populations throughout the world. Overweight and obesity are on the rise everywhere. Declines in physical activity and physical fitness are noted in all of the industrialized and industrializing nations (Eiben, 1998b). The health of the human population depends on the quality of life for all of its members. The goals of Healthy People 2010 or any similar program will be realized only if concern for the well-being of young people and adults takes precedence over short-term indicators of economic gain. Measures such as GDP may need to be replaced with demographic and physical growth indicators. Indeed, Morris (1979) developed a Physical Quality of Life Index. The index includes the infant mortality rate, life expectancy at one year of age, and literacy rates in a country. These measures are more direct indicators of health conditions for the majority of the people. In contrast, GDP is often unrelated to the real health conditions of the majority of the people (Cameron, 1991). The use of GDP is a reflection of an obsession with material comfort and financial security for the wealthy few. That narrow obsession will have to be replaced with a broad concern for personal physical fitness and health security. A proactive involvement with the well-being of other people will also be required.

It is my hope that this little book helps to provide its readers with the resources needed to understand some basics of human demography, human growth and development, and the interconnections between them. With such knowledge comes the ability to elucidate basic human needs and imagine endless human possibilities. With this knowledge also comes great responsibility to ensure that human needs are satisfied and that possibilities for the growth of humanity are freely explored.

GLOSSARY

Adolescence. A stage in the human life cycle, covering the five to eight years after the onset of puberty. The adolescent phase is characterized by a growth spurt in height and weight, virtually completion of permanent tooth eruption, development of secondary sexual characteristics, sociosexual maturation, intensification of interest and practice of adult social, economic, and sexual activities.

Adolescent growth spurt. The rapid and intense increase in the rate of growth in height and weight that occurs during the adolescent stage of the human life cycle.

Adulthood. The stage of the human life cycle that begins at about age 20 years. The prime of adulthood lasts until the end of childbearing years (late forties) and is a time of homeostasis in physiology, behavior, and cognition. Old age and senescence mark the period of decline in the function of many body tissues or systems during adulthood. This later phase lasts from about the end of childbearing years to death.

Adrenarche. The onset of secretion of androgen hormones from the adrenal gland, usually occurring at about six to eight years of age in most children.

Age-graded play group. A social group of children and juveniles in which the older individuals provide basic caretaker behavior and enculturation for the younger individuals. The play group frees adults for subsistence activities and other adult behaviors.

Age-specific central death rate. The probability that an individual who survives to age x will die within the next age interval,

Age-specific mortality rate. The number of deaths in an age interval per 1,000 persons surviving to age x (abbreviated as $1,000 m_x$).

Andropause. The decline in hormone production with age experienced by men.

Anthropological demography. The study of the biosocial characteristics of human populations and their development through time.

Apoptosis. Programmed cell death, a mechanism that allows cells to self-destruct when stimulated by the appropriate trigger. Cell deaths appear to be programmed by gene–environment interactions and are initiated for various reasons, such as when a cell is no longer needed within the body or when it becomes a threat to the health of the organism.

Biiliac width. The maximum linear distance between the iliac crests. Also called biiliac breadth or pelvic breadth.

Biocultural. Referring to a recurring interaction between the biology of human development and the sociocultural environment. Not only does the latter influence the former, but human developmental biology modifies social and cultural processes as well.

Biodemography. A field that analyzes the biological pattern to the dying out of individuals within a population, based heavily on evolution theory and genetics.

b_x. The average number of offspring produced during any given age interval.

Catch-up growth. The rapid increase in growth velocity following recovery from disease or refeeding after short-term starvation.

Census. A count of anything; in demography it refers to an enumeration of people.

Childhood. A stage in the human life cycle that occurs between the end of infancy and the start of the juvenile growth period (about the ages 3 to 10 years). Children are weaned from breast feeding (or bottle feeding) but must be provided specially prepared foods and require intensive care by older individuals. Childhood is characterized by relatively rapid neurological development and slow physical growth and development.

Chinanpas. A type of hydroponic field, with a mix of water canals and ponds between raised irrigated beds. Used by the Maya and Aztecs for intensive food production.

Closed population. One that experiences neither immigration nor emigration of people.

Congenital. States or conditions that exist in the individual at or prior to birth. The term is usually used to refer to hereditary or inborn medical conditions that are most often harmful.

Controlled fertility populations. Groups where family planning measures are routinely used.

Crown–rump length. The distance from the top of the head to the base of the buttocks, usually measured in the fetus or neonate.

Cultural animals. A phrase describing the human species, meaning that humans possess all of the potentials and limitations of any living creature but also add a cultural trilogy of (1) dependence on technology; (2) codified social institutions, such as kinship and marriage; and (3) ideology.

Culture. The technological, sociological, and ideological strategies that people use to exploit and enhance resources required for survival.

De facto census. A count of people living at a given location at the time of the census.

De jure census. A tally of people according to their regular or legal residence, even if they are living elsewhere at the time of the census.

Demographic transition. A model of population growth that holds that as a society becomes more economically developed there will be a reduction in mortality and, at some time later, there will be a reduction in fertility. The lag between reduced mortality and reduced fertility results in rapid population growth.

Deoxyribonucleic acid (DNA). One of the class of complex molecules called nucleic acids. DNA is found in the nucleus of virtually all living cells. DNA contains the genetic code needed for a cell to produce the proteins it requires to perform its function.

Development. Progression of changes from undifferentiated or immature state to a highly organized, specialized, or mature state.

Diaphysis. The shaft of a long bone.

Differential fertility. One of the two fundamental mechanisms of natural selection (the other being differential mortality), referring to variation in the reproductive success of mature organisms.

Differential mortality. One of the two fundamental mechanisms of natural selection (the other being differential mortality), referring to the death of some individuals of a population prior to their reproductive maturation.

d_x. The number of deaths occurring in a given age interval.

Ecology. The relationship that an individual organism, or group of individuals of a species, has with its physical, biological, and social environment.

Enamel hypoplasias. Malformation of the tooth crown, including pitting, linear furrowing, or complete lack of enamel. Used as indicators of malnutrition and disease stress during infancy and childhood.

Endemic. A disease that is restricted or peculiar to a locality or region and reoccurs persistently in that population.

Epidemic. A disease that spreads quickly and widely, almost without control, in a population.

Epidemiology. The study of the causes and transmission of disease.

Epiphysis. An ossification center of a long bone, separated from the shaft of the bone by cartilage.

Essential nutrients. A nutrient that cannot be manufactured by the human body from simpler elements and thus must be supplied from the diet.

Event history analysis. A mathematical method used to measure the duration of almost any process.

e_x. The life expectancy at age x.

Expanding tissues. Those tissues or cells that retain their mitotic potential even in the differentiated state. These tissues can increase in size and mass by cell division of all their cells. Examples include the liver, kidney, and endocrine glands.

Fecundity. The biological potential for childbearing.

Germinative cells. Undifferentiated cells, usually sequestered in well-defined regions within tissues, that give rise to the differentiated, specialized cells of mature tissues, organs, and subsytems in the body.

Gompertz equation. A simple formula that describes the exponential increase in mortality for the age range 20 to 60 years. In its modern formulation the equation takes the form $m(t) = \exp(mt)$, where m is the mortality rate and t is time as measured by age in years.

Gonadarche. Maturation of the gonads (testes or ovary) resulting in the secretion of gonadal hormones (androgens or estrogens).

Gross reproductive rate (GRR). The average number of female children that a woman would produce if she lived to the end of her potential reproductive years.

Growth. Quantitative increase in size or mass.

Growth plate region. The site of formation of bone tissue in a growing long bone. The growth plate consists of highly ordered rows of cartilage cells; the row farthest removed from the bony shaft is a germinative layer; it is responsible for cell replication and cartilage growth at the bone shaft. Over time the cartilage will be re-formed into true bone tissue.

Hazard rate. The probability per time unit that a "case" (person) that has survived to the beginning of the respective interval will "fail" (die) in that interval.

Heterochrony. Referring to several processes in biology that bring about evolutionary change between ancestral and descendant species by modifying characters present in the ancestor via changes in developmental timing.

Homeostasis. Any self-regulating process by which biological systems tend to maintain stability while adjusting to conditions that are optimal for survival.

Hominids. Living human beings and their extinct fossil ancestors characterized by habitual bipedal locomotion.

Hypermorphosis. A type of heterochrony that extends one or more stages of growth and development of the descendant species beyond that of the ancestral species.

Hyperplasia. Cellular growth by cell division (mitosis).

Hypertrophy. Cellular growth by an increase of material within each cell.

Hypothalamus. An evolutionarily ancient midbrain structure that in mammals provides a connection between the nervous system and the endocrine system—a neuroendocrine transducer. The human hypothalamus secretes hormones that stimulate or inhibit the production of other hormones by the pituitary that regulate growth and development.

Hypoxia. The lack of sufficient oxygen supplied to the tissues of the body. May be the result of disease or may be due to residence at high altitude (3,000 m or more above sea level).

Infancy. A stage in the life cycle of all mammals. For human beings it lasts from the second month after birth to end of lactation, usually by age 36. Human infancy is characterized by (1) rapid growth velocity with a steep deceleration in velocity with time, (2) feeding by lactation, (3) deciduous tooth eruption, and (4) many developmental milestones in physiology, behavior, and cognition.

Juvenile. A stage in the life cycle of most social mammals, including all of the higher primates. The juvenile stage is defined as the time of life when an individual is no longer dependent on adults (parents) for survival and prior to that individual's sexual maturation.

Law of mortality. An alleged universal progression of death for human beings, based on the Gompertz equation.

Life cycle. The stages of growth, development, and maturation from conception to death of any organism.

Life history. The major events that occur between the conception and death of an organism.

Life history theory. A field of biology concerned with the strategy an organism uses to allocate its energy toward growth, maintenance, reproduction, raising off-spring to independence, and avoiding death. For a mammal, it is the strategy of when to be born, when to be weaned, how many and what type of pre-reproductive stages of development to pass through, when to reproduce, and when to die.

Life tables. Mathematical devices designed to measure the duration of some phenomenon. In demography, life tables usually measure the duration of life.

Low birth weight. A weight at birth of 2,500 g or less for a neonate of normal gestation length (i.e., 37 to 40 weeks).

l_x. The size of the population at the beginning of an age interval.

L_x. The number of person-years lived during a given age interval.

Malthusian parameter (r). The intrinsic rate of natural increase of a population, equivalent to the number of births minus number of deaths per generation time.

Maternal depletion. A condition that results when the mother becomes pregnant again before she has been able to recover from the physiological drain caused by a previous pregnancy, birth, and lactation.

Maturity. The process and the state of reaching functional capacity in terms of biological, behavioral, and cognitive capacities.

Mean generation time (I). The average interval between the birth of an individual and the birth of its offspring for a given population.

Menarche. The first menstrual period.

Menopause. The sudden or gradual cessation of the menstrual cycle subsequent to the loss of ovarian function.

Midgrowth spurt. A relatively small increase in the rate of growth in height that occurs in many children between the ages of six and eight years.

Morbidity. States of ill health; disease.

M_x. The number of deaths in an age interval, also called the age-specific mortality rate.

Natural fertility populations. Societies without conscious family size limitations due to contraception or induced abortion.

Natural increase. A measure of the fertility of the local population, excluding contributions from immigration.

Natural selection. The process by which environmental constraints lead to varying degrees of reproductive success among individuals of a population of organisms. The individuals must vary in terms of genetically inherited characteristics. Natural selection determines the course of evolutionary change by maintaining favorable genotypes and phenotypes in a constant environment (stabilizing selection) or improving adaptation in a direction appropriate to environmental changes (directional selection). Charles Darwin and Alfred Wallace first proposed this concept in 1858.

Negative secular trend. A decrease in the mean size (e.g., height, weight, leg length) of the individuals of a population from one generation to the next. Negative secular trends usually indicate a deterioration in the quality of the biocultural environment for human development.

Neonatal period. A stage in the human life cycle lasting from birth to 28 days after birth.

Neonate. The newborn infant under 28 days of age.

Neoteny. A type of heterochrony that results in the retention of infantile or juvenile traits into adulthood. This is achieved by having sexual maturation take place while the individual is still in a preadult stage of phenotypic development.

Net reproductive rate (NRR). A demographic statistic calculated by multiplying the proportion of women surviving to each age (lx) by the average number of offspring produced at each age (bx) and then adding the products from all the age groups.

Organogenesis. The formation of body organs and systems during the first trimester of prenatal life.

Participant-observation. A methodology for the collection of demographic and other social data. Participant-observation requires the researcher to live with the people being studied and to learn their language and rules for behavior.

Pellagra. A nutritional disease caused by a lack of niacin (vitamin B_3).

Pelvic inlet. The bony opening of the birth canal through which the fetus must pass during parturition.

Phenotype (s). The physical or behavioral appearance of an individual, resulting from the interaction of the genes inherited at the moment of conception and the environment during growth and development.

Pituitary. An endocrine gland of vertebrate animals located at the base of the brain, below the hypothalamus, to which it is connected via blood vessels and nerves. The hormones secreted by the pituitary stimulate and control the functioning of almost all the other endocrine glands in the body.

Plastic. The capacity of a biological trait or behavior to be modified by the environment, usually during the period of growth and development.

Plasticity. The concept that the development of the phenotype is responsive to variations in the quality and quantity of environmental factors required for life. Such variations produce many of the differences in growth observed between individuals or groups of people.

Population. In biology, a group of individuals of a species that occupies a well-defined geographic area and, in sexually reproducing species, interbreeds.

Population census. The enumeration of a particular group of people, defined by location, nationality, citizenship, or some other common characteristic.

Population pyramid. A graphical representation of the number of males and females in a population by age groups.

Postpartum amenorrhea. The absence of menstrual cycles following birth.

Poverty. A scarcity of the necessities required for normal and adequate human physical and emotional growth, development, and maintenance.

Prematurity. A state at birth for human neonates who are born prior to 37 weeks of gestation.

Prolactin. A hormone that stimulates milk production in nursing women.

Puberty. An event of short duration (days or a few weeks) that marks the reactivation of the central nervous system regulation of sexual development. The onset of puberty is accompanied by a dramatic increase in secretion of sex hormones. In social mammals, including humans, puberty occurs at end of the juvenile stage.

Pull factor. In human migration studies, these are agents, or variables, at the new location that encourage people to move.

Push factor. In human migration studies, these are agents, or variables, at the current location that encourage or force people to move to a new location.

Qualitative data. In social science, information that describes the character and attributes of human beings and their behavior, without emphasis on numerical or statistical facts.

Quantitative data. Information that describes the amount, frequency, or other numerical or statistical aspects of human beings.

q_x. Abbreviation for age-specific central death rate (see above).

Renewing tissues. Those tissues, or cells, of the body that are replaced by a two-step process: (1) the mitotic division of germinative cells and (2) the differentiation of some of these newly divided cells into mature tissues. Examples of renewing tissues are the blood and the skin cells of the epidermis.

Secondary sexual characteristics. Physical traits associated with the onset of sexual maturation, including the development of facial hair and muscularity in boys and the development of the breast and adult fat distribution in girls.

Sedentes. People who remain in their place of birth.

Senescence. The period of the adult phase of the life cycle characterized by a decline in the function of many body tissues or systems. Senescence usually begins after the end of childbearing years and lasts until death.

Sibling competition. A condition when the brothers and sisters of multiple pregnancies are each vying for the same limited set of resources available from the mother.

Skeletal age and skeletal maturation. A measure of biological maturation (as distinguished from chronological age) based on stages of formation of the bones.

Socioeconomic status (SES). An indicator, often defined by measures of occupation and education of the parents or heads of household, used as a proxy for the general quality of the environment for growth and development of an individual.

Standard of living. The necessities, comforts, and luxuries enjoyed or aspired to by an individual or group.

Static tissues. Those tissues or cells that are incapable of growth by hyperplasia once they have differentiated from precursor germinative cells. Examples are nerve cells and striated muscle.

Swidden horticulture. A type of food production system in which garden plots are cut from the forest, the cut vegetation is burned, and crops are planted in the ashes.

Take-off. The point of increase in growth velocity that marks the start of the adolescent growth spurt.

Total reproductive rate (TRR). The average number of all offspring left by all women of a given birth cohort who survive to the oldest possible reproductive age for that population (generally 50 years).

Trade-offs. Life history strategies used when competition between two biological or behavioral traits requires partial allocation of energy or materials to each trait.

Trimesters. (Of pregnancy) The division of the nine calendar months of human pregnancy into three three-month periods. Usually called first, second, and third trimesters.

U-shaped curve. A model of health change during rural-to-urban migration for both individuals and groups. Health status begins at a high level, declines following migration, and then returns to a higher level after some time in the new environment.

Weaning. The termination of breast feeding.

REFERENCES

Abelson, A. E. (1976). Altitude and fertility. *Human Biology* **48**: 83–91.

Able, E. L. (1982). Consumption of alcohol during pregnancy: A review of effects on growth and development of offspring. *Human Biology* **54**: 421–453.

Aiello, L. C., and Wheeler, P. (1995). The expensive-tissue hypothesis. *Current Anthropology* **36**: 199–221.

Alexander, R. D., Hoogland, J. L., Howard, R. D., Noonan, K. M., and Sherman, P. W. (1979). Sexual dimorphisms and breeding systems in pinnipeds, ungulates, primates, and humans. In N. A. Chagnon and W. Irars (Eds.), *Evolutionary Biology and Human Social Behavior: An Anthropological Perspective.* North Scituate, MA: Duxbury, pp. 402–435.

Alley, T. R. (1983). Growth-produced changes in body shape and size as determinants of perceived age and adult caregiving. *Child Development* **54**: 241–248.

Altmann, J. (1980). *Baboon Mothers and Infants.* Cambridge: Harvard University Press.

Amaha, E. (1998). Baby blues. *Far Eastern Economic Review*, July **16**: 13.

Anderson, G. F., and Hussey, P. S. (2000). Population aging: A comparison among industrialized countries. *Health Affairs* **19**: 191–203.

Anderson, R. N., Ventura, S. J., Peters, K. D., and Matthews, T. J. (1998). Birth and deaths: United States, July 1996–June 1997. *Monthly Vital Statistics Report* **46**(12).

Andrieu, M. (1999). Population growth: Facing the challenge. *OECD Observer* **217/218**: 29–31.

Anonymous (2000). A multifaceted discussion of aging populations. *Focus Japan* **27**: 12–13.

Armelagos, G. J., Goodman, A. H., and Jacobs, K. H. (1991). The origins of agriculture: Population growth during a period of declining health. *Population and Environment* **13**: 9–22.

Austad, S. (1997). *Why We Age: What Science Is Discovering About the Body's Journey Through Life.* New York: Wiley.

Austad, S. N. (1994). Menopause: An evolutionary perspective. *Experimental Gerontology* **29**: 255–263.

Backman, G. (1934). Das Wachstum der Korperlange des Menchen. *Kunglicke Svenska Verenskapsakademiens Handlingar* **14**: 145.

Bailey, R. C., Jenike, M. R., Ellison, P. T., Bentley, G. R., Harrigan, A. M., and Peacock, N. R. (1992). The ecology of birth seasonality among agriculturalists in Central Africa. *Journal of Biosocial Science* **24**: 393–412.

Baker, P. (1977a). Problems and strategies. In P. T. Baker (Ed.), *Human Population Problems in the Biosphere: Some Research Strategies and Designs*, MAB Technical Notes 3. Paris: UNESCO, pp. 11–32.

Baker, P. (1977b). Biological and social aspects of migration of the Andes population. *Archivos de Biologia Andina* **7**: 63–82.

Baker, P. (1984). Migration, genetics, and the degenerative diseases of South Pacific Islanders. In A. J. Boyce (Ed.), *Migration and Mobility*. London: Taylor and Francis, pp. 209–239.

Barker, D. J. P. (Ed.). (1992). *The Fetal and Infant Origins of Adult Disease*. London: British Medical Journal Books.

Barker, D. J. P. (1994). *Mothers, Babies and Disease in Later Life*. London: British Medical Journal Publications.

Barnicot, N. A. (1977). Biological variation in modern populations. In G. A. Harrison, J. S. Weiner, J. M. Tanner, and N. A. Barnicot (Eds.), *Human Biology*, 2nd ed. Oxford: Oxford University Press, pp. 181–298.

Baughan, B., Brault-Dubuc, M., Demirjian, A., and Gagnon, G. (1980). Sexual dimorphism in body composition changes during the pubertal period: As shown by French-Canadian children. *American Journal of Physical Anthropology* **52**: 85–94.

Beck, B. B. (1980). *Animal Tool Behavior*. New York: Garland.

Bekoff, M., and Byers, J. A. (1985). The development of behavior from evolutionary and ecological perspectives in mammals and birds. *Evolutionary Biology* **19**: 215–286.

Benedict, B. (1972). Social regulation of fertility. In G. A. Harrison and A. J. Boyce (Eds.), *The Structure of Human Populations*. Oxford: Clarendon, pp. 73–89.

Benfer, R. (1984). The challenges and rewards of sedentism: The preceramic village of Paloma, Peru. In M. N. Cohen and G. J. Armelagos (Eds.), *Paleopathology at the Origins of Agriculture*. New York: Academic, pp. 531–558.

Benfer, R. (1990). The preceramic period site of Paloma, Peru: Bioindications of improving adaptation to sedentism. *Latin American Antiquity* **1**: 284–318.

Bierman, J. M., Siegel, E., French, F. E., and Simonian, K. (1965). Analysis of the outcome of all pregnancies in a community. *American Journal of Obstetrics and Gynecology* **91**: 37–45.

Bindon, J. R., and Baker, P. T. (1985). Modernization, migration and obesity among Samoan adults. *Annals of Human Biology* **12**: 67–76.

Binford, L. R. (1984). *Faunal Remains from the Klasies River Mouth*. New York: Academic.

Binford, L. R. (1987). American Association of Physical Anthropologists annual luncheon address, April 1986: The hunting hypothesis, archaeological methods, and the past. *Yearbook of Physical Anthropology* **30**: 1–9.

Blumenschine, R. J., and Cavallo, J. A. (1992). Scavenging and human evolution. *Scientific American* **267**(10): 90–96.

Blurton-Jones, N. G. (1993). The lives of hunter-gather children: Effects of parental behavior and parental reproductive strategy. In M. E. Pereira and L. A. Fairbanks (Eds.), *Juvenile Primates*. Oxford: Oxford University Press, pp. 309–326.

Blurton-Jones, N. G., Smith, L. C., O'Connel, J. F., and Handler, J. S. (1992). Demography of the Hadza, an increasing and high density population of savanna foragers. *American Journal of Physical Anthropology* **89**: 159–181.

Boas, F. (1911). *Changes in the Bodily Form of Descendants of Immigrants*. 61st Congress, 2nd session. S. Doc. 208. Washington, DC: U.S. Government Printing Office.

Boas, F. (1912). Changes in the bodily form of descendents of immigrants. *American Anthropologist* **14**: 530–563.

Boas, F. (1922). Report on an anthropometric investigation of the population of the United States. *Journal of the American Statistical Association* **18**: 181–209.

Boas, F. (1930). Observations on the growth of children. *Science* **72**: 44–48.

Boas, F. (Ed.). (1940). *Race, Language and Culture*. New York: Free Press.

Boerma, J. T., Nunn, A. J., and Whitworth, J. A. (1998). Mortality impact of the AIDS epidemic: Evidence from community studies in the less developed countries. *AIDS* **12**(Suppl. 1): S3–S14.

Bogin, B. (1985). The extinction of *Homo sapiens*. *Michigan Quarterly Review* **24**: 329–343.

Bogin, B. (1988). Rural-to-urban migration. In C. G. N. Mascie-Taylor and G. W. Lasker (Eds.), *Biological Aspects of Human Migration*. Cambridge: Cambridge University Press, pp. 90–129.

Bogin, B. (1993). Biocultural studies of ethnic groups. In G. W. Lasker and C. G. N. Mascie-Taylor (Eds.), *Research Strategies in Human Biology*. Cambridge: Cambridge University Press, pp. 33–61.

Bogin, B. (1994). Adolescence in evolutionary perspective. *Acta Paediatrica* **406**(Suppl.): 29–35.

Bogin, B. (1995). Growth and development: Recent evolutionary and biocultural research. In N. Boaz and D. Wolfe (Eds.), *Biological Anthropology: The State of the Science*. Bend, OR: International Institute for Human Evolutionary Research, pp. 9–70.

Bogin, B. (1997). The evolution of human nutrition. In L. Romanucci-Ross, D. Moerman, and L. R. Tancredi (Eds.), *The Anthropology of Medicine*, 3rd ed. South Hadley, MA: Bergen & Garvey, pp. 96–142.

Bogin, B. (1998a). The tall and the short of it. *Discover* **19**(Feb.): 40–44.

Bogin, B. (1998b). Milk and human development: An essay on the "milk hypothesis." *Antropolgica Portuguesa* **15**: 22–36.

Bogin, B. (1999a). *Patterns of Human Growth*, 2nd ed. Cambridge: Cambridge University Press.

Bogin, B. (1999b). Evolutionary perspective on human growth. *Annual Review of Anthropology* **28**: 109–153.

Bogin, B., and Keep, R. (1998). Eight thousand years of human growth in Latin America: Economic and political history revealed by anthropometry. In J. Komlos and J. Baten (Eds.), *The Biological Standard of Living and Economic Development: Nutrition, Health, and Well Being in Historical Perspective*. Munich: Fritz Steiner, pp. 268–293.

Bogin, B., and Keep, R. (1999). Eight thousand years of economic and political history in Latin America revealed by anthropometry. *Annals of Human Biology* **26**: 333–351.

Bogin, B., and Loucky, J. (1997). Plasticity, political economy, and physical growth status of Guatemala Maya children living in the United States. *American Journal of Physical Anthropology* **102**: 17–32.

Bogin, B., and MacVean, R. B. (1978). Growth in height and weight of urban Guatemalan primary school children of high and low socioeconomic class. *Human Biology* **50**: 477–488.

Bogin, B., and MacVean, R. B. (1981a). Body composition and nutritional status of urban Guatemalan children of high and low socioeconomic class. *American Journal of Physical Anthropology* **55**: 543–551.

Bogin, B., and MacVean, R. B. (1981b). Nutritional and biological determinants of body fat patterning in urban Guatemalan children. *Human Biology* **53**: 259–268.

Bogin, B., and MacVean, R. B. (1981c). Bio-social effects of migration on the development of families and children in Guatemala. *American Journal of Public Health* **71**: 1373–1377.

Bogin, B., and MacVean, R. B. (1983). The relationship of socioeconomic status and sex to body size, skeletal maturation, and cognitive status of Guatemala City schoolchildren. *Child Development* **54**: 115–128.

Bogin, B., and MacVean, R. B. (1984). Growth status of non-agrarian, semi-urban living Indians in Guatemala. *Human Biology* **56**: 527–538.

Bogin, B., and Smith, B. H. (1996). Evolution of the human life cycle. *American Journal of Human Biology* **8**: 703–716.

Bogin, B., Wall, M., and MacVean, R. B. (1992). Longitudinal analysis of adolescent growth of Ladino and Mayan school children in Guatemala: Effects of environment and sex. *American Journal of Physical Anthropology* **89**: 447–457.

Bogin, B., Loucky, J., Leskie, S., MacNee, S., Kapell, M., and Smith, P. K. (2000). Body proportion changes in Maya refugees in the United States (abstract). *American Journal of Human Biology* **12**: 292.

Bolk, L. (1926). *Das Problem der Menschwerdung*. Jena: Gustav Fischer.

Bonner, J. T. (1965). *Size and Cycle*. Princeton, NJ: Princeton University Press.

Bonner, J. T. (1993). *Life Cycles: Reflections of an Evolutionary Biologist*. Princeton, NJ: Princeton University Press.

Bonturi, M. (1998). Portugal: The health system. *The OECD Observer* **210**: 43–44.

Borkan, G. A., Hults, D. E., Cardarelli, J., and Burrows, B. A. (1982). Comparison of ultrasound and skinfold measurements in assessment of subcutaneous and total fatness. *American Journal of Physical Anthropology* **58**: 307–313.

Boserup, E. (1965). The Conditions of Agricultural Growth. Chicago: Aldine.

Bowlby, R. (1969). *Attachment and Loss*. New York: Basic Books.

Boyce, A. J. (Ed.). (1984). *Migration and Mobility*. London: Taylor and Francis.

Boyd, E. (1980). *Origins of the Study of Human Growth* (B. S. Savara and J. F. Schilke, Eds.). Eugene: University of Oregon Press.

Boyden, S. V. (Ed.). (1970). *The Impact of Civilization on the Biology of Man.* Toronto: University of Toronto Press.

Boyden, S. V. (1972). Ecology in relation to urban population structure. In G. A. Harrison and A. J. Boyce (Eds.), *The Structure of Human Populations.* Oxford: Clarendon Press, pp. 411–441.

Brain, C. K. (1981). *The Hunters or the Hunted? An Introduction to African Cave Taphonomy.* Chicago: Chicago University Press.

Brettell, C. B. (1986). *Men Who Migrate, Women Who Wait.* Princeton: Princeton University Press.

Briggs, A. (1983). The environment of the city. In D. J. Ortner (Ed.), *How Humans Adapt: A Biocultural Odyssey.* Washington, DC: Smithsonian, pp. 371–387.

Brockerhoff, M. (1994). The impact of rural-urban migration on child survival. *Health Transition Review* **4**: 127–149.

Brockerhoff, M., and Yang, X. (1994). Impact of migration on fertility in sub-Saharan Africa. *Social Biology* **41**: 19–43.

Brody, H. (1974). *Inishkillane: Change and Decline in the West of Ireland.* New York: Schocken Books.

Brody, S. (1924). The kinetics of senescence. *Journal of General Physiology* **6**: 245–257.

Brody, S. (1945). *Bioenergetics and Growth.* New York: Reinhold Publishing.

Bromage, T. G., and Dean, M. C. (1985). Re-evaluation of the age at death of immature fossil hominids. *Nature* **317**: 523–527.

Brown, D. E. (1982). Physiological stress and culture change in a group of Filipino-Americans: A preliminary investigation. *Annals of Human Biology* **9**: 553–563.

Brown, F., Harris, J., Leakey, R., and Walker, A. (1985). Early *Homo erectus* skeleton from west Lake Turkana, Kenya. *Nature* **316**: 788–792.

Bryant, V. M., Jr. (1974). Prehistoric diet in southwest Texas: The coprolite evidence. *American Antiquity* **39**: 407–420.

Bryant, V. M., Jr., and Williams-Dean, G. (1975). The coprolites of man. *Scientific American* **232**: 100–109.

Buckler J. (1990). *A Longitudinal Study of Adolescent Growth.* London: Springer-Verlag.

Bunker, J. P., Houghton, J., and Baum, M. (1998). Putting the risk of breast cancer in perspective. *British Medical Journal* **317**: 1307–1309.

Burghart, R. (1990). The cultural context of diet, disease and the body. In G. A. Harrison and J. C. Waterlow (Eds.), *Diet and Disease in Traditional and Developing Societies.* Cambridge: Cambridge University Press, pp. 307–325.

Butler, G. E., McKie, M., and Ratcliffe, S. G. (1990). The cyclical nature of prepubertal growth. *Annals of Human Biology* **17**: 177–198.

Butler, S. (1998). Japan's baby bust. *U.S. News & World Report,* October **5**: 42–44.

Butterworth, D. (1977). Selectivity of out-migration from a Mixtec community. *Urban Anthropology* **6**: 129–139.

Butterworth, D., and Chance, J. K. (1981). *Latin American Urbanization.* Cambridge: Cambridge University Press.

Cabana, T., Jolicoeur, P., and Michaud, J. (1993). Prenatal and postnatal growth and allometry of stature, head circumference, and brain weight in Québec children. *American Journal of Human Biology* **5**: 93–99.

Cameron, N. (1991). Human growth, nutrition, and health status in sub-Sahara Africa. *Yearbook of Physical Anthropology* **34**: 211–250.

Cameron, N. (1997). Growth and health in a developing country: The South African Experience 1984–1994. In D. F. Roberts, P. Rudan, and T. Skaric-Juric (Eds.), *Growth and Development in a Changing World.* Zagreb: Croatian Anthropological Society, pp. 131–156.

Cameron, N., Mitchell, J., Meyer, D., Moodie, A., Bowie, M. D., Mann, M. D., and Hansen, J. D. L. (1988). Secondary sexual development of "Cape Coloured" girls following kwashiorkor. *Annals of Human Biology* **15**: 65–76.

Cameron, N., Mitchell, J., Meyer, D., Moodie, A., Bowie, M. D., Mann, M. D., and Hansen, J. D. L. (1990). Secondary sexual development of "Cape Coloured" boys following kwashiorkor. *Annals of Human Biology* **17**: 217–228.

Cameron, N., Grieve, C. A., Kruger, A., and Leschner, K. F. (1993). Secondary sexual development in rural and urban South African black children. *Annals of Human Biology* **20**: 583–593.

Caraway, C. (1981). *The Mayan Design Book*. Owing Mills, MD: Stemmer House Publishers.

Carlson, D. S., Armelagos, G. J., and Van Gerven, D. P. (1976). Patterns of age-related cortical bone loss (osteoporosis) within the femoral diaphysis. *Human Biology* **48**: 295–314.

Carlstram, G., and Levi, L. (1971). *Urban Conglomerates as Psychosocial Human Stressors*. Stockhlom: Royal Ministry for Foreign Affairs.

Carreira, A. (1982). *The people of the Cape Verde Islands: Exploitation and Emigration*. North Haven, CT: Shoe String Press.

Carreira, A. (1984). *Cabo Verde (Aspectos sociais. Secas e fomes do século XX)*. Lisboa: Edições Ulmeiro.

Cartmill, M. (1974). Rethinking primate origins. *Science* **184**: 436–443.

Case, T. J. (1978). On the evolution and adaptive significance of postnatal growth rates in terrestrial vertebrates. *Quarterly Review of Biology* **53**: 243–282.

Cavalli-Sforza, L. L., Menozzi, P., and Piazza, A. (1994). *The History and Geography of Human Genes*. Princeton: Princeton University Press.

Cavallo, J. A. (1990). Cat in the human cradle. *Natural History* **2**: 52–60.

Chagnon, N. A. (1983). *Ynomaö: The Fierce People*, 3rd ed. New York: Holt, Rinehart, Winston.

Chandra, R. K. (1990). McCollum Award Lecture: Nutrition and immunity: Lessons from the past and new insights into the future. *American Journal of Clinical Nutrition* **53**: 1087–1101.

Charlesworth, B. (1980). *Evolution in Age-Structured Populations*. Cambridge: Cambridge University Press.

Chaundhury, R. H. (1978). Female status and fertility behavior in a metropolitan urban area of Bangladesh. *Population Studies* **32**: 261–273.

Cheek, D. B. (1968). Muscle cell growth in normal children. In D. B. Cheek (Ed.), *Human Growth*. Philadelphia: Lea & Febiger, pp. 337–351.

Childe, V. G. (1942). *What Happened in History*. London: Penguin Books.

Clegg, E. J. (1979). ABO and Rh blood groups in Outer Hebrides. *Annals of Human Biology* **6**: 457–470.

Clegg, E. J., and Garlick, J. P. (Eds.). (1980). *Disease and Urbanization: Symposia of the Society for the Study of Human Biology*, Vol. 20. Atlantic Highlands, NJ: Humanities.

Cockburn, T. A. (Ed.). (1967). *Infectious Disease: Their Evolution and Eradication*. Springfield, IL: Charles C. Thomas.

Cohen, M. N., and Armelagos, G. J. (Eds.). (1984). *Paleopathology at the Origins of Agriculture*. London: Academic.

Cohen, M. N., O'Connor, K., Danforth, M., Jacobi, K., and Armstrong, C. (1994). Health and death at Tipu. In C. S. Larsen and G. R. Milner (Eds.), *In the Wake of Conquest*. New York: Wiley-Liss, pp. 121–133.

Cole, L. C. (1954). The population consequence of life history phenomena. *Quarterly Review of Biology* **19**: 103–137.

Coleman, D. (1994). Trends in fertility and intermarriage among immigrant populations in Western Europe as measures of integration. *Journal of Biosocial Science* **26**: 107–136.

Coleman, D., and Salt, J. (1992). *The British Population: Patterns, Trends, and Processes*. Oxford: Oxford University Press.

Collins, J. W., Jr., and David, R. J. (1993). Race and birthweight in biracial infants. *American Journal of Public Health* **83**: 1125–1129.

Condon, R. G. (1990). The rise of adolescence: Social change and life stage dilemmas in the Central Canadian Arctic. *Human Organization* **49**: 266–279.

Connell, K. H. (1968). *Irish Peasant Society: Four Historical Essays*. Oxford: Clarendon.

Conroy, G. C. (1990). *Primate Evolution*. New York: Norton.

Conroy, G. C., and Vannier, M. W. (1991). Dental development in South African australopithecines. Part I: Problems of pattern and chronology. *American Journal of Physical Anthropology* **86**: 121–136.

Cook, S. F., and Borah, W. W. (1979). *Essays in Population History: Mexico and California.* Berkeley: University of California Press.

Crooks, D. L. (1995). American children at risk: Poverty and its consequences for children's health, growth, and school achievement. *Yearbook of Physical Anthropology* **38**: 57–86.

Cutler, G. B., Jr., Glenn, M., Bush, M., Hodgen, G. D., Graham, C. E., and Loriaux, D. L. (1978). Adrenarche: A survey of rodents, domestic animals, and primates. *Endocrinology* **103**: 2112–2118.

Dart, R. A. (1957). The Osteodontokeratic culture of *Australopithecus prometheus.* Pretoria: Transvaal Museum Memoirs, No. 10.

Darwin, C. (1859). *The Origin of Species by Means of Natural Selection.* London: J. Murry. Reprinted by Avenel Books, New York, 1979.

Darwin, C. (1871). *The Descent of Man, and Selection in Relation to Sex.* Princeton: Princeton University Press; reprinted 1981.

Dasgupta, P. (1993). *An Inquiry into Well-Being and Destitution.* Oxford: Clarendon.

Datta, A. K. (1998). Computer-aided engineering in food process and product design. *Food Technology* **10**: 44–48.

Davies, C. T. M., Mbelwa, D., and Dore, C. (1974). Physical growth and development of urban and rural East African children, aged 7–16. *Annals of Human Biology* **1**: 257–268.

Davies, P. S. W., Jones, P. R. M., and Norgan, N. G. (1986). The distribution of subcutaneous and internal fat in man. *Annals of Human Biology* **13**: 189–192.

Davis, K. (1945). The world demographic transition. *Annals of the American Academy of Political and Social Science* **273**: 1–11.

Demirjian, A. (1986). Dentition. In F. Falkner and J. M. Tanner (Eds.), *Human Growth*, Vol. 2: *Postnatal Growth*. New York: Plenum, pp. 269–298.

Dettwyler, K. A. (1995). A time to wean: The hominid blueprint for the natural age of weaning in modern human populations. In P. Stuart-Macadam and K. A. Detwyller (Eds.), *Breastfeeding: Biocultural Perspectives.* New York: Aldine de Gruyter, pp. 39–74.

Devilliers, H. (1971). A study of morphological variables in urban and rural Venda male populations. In D. J. M. Vorster (Ed.), *Human Biology of Environmental Change.* London: International Biological Program.

Dietz, W. H., Marino, B., Peacock, N. R., and Bailey, R. C. (1989). Nutritional status of Efe pygmies and Lese horticulturalists. *American Journal of Physical Anthropology* **78**: 509–518.

Dittus, W. P. J. (1977). The social regulation of population density and age-sex distribution in the Toque Monkey. *Behaviour* **63**: 281–322.

Dobzhansky, T. (1962). *Mankind Evolving.* New Haven: Yale University Press.

Draper, P. (1976). Social and economic constraints on child life among the !Kung. In R. B. Lee and I. DeVore (Eds.), *Kalahari Hunter-Gatherers.* Cambridge: Harvard University Press, pp. 199–217.

Dubisch, J. (1977). The city as resource: Migration from a Greek island village. *Urban Anthropolgy* **6**: 65–81.

Dubos, R. (1965). *Man Adapting.* New Haven: Yale University Press.

Eagleton, T. (1995). Indigestible truths. *New Statesman & Society London* **8**: 22–23.

Eiben, O. G. (1998a). Growth and maturation problems of children and social inequality during the economic liberalization in Central and Eastern Europe. In S. S. Strickland and P. S. Shetty (Eds.), *Human Biology and Social Inequality.* Cambridge: Cambridge University Press, pp. 76–95.

Eiben, O. G. (1998b). Growth and physical fitness of children and youth at the end of the XXth century: Preliminary report. *International Journal of Anthropology* **13**: 129–136.

Ellison, P. T. (1982). Skeletal growth, fatness, and menarcheal age: A comparison of two hypotheses. *Human Biology* **54**: 269–281.

Ellison, P. T. (1990). Human ovarian function and reproductive ecology: New hypotheses. *American Anthropologist* **92**: 933–952.

Ellison, P. T., and O'Rourke, M. T. (2000). Population growth and fertility regulation. In S. Stinson, B. Bogin, R. Huss-Ashmore, and D. O'Rourke (Eds.), *Human Biology: An Evolutionary and Biocultural Perspective.* New York: Wiley, pp. 553–586.

Eltis, D. (1982). Nutritional trends in Africa and the Americas: Heights of Africans, 1819–1839. *Journal of Interdisciplinary History* **12**: 453–475.

Emanuel, I., Hale, C. B., and Berg, C. J. (1989). Poor birth outcomes of American black women: An alternative hypothesis. *Journal of Public Health Policy* **10**: 299–308.

Emanuel, I., Filakti, H., Alberman, E., and Evans, S. J. W. (1992). Intergenerational studies of human birthweight from the 1958 birth cohort. 1. Evidence for a multigenerational effect. *British Journal of Obstectrics and Gynecology* **99**: 67–74.

Enlow, D. H. (1963). *Principles of Bone Remodeling.* Springfield, IL: C. C. Thomas.

Ericksen, J. A., Ericksen, E. P., Hostetler, J. A., and Huntington, G. E. (1979). Fertility patterns and trends among the Old Order Amish. *Population Studies* **33**: 255–276.

Estatísticas Demográficas. (1998). Lisboa: Instituto Nacional de Estatística.

Etkin, N. L., and Ross, P. J. (1997). Malaria, medicine, and meals: A biobehavioral perspective. In L. Romanucci, D. Moerman, and L. R. Tancredi (Eds.), *The Anthropology of Medicine.* New York: Praeger, pp. 169–209.

Eveleth, P. B., and Tanner, J. M. (1976). *World-Wide Variation in Human Growth.* Cambridge: Cambridge University Press.

Eveleth, P. B., and Tanner. J. M. (1990). *World-Wide Variation in Human Growth,* 2nd ed. Cambridge: Cambridge University Press.

Ewer, R. F. (1973). *The Carnivores.* Ithaca, NY: Cornell University Press.

Feder, K. (1996). *Frauds, Myths and Mysteries: Science and Pseudoscience in Archaeology.* Mountain View, CA: Mayfield.

Fedigan, L. M., and Pavelka, M. S. M. (1994). The physical anthropology of menopause. In A. Herring and M. S. M. Pavelka (Eds.), *Strength in Diversity.* Toronto: Canadian Scholars Press, pp. 103–126.

Fellague-Ariouat, J., and Barker, D. J. P. (1993). The diet of girls and young women at the beginning of the century. *Nutrition and Health* **9**: 15–23.

Figueroa, R. (1986). Leyenda de la formación de los hombres de maiz (summary). In C. Figueroa (Ed.), *Cocina Guatemalteca.* Guatemala City: Editorial Piedra Santa, pp. xiii–xiv.

Filho, J. L. (1981). *Cabo-Verde. Subsídios para um levantamento cultural.* Lisboa: Plátano Editora.

Fitzpatrick, M. L. (1998). *The Long March: The Choctaw's Gift to Irish Famine Relief.* Hillsboro, OR: Beyond Words.

Floud, R., Wachter, K., and Gregory, A. A. (1990). *Height, Health and History: Nutritional Status in the United Kingdom, 1750–1980.* Cambridge: Cambridge University Press.

Fogel, R. W. (1986). Physical growth as a measure of the economic wellbeing of populations: The eighteenth and nineteenth centuries. In F. Falkner and J. M. Tanner (Eds.), *Human Growth,* 2nd ed., Vol. 3. New York: Plenum, pp. 263–281.

Fomon, S. J., Owen, G. M., Filer, L. J., and Maresh, M. (1966). Body composition of the infant, parts I and II. In F. Falkner (Ed.), *Human Development.* Philadelphia: Saunders, pp. 239–253.

Forbes, G. (1986). Body composition during adolescence. In F. Falkner and J. M. Tanner (Eds.), *Human Growth,* 2nd ed., Vol. 2. New York: Plenum, pp. 119–146.

Foster, P. (1992). *The World Food Problem.* Boulder, CO: Lynne Raienner.

Foxman, B., Frerichs, R. R., and Becht, J. N. (1984). Health status of migrants. *Human Biology* **56**: 129–141.

França, L. (1992). *A comunidade Cabo-Verdiana em Portugal.* Lisbon: Instituto de Estudos para o Desenvolvimento.

Frank, D. A., Klass, P. E., Earls, F., and Eisenberg, L. (1996). Infants and young children in orphanages: One view from pediatrics and child psychiatry. *Pediatrics* **97**(4): 569–578.

Franken, R. E. (1988). *Human Motivation,* 2nd ed. Pacific Grove, CA: Brooks/Cole.

Freedman, R., Whelpton, P. K., and Campbell, A. A. (1959). *Family Planning, Sterility and Population Growth.* New York: McGraw-Hill.

Friedlander, D., Okun, B. S., and Segal, S. (1999). The demographic transition then and now: Process, perspectives, and analyses. *Journal of Family History* **24**: 493–533.

Frisancho, A. R. (1990). *Anthropometric Standards for the Assessment of Growth and Nutritional Status.* Ann Arbor, MI: University of Michigan Press.

Frisancho, A. R., Klayman, J. E., and Matos, J. (1976). Symbiotic relationship of high fertility, high childhood mortality and socio-economic status in an urban Peruvian population. *Human Biology* **48**: 101–111.

Frisancho, A. R., Matos, J., Leonard, W. R., and Yaroch, L. A. (1985). Developmental and nutritional determinants of pregnancy outcome among teenagers. *American Journal of Physical Anthropology* **66**: 247–261.

Froggatt, P. (1999). Medicine in Ulster in relation to the great famine and "the troubles." *British Medical Journal* **319**: 1636–1639.

Fry, W. E., and Goodwin, S. B. (1997). Resurgence of the Irish potato famine fungus. *BioScience* **47**: 363–371.

Fulwood, R. (1981). Height and weight of adults, ages 18–74, by socioecomic and geographic variables, United States. *Vital and Health Statistics*, Series 11, no. 224. DHHS publication number (PHS) 81-1674. Hyattsville, MD: National Center for Health Statistics.

Gage, T. B. (1998). The comparative demography of primates: With some comments on the evolution of life histories. *Annual Review of Anthropology* **27**: 197–221.

Gage. T. B. (2000). Demography. In S. Stinson, B. Bogin, R. Huss-Ashmore, and D. O'Rourke (Eds.), *Human Biology: An Evolutionary and Biocultural Perspective.* New York: Wiley, pp. 507–551.

Galdikas, B. M., and Wood, J. W. (1990). Birth spacing patterns in humans and apes. *American Journal of Physical Anthropology* **83**: 185–191.

Garine, I. de (1987). Food, culture and society. *Courier* **40**: 4–7.

Garine, I. de (1994). The diet and nutrition of human populations. In T. Ingold (Ed.), *Companion Encyclopedia of Anthropology.* London: Routledge, pp. 226–264.

Garn, S. M. (1970). *The Earlier Gain and Later Loss of Cortical Bone in Nutritional Perspective.* Springfield, IL: Charles C. Thomas.

Garn, S. M. (1985). Smoking and human biology. *Human Biology* **57**: 505–523.

Garn, S. M., Pesick, S. D., and Pilkington, J. J. (1984). The interaction between prenatal and socioeconomic effects on growth and development on childhood. In J. Borms, R. Hauspie, A. Sand, C. Susanne, and M. Hebbelinck (Eds.), *Human Growth and Development.* New York: Plenum, pp. 59–70.

Geertz, C. (1963). *Agricultural Involution.* Berkely: University of California Press.

Gibson, C. J., and Lennon, E. (1999). *Historical Census Statistics on the Foreign-Born Population of the United States: 1850–1990.* Population Division Working Paper No. 29. Washington, DC: U.S. Bureau of the Census.

Goldscheider, C. (1971). *Population, Modernization and Social Change.* Boston: Little, Brown.

Goldstein, A., White, M., and Goldstein, S. (1997). Migration, fertility, and state policy in Hubei Province, China. *Demography* **34**: 481–491.

Goldstein, M. S. (1943). *Demographic and Bodily Changes in Descendants of Mexican Immigrants.* Austin: Institute of Latin American Studies.

Goldstein, S. (1973). Interrelations between migration and fertility in Thailand. *Demography* **10**: 225–258.

Gompertz. B. (1825). On the nature of the function expressive of the law of human mortality and on a new mode of determining life contingencies. *Philosophical Transactions of the Royal Society of London* **115**: 513–585.

Goodall, J. (1983). Population dynamics during a 15-year period in one community of free-living chimpanzees in the Gombe National Park, Tanzania. *Zietschrift fur Tierpsychologie* **61**: 1–60.

Goodman, A. H., and Leatherman, T. L., (Eds). (1998). *Building a New Biocultural Synthesis.* Ann Arbor: University of Michigan Press.

Goodman, A. H., Thomas, R. B., Swedlund, A. C., and Armelagos, G. J. (1988). Biocultural perspectives on stress in prehistoric, historical, and contemporary population research. *Yearbook of Physical Anthropology* **31**: 169–202.

Goss, R. (1964). *Adaptive Growth.* New York: Academic.

Goss, R. (1978). *The Physiology of Growth.* New York: Academic.

Goss, R. (1986). Modes of growth and regeneration. In F. Falkner and J. M. Tanner (Eds.), *Human Growth*, 2nd. ed. Vol. 1. New York: Plenum, pp. 3–26.

Gould, R. A. (1981). Comparative ecology of food-sharing in Australia and Northwest California. In R. S. O. Harding and G. Teleki (Eds.), *Omnivorous Primates.* New York: Columbia University Press, pp. 422–454.

Gould, S. J. (1977). *Ontogeny and Phylogeny.* Cambridge: Belknap.

Gould, S. J. (1979). Mickey Mouse meets Konrad Lorenz. *Natural History* **88**(4): 30–36.

Gould, S. J. (1981). *The Mismeasure of Man.* New York: Norton.

Graham, G. G., MacLean, W. C., Jr., Kallman, C. H., Rabold, J., and Mellits, E. D. (1979). Growth standards for poor urban children in nutrition studies. *American Journal of Clinical Nutrition* **32**: 703–710.

Gregson, S., Garnett, G. P., and Zaba, B. W. (1998). Trends in family structure in African populations affected by HIV. *International Conference on AIDS, 1998* **12**: 482 (abstract).

Greil, H. (1997). Sex, body type and timing in bodily development—trend statements based on a cross-sectional anthropometric study. In D. F. Roberts, P. Rudan, and T. Škaric-Juric (Eds.), *Growth and Development in a Changing World.* Zagreb: Croatian Anthropological Soiciety, pp. 59–88.

Greulich, W. W., and Pyle, S. I. (1959). *Radiographic Atlas of Skeletal Development of the Hand and Wrist*, 2nd. ed. Stanford: Stanford University Press.

Guatemala News Watch. (1995). Official census results. *Guatemala News Watch* **10**(6): 3.

Guinnane, T. W. (1994). The great Irish famine and population: The long view. *AEA Papers and Proceedings* **84**: 303–308.

Gullahorn, J. T., and Gullahorn, J. E. (1963). An extension of the U-curve hypothesis. *Journal of Social Issues* **19**: 33–47.

Gurney, J. M., and Jelliffe, D. B. (1973). Arm anthropometry in nutritional assessment: Nomogram for the rapid calculation of muscle circumference and cross-sectional muscle and fat areas. *American Journal of Clinical Nutrition* **26**: 912–915.

Gurri, F. D., and Dickinson, F. (1990). Effects of socioeconomic, ecological, and demographic conditions on the development of the extremities and the trunk: A case study with adult females from Chiapas. *Journal of Human Ecology* **1**: 125–138.

Guthrie, H., and Picciano, M. F. (1995). *Human Nutrition.* St. Louis: Mosby.

Habicht, J. P., Yarbrough, C., Martorell, R., Malina, R. M., and Klein, R. E. (1974). Height and weight standards for preschool children. *Lancet* **1**: 611–615.

Haines, M. R., and Avery, R. C. (1982). Differential infant and child mortality in Costa Rica: 1968–1973. *Population Studies* **36**: 1–13.

Hajat, A., Lucas, J. B., and Kingston, R. (2000). Health outcomes among Hispanic subgroups: Data from the National Health Interview Survey, 1992–95. *Advance Data from Vital and Health statistics*, No. 310. Hyattsville, MD: National Center for Health Statistics.

Halder, G., Callaerts, P., and Gehring, W. J. (1995). New perspectives on eye evolution. *Current Opinion in Genetics and Development* **5**: 602–609.

Halfon, N., Mendonca, A., and Berkowitz, G. (1995). Health status of children in foster care. The experience of the Center for the Vulnerable Child. *Archives of Pediatric and Adolescent Medicine* **149**(4): 386–392.

Halpern, C. T., Udry, R. J., Campbell, B., and Suchinddran, C. (1993). Testosterone and pubertal development as predictors of sexual activity: A panel analysis of adolescent males. *Psychosomatic Medicine* **55**: 436–447.

Hamill, P. V. V., Johnson, C. L., Reed, R. B., and Roche, A. F. (1977). *NCHS Growth Curves for Children Birth–18 years, United States.* DHEW Publications (PHS) 78-1650. Washington, DC: U.S. Government Printing Office.

Hamilton, E. M. N., Whitney, E. N., and Sizer, F. S. (1988). *Nutrition: Concepts and Controversies*, 4th ed. St. Paul: West.

Hamilton, W. (1966). The moulding of senescence by natural selection. *Journal of Theoretical Biology* **12**: 12–45.

Hammer, M. F., and Horai, S. (1995). Y chromosomal structure model for the population history of the peopling of Japan. *American Journal of Human Genetics* **56**: 951–962.

Hanna, J. M., and Baker, P. T. (1979). Biocultural correlates to the blood pressure of Samoan migrants to Hawaii. *Human Biology* **51**: 461–497.

Hansman, C. (1970). Anthropometry and related data: Anthropometry, skinfold thickness measurements. In R. W. McCammon (Ed.), *Human Growth and Development*. Springfied, IL: Charles C. Thomas, pp. 101–154.

Harding, R. S. O. (1981). An order of omnivores: Nonhuman primate diets in the wild. In R. S. O. Harding and G. Teleki (Eds.), *Omnivorous Primates*. New York: Columbia University Press, pp. 191–214.

Harris, M. (1993). *Culture, People, Nature*, 6th ed. New York: Addison-Wesley.

Harrison, G. A., and Gibson, J. B. (Eds.). (1976). *Man in Urban Environments*. Oxford: Oxford University Press.

Harrison, G. A., and Jeffries, D. J. (1977). Human biology in urban environments: A review of research strategies. In P. Baker (Ed.), *Problems in the Biosphere: Some Research Strategies and Designs*, MAB Technical Notes 3. Paris: UNESCO, pp. 65–82.

Harvey, P. H., Martin, R. D., and Clutton-Brock, T. H. (1986). Life histories in comparative perspective. In B. B. Smuts, D. L. Cheney, R. M. Seyfarth, R. W. Wrangham, and T. T. Struhsaker (Eds.), *Primate Societies*. Chicago: University of Chicago Press, pp. 181–196.

Haub, C. (1995). How many people have ever lived on Earth? *Population Today* **23**: 4.

Hauser, P. M., and Schnore, L. F. (1965). *The Study of Urbanization*. New York: Wiley.

Haviland, W. A., and Moholy-Nagy, H. (1992). Distinguishing the high and mighty from the hoi polloi at Tikal, Guatemala. In: A. F Chase and D. Z. Chase (Eds.), *Mesoamerican Elites: An Archaeological Assessment*, pp. 50–60. Norman, Oklahoma: University of Oklahoma Press.

Hayden, B. (1981). Subsistence and ecological adaptations of modern hunter/gatherers. In R. S. O. Harding and G. Teleki (Eds.), *Omnivorous Primates*. New York: Columbia University Press, pp. 344–421.

Hayflick, L. (1980). The cell biology of human aging. *Scientific American* **242**: 58–65.

Henneberg, M. (1988). Decrease of human skull size in the Holocene. *Human Biology* **60**: 395–405.

Henneberg, M., and Van Den Berg, E. R. (1990). Test of socioeconomic causation of secular trend: Stature changes among favored and oppressed South Africans are parallel. *American Journal of Physical Anthropology* **83**: 459–465.

Henry, L. (1961). Some data on natural fertility. *Eugenics Quarterly* **8**: 81–91.

Hermanussen, M. (1998). Patagonian giants: Myths and possibilities. In S. J. Ulijaszek, F. E. Johnston, and M. A. Preece (Eds.), *The Cambridge Encyclopedia of Human Growth and Development*. Cambridge: Cambridge University Press, p. 390.

Hern, W. M. (1993). Is human culture carcinogenic for uncontrolled population growth and ecological destruction? *BioScience* **43**: 768–773.

Higham, E. (1980). Variations in adolescent psychohormonal development. In J. Adelson (Ed.), *Handbook of Adolescent Psychology*. New York: Wiley, pp. 472–494.

Hill, J. P., and Lynch, M. E. (1983). The intensification of gender-related role expectations during early adolescence. In J. Brooks-Gunn and A. C. Petersen (Eds.), *Girls at Puberty*. New York: Plenum, pp. 201–228.

Hill, K., and Hurtado, A. M. (1989). Hunter-gatherers of the New World. *American Scientist* **77**: 436–443.

Hill, K., and Hurtado, A. M. (1991). The evolution of premature reproductive senescence and menopause in human females: An evaluation of the "Grandmother Hypothesis." *Human Nature* **2**: 313–350.

Hill, K., and Kaplan, H. (1988). Trade offs in male and female reproductive startegies among the Ache. Parts 1 and 2. In: L. Betzig, M. Borgerhoff-Mulder, and P. Turke (Eds.), *Human Reproductive*

Behavior: A Darwininian Perspective, pp. 277–89, 291–305. Cambridge: Cambridge University Press.

Hill, K., and Kaplan, H. (1999). Life history traits in humans: Theory and empirical studies. *Annual Review of Anthropology* **28**: 397–430.

Hinday, V. A. (1978). Migration, urbanization and fertility in the Philippines. *International Migration Review* **12**: 370–385.

Hoey, H. M., Tanner, J. M., and Cox, L. A. (1987). Clinical growth standards for Irish children. *Acta Paediatrica Scandinavia* **338**(Suppl.): 1–31.

Hoff, C. J., and Abelson, A. E. (1976). Fertility. In P. T. Baker and M. A. Little (Eds.), *Man in the Andes: A Multidisciplinary Study of High Altitude Quechua*. Stroudsberg, PA: Dowden, Hutchinson and Ross, pp. 128–146.

Hollingsworth, P. (1998). Silicon chips: Food trend for the new millennium. *Food Technology* **52**: 54.

Hollnsteiner, M. R., and Tacon, P. (1982). Urban migration in developing countries: Consequences for families and children. Paper presented at the annual meeting of the American Association for the Advancement of Science, January 4, Washington, DC.

Holmes, D. N. (1976). Migration and fertiliy: Introduction. In *The Dynamics of Migration: Internal Migration and Fertility*. Occasional monograph series, No. 5, Vol. 1. Washington, DC: Interdisciplinary Communications Program, Smithsonian.

Howell, N. (1979). *Demography of the Dobe !Kung*. New York: Academic.

Hulanicka, B., and Kotlarz, K. (1983). The final phase of growth in height. *Annals of Human Biology* **10**: 429–434.

Hulse, F. (1969). Migration and cultural selection in human genetics. In P. C. Biswas (Ed.), *The Anthroplogist*. Delhi, India: University of Delhi, pp. 1–21.

Hutchinson, B. (1961). Fertility, social mobility and urban migration in Brazil. *Population Studies* **14**: 182–189.

Huttley, S. R., Victoria, C. G., Barros, F. C., and Vaughn, J. P. (1992). Birth spacing and child health in urban Brazilian children. *Pediatrics* **89**: 1049–1054.

IBNMRR. (1995). *Third Report on Nutrition Monitoring in the United States: Executive Summary*. Washington, DC: U.S. Government Printing Office (report of the Interagency Board for Nutrition Monitoring and Related Research).

Illsley, R., Finlayson, A., and Thompson, B. (1963). The motivation and characteristics of internal migrants: A socio-medical study of young migrants in Scotland. *Milbank Memorial Fund Quarterly* **41**: 115–144, 217–248.

Imbelloni, J. (1949). Los Patagones. *Runa* **7**: 5–58.

Inoue, K., Asao, T., and Shimada, T. (2000). Ethnic-related differences in the frequency distribution of genetic polymorphisms in the CYP1A1 and CYP1B1 genes in Japanese and Caucasian populations. *Xenobiotica* **30**: 285–295.

Instituto Nacional de Estatística. (1999). *Gerações mais idosas*. Lisbon: Instituto Nacional de Estatística.

Issac, G. L. (1978). The food sharing behavior of proto-human hominids. *Scientific American* **238**(4): 90–108.

Jackson, F. L. (1990). Two evolutionary models for the interactions of dietary organic cyanogens, hemoglobins, and falciparum malaria. *American Journal of Human Biology* **2**: 521–532.

Jaswal, S. (1983). Age and sequence of permanent tooth emergence among Khasis. *American Journal of Physical Anthropology* **62**: 177–186.

Jenkins, J. C. (1977). Push/pull in recent Mexican to the U.S. migration. *International Migration Review* **11**: 178–189.

Johnson, C. L., Fulwood, R., Abraham, S., and Bryner, J. D. (1981). *Basic Data on Anthropometric Measurements and Angular Measurements of the Hip and Knee Joints for Selected Age Groups 1–74 Years of Age*. DHHS Publication, no. (PHS) 81-1669. Washington DC: U.S. Government Printing Office.

Johnson, T. O. (1970). Height and weight patterns of an urban African population sample in Nigeria. *Tropical Geography and Medicine* **22**: 65–76.

Johnston, F. E., and Beller, A. (1976). Anthropometric evaluation of the body composition of black, white, and Puerto Rican newborns. *American Journal of Clinical Nutrition* **29**: 61.

Johnston, F. E., Borden, M., and MacVean, R. B. (1973). Height, weight and their growth velocities in Guatemalan private schoolchildren of high socio-economic class. *Human Biology* **45**: 627–641.

Johnston, F. E., Bogin, B., MacVean, R. B., and Newman, B. C. (1984). A comparison of international standards versus local reference data for the triceps and subscapular skinfolds of Guatemalan children and youth. *Human Biology* **56**: 157–171.

Jolly, A. (1985). *The Evolution of Primate Behavior*, 2nd ed. New York: Macmillan.

Jorde, L. B., and Durbize, P. (1986). Opportunity for natural selection in Utah Mormons. *Human Biology* **58**: 97–114.

Käferstein, F. K., Motarjrmi, Y., and Bettcher, D. W. (1997). Foodborne disease control: A transnational challenge. *Emerging and Infectious Diseases* **3**: 503–510.

Kaplan, B. (1954). Environment and human plasticity. *American Anthropologist* **56**: 780–799.

Katz, S. H., Heideger, M. L., and Valleroy, L. A. (1974). Traditional maize processing techniques in the New World. *Science* **184**: 765–773.

Katz, S. H., Hediger, M. L., Zemel, B. S., and Parks, J. S. (1985). Adrenal androgens, body fat and advanced skeletal age in puberty: New evidence for the relations of adrenarche and gonadarche in males. *Human Biology* **57**: 401–413.

Katzenberg, M. A. (1992). Advances in stable isotope analysis of prehistoric bone. In S. R. Saunders and M. A. Katzenberg (Eds.), *Skeletal Biology of Past Peoples: Research Methods*. New York: Wiley-Liss, pp. 135–147.

Kay, R. F. (1985). Dental evidence for the diet of *Australopithecus*. *Annual Review of Anthropology* **14**: 315–341.

Kennedy, R. E. (1973). *The Irish: Emigration, Marriage, and Fertility*. Berkeley: University of California Press.

Ketkar, S. L. (1979). Determinants of fertility in a developing society: The case of Sierra Leone. *Population Studies* **23**: 479–488.

Keyfitz, N. (1982). Development and the elimination of poverty. *Economic Development and Culture Change* **30**: 649–670.

Kirkwood, T. B. L. (1977). Evolution of aging. *Nature* **270**: 301–304.

Kirkwood, T. B. L., and Holliday, R. (1986). Selection for optimal accuracy and the evolution of aging. In T. B. L. Kirkwood, R. F. Rosenberger, and D. J. Galas (Eds.), *Accuracy in Molecular Processes*. New York: Chapman and Hall, pp. 363–379.

Klein, R. G. (1989). *The Human Career: Human Biological and Cultural Origins*. Chicago: University of Chicago Press.

Kliegman, R. M. (1995). Neonatal technology, perinatal survival, social consequences, and the perinatal paradox. *American Journal of Public Health* **85**: 909–913.

Kobyliansky, E., and Arensburg, B. (1977). Changes in morphology of human populations due to migrations and selection. *Annals of Human Biology* **4**: 57–71.

Komlos, J. (1991). Anthropometric history: What is it? *Journal of Social and Biological Structures* **14**: 353–356.

Komlos, J. (1993). The secular trend in the biological standard of living in the United Kingdom, 1730–1860. *Economic History Review* **46**: 115–144.

Komlos, J. (Ed.). (1994). *Stature, Living Standards, and Economic Development: Essays in Anthropometric History*. Chicago: Chicago University Press.

Komlos, J. (1998). Shrinking in a growing economy? The mystery of physical stature during the industrial revolution. *Journal of Economic History* **58**: 779–802.

Koningsberg, L., and Frankenberg, S. R. (1994). Paleodemography: Not quite dead. *Evolutionary Anthropology* **3**: 92–105.

Konner, M. (1976). Maternal care, infant behavior and development among the !Kung. In R. B. Lee and I. DeVore (Eds.), *Kalahari Hunter-Gatherers*. Cambridge: Harvard University Press, pp. 218–245.

Kramer, P. (1998). The costs of human locomotion: Maternal investment in infant transport. *American Journal of Physical Anthropology* **107**: 71–85.

Kristof, N. D. (1999). Empty isles are signs Japan's sun might dim. *New York Times on the Web*, August 1: www.nytimes.com/library/world/asia/080199japan-decline.html

Kumudini, D. (1965). The effect of education on fertility. *Proceedings of the World Population Conference, Belgrade* **4**: 146–149.

Lai, D., Tsai, S. P., and Hardy, R. J. (1997). Impact of HIV/AIDS of life expectancy in the United States. *AIDS* **11**(2): 203–207.

Lamar, J. (2000). Japan to allow in foreign nurses to care for old people. *British Medical Journal* **320**: 825.

Lancaster, J. B., and Lancaster, C. S. (1983). Parental investment: The hominid adaptation. In D. J. Ortner (Ed.), *How Humans Adapt*. Washington, DC: Smithsonian Institution Press, pp. 33–65.

Largo, R. H., Gasser, T. H., Prader, A., Stutzle, W., and Huber, P. J. (1978). Analysis of the adolescent growth spurt using smoothing spline functions. *Annals of Human Biology* **5**: 421–434.

Laron, Z., Arad, J., Gurewitz, R., Grunebaum, M., and Dickerman, Z. (1980). Age at first conscious ejaculation—a milestone in male puberty. *Helvatica Paediatrica Acta* **35**: 13–20.

Larsen, C. S., and Milner, G. R. (Eds.). (1994). *In the Wake of Contact: Biological Responses to Conquest*. New York: Wiley-Liss.

Lasker, G. W. (1946). Migration and physical differentiation. *American Journal of Physical Anthropology* **4**: 273–300.

Lasker, G. W. (1952). Environmental growth factors and selective migration. *Human Biology* **24**: 262–289.

Lasker, G. W. (1969). Human biological adaptability. *Science* **166**: 1480–1486.

Lasker, G. W., and Evans, F. G. (1961). Age, environment and migration: Further anthropometric findings on migrant and non-migrant Mexicans. *American Journal of Physical Anthropology* **19**: 203–211.

Laughlin, W. S. (1972). Ecology and population structure in the Arctic. In G. A. Harrison and A. J. Boyce (Eds.), *The Structure of Human Populations*. Oxford: Clarendon, pp. 379–392.

Lee, B. S., and Farber, S. C. (1984). Fertility adaptation by rural-urban migrants in developing countries: The case of Korea. *Population Studies* **38**: 141–155.

Lee, P. C., Majluf, P., and Gordon, I. J. (1991). Growth, weaning, and maternal investment from a comparative perspective. *Journal of the Zoological Society of London* **225**: 99–114.

Lee, R. B. (1968). What hunters do for a living, or, how to make out on scarce resources. In R. B. Lee and I. DeVore (Eds.), *Man the Hunter*. Cambridge, MA: Harvard University Press.

Lee, R. B. (1984). *The Dobe !Kung*. New York: Holt, Rinehart & Winston.

Lee, R. B., and DeVore, I. (1968). *Man the Hunter*. Cambridge MA: Harvard University Press.

Leonard, W. R., and Robertson, M. L. (1992). Nutritional requirements and human evolution: A bioenergetics model. *American Journal of Human Biology* **4**: 179–195.

Leonard, W. R., and Robertson, M. L. (1994). Evolutionary perspectives on human nutrition: The influence of brain and body size on diet and metabolism. *American Journal of Human Biology* **6**: 77–88.

Leslie, P. W., Campbell, K. L., Campbell, B. C., Kigondu, C. S., and Kirumbi, L. W. (1999). Fecundity and fertility. In M. A. Little and P. W. Leslie (Eds.), *Turkana Herders of the Dry Savanna: Ecology and Biobehavioral Response of Nomads to an Uncertain Environment*. Oxford: Oxford University Press, pp. 249–280.

LeVine, R. (1977). Child rearing as a cultural adaptation. In P. H. Leiderman, S. Tulkin, and A. Rosenfeld (Eds.), *Culture and Infancy: Variations in the Human Experience*. New York: Academic, pp. 15–27.

Liberty, M., Hughey, D., and Scaglion, R. (1976a). Rural and urban Omaha fertility. *Human Biology* **48**: 59–71.

Liberty, M., Scaglion, R., and Hughey, D. (1976b). Rural and urban Seminole fertility. *Human Biology* **48**: 741–755.

Lieberman, L. S. (1991). The biocultural consequences of contemporary and future diets in developed countries. *Collegium Antropologicum* **15**: 73–85.

Lipton, M. (1977). *Why Poor People Stay Poor: Urban Bias in World Development*. Cambridge, MA: Harvard University Press.

Little, M. A., and Leslie, P. W. (Eds.). (1999). *Turkana Herders of the Dry Savanna: Ecology and Biobehavioral Response of Nomads to an Uncertain Environment*. Oxford: Oxford University Press.

Little, M. A., Galvin, K., and Mugambi, M. (1983). Cross-sectional growth of nomadic Turkana pastoralists. *Human Biology* **55**: 811–830.

Livi-Bacci, M. (1997). *A Concise History of World Population*, 2nd ed. Oxford: Blackwell.

Livingstone, F. B. (1958). Anthropological implications of sickle cell gene distribution in West Africa. *American Anthropologist* **60**: 533–562.

Lorenz, K. (1971). Part and parcel in animal and human societies: A methodological discussion. In *Studies in Animal and Human Behavior*, Vol. II (Trans. R. Martin). Cambridge: Harvard University Press, pp. 115–195.

Loue, S., and Bunce, A. (1999). *The Measurement of Immigration Status in Health Research*. Vital Health Stat 2 (127). Hyattsville, MD: National Center for Health Statistics.

Lovejoy, O. (1981). The origin of man. *Science* **211**: 341–350.

Lovell, W. G., and Lutz, C. H. (1994). Conquest and population: Maya demography in historical perspective. *Latin American Research Review* **29**: 133–140.

Lovell, W. G., and Lutz, C. H. (1996). "A dark obverse": Maya survival in Guatemala, 1520–1994. *The Geographical Review* **86**: 398–407.

Low-Beer, D., Stoneburner, R., and Mukulu, A. (1996). The demographic impact of HIV mortality on population structure: Empirical evidence from the 1991 Ugandan census. *International Conference on AIDS, 1996* **11**(1): 39 (abstract).

Lowery, G. H. (1986). *Growth and Development of Children*, 8th ed. Chicago, IL: Yearbook Medical Publishers.

Lutz, W., Sanderson, W., and Scherbow, S. (1997). Doubling of world population unlikely. *Nature* **387**: 803–804.

MacBeth, H. M. (1984). The study of biological selectivity in migrants. In A. J. Boyce (Ed.), *Migration and Mobility*. London: Taylor and Francis, pp. 195–207.

Macisco, J. J., Bouvier, L. F., and Renzi, M. J. (1969). Migration status, education and fertility in Puerto Rico, 1960. *Milbank Memorial Fund Quarterly* **47**: 167–187.

Macisco, J. J., Bouvier, L. F., and Weller, R. H. (1970). The effect of labor force participation on the relation between migration status and fertility in San Juan, Puerto Rico. *Milbank Memorial Fund Quarterly* **48**: 51–70.

Maki, K., Morimoto, A., Nishioka, T., Kimura, M., and Braham, R. L. (1999). The impact of race on tooth formation. *ASDC Journal of Dentistry in Childhood* **66**: 353–356, 294–295.

Malina, R. M. (1986). Growth of muscle tissue and muscle mass. In F. Falkner and J. M. Tanner (Eds.), *Human Growth*, Vol. 2: *Postnatal Growth*. New York: Plenum, pp. 77–99.

Malina, R. M., Himes, J. H., Stepick, C. D., Lopez, F. G., and Buschang, P. H. (1981). Growth of rural and urban children in the Valley of Oaxaca, Mexico. *American Journal of Physical Anthropology* **55**: 269–280.

Malina, R. M., Bushang, P. H., Aronson, W. L., and Selby, H. (1982). Childhood growth status of eventual migrants and sedentes in a rural Zaputec community in the valley of Oaxaca, Mexico. *Human Biology* **54**: 709–716.

Malinowski, A., and Wolanski, N. (1985). Anthropology in Poland. *Teoria I Emperia W Polskiej Szkole Antropologicznej* **11**: 35–69.

Malthus, T. R. (1798). *An Essay of the Principle of Population, as it Affects the future Improvement of Society with Remarks on the Speculations of Mr. Godwin, M. Condorcet, and Other Writers*. St. Paul's Church-Yard, London: J. Johnson.

Mann, A. E., Lampl, M., and Monge, J. (1990). Patterns of ontogeny in human evolution: Evidence from dental development. *Yearbook of Physical Anthropology* **33**: 111–150.

Marshall, W. A., and Tanner, J. M. (1970). Variation in the pattern of pubertal changes in boys. *Archives of the Diseases of Childhood* **45**: 13–23.

Marsiglio, W. (1987). Adolescent fathers in the United States: Their initial living arrangements, marital experience and educational outcomes. *Family Planning Perspectives* **19**: 240–251.

Martin, R. D. (1983). Human brain evolution in an ecological context. *Fifty-second James Arthur Lecture.* New York: American Museum of Natural History.

Martin, R. D. (1990). *Primate Origins and Evolution: A Phylogenetic Reconstruction.* Princeton: Princeton University Press.

Martin, W. J. (1949). *The Physique of Young Adult Males.* Medical Research Council Memorandum, No. 20. London: HMSO.

Mascie-Taylor, C. G. N. (1984). The interaction between geographical and social mobility. In A. J. Boyce (Ed.), *Migration and Mobility.* London: Taylor and Francis, pp. 161–178.

Mascie-Taylor, C. G. N., and Bogin, B. (Eds.). (1995). *Human Variability and Plasticity. Cambridge Studies in Biological Anthropology.* Cambridge: Cambridge University Press.

Mathers, K., and Henneberg, M. (1995). Were we ever that big? Gradual increase in hominid body size over time. *Homo* **46**: 141–173.

Mattos, A. M. (1994). Reconstrução das identidades no processo de emigração. A população Cabo-Verdiana residente em Portugal. Ph.D. dissertation, Instituto Superior de Ciências do Trabalho eda Empresa, Lisbon.

McCabe, V. (1988). Facial proportions, perceived age, and caregiving. In T. R. Alley (Ed.), *Social and Applied Aspects of Perceiving Faces.* Hillsdale, NJ: Lawerence Earlbaum Associates, pp. 89–95.

McGarvey, S. T., and Baker, P. T. (1979). The effects of modernization and migration on Samoan blood pressures. *Human Biology* **51**: 461–479.

McNeill, W. H. (1976). *Plagues and Peoples.* New York: Doubleday.

McNeill, W. H. (1979). Historical patterns of migration. *Current Anthropology* **20**: 95–102.

Meadows, D. H., Medows, D. L., Randers, J., and Behrens, W. W., III. (1972). *The Limits to Growth.* New York: Universe Books.

Medwar, P. B. (1952). *An Unsolved Problem in Biology.* London: HK Lewis.

Meindl, R. S., and Swedlund, A. C. (1977). Secular trends in mortality in the Connecticut Valley, 1700–1850. *Human Biology* **49**: 389–414.

Meredith, H. V. (1979). Comparative findings on body size of children and youths living at urban centers and in rural areas. *Growth* **43**: 95–104.

Meyers, G. C., and Morris, E. W. (1966). Migration and fertility in Puerto Rico. *Population Studies* **20**: 85–96.

Michelson, W. H. (1970). *Man and His Urban Environment: A Sociological Approach.* Reading, MA: Addison-Wesley.

Migone, A., Emanuel, I., Mueller, B., Daling, J., and Little, R. E. (1991). Gestational duration and birthweight in White, Black, and mixed-race babies. *Pediatric and Perinatal Epidemiology* **5**: 378–391.

Mills, M. G. L. (1990). *Kalahari Hyenas.* London: Unwin Hyman.

Ministerio de Salud Publica. (1989). *Encuesta Nacional de Salud Materno Infantil 1987.* Guatemala City: Minesterio de Salud Publica.

Moerman, D. E. (1986). *Medicinal Plants of Native America.* Ann Arbor, MI: Museum of Anthropology, University of Michigan.

Moerman, M. L. (1982). Growth of the birth canal in adolescent girls. *American Journal of Obstetrics and Gynecology* **143**: 528–532.

Mokyr, J. (1983). *Why Ireland Starved: A Quantitative and Analytical History of the Irish Economy, 1800–1850.* London: George Allen & Unwin.

Moore, L. G., Niermeyer, S., and Zamudio, S. (1998). Human adaptation to high altitude: Regional and life-cycle perspectives. *Yearbook of Physical Anthropology* **41**: 25–64.

Morales, A., Heaton, J. P., and Carson, C. C., III. (2000). Andropause: A misnomer for a true clinical condition. *Journal of Urology* **163**: 705–712.

Morley, D. C., Woodland, M., Martin, W. J., and Allen, I. (1968). Heights and weights of west African children from birth to age of five. *West African Medical Journal* **17**: 8–13.

Morris, M. D. (1979). *Measuring the Condition of the World's Poor: The Physical Quality of Life Index.* New York: Pergamon.

Morrison, T. (1970). *The Bluest Eye*. Plume Edition with new afterword, 1994. New York: Plume/ Penguin.

Mueller, W. H., Murillo, F., Palamino, H., Badzioch, M., Chakraborty, R., Fuerst, P., and Schull, W. J. (1980). The Aymara of Western Bolivia: V. Growth and development in an hypoxic environment. *Human Biology* **52**: 529–546.

Muller, J., Nielsen, C. T., and Skakkebaek, N. E. (1989). Testicular maturation and pubertal growth and development in normal boys. In J. M. Tanner and M. A. Preece (Eds.), *The Physiology of Human Growth*. Cambridge: Cambridge University Press, pp. 201–207.

Mumford, L. (1956). The natural history of urbanization. In W. E. Thomas (Ed.), *Man's Role in Changing the Face of the Earth*. Chicago: University of Chicago Press.

Nag, M. (1980). How modernization can also increase fertility. *Current Anthropology* **21**: 571–587.

Nakano, Y., and Kimura, T. (1992). Development of bipedal walking in *Macaca fuscata* and *Pan troglodytes*. In S. Matano, R. H. Tuttle, H. Ishida, and M. Goodman (Eds.), *Topics in Primatology*, Vol. 3. Tokyo: University of Tokyo, pp. 177–190.

National Academy of Sciences. (1989). *Recommended Dietary Allowances*, 10th ed. Washington, DC: National Academy Press.

National Center for Health Statistics. (1994). *Vital Statistics of the United States*, Vol. 1: *Natality*. Washington, DC: Public Health Service.

National Center for Health Statistics. (1999). Vital Statistics of the United States, 1993, Volume 1, natality. Hyattsville: Maryland.

Neel, J. V., and Weiss, K. (1975). The genetic structure of a tribal population, the Yanomamo Indians. Biodemographic studies XII. *American Journal of Physical Anthropology* **42**: 25–52.

Nellhaus, G. (1968). Head circumference from birth to eighteen years. *Pediatrics* **41**: 106.

Newsinger, J. (1996). The Great Irish Famine: A crime of free market economics. *Monthly Review* **47**: 11–19.

Nichols, S., and Steckel, R. H. (1997). Tall but poor: Living standards of men and women in pre-famine Ireland. *Journal of European Economic History* **26**: 105–134.

Nishida, T., Takasaki, H., and Takahata, Y. (1990). Demography and reproductive profiles. In T. Nishida (Ed.), *The Chimpanzees of the Mahale Mountains: Sexual and Life History Strategies*. Tokyo: University of Tokyo Press, pp. 63–97.

Noboru, M. (1999). Four crises confronting Japan. *Japan Echo*, February: 13–14.

Norton, N. (1997). *Guatemala*. Cadogan: London.

Oates, J. F. (1987). Food distribution and foraging behavior. In B. B. Smuts, D. L. Cheney, R. M. Seyfarth, R. W. Wrangham, and T. T. Struhsaker (Eds.), *Primate Societies*. Chicago: University of Chicago Press, pp. 197–209.

O'Dell, M. E. (1984). The children of conquest in the new age: Ethnicity and change among the highland Maya. *Central Issues in Anthropology* **5**: 1–15.

OECD. (1999). The city in the global village. *The OECD (Organization for Economic Cooperation and Development) Observer* **217/218**: 33–35.

O'Grada, C. (1989). Poverty, population and agriculture, 1800–1845. In W. E. Vaughan (Ed.), *A New History of Ireland*. Vol. V: *Ireland under the Union I. 1801–1870*. Oxford: Clarendon.

O'Grada, C. (1999). *Black '47 and Beyond: The Great Irish Famine in History, Economy, and Memory*. Princeton, NJ: Princeton University Press.

Olshansky, S. J., and Carnes, B. A. (1997). Ever since Gompertz. *Demography* **34**: 1–15.

Olshansky, S. J., Carnes, B. A., and Grahn, D. (1998). Confronting the boundaries of human longevity. *American Scientist* **86**: 52–61.

Oppenheim, A. L. (1974). *Ancient Mesopotamia*. Chicago: University of Chicago Press.

Orlansky, D., and Dubrovsky, S. (1978). *The Effects of Rural-Urban Migration on Women's Role and Status in Latin America*. Reports and Papers in the Social Sciences, No. 41. Paris: UNESCO.

Oyhenart, E. E., Torres, M. F., Pucciarelli, H. M., Dahinten, S. L., and Carnese, F. R. (in press). Growth and sexual dimorphism in aborigines from Chubut (Argentina) I: Body Analysis. *Acta Medica Auxologica* **32**.

Padez, C. (2000). What can your height tell about you: Educational level and body height in Portuguese young males (abstract). *American Journal of Physical Anthropology* **30**(Suppl.): 244.

Padez, C., and Johnston, F. E. (1999). Secular trends in male adult height 1904–1996 in relation to place of residence and parent's educational level in Portugal. *Annals of Human Biology* **26**: 287–298.

Paigen, B., Goldman, L. R., Magnant, M. M., Highland, J. H., and Steegmann, A. T., Jr. (1987). Growth of children living near the hazardous waste site, Love Canal. *Human Biology* **59**: 489–508.

Panek, S., and Piasecki, M. (1971). Nowa Huta: Integration of the population in the light of anthropometric data. *Materialyi i Prace Anthropologiczne* **80**: 1–249 (in Polish with English summary).

Panter-Brick, C., Todd, A., and Baker, R. (1996). Growth status of homeless Nepali boys: Do they differ from rural and urban controls? *Social Science and Medicine* **43**: 441–451.

Parker, L. N. (1991). Adrenarche. *Endocrinology and Metabolism Clinics of North America* **20**: 71–83.

Parker, S. T. (1996). Using cladistic analysis of comparative data to reconstruct the evolution of cognitive development in hominids. In E. Martins (Ed.), *Phylogenies and the Comparative Method in Animal Behavior*. Oxford: Oxford University Press, pp. 433–448.

Pavelka, M. S., and Fedigan, L. M. (1991). Menopause: A comparative life history perspective. *Yearbook of Physical Anthropology* **34**: 13–38.

Pearl, R. (1925). *The Biology of Population Growth*. New York: Knopf.

Pearl, R., and Miner, J. R. (1935). Experimental studies on the duration of life. XIV. The comparative mortality of certain lower organisms. *Quarterly Review of Biology* **10**: 60–79.

Pelletier, D. L., Frongillo, E. A., Schroeder, D. G., and Habicht, J. P. (1995). The effects of malnutrition on child mortality in developing countries. *Bulletin of the World Health Organization* **73**: 443–448.

Pelto, G. H., and Pelto, P. J. (1989). Small but healthy? An anthropological perspective. *Human Organization* **48**: 11–15.

Pelto, J. P., and Pelto, G. H. (1983). Culture, nutrition, and health. In L. Romanucci, D. Moerman, and L. R. Tancredi (Eds.), *The Anthropology of Medicine*. New York: Praeger, pp. 173–200.

Pereira, M. E., and Altman, J. (1985). Development of social behavior in free-living nonhuman primates. In E. S. Watts (Ed.), *Nonhuman Primate Models for Human Growth and Development*. New York: Alan R. Liss, pp. 217–309.

Pereira, M. E., and Fairbanks, L. A. (Eds.). (1993). *Juvenile Primates: Life History, Development, and Behavior*. New York: Oxford University Press.

Peschel, R. E., and Peschel, E. R. (1987). Medical insights into the castrati of opera. *American Scientist* **75**: 578–583.

Petersen, A. C., and Taylor, B. (1980). The biological approach to adolescence: Biological change and psychological adaptation. In J. Adelson (Ed.), *Handbook of Adolescent Psychology*. New York: Wiley, pp. 117–155.

Plant, T. M. (1994). Puberty in primates. In E. Knobil and J. D. Neill (Eds.), *The Physiology of Reproduction*, 2nd ed. New York: Raven, pp. 453–485.

Potts, R. (1988). *Early Hominid Activities at Olduvai*. New York: Aldine de Gruyter.

Potts, R. B., and Shipman, P. (1981). Cutmarks made by stone tools on bones from Olduvai gorge, Tanzania. *Nature* **291**: 577–580.

Prader, A. (1984). Biomedical and endocrinological aspects of normal growth and development. In J. Borms, R. Hauspie, A. Sand, C. Susanne, and M. Hebbelinck (Eds.), *Human Growth and Development*. New York: Plenum, pp. 1–22.

Prader, A., Tanner, J. M., and Von Harnack, G. A. (1963). Catch-up growth following illness or starvation. *Journal of Paediatrics* **62**: 646–659.

Preston, S. H. (1975). The changing relation between mortality and level of economic development. *Population Studies*, **29**: 231–248.

Preston, S. H., Haines, M. R., and Panuk, E. (1981). Effect of industrialization and urbanization on mortality in developed countries. In *International Population Conference, Manila, 1981, Proceedings*, Vol. 2. Liege: International Union for the Scientific Study of Population, pp. 233–253.

Prince, J. M., and Steckel, R. H. (1998). Tallest in the world: Native Americans of the Great Plains in the nineteenth century. *National Bureau of Economic Research Working Paper Series, Historical Paper* **112**: 1–35.

Puga, D. (1998). Urbanization patterns: European versus less developed countries. *Journal of Regional Science* **38**: 231–252.

Ravenstein, E. G. (1885). The laws of migration. *Royal Statistical Society* **48**(Pt. 2): 167–277.

Relethford, J. H. (1995). Re-examination of secular change in adult Irish stature. *American Journal of Human Biology* **7**: 249–253.

Relethford, J. H., Lees, F. C., and Crawford, M. H. (1980). Population structure and anthropometric variation in rural western Ireland: Migration and biological differentiation. *Annals of Human Biology* **7**: 411–428.

Rindfuss, R. R. (1976). Fertility and migration: The case of Puerto Rico. *International Migration Review* **10**: 191–203.

Robinson, W. C. (1963). Urbanization and fertility: The non-western experiences. *Milbank Memorial Fund Quarterly* **4**: 291–308.

Robson, E. B. (1978). The genetics of birth weight. In F. Falkner and J. M. Tanner (Eds.), *Human Growth*, Vol. 1. New York: Plenum, pp. 285–297.

Roche, A. F., and Davila, G. H. (1972). Late adolescent growth in stature. *Pediatrics* **50**: 874–880.

Roche, A. F., Wainer, H., and Thissen, D. (1975). *Skeletal Maturity. The Knee Joint as a Biological Indicator.* New York: Plenum.

Rodriguez, P. M., Waller, J. M., and Edwards, C. (2000). U.N. now fears underpopulation. *Insight*, May 15: 6.

Roede, M. J., and van Wieringen, J. C. (1985). Growth diagrams 1980. *Tijdschrift voor Sociale Gezondheidszorg*, Supplement 1985: 1–34.

Rogers, A. (1982). Sources of urban population growth and urbanization, 1950–2000: A demographic accounting. *Economic Development and Culture Change* **30**: 483–506.

Rogers, A., and Williamson, J. C. (1982). Migration, urbanization, and third world development: An overview. *Economic Development and Cultural Change* **30**: 463–482.

Rogoff, B., Seller, M. J., Pirrotta, S., Fox, N., and White, S. H. (1975). Age assignment of roles and responsibilities of children: A cross cultural survey. *Human Development* **18**: 353–369.

Rousham, E. K., and Gracey, M. (1998). Differences in growth among remote and town-dwelling aboriginal children in the Kimberly region of Western Australia. *Australia and New Zealand Journal of Public Health* **22**: 690–694.

Ruff, C. B. (1991). *Aging and Osteoporosis in Native Americans from Pecos Pueblo, New Mexico: Behavioral and Biomechanical Effects.* New York: Garland.

Ruff, C. B., and Walker, A. (1993). Body size and body shape. In A. C. Walker and R. F. Leakey (Eds.), *The Nariokotome Homo erectus Skeleton.* Cambridge, MA: Belknap, pp. 234–265.

Ruff, C. B., Trinkhaus, E., Walker, A., and Larsen, C. S. (1993). Postcranial robusticity in Homo. I: Temporal trends and mechanical interpretation. *American Journal of Physical Anthropolology* **91**: 21–53.

Saba, J. (1999). O Brazil! *MC Technology Marketing Intelligence* **19**: 42–52.

Sabagh, G., and Yim, S. B. (1980). The relationship between migration and fertility in a historical context: The case of Morocco in the 1960's. *International Migration Review* **14**: 525–538.

Sacher, G. A. (1975). Maturation and longevity in relation to cranial capacity in hominid evolution. In R. Tuttle (Ed.), *Primate Functional Morphology and Evolution.* The Hague: Mouton, pp. 417–441.

Saenz de Tejada, E. (1988). Analytical description of the food patterns in Mesoamerica since prehistoric times to the present, with special attention to the triada (translated from the Spanish title). Thesis, Universidad del Valle de Guatemala, Guatemala City.

St. George, D., Everson, P. M., Stevenson, J. C., and Tedrow, L. (2000). Birth intervals and early childhood mortality in a migrating Mennonite community. *American Journal of Human Biology* **12**: 50–63.

Sanderson, M., Emanuel, I., and Holt, V. (1995). The intergenerational relationship between mother's birthweight, infant birthweight and infant mortality in black and white mothers. *Paediatric and Perinatal Epidemiology* **9**: 391–405.

Satake, T., Malina, R. M., Tanaka, S., and Kirutka, F. (1994). Individual variation in the sequence of ages at peak velocity in seven body dimensions. *American Journal of Human Biology* **6**: 359–367.

Scammon, R. E. (1927). The first seriation study of human growth. *American Journal of Physical Anthropology* **10**: 329–336.

Scammon, R. E. (1930). The measurement of the body in childhood. In J. A. Harris and others (Eds.), *The Measurement of Man*. Minneapolis: University of Minnesota Press, pp. 173–215.

Scammon, R. E., and Calkins, L. A. (1929). *The Development and Growth of the External Dimensions of the Human Body in the Fetal Period*. Minneapolis: University of Minnesota Press.

Schaller, G. B., and Lowther, G. R. (1969). The relevance of carnivore behavior to the study of early hominids. *Southwest Journal of Anthropology* **25**: 307–341.

Schally, A. V., Kastin, A. J., and Arimura, A. (1977). Hypothalmic hormones: The link between brain and body. *American Scientist* **65**: 712–719.

Schell, L. M. (1991). Effects of pollutants on human prenatal and postnatal growth: Noise, lead, polychlorinated compounds and toxic wastes. *Yearbook of Physical Anthropology* **34**: 157–188.

Schell, L. M. (1997). Culture as a stressor: A revised model of biocultural interaction. *American Journal of Physical Anthropology* **102**: 67–77.

Schell, L. M., and Hodges, D. C. (1985). Variation in size at birth and cigarette smoking during pregnancy. *American Journal of Physical Anthropology* **68**: 549–554.

Schlegel, A. (Ed.). (1995). Special issue on adolescence. *Ethos* **23**: 3–103.

Schlegel, A., and Barry, H. (1991). *Adolescence: An Anthropological Inquiry*. New York: Free Press.

Schoeninger, M. J. (1979). Diet and status at Chalcatzingo: Some empirical and technical aspects of strontium analysis. *American Journal of Physical Anthropology* **51**: 295–310.

Schoeninger, M. J. (1982). Diet and the evolution of modern human form in the Middle East. *American Journal of Physical Anthropology* **58**: 37–52.

Scholl, T. O., O'Dell, M. E., and Johnston, F. E. (1976). Biological correlates of modernization in a Guatemala highland municipio. *Annals of Human Biology* **3**: 23–32.

Scrimshaw, N. S., and Young, V. R. (1978). The requirements of human nutrition. In N. Kretchmer and W. van B Robertson (Eds.), *Human Nutrition*, San Francisco: W. H. Freeman, pp. 156–170.

Scrimshaw, S. C. M. (1978). Infant mortality and behavior in the regulation of family size. *Population and Development Review* **4**: 383–403.

Seckler, D. (1980). Malnutrition: An intellectual odyssey. *Western Journal of Agricultural Economics* **5**: 219–227.

Seckler, D. (1982). "Small but healthy": A basic hypothesis in the theory, measurement, and policy of malnutrition. In P. V. Sukhatme (Ed.), *Newer Concepts of Nutrition and Their Implication for Policy*. Pune, India: Maharashta Association for the Cultivation of Science Research Institute, pp. 127–137.

Shams, M., and Williams, R. (1997). Generational changes in height and body mass differences between British Asians and the general population in Glasgow. *Journal of Biosocial Science* **29**: 101–109.

Shapiro, H. L. (1939). *Migration and Environment*. Oxford: Oxford University Press.

Shapiro, S., and Unger, J. (1965). *Relation of Weight at Birth to Cause of Death and Age at Death in the Neonatal Period: United States, Early 1950*. Public Health Service Pub. No. 1000, Series 21, No. 6. Washington DC: U.S. Government Printing Office.

Shea, B. T. (1989). Heterochrony in human evolution: The case for neoteny reconsidered. *Yearbook of Physical Anthropology* **32**: 69–101.

Shephard, R. J., and Rode, A. (1996). *The Health Consequences of "Modernization."* Cambridge: Cambridge University Press.

Shields, D. L. L. (1995). *The Color of Hunger*. London: Rowman and Littlefield.

Short, R. V. (1976). The evolution of human reproduction. *Proceedings, Royal Society* **195**(Ser. B): 3–24.

Shrestha, L. B. (2000). Population aging in developing countries. *Health Affairs* **19**: 204–212.

Sillen, A., and Kavanagh, M. (1982). Strontium and paleodietary research: A review. *Yearbook of Physical Anthropology* **25**: 67–90.

Silvestre, A. (1994). *Cabo-Verde. Na rota da internacionalização.* Lisbon: Grupo de Cooperação de Língua Portuguesa do Instituto Internacional de Caixas Económicas.

Simons, E. L. (1989). Human origins. *Science* **245**: 1343–1350.

Singer, C. (1959). *A Short History of Scientific Ideas to 1900.* London: Oxford University Press.

Singh, G. K., and Yu, S. M. (1995). Infant mortality in the United States: Trends, differentials, and projections 1950 through 2010. *American Journal of Public Health* **85**: 957–964.

Skjaerven, R., Wilcox, A. J., Oyen, N., and Magnus, P. (1997). Mothers' birth weight and survival of their offspring: Population based study. *British Medical Journal* **314**: 1376–1380.

Smail, P. J., Faiman, C., Hobson, W. C., Fuller, G. B., and Winter, J. S. (1982). Further studies on adrenarche in nonhuman primates. *Endocrinology* **111**: 844–848.

Smith, B. H. (1991a). Age at weaning approximates age of emergence of the first permanent molar in non-human primates. *American Journal of Physical Anthropology* **12**(Suppl.): 163–164 (abstract).

Smith, B. H. (1991b). Dental development and the evolution of life history in Hominidae. *American Journal of Physical Anthropology* **86**: 157–174.

Smith, B. H. (1992). Life history and the evolution of human maturation. *Evolutionary Anthropology* **1**: 134–142.

Smith, B. H. (1993). Physiological age of KMN-WT 15000 and its significance for growth and development of early Homo. In A. C. Walker and R. F. Leakey (Eds.), *The Nariokotome Homo erectus Skeleton.* Cambridge, MA: Belknap, pp. 195–220.

Smith, B. H., and Tompkins, R. L. (1995). Toward a life history of the hominidae. *Annual Review of Anthropology* **25**: 257–279.

Smith, B. H., Crummett, T. L., and Brandt, K. L. (1994). Ages of eruption of primate teeth: A compendium for aging individuals and comparing life histories. *Yearbook of Physical Anthropology* **37**: 177–231.

Smith, M. T. (1984). The effects of migration on sampling in genetical surveys. In A. J. Boyce (Ed.), *Migration and Mobility.* London: Taylor and Francis, pp. 97–110.

Sokal, R. R., and Thomson, B. A. (1998). Spatial genetic structure of human populations in Japan. *Human Biology* **70**: 1–22.

Sommerville, J. (1982). *The Rise and Fall of Childhood.* Beverly Hills, CA: Sage.

SoRelle, R. (2000). Gap between death rates for blacks and whites remains as large as in 1950. *Circulation* **101**(12): E9026.

Spencer, H. (1886). *The Principles of Biology*, Vols. I and II. New York: D. Appleton.

Stearns, S. C. (1992). *The Evolution of Life Histories.* Oxford: Oxford University Press.

Steckel, R. H. (1998). Strategic ideas in the rise of the new anthropometric history and their implications for interdisciplinary research. *Journal of Economic History* **58**: 803–821.

Steegmann, A. T., Jr. (1985). 18th century British military stature: Growth cessation, selective recruiting, secular trends, nutrition at birth, cold and occupation. *Human Biology* **57**: 77–95.

Stein, Z., Susser, M., Saenger, G., and Marolla, F. (1975). *Famine and Human Development. The Dutch Hunger Winter of 1944–1945.* London: Oxford University Press.

Stinson, S. (1982). The interrelationship of mortality and fertility in rural Bolivia. *Human Biology* **54**: 299–313.

Storey, R. (1985). An estimate of mortality in a pre-Columbian urban population. *American Anthropologist* **83**: 519–535.

Stover, J., and Way, P. (1998). Projecting the impact of AIDS on mortality. *AIDS* **12**(Suppl. 1): S29–S39.

Strassman, B. (1998). Predictors of fecundability and conception waits among the Dogon of Mali. *American Journal of Physical Anthropology* **105**: 167–184.

Stratz, C. H. (1909). Wachstum und Proportionen desMenschen vor und nach der Geburt. *Archiv für Anthropologie* **8**: 287–297.

Strum, S. (1981). Processes and products of change: Baboon predatory behavior at Gilgil, Kenya. In R. S. O. Harding and G. Teleki (Eds.), *Omnivorous Primates.* New York: Columbia University Press, pp. 255–302.

Styne, D. M., and McHenry, H. (1993). The evolution of stature in humans. *Hormone Research* **39**(Suppl. 3): 3–6.

Susanne, C. (1984). Biological differences between migrants and non-migrants. In A. J. Boyce (Ed.), *Migration and Mobility*. London: Taylor and Francis, pp. 179–195.

Swanbrow, D. (2000). Black-white health gap is as large as it was in 1950, new U-M study says. *The University Record*, March 13, 2000. Ann Arbor: University of Michigan, p. 13.

Swedlund, A. C., Meindl, R. S., and Gradie, M. I. (1980). Family reconstitution in the Connecticut Valley: Progress on record linkage and the mortality survey. In B. Dyke and W. Morril (Eds.), *Genealogical Demography*. New York: Academic, pp. 139–155.

Szreter, S., and Mooney, G. (1998). Urbanization, mortality, and the standard of living debate: New estimates of the expectation of life at birth in nineteenth-century British cities. *Economic History Review* **51**: 84–112.

Taffel, S. (1980). *Factors Associated with Low Birth Weight. United States, 1976*. DHEW Publication No. (PHS) 80-1915. Washington, DC: U.S. Government Printing Office.

Tague, R. G. (1994). Maternal mortality or prolonged growth: Age at death and pelvic size in three prehistoric Amerindian populations. *American Journal of Physical Anthropology* **95**: 27–40.

Takasaki, Y., Pieddeloup, C., and Anzai, S. (1987). Trends in food intake and digestive cancer mortalities in Japan. *Human Biology* **59**: 951–957.

Tanner, J. M. (1947). The morphological level of personality. *Proceedings of the Royal Society of Medicine* **40**: 301–303.

Tanner, J. M. (1962). *Growth and Adolescence*, 2nd ed. Oxford: Blackwell Scientific Publications.

Tanner, J. M. (1963). The regulation of human growth. *Child Development* **34**: 817–847.

Tanner, J. M. (1978). *Fetus into Man*. Cambridge: Harvard University Press.

Tanner, J. M. (1981). *A History of the Study of Human Growth*. Cambridge: Cambridge University Press.

Tanner, J. M. (1986). Growth as a mirror for the conditions of society: Secular trends and class distinctions. In A. Demirjian (Ed.), *Human Growth: A Multidisciplinary Review*. London: Taylor and Francis, pp. 3–34.

Tanner, J. M. (1990). *Fetus into Man*, 2nd ed. Cambridge: Harvard University Press.

Tanner, J. M., Whitehouse, R. H., Cameron, N., Marshall, W. A., Healy, M. J. R., and Goldstein, H. (1983). *Assessment of Skeletal Maturity and Prediction of Adult Height*, 2nd ed. London: Academic.

Tardieu, C. (1998). Short adolescence in early hominids: Infantile and adolescent growth of the human femur. *American Journal of Physical Anthropology* **197**: 163–178.

Taylor, J. (1999). Editorial. *Food Review: Official Journal of the South African Association for Food Science & Technology* **26**: 37–44.

Tedlock, D. (Transl.) (1985). *Popol Vuh*. New York: Simon and Schuster.

Teleki, G. (1981). The omnivorous diet and eclectic feeding habits of chimpanzees in Gombe National Park, Tanzania. In R. S. O. Harding and G. Teleki (Eds.), *Omnivorous Primates*. New York: Columbia University Press, pp. 303–343.

Teleki, G. E., Hunt, E., and Pfifferling, J. H. (1976). Demographic observations (1963–1973) on the chimpanzees of the Gombe National Park, Tanzania. *Journal of Human Evolution* **5**: 559–598.

Thompson, J. L. (1995). Terrible teens: The use of adolescent morphology in the interpretation of Upper Pleistocene human evolution. *American Journal of Physical Anthropology* **20**(Suppl.): 210.

Thompson, J. L., and Bilsborough, A. (1997). The current state of the Le Moustier 1 skull. *Acta Perhistorica et Archaeologica* **29**: 17–38.

Thompson, J. L., and Nelson, A. J. (1997). Relative postcranial development of Neandertal. *Journal of Human Evolution* **32**: A23–A24.

Thompson, J. N. (1999). Population ecology. *Encyclopædia Britannica Online*, http://www.eb.com:180/bol/topic?eu = 127611.

Thompson, W. S. (1929). Recent trends in world population. *American Journal of Sociology* **34**: 959–979.

Timiras, P. S. (1972). *Developmental Physiology and Aging*. New York: MacMillan Publishing Co.

Tobias, P. V. (1970). Puberty, growth, malnutrition and the weaker sex—and two new measures of environmental betterment. *Leech* **40**: 101–107.

Tobias, P. V. (1985). The negative secular trend. *Journal of Human Evolution* **14**: 347–356.

Todd, J. T., Mark, L. S., Shaw, R. E., and Pittenger, J. B. (1980). The perception of human growth. *Scientific American* **242**(2): 132–144.

Trevathan, W. R. (1987). *Human Birth: An Evolutionary Perspective.* New York: Aldine de Gruyter.

Trevathan, W. R. (1996). The evolution of bipedalism and assisted birth. *Medical Anthropology Quarterly* **10**: 287–298.

Trinkaus, E., Churchill, S. E., and Ruff, C. B. (1994). Postcranial robusticity in Homo. II: Humeral bilateral asymmetry and bone plasticity. *American Journal of Physical Anthropology* **93**: 1–34.

Tuan, Y. F. (1978). The city: Its distance from nature. *Geographical Review* **68**: 1–12.

Turnbull, C. M. (1983a). *The Human Cycle.* New York: Simon & Schuster.

Turnbull, C. M. (1983b). *The Mbuti Pygmies.* New York: Holt, Rinehart & Winston.

Tzian, L. (1994). *Mayas and Ladinos en Cifras: El Caso de Guatemala.* Cholsamaj: Guatemala City.

U.S. Department of Health and Human Services. (2000). Healthy People 2010 (Conference Edition, in two volumes). Washington, D.C.: U.S. Department of Health and Human Services (available at http://www.health.gov/healthypeople.

Ubelaker, D. H. (1994). The biological impact of European contact in Ecuador. In C. S. Larsen and G. R. Milner (Eds.), *In the Wake of Conquest.* New York: Wiley-Liss, pp. 147–160.

Ubelaker, D. H., Katzenberg, M. A., and Doyon, L. G. (1995). Status and diet in precontact highland Ecuador. *American Journal of Physical Anthropology* **97**: 403–411.

Ulijaszek, S. J., and Strickland, S. S. (1993). *Nutritional Anthropology: Prospects and Perspectives.* London: Smith Gordon.

Umezaki, M., and Ohtsuka, R. (1998). Impact of rural-urban migration on fertility: A population ecology analysis in the Kombio, Papua New Guinea. *Journal of Biosocial Science* **30**: 411–422.

United Nations. (1975). *Status of Women and Family Planning.* Department of Economic and Social Affairs. New York: United Nations.

United Nations. (1980). *Patterns of Urban and Rural Growth.* Population Studies, No. 68. New York: United Nations.

U.S. Bureau of Census. (1999). *World Population at a Glance: 1998 and Beyond.* Publication IB/98-4, January, 1999. Washington, DC: U.S. Department of Commerce.

Van de Walle, F. (1986). Infant mortality and the European demographic transition. In A. J. Coale and S. C. Watkins (Eds.), *The Decline of Fertility in Europe.* Princeton, NJ: Princeton University Press, pp. 201–233.

Van Gerven, D. P., Sheridan, S. G., and Adams, W. Y. (1995). The health and nutrition of a medieval Nubian population. *American Anthropologist* **97**: 468–480.

Van Loon, H., Saverys, V., Vuylsteke, J. P., Vlietinck, R. F., and Eeckels, R. (1986). Local versus universal growth standards: The effect of using NCHS as a universal reference. *Annals of Human Biology* **13**: 347–357.

Varela-Silva, M. I. (1996). Influência de variáveis bioculturais na motivaçá para a participação desportiva. Estudo de vários grupos étnicos durante a adolescência. Masters dissertation, Lisbon: Universidade Tecnica de Lisboa-FMH.

Vavra, H. M., and Querec, L. J. (1973). *A Study of Infant Mortality from Linked Records by Age of Mother, Total-Birth Order, and Other Variables.* DHEW Publication No. (HRA). 74-1851. Washington, DC: U.S. Government Printing Office.

Velimirovic, B. (1979). Forgotten people—the health of migrants. *Bulletin of the Pan American Health Organization* **13**: 66–85.

Vermeulen, A. (2000). Andropause. *Maturitas* **15**: 5–15.

Villar, J., and Belizan, J. M. (1982). The relative contribution of prematurity and fetal growth retardation to low birth weight in developing and developed countries. *American Journal of Obstetrics and Gynecology* **143**: 793–798A.

Villarijos, V. M., Osborn, J. A., Payne, F. J., and Arguedes, J. A. (1971). Heights and weights of children in urban and rural Costa Rica. *Environmental Child Health* **17**: 31–43.

Walcher, G. (1905). Ueber die Entstehung von Brachy-und Dolichocephalie durch willkürliche Bein-flussung des kindlichen Schadels. *Zentralblatt für Gynakologie* **29**: 193–196.

Walker, A., Zimmerman, M. R., and Leakey, R. E. F. (1982). A possible case of hypervitaminosis A in *Homo erectus*. *Nature* **296**: 248–250.

Walker, A. C. (1981). Dietary hypotheses and human evolution. *Philosophical Transactions of the Royal Society* **B292**: 58–64.

Walker, A. C., and Leakey, R. F. (Eds.). (1993). *The Nariokotome* Homo erectus *Skeleton*. Cambridge, MA: Belknap.

Washburn, S. L., and Lancaster, C. H. (1968). The evolution of hunting. In R. B. Lee and I. DeVore (Eds.), *Man the Hunter*. Cambridge, MA: Harvard University Press, pp. 293–303.

Washburn, S. L., and Moore, R. (1980). *Ape into Human: A Study of Human Evolution*, 2nd ed. Boston: Little, Brown.

Waterlow, J. C., Buzina, R., Keller, W., Lane, J. M., Nichaman, M. Z., and Tanner, J. M. (1977). The presentation and use of height and weight data for comparing the nutritional status of groups of children under the age of 10 years. *Bulletin of the World Health Organization* **55**: 489–498.

Watts, D. P., and Pusey, A. E. (1993). Behavior of juvenile and adolescent great apes. In M. E. Pereira and L. A. Fairbanks (Eds.), *Juvenile Primates*. Oxford: Oxford University Press, pp. 148–170.

Watts, E. S. (1985). Adolescent growth and development of monkeys, apes and humans. In E. S. Watts (Ed.), *Nonhuman Primate Models for Human Growth and Development*. New York: Alan R. Liss, pp. 41–65.

Watts, E. S. (1990). Evolutionary trends in primate growth and development. In C. J. DeRousseau (Ed.), *Primate Life History and Evolution*. New York: Wiley-Liss, pp. 89–104.

Way, A. A. (1976). Morbidity and post neonatal mortality. In P. T. Baker and M. A. Little (Eds.), *Man in the Andes: A Multidisciplinary Study of High Altitude Quechua*. Stroudsberg, PA: Dowden, Hutchinson and Ross, pp. 147–160.

Way, P., and Stover, J. (1998). The demographic impact of AIDS: Projecting the impact of AIDS on mortality and other demographic measures. *International Conference on AIDS, 1998* **12**: 943 (abstract).

Way, P. O., and Stanecki, K. A. (1992). AIDS and population: Prospects for negative population growth. *International Conference on AIDS, 1992* **8**(2): C326 (abstract).

Webster, D. L., Evans, S. T., and Sanders, W. T. (1993). *Out of the Past: An Introduction to Archaeology*. Mountain View, CA: Mayfield.

Weindruch, R. (1996). Caloric restriction and aging. *Scientific American* **274**(1): 46–52.

Weirman, M. E., and Crowley, W. F., Jr. (1986). Neuroendocrine control of the onset of puberty. In F. Falkner and J. M. Tanner (Eds.), *Human Growth*, 2nd ed, Vol. 2. New York: Plenum, pp. 225–241.

Weisner, T. S. (1987). Socialization for parenthood in sibling caretaking societies. In J. B. Lancaster, J. Altmann, A. S. Rossi, and L. R. Sherrod (Eds.), *Parenting Across the Life Span: Biosocial Dimensions*. New York: Aldine de Gruyter, pp. 237–270.

Weisner, T. S. (1996). The 5–7 transition as an ecocultural project. In A. Samaroff and M. Haith (Eds.), *Reason and Responsibility: The Passage through Childhood*. Chicago: University of Chicago Press, pp. 295–326.

Weiss, K. (1990). The biodemography of variation in human frailty. *Demography* **27**: 185–206.

Weiss, K. M., Ferrell, R. E., and Hanis, C. L. (1984). A New World syndrome of metabolic diseases with a genetic and evolutionary basis. *Yearbook of Physical Anthropology* **27**: 153–178.

Weissman, I. L., Hood, L. E., and Wood, W. B. (1978). *Essential Concepts in Immunology*. Melno Park: Benjamin/Cummings.

Werner, E. E., Bierman, J. M., and French, F. E. (1971). *The Children of Kauai*. Honolulu: University of Hawaii Press.

White, S. H. (1965). Evidence for a hierarchical arrangement of learning processes. In L. P. Lipsitt and C. C. Spiker (Eds.), *Advances in Child Development and Behavior*, Vol. 2. New York: Academic, pp. 187–220.

Whiting, B. B., and Edwards, C. P. (1988). *Children of Different Worlds*. Cambridge: Harvard University Press.

Whitworth, D. (1999). Faithful live longer. *London, Times* July 3: 13.

Whyte, R. O. (1974). *Rural Nutrition in Monsoon Asia.* Kuala Lampoor: Oxford University Press.

Widdowson, E. M. (1970). The harmony of growth. *Lancet* **1**: 901–905.

Williams, G. C. (1957). Pleiotropy, natural selection and the evolution of senescence. *Evolution* **11**: 398–411.

Williams, G. C. (1966). Natural selection, the cost of reproduction, and a refinement of Lack's principle. *American Naturalist* **100**: 687–690.

Winkler, L. A., and Anemone, R. L. (1996). Recent development in hominoid ontogeny: An overview and summation. *American Journal of Physical Anthropology* **99**: 1–8.

Wolanski, N., and Bogin, B. (Eds.). (1996). *Family as an Environment for Human Development.* New Delhi: Kamal Raj.

Wood, J. W., O'Connor, K. A., and Holman, D. J. (1999). Biodemographic models of menopause. *American Journal of Human Biology* **11**: 133–134.

Woods, R. (1985). The effects of population redistribution on the level of mortality in nineteenth-century England and Wales. *Journal of Economic History* **45**: 645–651.

World Bank. (1996). *Urbanization: The Challenge for the Next Century.* Finance & Development, http://www.worldbank.org/fandd/english/0696/articles/0180696.htm.

World Resources Institute. (1994). *World Resources 1994–96.* Oxford: Oxford University Press.

Worthman, C. M. (1986). Later-maturing populations and control of the onset of puberty. *American Journal of Physical Anthropology* **69**: 282 (abstract).

Worthman, C. M. (1993). Biocultural interactions in human development. In M. E. Pereira and L. A. Fairbanks (Eds.), *Juvenile Primates: Life History, Development, and Behavior.* New York: Oxford University Press, pp. 339–357.

Wrigley, E. A. (1998). Explaining the rise in marital fertility in England in the "long" eighteenth century. *Economic History Review LI* **3**: 435–464.

Wyatt, D. T., Simms, M. D., and Horwitz, S. M. (1997). Widespread growth retardation and variable growth recovery in foster children in the first year after initial placement. *Archives of Pediatric and Adolescent Medicine* **151**(8): 813–816.

Young, V. R., Steffee, W. P., Pencharz, P. B., Winterer, J. C., and Scrimshaw, N. S. (1975). Total human body protein synthesis in relation to protein requirements at various ages. *Nature* **253**: 192–194.

Zaba, B. (1998). Evidence for the impact of HIV on fertility in Africa. *International Conference on AIDS, 1998* **12**: 479 (abstract).

Zarate, A., and Zarate, A. U. (1975). On the reconciliation of research findings of migrant-nonmigrant fertility differentials in urban areas. *International Migration Review* **9**: 115–156.

Zavattaro, M., Susanne, C., and Vercauteren, M. (1997). International migration and biogeographical behaviour: A study of Italians in Belgium. *Journal of Biosocial Science* **26**: 345–354.

Zhang, J., and Bowes, W. A. (1995). Birth-weight-for-gestational-age patterns by race, sex, and parity in the United States population. *Obstetrics and Gynecology* **86**: 200–208.

Zihlman, A. L. (1981). Women as shapers of human adaptation. In F. Dahlberg (Ed.), *Woman the Gatherer.* New Haven: Yale University Press, pp. 75–120.

Zihlman, A. L. (1997). Women's bodies, women's lives: An evolutionary perspective. In M. E. Morbeck, A. Galloway, and A. L. Zihlman (Eds.), *The Evolving Female: A Life History Perspective.* Princeton: Princeton University Press, pp. 185–197.

Index